BEHIND JAPAN'S
SURRENDER

The Secret Struggle
That Ended an Empire

by Lester Brooks

with a Foreword by Fumihiko Togo

Carpe Veritas Books, De Gustibus Press, Ltd., Stamford, CT

I am reading about some persons, long dead. Surreptitiously, other names insert themselves into the text, and, presently, I am reading about us, as we shall be when we are the past. Most has utterly vanished. Problems which were once so vital, spread themselves over the pages as cold abstractions—simple ones, but we failed to understand them. We appear as rather stupid, foolish, self-seeking puppets, moved by obvious strings, which, now and again, get tangled up.
—DAG HAMMARSKJÖLD, 1950
(from *Markings*. New York; Knopf, 1964)

This book is dedicated to Patricia, James, Jonathan and Christopher.

Other books by Lester Brooks include:
   African Achievements: Leaders, Civilizations & Cultures of Ancient
      Africa
   Blacks in the City, A History of the National Urban League (with
      Guichard Parris)

BEHIND JAPAN'S SURRENDER

Published in the United States by Carpe Veritas Books, a division of
   De Gustibus Press, Ltd., Stamford, Connecticut, February, 1995.
First published in the United States in 1968 by McGraw-Hill Book
   Company.

Library of Congress Catalog Card Number: 67-25808

ISBN 0-9626946-8-1
   1. Brooks, Lester. 2. World War II -- Japan, 3. Japan, surrender of,
1945. 4. Great Pacific War, 1941 - 1945.

FIRST 1995 EDITION

Contents

Preface

While millions around the world celebrated the end of World War II, a handful of men, the leaders of Japan, battled among themselves. The issue was whether to continue the war or surrender. Their struggle continued for four days *after* the first official Japanese offer to surrender set off the bells, the dancing and the wild cheering around the globe.

This narrative tells why those celebrations were premature and how, very narrowly, Japan's peacemakers overcame terrorism, assassinations and an armed *coup d'état*.

In 1945 the officers of the Japanese army were determined almost to a man to prevent what they thought would be the end of 2,600 years of their Emperor-god system. Powerful men in the Japanese navy were preparing their forces for suicide onslaughts against the Allied invaders. Civilian extremists were whipping up their followers not only to resist to the death, but to smash the "peacemongers" with gun, sword, and torch. The head of Japan's police expected the masses to rise in revolt. The commandant of the *kempeitai* (military police) predicted that the troops would revolt.

Japan at that time was a nation of 80,000,000 tattered, almost starving humans, sick of war but dedicated to continuing it until signaled to halt. Their workplaces, homes, supplies, and friends were consumed daily in the ever-increasing firebomb raids. Their crops were failing. Their health was borderline. They were cut off from the mainland by mines, submarines, surface ships, and planes. Even travel between the home islands was becoming terribly dangerous. Still the military men were committed to fight a "decisive battle in the homeland."

These military leaders were not blind. They were not stupid. They were normal human beings acting in a perfectly normal fashion, responding in completely understandable ways to the pressures upon them. Their behavior was normal and understandable, that is, in the Japan of 1945. It is this point that makes that macabre interlude in the now-distant past—the fight within Japan over surrender —relevant today: the appearance of the outside world as seen by the Japanese leaders mirrored their own requirements. But that pattern of needs, that view of life, was riveted on them by themselves.

If we had been able to see more clearly what the Japanese view of the world was we might have helped them overcome objections to surrender at an earlier time. Ours is an era when negotiated peaces or uneasy truces—anything but all-out war—are the only ways to wind up armed conflicts. Since this is so, the need to understand the adversary's view of the world is crucially important. The Japanese experience in World War II gives us insight into this.

At the top the leaders were not megalomaniacs with closed minds. They knew, deep within, that they could not win. They knew it even before the Nazi collapse made it certain that the Allies would pour vastly superior forces and weapons into the final assault. They knew defeat was inescapable (but inadmissible) before the A-bombs and the Soviet attack. Yet they rejected surrender as a logical choice.

There is a demonstration of hypnosis as old, perhaps, as hypnosis itself. The hypnotist, the subject, and a third person are on stage. The subject, in a trance, is told that he and the hypnotist are alone. When he is awakened, the subject acts as though the third person does not exist. Almost. But when the subject is asked to sit in the third chair, he makes excuses. When bidden to take something to or from the third person, he evades. Does he not see the other person? Unquestionably his senses tell him that there is another person present. Then why does he not acknowledge this and act rationally—as though the person existed?

The suggestion, implanted in hypnosis, that the subject and hypnotist are alone, does not allow room for the existence of a third person. The subject's view of the immediate world conforms to the requirements, the needs-pattern established in hypnosis. His senses and his responses conform defensively and protectively. The hypnotized subject's clouded perception refuses to admit what appears to the audience to be indisputable reality.

Japan's military masters were in a similar, self-hypnotized condition in 1945. It was defeat, utter and absolute, that their perception refused to allow.

Their bitter "awakening" is the subject of this book.

Acknowledgments

Thanks are due. . . .

In a sense, this book began in a U.S. army replacement depot (i.e., a staging area) on Lingayen Gulf on the Philippine island of Luzon in 1945. I was there as a G.I. and if the events in this book had not taken place, like thousands of other American soldiers I would have been one of the ground troops thrown into the all-out assault on Japan that fall or the following spring. Instead, I arrived in the burned-out capital of the defunct Japanese Empire that winter as one of its "conquerors."

Fortunately, I had been transferred from my engineer outfit to GHQ, SCAP and was assigned to edit an army magazine. I had one deadline per week and this gave me freedom to journey and observe throughout the length of Japan. I had traveled widely in the Philippines and seen the shambles the fighting had made of Manila, Baguio and many provincial towns. But the extent of the destruction in Japan and the scavenger existence of its dazed people had unexpected impact. They etched questions in the brain. The spectacle of these bewildered, undernourished people in the ashes of their homes and ruins of their often primitive factories, soon melted the views instilled by years of "hate the enemy" propaganda. Seeing a shivering shack-and-soup-kitchen society limping along on tricycles, ancient (and scarce) charcoal-burning vehicles and patched trains raised the question of how, in the first place, they ever could have seriously considered war on the U.S. And again and again another question flashed: "Why didn't they quit before it came to this?"

I went back to civilian pursuits and these questions were superseded by others that, for me, were more immediate. But in 1949 while I was at Columbia University the questions received a dusting and additional illumination. I managed for Columbia's Bureau of Applied Social Research a Rockefeller Foundation project in which six Japanese broadcasters were brought to the United States to observe the workings of radio in a democracy. One of these six was Hiroshi Niino and he had a remarkable story to tell of the events leading up to Japan's surrender. He was one of those at Radio Tokyo who was locked up when insurgents took over the broadcasting facilities. It was he who first told me about the *coup d'état* and the desperate attempts to prevent surrender.

Three years later when I was in Japan again Niino-san told me more and showed me the scenes of action. But because of other commitments, it was not until 1965 that I was able to devote the necessary time to the questions that had haunted me. Again, Niino-san played an important role as adviser and recounted in detail the incredible events of the August 15 Incident as experienced by the broadcasters.

Many others in Japan also assisted generously. Foremost of these was Miss Naomi Fukuda, the ever-charming and intrepid librarian of International House of Japan who arranged for help and almost magically materialized needed reference items. Miss Florence Takahashi was a model of genial efficiency in the essential and difficult role of Girl Friday. Riiche Inagaki, McGraw-Hill's resident manager in Japan opened doors and counseled wisely. At the National Diet Library I was fortunate to have the diligent assistance of Konosuke Hayashi and the cooperation of Makoto Kuwabara. Four scholars, Atsushi Oi, Masao Inaba, Ikuhiko Hata and Noburo Kojima provided valuable insights and directed my attention to significant sources. Messrs. Kato and Kikuchi of the International House staff gave indispensable help with translations and interview arrangements, as did John Ishizaki and Mitsuko Yamada and their associates, Shishikura Tsunetaka and Yuichiro Matsushima at *Asahi Shimbun*. Masaru Ogawa kindly made available the facilities of the *Japan Times* and Sadao Otake did likewise at *Kyodo* news agency. Robert Klaverkamp of *Reader's Digest* and John Randolph of the *Seattle Times* were extremely generous in their aid and counsel, as were Professors Herschel Webb, James Crowley, Robert J. C. Butow, James Morley, Ardath Burks, George Akita, and Richard Storry.

In the United States, the interest and enthusiasm of Robert Gutwillig launched this project; the friendly encouragement and invaluable assistance of Prof. Lawrence Olson and Japan Society executive director Douglas Overton moved it forward. The splendid cooperation of Len Giovannitti of National Broadcasting Co. was particularly helpful because he had just completed a parallel project. I was fortunate to have the advice and views of Hon. Fumihiko and Mrs. Togo. Grateful bows of appreciation are due for the resources and professional help made available by Andrew Y. Kuroda, chief of the Japanese Section, Library of Congress; F. Kent Loomis, acting director of Naval History, and his associate in the Office of Naval History, Dean Allard; Wilbur Nigh of the World War II Reference Branch, National Archives; Col. Grover Heiman, Jr., of the Defense Department's Magazine and Book Division; and the Office of the Chief of Military History, Department of the Army.

I was fortunate to have the candid and penetrating suggestions of Ansei Uchima, Malcolm Reiss and Patricia Brooks on the manuscript. The indefatigable Marion Dettloff transcribed the hours and hours of tape recorded interviews and developed a delightful Japanese accent in the process.

If it had not been for all of these and the many others who aided in so many ways, this book would have been impossible. To them major credit is due for the virtues it may possess; obviously, for the shortcomings I alone am responsible.

Among Those Present...

*the following men played important roles
in the final days of Imperial Japan:*

HIROHITO, 124th descendant of the sun goddess, Amaterasu, hence son of heaven—Tenno of Japan. *Showa* (enlightened peace) is the name chosen for his reign by Hirohito. He was in the 20th year of his reign in 1945, his 44th year.

MARQUIS KOICHI KIDO, lord keeper of the privy seal, closest adviser-confidante of the Emperor.

ADMIRAL BARON KANTARO SUZUKI, prime minister from April 6 to August 16, 1945; Sino-Japanese and Russo-Japanese war hero; former grand chamberlain to the Emperor, then president of the privy council and member of the *jushin* (senior statesmen).

SHIGENORI TOGO, foreign minister in Suzuki's cabinet; had served as foreign minister October 1941–September 1942.

GENERAL KORECHIKA ANAMI, war minister, Suzuki cabinet; had served as a military aide-de-camp to the Emperor in the late twenties.

ADMIRAL MITSUMASA YONAI, navy minister, Suzuki cabinet and in the preceding and succeeding cabinets; former prime minister of Japan; member of *jushin*.

HISATSUNE SAKOMIZU, chief cabinet secretary, Suzuki cabinet; former finance ministry bureaucrat; son-in-law of former Prime Minister Admiral Okada, a leader of peace faction.

GENERAL YOSHIJIRO UMEZU, chief of staff of Imperial Japanese Army; former commandant of Kwantung army and ambassador to Manchukuo.

ADMIRAL SOEMU TOYODA, chief of staff of Imperial Japanese Navy.

KIICHIRO HIRANUMA, president of the privy council, former prime minister, member of *jushin;* head of right-wing society and ardent nationalist.

LIEUTENANT GENERAL TAKESHI MORI, commandant of the Imperial Guards Division.

LIEUTENANT GENERAL SHIZUICHI TANAKA, commandant of the Eastern District Army (covering Tokyo-Yokohama area).

LIEUTENANT GENERAL KENJI OKIDO, commandant of the *kempeitai,* Japan's omnipresent, oppressive military police.

LIEUTENANT GENERAL MASAO YOSHIZUMI, chief, Military Affairs Bureau, IJA-war ministry, the powerful political action center of the army.

VICE-ADMIRAL ZENSHIRO HOSHINA, chief, Military Affairs Bureau, IJN-navy ministry.

LIEUTENANT GENERAL SUMIHISA IKEDA, chief, Cabinet Planning Bureau, former G-5, Kwantung army and close associate of General Umezu.

COLONEL OKIKATSU (KOKO) ARAO, chief, War Affairs Section, Military Affairs Bureau of the army. One of original plotters of *coup d'état.*

LIEUTENANT COLONEL MASAHIKO TAKESHITA, brother-in-law of General Anami, the war minister, and head of domestic affairs sub-section of Arao's unit. Planned *coup.*

LIEUTENANT COLONEL JIRO SHIIZAKI, member of Takeshita's staff. Participated in *coup.*

MAJOR KENJI HATANAKA, fanatical nationalist. Member of Takeshita's staff. Led *coup.*

LIEUTENANT COLONEL MASAO INABA, head, mobilization and budget sub-sections of Military Affairs Bureau of the army; speech-writer for Anami. Planned *coup.*

LIEUTENANT COLONEL MASATAKA IDA, member of Inaba's staff, assigned to budget sub-section. Participated in *coup.*

COLONEL SABURO HAYASHI, secretary to the war minister.

DOCTOR HIROSHI (KAINAN) SHIMOMURA, president of Board of Information and member of Suzuki cabinet; former editior of Asahi newspapers.

WHO RAN JAPAN IN 1945?

From the outside, it appeared that power in Japan was held — and exercised — as follows:

Hirohito, *the Emperor*, made the decisions.

The Diet (Japan's parliament) passed the legislation.

The premier and his cabinet recommended legislation and ran the country.

The privy council, men appointed for life by the Emperor, reviewed and passed on legislation, treaties and appointments.

The jushin, a panel of senior statesmen appointed by the Emperor, advised him on current matters. The *jushin* were former premiers and the president of the privy council.

Supreme Council for Direction of the War was a coordinating conference which, with Imperial General Headquarters, decided war policy.

Zaibatsu, the mammoth industrial and commercial cartels, exercised strong influence on government through their adherents in the Diet and the bureaucracy.

Army and navy chiefs of staff and the *ministers of war and navy* had more influence on policy than in Western nations. They were among the dozen men who had unlimited access to the Throne.

Palace retainers—the lord keeper of the privy seal, grand chamberlain, keeper of the imperial household and chief aide-de-camp—were advisers to the Emperor.

However, on the inside, by 1945 power was held and exercised this way:

Hirohito, the Emperor, was powerless to make the real decisions. He was a figurehead of paramount importance—the moral and spiritual leader of Nippon whose signature was required on and could not be withheld from orders, legislation, documents, or appointments.

War Minister Korechika Anami and **Army Chief of Staff** General Yoshijiro Umezu, were the two most powerful men in Japan. With their constitutional powers they could dictate what the government must do — and they had millions of battle-seasoned veterans and the police weight of the *kempeitai* to back up their demands.

Chief Cabinet Secretary Hisatsune Sakomizu was not merely an administrator of government machinery. He was the premier's chief adviser and political strategist.

Foreign Minister Shigenori Togo and his foreign affairs colleagues found themselves in demand. In 1945 the military began to look to diplomacy, which they had despised for fifteen years, to accomplish what Japanese arms could not.

The cabinet consisted of fifteen men whose agreement on policy matters had to be unanimous. This impractical requirement paralyzed cabinet action and nearly destroyed the Suzuki government. The cabinet decided matters and presented them to the privy council and the Emperor for his signature and formal promulgation.

The Diet was moribund. Opposition had long been silenced; it was called into session only to provide a means of rallying public opinion behind programs the military considered necessary.

Lord Keeper of the Privy Seal Marquis Koichi Kido, the Emperor's closest adviser, counseled Hirohito's actions and pronouncements, decided who should and should not see the Emperor and carefully guarded and used the prestige of the Imperial House and the Emperor. In 1945 he worked to bring about surrender.

Prime Minister Admiral Baron Kantaro Suzuki might have maneuvered his government to an earlier surrender through vigorous leadership, aggressive and determined political action.

Supreme Council for Direction of the War—the "Big Six"—consisted of the premier, ministers of war, navy, foreign affairs and chiefs of staff of army and navy. This extra-constitutional body made top-level decisions about war and negotiations to end it. Because it consisted of the most powerful men in the land, its decisions carried.

Navy Minister Mitsumasa Yonai and **Navy Chief of Staff Soemu Toyoda** had lost nearly all offensive naval power and their importance had dwindled also. Still, they had direct access to the Emperor and had millions of armed men under orders.

The privy council's scope included approval of all national laws, treaties, appointments to high office and Imperial pronouncements. In spite of its broad powers, it had dwindled to rubber-stamp duty.

The zaibatsu were demoralized, their physical plants largely destroyed by unrelenting enemy air raids. The big business groups used what influence they could muster to end the war. But, their influence, too, had dwindled.

Foreword

Japan has fought two wars in this century. One ended in victory, and the other in defeat. The story of the Russo-Japanese war of 1904–1905 is now a part of history, but the events leading up to the Imperial decision to end the Pacific War have not quite been buried in the pages of history.

We had, twenty-two years ago, six members of the Supreme Council for the Direction of War who were responsible for ending the war. Their situation was somewhat different from Prime Minister Katsura's and Foreign Minister Komura's at the end of the Russo-Japanese war. In the summer of 1905, Japan was victorious on land and sea, even though her military was on the verge of exhaustion. Field Marshal Ohyama and his chief-of-staff, General Kodama, had admitted that the time had come for peace; in addition, there was the intermediary of President Theodore Roosevelt. In contrast to this, forty summers later when the tide of war was overwhelmingly against Japan, the Allies demanded "unconditional surrender" while the Japanese sloganized "one hundred million deaths of honor."

Under these circumstances, in the early part of May, my father-in-law, Foreign Minister Togo, initiated a series of private meetings with the five other members of the Supreme Council: Prime Minister Admiral Suzuki, War Minister Anami, Navy Minister Yonai, Army Chief-of-Staff Umezu, Navy Chief-of-Staff Toyoda. The credit due him for this patient and painstaking groundwork can only be known by those who were his immediates. In many ways this initiative of Mr. Togo's was the first substantial step toward the three-month path leading to the end of the war. For, while in the last few days of war the foreign minister was caught between the demand of "unconditional surrender" by the Allies and the insistence on a "final battle on the beach" by the military services at home, and the war minister between the Imperial wishes to end the war and his subordinates' pressure for continuation of war to save the national polity, each of these six leaders knew by late spring what the other had in mind. It was solely because there had been a unity of spirit achieved among the team of the Big Six that a final decision could have been made at the Imperial command to accept the terms of the Potsdam declaration thereby ending the war.

In retrospect it is hard to imagine how the military leaders could have insisted on the continuation of the war when the war potential had been all but completely shattered—and all this compounded by the atomic bomb and the Soviet Union's entry into the war. One cannot, however, dismiss this insistence simply as wild fanaticism. It is only fair, as Lester Brooks has shown in this book, to endeavor to reproduce the series of events in proper perspective so that readers will be able to put themselves in the places of persons who played major roles in this historic moment.

It was a sudden anti-climax when the Suzuki cabinet resigned within two hours after the Emperor's broadcast ending the war, although evidently this action was only perfectly natural to Admiral Suzuki. It is no use now to ponder over whether these leaders in the cabinet should not have continued to serve the country in the hard days that followed the surrender. But they had retired honorably from the scene—General Anami having committed suicide like a classic warrior and Foreign Minister Togo later dying a lonely death in a prison hospital—entrusting the task of Japan's reconstruction to the hands of the "young and capable," as Admiral Suzuki put it. It will be long remembered, however, that because these leaders had successfully brought the war to an end at that moment, the status of the Imperial Household remained intact while the country was left undivided—a fate unlike that which befell other countries at the war's end.

There have now been published many memoirs and accounts of the Pacific War. Nevertheless, the story of the last days of the holocaust cannot be told and retold too often. No one person alone has the knowledge of everything that happened, nor can one be absolutely objective in telling a story of one's own. *Behind Japan's Surrender,* by Lester Brooks, is a most valuable work which reveals the part played by a small number of Japanese leaders in a crucial moment in the history of Japan.

FUMIHIKO TOGO

Tokyo, August 15, 1967

[*Mr. Togo was secretary to Foreign Minister Shigenori Togo in 1945. He is now head of the North American desk of* Gaimusho, *Japan's Ministry of Foreign Affairs.*]

Behind Japan's Surrender

Chapter 1

Twilight or Gyokusai?*

CROWDS THRONG THE WEST END

SPONTANEOUS GAIETY

Thousands of Londoners and service men and women disregarded the official request that the Japanese reported surrender should be treated with reserve and made merry last night. From Aldwych to Oxford Circus all the main streets were filled with men and women celebrating what to them was final victory . . . coloured streamers floated down from tall buildings and the sunlit streets were soon carpeted by shredded paper and books thrown from windows. . . .

The crowds grew in Piccadilly Circus and in all the streets leading there . . . dancing became general . . . hand-in-hand groups of service men and women and civilians wound their way between buses and lampposts.

Men scaled lampposts and affixed at the top allied flags. One girl sat on the top of traffic lights and displayed the announcement "Japan Surrenders" for all to see.

Australian airmen . . . whooped their way into the center of a crowd in Aldwych . . . popular war-time airs soon had the crowds swinging and swaying in joyous abandon.

Before 7 o'clock, when no confirmation of the Tokyo broadcast was forthcoming, the crowds gradually thinned and soon the litter-strewn pavements had little more than the normal number of pedestrians. Later the crowds increased again, determined to enjoy themselves. Many fireworks were thrown.

—*Times* (London), August 11, 1945

* *Gyokusai:* Japanese equivalent of Armageddon.

The war in the Pacific was over.

Or was it?

In the Allied nations wherever people congregated, celebrations, ranging from prayerful to frenzied, had been unleashed August 11, 1945, when the outside world first heard that Japan had tentatively accepted the Allied terms for surrender.

By August 13 the unofficial victory celebrations were in their third day. But they were premature.

At the fronts, men were still fighting and dying.

In Japan, only a handful knew that surrender was even a possibility. Most believed that all Japanese must fight on, with *Yamato* spirit if not with modern weapons. Even many of those who knew the nation was on the brink of surrender flung back the likelihood, refusing to consider it. There were others who not only rejected surrender but intended to prevent it. A delegation of these fanatics called on the most powerful man in Japan the evening of August 13.

In the heat and querulous storminess of the summer night they arrived khaki-clad and panting at the door, like leaves unseasonably loosened, splayed against the entryway by a sudden burst of chilling wind.

Three had been expected. All six were welcome. They were the archetypes of "young officers," the hotspurs whose impatience, ruthlessness, and unbridled ambition had driven Japan to military adventure, had captured and held hostage to fear the moderates—the responsible opposition and statesmanship in the nation.

There, on the threshold of the war minister's official residence, on the short street between the moribund Diet in its stone mausoleum and the impotent Emperor surrounded by the charred ruins of his palace, they paused. While the servant carried word to Japan's minister of war that they were there, they shivered in anticipation of the risk-all throw they were about to attempt. Theirs was a delegation for total destruction and national suicide, and the war minister, General Korechika Anami, was the pivot of their plans.

General Anami had arrived at the house only shortly before, back for a brief respite from the conferences that seemed never to end. His day had started early, with a call on the lord privy seal. Then came the wrangling in the morning session of the Supreme Council for

Direction of the War (SCDW) and the full cabinet session that followed. These plus the pressures of his work and the demands from the junior officers would have exhausted a horse. Anami, however, had the constitution of an ox. His tough hide was able to take the rain of blows that seemed to increase daily. On this thirteenth of August 1945, these blows included day-long bombing and strafing of central Japan by carrier-based enemy planes, shelling of coastal towns by enemy task forces, surging advances by Soviet troops in Manchuria, and somewhat less staggering setbacks on a score of fronts from Burma to Sakhalin. But his day was not yet ended.

Suddenly Anami emerged into the Western-style reception room like a locomotive in khaki. With a wide smile and ebullient warmth he welcomed his callers, put them at ease after they snapped to attention. They were actually more trusted followers and disciples than subordinates, and between Anami and them there existed an openness and the free exchange for which the war minister was famous in the army. He was in a sense the head of the family and they all were like sons to him.

With all and each of the six men present Anami shared beliefs, ties, and loyalties. All were members of the war ministry's Military Affairs Bureau, the nerve center, that cerebrum, of the Japanese military establishment. Masahiko Takeshita, the lieutenant colonel in charge of political liaison branch of its Army Affairs Section, shared family responsibilities and camaraderie as Anami's brother-in-law, longtime neighbor, occasional *kendo* partner, and confidant.

Lieutenant Colonel Masao Inaba was chief of the budget branch of the Army Affairs Section. In this spot Inaba sought and expressed Anami's attitudes and decisions in speeches, budget messages, and news statements. Like the devoted and efficient "ghost" he was, Inaba identified with Anami's views (as he saw them) as closely as carbon paper.

The chief of the Army Affairs Section, Colonel Okikatsu (Koko) Arao, was the senior officer of the young tigers and headed the original delegation of three.

These three had been joined at the last minute by three of Anami's younger and most enthusiastic admirers, Major Kenji Hatanaka,

Lieutenant Colonel Jiro Shiizaki (both of whom reported to Take-shita), and Lieutenant Colonel Masataka Ida, who reported to Inaba.

Hatanaka was slight, intense, driven by unreserved superpatrio-tism. Shiizaki was solid and quiet, a reliable follower. Ida's slim figure was topped by a pleasing face as malleable as a dumpling.

Ida and Hatanaka were dedicated followers of the extremist Professor Hiraizumi, who lectured at Tokyo University. Anami too was impressed by the Professor's historical-mythical synthesis of Japan's destiny and his thesis that it was the responsibility of subjects to guard the Imperial Way, even against the will of the Emperor himself. The war minister had attended Hiraizumi's lectures and had made it possible for him to address officer groups at Ichigaya Heights—the Japanese Pentagon.

Ida and Hatanaka were members of a study group led by Hirai-zumi. They met regularly with about ten others at the Professor's home for private classes. Ida and Hatanaka had been attending for years and had thoroughly soaked up the Professor's heady blend of mythology and ultranationalism that condoned any bloody means to an end, if the end was pure. The Professor had been a key figure in ultranationalist circles for a dozen years and many of his most de-voted students were army men.

The night before Ida had received an alarming report. The pro-peace faction, he had heard, now believed that if it assassinated General Anami it would be able to strike the army powerless. This, Ida believed, was quite accurate. As a precaution, to protect the war minister, the *kempeitai* (military police) guard around him was increased to twenty. And Ida and Hatanaka, concerned about their idol, had made the lengthy trip to the General's home in the remote Tokyo suburb of Mitaka that sultry Sunday evening to make sure he was safe. It was a demonstration of their devotion and Anami appreciated it and them accordingly.

Now, on Monday the thirteenth, the delegation of six represented conspirators from the Military Affairs Bureau and the Second Section of Army General Headquarters. The purpose of the group was clear-cut: to install Anami as the military dictator of Japan and continue the fight against the Allies. The time was 10 P.M.; the place was Tokyo, burned-out capital of a besieged, broken country.

Anami had a general idea of their purpose. The afternoon of the twelfth, as he was about to rush to a cabinet meeting, members of this same group had detained him in his office, patient but distracted. Takeshita, as spokesman, in a fiery presentation charged the war minister to reject the Potsdam terms, continue the war, and order the Eastern District Army to prepare for martial law. Others in Anami's office at the time included Vice-minister General Wakamatsu and his secretary, Lieutenant Colonel Hirose; Chief of the Military Services Bureau Nasu; Colonel Hiroo Sato, Chief of the War Preparations Section; Anami's secretary, Colonel Saburo Hayashi; and Colonel Arao, the chief of the Army Affairs Section.

Under extreme pressure to reach the cabinet meeting before discussion began, Anami ordered the vice-minister of war, Wakamatsu, to take the necessary steps and dashed away. Wakamatsu wisely sat on the matter until he had further instructions. The conspirators tried to reach Anami during the day of the thirteenth, but he had been beyond reach—in conference all day. Now, at last, the General was ready to hear them out. In a corner of the room was his secretary Colonel Hayashi, who gave the meeting an air of outrageousness even before it began. His face carried an expression of incredulous bewilderment, a look indelibly stamped on his features at an early age. Hayashi's experience as a Japanese citizen and military officer had done nothing to lessen it.

Colonel Arao, his heavy, flat face waggling in the light as he emphasized his words, told Anami they had called now because they considered the time ripe to launch a *coup d'état*. Since the government leaders had decided the Potsdam declaration should be accepted, he said, the only possible thing to do was to change the government. To bring this about quickly and with a minimum of difficulty and—most important—to make certain that the new government would fight the "decisive battle of the homeland" to the last Japanese, these were the objectives of the plan Arao and his five companions carried.

As Arao explained the plan, Anami sat silently erect in the sticky heat, his eyes shut tight in deep meditation.

The entire scheme was based on a paragraph in the imperial ordinance concerning martial law. It authorized local garrison commanders to proclaim martial law *provisionally and without Imperial sanction* in case of emergency. So the plan would place Tokyo under martial law, "isolate" the Emperor from the peace faction, and "request" him to issue such orders as might be necessary to continue World War II.

This would have been reversion in form as well as fact to the situation existing when Commodore Perry had arrived at Japan's shores ninety years before. Perry sent his envoys to the ruler of Japan, the military Shogun at that time. Not until years later, when the U.S. sent Townsend Harris as American consul, was it learned that there was an Emperor living at Kyoto in isolation enforced by the Shogun.

The Meiji Restoration of 1868 had overthrown the Shogunate and placed the Emperor at the center of Japanese life. Although it did not restore him to absolute power, he became the figurehead and carried out ceremonial and religious functions. As the Divine Son of Heaven, high priest of the state religion, and central symbol of power, his sanction was mandatory to legitimatize government actions. The Restoration had been planned that way; the military ever since 1868 had promoted this symbolism and benefited from it.

Now this small band of patriotic plotters planned that theirs would be the only voices to reach the Emperor and theirs the only hands to use him as a rubber stamp.

Their scheme was simple:

1. *Purpose.* The surrender will not be made until a definite assurance is given as to our conditions regarding the Emperor. Negotiations will be continued. To elicit from the Emperor sanction to continue negotiations until the desired peace conditions are met. [This meant reversing the Emperor's personally stated decision that the Potsdam Declaration should be accepted. It meant that fighting would continue until the Allies accepted conditions laid down by the Japanese army, conditions that were impossible.]

2. *Procedure.* The *coup* will be executed by virtue of the war minister's authority to dispatch local troops for emergency security purposes as the occasion demands.

3. *Measures to be taken:* The Emperor will be restricted to the Imperial Court and other advocates of peace such as Kido [lord privy seal], Suzuki [prime minister], the foreign minister and navy minister will be segregated by the troops. Then martial law will be enforced.

4. *Conditions and Prerequisites:* The *coup* will be carried out on condition that the war minister, the chief of staff of the army, the
Commander of the Eastern District Army, and the Commander of
the Imperial Guards Division all agree.

For the success of the scheme General Anami, the war minister,
had to agree. He was the kingpin; without him this plan was useless.
There was no other military figure in the nation of comparable stature
about whom a resistance movement could be rallied.

The army chief of staff also was essential, because his opposition
could bring to bear the army forces that might destroy the attempt.

The commander of the Eastern District Army had in his grip all
Tokyo and was responsible for its protection and defense. His cooperation, therefore, was all-important too.

The Imperial Guards Division theoretically was responsible only to
the Emperor and was assigned to protect him and guard the palace
and the imperial establishment therein. If the Guards were not in the
plot, a battle could not be avoided. Thus the commandant of the
Guards was essential also.

The conspirators hoped that the falling-domino phenomenon might
work in their favor in bringing the entire army into the scheme.

Anami, listening with eyes closed, was the focus of the plotters'
minute attention and limitless hopes. As the plan unfolded he had
interjected from time to time a weighty "I will dedicate my life to
your cause" and a solemn "I can well understand what Saigo felt."
(Takamori Saigo was popularly believed to have been forced unwillingly and heroically to lead the only serious revolt against the Meiji
regime in 1872. It had failed; he paid with his life.)

With the conspirators seated around him, Anami slowly confided
that he had been dissatisfied with the peace group's behavior since
August 9, when the first day-long cabinet debate of the Potsdam
terms had taken place. Then Anami asked Colonel Arao for the plan.
He studied it closely in silence. "What about the scheme of communications?" he queried.

Arao described how they planned to seal off the palace, cutting the
telephone lines and shutting the gates. He told how they would take
over the broadcasting network and control the press.

Sweeping a handkerchief over his perspiring brow, Anami said
"The plan is very incomplete." He closed his eyes again, then said for

the second time: "I can well understand the feelings of Takamori Saigo on the one hand—" He paused. The plotters hung on his words. "But on the other hand," he mused, "I have offered my life to the Emperor." His listeners eagerly concluded that the war minister had decided to back them in executing the *coup.*

Anami sighed. "The communications plan concerning the palace is too important. It needs work. I will give you an answer after I have thought about the matter."

But this put-off did not suit his visitors. The plotters pressed him for a decision and pleaded with him to go to his office at the war ministry at midnight and give Colonel Arao his answer. Anami agreed. Their scheme had originally been planned to trigger at midnight. Now it would have to be delayed. They had heard that a cabinet meeting was scheduled for ten o'clock the next morning. They decided to make that the new target time.

The meeting began to break up. Anami impressed the young officers with his concern for them. He accompanied them to the porch to see them off, and he cautioned them to return to their quarters in small groups rather than all together. "Be careful," he warned, "since they may be watching you tonight." They were touched at this solicitude, thinking that Anami was afraid the peace faction had set the police or some other agents on their trail and that it showed his resentment and suspicion of the peace faction.

It was after ten when all but one of the conspirators scattered from Anami's residence in three different directions, scurrying before the approaching rain. Takeshita remained behind. He asked his brother-in-law his frank opinion of the *coup* plan. Anami shrugged and replied noncommittally that "one cannot reveal his true thoughts in the presence of such a large group." Takeshita, who was familiar with Anami's manner of speech, was satisfied from this that Anami meant to participate in the *coup.* Immensely encouraged, he left, ducking through the showers.

Anami's secretary Colonel Hayashi had sat silent and observant through all this, as an aide to a Japanese general should. He wasn't satisfied with Anami's words. In fact, he couldn't figure out his chief's intentions and he told him so.

"Although I don't know if you approved of the plan because I was only listening from the side, I think you gave them the impression you agreed with it. You didn't say the plan was right or wrong, but since they were brooding over it excitedly, I think they left with the impression you agreed. If you disapprove, it's necessary to say so definitely. The discussion of the Potsdam declaration is leaking out to the people. Furthermore, only sixty per cent of the workers in the nation's war-munitions plants are reporting to work. Since this is the case, I believe it is useless for the army to insist on continuing the war because the people simply will not follow."

Hayashi had pinpointed a major problem. The Japanese language is inherently a tongue of allusion, ambiguity, and infinite subtlety. It is at its best in poetry, where a few words convey a wide range of sometimes quite contradictory meanings. But it often requires a great many words to convey one meaning and one alone. Anami was making no strenuous effort to avoid misunderstanding. Added to this, the inexactitude of the language made it even more likely that he had been misunderstood.

The war minister regarded Hayashi impassively but said nothing. Hayashi, realizing that the subject was closed, excused himself and left for his billet next door. Anami called for his orderly, had his nightly vitamin shot, followed by a hot bath. The day had been like one long *kendo* session, and he needed the relaxation. The ancient ritual of the *kendo* fencing tournament with the punishing bamboo swords was an art Anami enjoyed; he had in fact attained the fifth rank in proficiency.

Kendo is a grueling sport in which opponents protect their faces, hands, and bodies with armor and wield sturdy bamboo staves. Much cudgeling is inevitable as the opponents try to score points by striking the crown, throat, armpits, or sword hand. But more than the simple win, the greatest achievement in *kendo* is the maintainance of a calm attitude when heavily pressed, meanwhile leaving no opening for the opponent.

In a lengthy day of verbal fencing with Foreign Minister Togo, Navy Minister Yonai, and other peace advocates, Anami had scored few points, taken much punishment. But he had succeeded in remaining calm, in pressing on, and—he believed—leaving no openings.

Driving from his residence to his office through the sweltering blanket of darkness and skittering showers just before midnight, War

Minister Anami was accompanied by Colonel Hayashi, as usual. General Anami was on his way to meet Colonel Arao. As the representative of the plotters, "Koko" Arao expected that the General would give him his final decision about participation in the *coup*. The *coup* would determine whether there would be a *gyokusai*—an Armageddon; whether Japan's cities and towns would be transformed into plantations; whether the nation would be turned back to the Stone Age—to an agricultural, food-hunt society—from its once highly sophisticated industrial complex.

Meanwhile, trusting, hopeful, peace-drunk crowds had been snake-dancing and celebrating V-J day unofficially in London's Piccadilly Circus, New York's Times Square, in San Francisco, Melbourne, and scores of other Allied cities for the past three days. The war minister knew this and, like some of his fellow officers, believed this popular pressure would influence the Allied nations to moderate their terms. His decision at midnight could turn off those victory celebrations abruptly—or make them official.

Bringing down the roof of Japanese civilization in a Samsonesque finale was the unique opportunity open to Anami at this point. He could take over by *coup,* proclaiming martial law. Or he could bring the government down by handing in his resignation—then pick up the pieces as head of the military government that surely would succeed it. With the dictatorial power that would be his in either case the war minister could neutralize the peace faction, isolate the Emperor, and continue the defense of Japanese national polity (the Emperor system) down to the last spear-armed Japanese in the last remote grotto of the homeland. The grinding final battles would be fought with the expectation that the more enemy blood drawn the better the chances that the Allies would settle for less in order to stop the slaughter.

Anami's other options were potent but equally negative: he could continue to fight a skillful delaying action in the cabinet and Supreme Council for Direction of the War sessions. His untiring, passionate opposition to the Potsdam declaration terms had tied up the end of the war since the tenth of August, when the Emperor had said flatly that the terms should be accepted. If Anami made the discussions drag on long enough it would inevitably cause the peace negotiations with the Allies to collapse.

Anami could withdraw from the SCDW meetings—simply refuse to attend them—thereby bringing all discussion to a halt and an inevitable cabinet collapse. He could refuse to sign the imperial rescript, the official document proclaiming the acceptance of the Potsdam terms when and if it was drawn up. This would invalidate the rescript and bring the government down.

Meanwhile, the Japanese army was under Anami's orders of August 10 to:

. . . carry through to its end the holy war for the protection of the Land of the Gods . . . to fight resolutely although that may involve our nibbling grass, eating earth and sleeping in the fields. It is our belief that there is life in death. This is the spirit of the great Nanko who wanted to be reborn seven times in order to serve the country, or the indomitable spirit of Tokimune who refused to entertain delusions and pressed on vigorously with the work of crushing the Mongolian horde. All officers and men of the entire Army without exception should realize the spirit of Nanko and Tokimune and march forward to encounter the mortal enemy.

Now, at midnight on August 13, the war minister arrived amid heat-lightning at his office. His secretary, Colonel Hayashi was at his side. General Anami found Colonel Arao practically hopping in anticipation. Hayashi settled down in the outer office as Arao and the general went into the war minister's room.

In a haze of cigarette smoke and rambling phrases Anami again endorsed the goal of "an inviolable national polity" (i.e., a continuation of Japan's Emperor system) and swore his dedication to the Emperor. Then he told Arao that with war-production efficiency under 60 per cent it was now difficult even to manufacture shells and bullets. He wound up by asking Arao to be prepared to meet with him the next morning at seven to see General Umezu, the army chief of staff, with whom they would discuss the plan. This must mean, concluded Arao, that the war minister is going to participate in the *coup* and is going to persuade General Umezu to cooperate. The Colonel was elated and hurried with this good news to his fellow plotters.

General Anami returned to the car with Hayashi. The sky had cleared. As they drove back to his residence through the now-moonlit vistas of brick chimneys, naked trees, and debris, the war minister described the meeting to Hayashi. "I told Arao what you said to me," Anami said quietly. The force seemed to have gone out of him momentarily. "But I wonder if he will interpret it to mean that I am against the *coup*. What do you think about it?"

Hayashi studied Anami's face in the dim light. He could see no indications of tenseness or strain. The General was in robust health and even with his staggering burden seemed serene. They now had arrived back at the war minister's official residence. Stepping out of the car, the Colonel thought about the fanaticism of the plotters and about Anami's indirectness. "I just wonder," said Hayashi, saluting.

Then Anami was gone in the soft August night.

While the war minister headed for his pillow, his brother-in-law Takeshita and fellow plotters were feeding eagerly on Arao's news. Now that General Anami was with them they could move ahead. The war minister would unquestionably persuade General Umezu to cooperate.

But with the cabinet meeting and the zero hour set for ten o'clock they would have to work fast. They still needed the commanders of the Guards and the Eastern District Army. The conspirators decided to call these two officers and the head of the *kempeitai* (the dreaded military police) to the war minister's office to meet with the General immediately after his talk with Umezu. Then Anami could order them to cooperate. And, of course, if they hesitated to participate, they could be easily disposed of and appropriate orders sent to their deputy commanders.

The conspirators sent word, ostensibly from the war minister, to General Tanaka, commander of the Eastern District Army, to General Mori, commander of the Imperial Guards Division, and General Okido, the *kempeitai* chief to report to General Anami's office at 7:15 A.M. Meanwhile the plotters set about preparing the necessary orders and instructions to the troops.

At last they were in motion! Within half a day they would be in complete command and there would be no further need to tolerate the insolent, sacrilegious peace faction. Then on with the war! until the enemy agreed to reasonable terms—the military's terms.

Chapter 2

The Thief at the Fire

On August 13, 1945, the war minister of Japan was visited by six conspirators determined to take over the government and continue the war in his name. Why he should receive them warmly (as he did) and encourage them (as he did) can be traced back infinitely.

The roots of his action could be found in the mythological origin of Japan, of the peculiar institutions that grew in that isolated land; in the separation of Emperor and ruler; in the prodigious Meiji Restoration; in the ascendancy of the aggressive militarists—and in the recent history of Japan in World War II. His actions could be seen somewhat more clearly, however, by reviewing the events of the preceding four days—since August 9, 1945.

"At present things are in a crude and obscure condition and the people's minds are unsophisticated. They roost in nests or dwell in caves. Their manners are simply what is customary." So it was with the Japanese in August 1945, as it had been when Emperor Jimmu made the observation twenty-six centuries earlier, in 660 B.C.

It was the eighth year of war for Japan. In Tokyo, the sprawling capital city, the bake-oven heat of August was coaxing patches of sweet potatoes to ripeness where hundreds of the city's schools, shops, offices, and homes had formerly stood. Tokyo's history stretched back more than five centuries, but its future looked bleak in this twentieth year of Showa, Hirohito's reign.

Once Tokyo had been the world's third largest city; now more than half of its seven million citizens had fled, been shipped out, conscripted and assigned elsewhere, or killed or maimed in the massive air attacks that had seared the ancient metropolis and burned out half of its buildings. Furthermore, the July edict under which all but 200,000 residents were to evacuate it would leave Tokyo a ghost city.

The capital reeked of char, even though on the morning of August 9 there were no incendiary bombs actively doing their devilry. The billowing, choking smoke had subsided after the last fire raid, but its ashen residue was ground into the fabric of life. Clothing, bedding, walls, food, the earth exuded the invisible carbon essences they had soaked up from the saturated air during and after the fires. Nothing and no one seemed free of them.

The city itself was the heart of a country under siege. More efficiently and intensely than in any other siege in history, the enemy was grinding down the people and every material thing Japanese. Ringed by a blockade of hundreds of surface warships and under-water craft, sealed off by mines and vigilant enemy aircraft, pounded, burned, and ripped by the bombers and guns of the Allies, the Japanese people were rapidly advancing backward. From the most modern industrial nation in Asia Japan was being transformed into a helpless, fragmented society one stage away from the Stone Age.

Children had been among the first evacuees from the cities. Often entire classes went with their teachers to "safe" towns in the country. On the outskirts of Tokyo in one rustic primary schoolhouse there was nevertheless unusual activity on the morning of August 9, 1945. The school had been closed for weeks, but the building was now the site of the radio monitoring operation of Japan's official news service, Domei. Here the receivers were tuned to the world's capitals and here at 4 A.M., in the predawn of this sultry summer day, the operator on the Moscow frequency was shocked from his torpor.

When the Tass broadcast began he was sleepy; by the time it was over he was trembling from head to foot. The operator grabbed the telephone and called Domei's overseas editor at his room in the Imperial Hotel. "Hasegawa," he gasped, "the Russians have attacked us!"

The Russians had declared war, effective at midnight August 8. Russian troops were already rolling across the Manchurian borders of Siberia in three different sectors in a massive triple pincers.

The Domei intercept was relayed to the foreign ministry and its radio section immediately telephoned the foreign minister, aloof, wooden-faced Shigenori Togo. He listened, grim and outraged, to the text:

After the defeat and surrender of Hitlerite Germany, Japan became the only great power that still stood for the continuation of the war.

The demand of the three powers, the United States, Great Britain, and China on July 26 for the unconditional surrender of the Japanese armed forces was rejected by Japan, and thus the proposal of the Japanese Government to the Soviet Union on mediation in the war in the Far East loses all basis.

Taking into consideration the refusal of Japan to capitulate, the Allies submitted to the Soviet Government a proposal to join the war against Japanese aggression and thus shorten the duration of the war, reduce the number of victims, and facilitate the speedy restoration of universal peace.

Loyal to its Allied duty, the Soviet Government accepted the proposal of the Allies and has joined in the declaration of the Allied Powers of July 26.

The Soviet Government considered that this policy is the only means able to bring peace nearer, free the people from further sacrifice and suffering, and give the Japanese people the possibility of avoiding those dangers and destruction suffered by Germany after her refusal to capitulate unconditionally.

In view of the above, the Soviet Government declares that from tomorrow, that is August 9, the Soviet Government will consider itself to be at war with Japan.

This Soviet move, less than seventy-two hours after the Hiroshima bombing, was staggering. None knew this better than Togo—who, through the Japanese ambassador in Moscow, had been trying since Germany's surrender in May to get the Soviets to act as peace mediator with the Allies.

The Americans knew this also, because the U.S. had cracked the Japanese code and was diligently monitoring and reading Japanese communications. One of the most important messages of the war was Togo's cable of July 12 to Sato in Moscow: ". . . it is His Majesty's heart's desire to see the swift termination of the war. In the Greater East Asia War, however, as long as America and England insist on unconditional surrender our country has no alternative but to see it through in an all-out effort for the sake of survival and the honor of the homeland." Though this flat statement of the Emperor's intentions should have caused the U.S. to make quick and direct diplomatic efforts to end the war at that point, no action was taken to capitalize on this golden opportunity.

The Russians kept Sato, Japan's ambassador, at arm's length so that he could not get a straight yes-or-no answer to his attempts to arrange for mediation: The Japanese listed no specifications in their request. What did they wish? Sato said they wished permission for Prince Konoye to come to Moscow on a special mission as the Emperor's personal representative. The Soviets countered with questions about the purpose of the mission, then about specifics and details. The real purpose of these Soviet responses, as Stalin told Truman at Potsdam, was to lull the Japanese, to lead them to believe that the request was under active consideration—until the Soviets were ready to strike.

The Japanese leaders had fastened their sights and hopes single-mindedly on this straw. They hoped the Soviets might be an avenue to the Allies and that through this channel the unconditional surrender demand could be modified. And they hoped that this admission of defeat would encourage the Soviets to stay neutral.

These hopes were built on the shifting sands of Soviet expediency. Sato had sent back a long series of explicit notes to the foreign minister telling him how useless this effort was likely to be. He entreated Togo to make peace before Japan suffered Germany's fate. One of Sato's notes estimated that Russia would attack Japan sometime after August 1. These notes had not boosted Sato's popularity either in the foreign ministry or in the Japanese cabinet. Nor was the fact that he was now proved an accurate observer destined to enlarge his circle of admirers. Bitter prophecy proved accurate brings no applause.

What had been dreaded in Japan had finally happened. The Soviets had dropped the first shoe in April 1945, when they denounced the Japan–Soviet Neutrality Pact. Now they had dropped the other shoe. While Japan's cities were going up in flames or evaporating in mushroom clouds, the Soviet Union struck like a thief at a fire. The suspense, at least, was over. The slaughter had spread to still another quarter.

"Before dawn I was notified by the foreign ministry radio operator that Russia had declared war on Japan and invaded Manchuria," noted Togo. "I went immediately to call on the prime minister [Admiral Baron Kantaro Suzuki] who had been bombed out. . . . I reminded the PM that I had asked him to call together members of the Supreme Council for Direction of the War to discuss the atom bombing of Hiroshima and added that I felt it more urgent than ever, now, that a decision be made to terminate the war immediately. The PM agreed."

The venerable premier tended to agree with whatever was said. It was one of his most confusing and infuriating characteristics. Now he turned to the young chief cabinet secretary, Hisatsune Sakomizu, who had arrived shortly before, and told him to summon the members of the SCDW to the earliest possible meeting.

Then Suzuki thought of Lieutenant General Sumihisa Ikeda, chief of the Cabinet Planning Bureau. Ikeda had been with the Kwantung army in Manchuria until three weeks ago, therefore was familiar with its ability to resist the Soviet advance. The premier telephoned Ikeda and asked the large-boned, statistically minded soldier "Is the Kwantung army capable of repulsing the Soviet advance?"

"The Kwantung army is hopeless," responded Ikeda. "Within two weeks Changchu [the major city in central Manchuria] will be occupied."

Suzuki, by now resigned to unpleasant news, sighed. "Is the Kwantung army that weak? Then the game is up."

"The greater the delay in making the final decision," Ikeda advised, "the worse the situation will be for us."

"Absolutely correct," concurred the premier.

It is strange, mused Ikeda, that the premier never expresses any opinion of his own, either at the cabinet meetings or at the imperial conferences.

In his billet southeast of the palace Lieutenant Colonel Masahiko Takeshita was dozing when the plaintive ring of the telephone pierced his sleep and ousted him from bed. Takeshita was handsome, hotheaded and bristling with energy.

The telephone call was from the war ministry: A report is just in from the Kwantung army (Japan's major military force in China and

Manchuria). The Russians have attacked. Get over here right away.

Takeshita jumped into his uniform, hailed one of the charcoal-burning staff cars and putted noisily to the war ministry building. He found discussion raging full blast. It centered around the Russian invasion; the treachery of the Soviets in striking without warning; their lies in justifying their attack; the strength of the Kwantung army to resist; the fate of the Emperor if they won; fate of the empire if they won; fate of the army leaders if they won.

Suddenly it was a different war. Though Russia's attack had long been feared Japan was not prepared for it, according to Lieutenant General Kawabe, the army's vice chief of staff: "Russian entry was a great shock when it actually came, whereas the atom bomb impact was not so readily apparent. Since Tokyo was not directly affected by the bombing, the full force of the shock was not felt. . . . [But] reports reaching Tokyo described Russian forces as 'invading in swarms.' It gave us all the more severe shock and alarm because we had been in constant fear of it with a vivid imagination that 'the vast Red army forces in Europe were now being turned against us.' "

The Soviet attack should not have been a shock. Japanese intelligence reports stated that Russian troops, guns, tanks, and other equipment were being shipped to Siberia beginning in February 1945. Even the rate was reported: thirty carloads a day. By the end of May, intelligence estimated that shipments totaled 870 guns, 1200 tanks, 1300 planes, and more than 160,000 men. Of course the shipments had increased after the German collapse in May. One significant point reported was that these troops were not equipped for winter fighting. Apparently they were planning for a short and sweet campaign—soon.

The Russians could well remember their clashes with Japan, and vice versa. Well within the memory of living men Russia had suffered severe casualties at Japan's hands on three previous occasions. And there had been continued friction between them.

Japan had traded her claims to Sakhalin for the Kurile Islands in 1875. Twenty years later Russia stepped in when Japan defeated China and seemed about to enlarge her mainland empire. That same year Japan was forced by the triple intervention of Russia, France, and Germany to give up claims to Port Arthur and evacuate that city in exchange for considerable silver. It rankled the sensitive Japanese that only three years later Russia took over Port Arthur (leasing it from China).

This was one of the elements that had fueled the Russo-Japanese war of 1904. In it, Japan attacked Russia by surprise and quickly finished off the Russian navy and Siberian army. Japan exhausted herself in the process, however, and was delighted when Theodore Roosevelt stepped in as peacemaker. The Treaty of Portsmouth gave half of Sakhalin to Japan and Russia surrendered her lease on the Kwantung Peninsula and Port Arthur, packed up and left Manchuria, and recognized Japan's sphere of influence in Korea.

When the Russian Revolution occurred in 1917, the Japanese were "invited" by the British and Americans to send troops into Siberia to "maintain the *status quo.*" The request was for 7000 troops from each Allied power for this expedition. The Japanese enthusiastically cooperated—so much so that they lost count until ten times 7000 had been dispatched. And then they lost track of the time.

When the other Allies withdrew their troops the Japanese stayed on and on. And on. Only after polite but firm diplomatic pressure from Britain and the U.S. were the Japanese troops withdrawn from Siberia two years after other Allied forces had been pulled out, and it took Japan an additional two years to withdraw troops from Russian Sakhalin. Japanese forces had reached the central Siberian city of Irkutsk, nearly 1400 miles from the Sea of Japan, before their withdrawal.

Border brushes between Japan and the Russians were frequent after Japan took over Korea, set up its puppet Manchukuo empire in Manchuria in 1931, and swept Chinese resistance aside as it advanced into Inner Mongolia. Japan also squeezed oil and fishing concessions from Russia.

By mid-1938, Japan's military leaders in Manchuria thought it time to test Russian strength. They launched a sizable border probe at Changkufeng at the corner where Korea, Manchuria, and Siberia meet. The Soviets gave them a stinging defeat. The following spring the Japanese tried another border adventure. The Kwantung army itself attacked Soviet positions in Outer Mongolia at Nomonhan. This rapidly escalated into a small war, with 300,000 troops battling in what was the world's largest clash of mechanized armies up to that time. After an estimated 50,000 casualties, the Japanese decided to call the whole thing off.

With this history of Russo-Japanese abrasion, there was little question in the minds of Japanese officers that sulfurous morning of August 9, 1945, that the Soviets would be after all they could grab. And the Japanese officers at GHQ knew what the world suspected but the Japanese people did not know: that the vaunted Kwantung army had been tapped for troops and weapons for the other Japanese campaigns until little was left. It was even said the troops had but one rifle for three men. The beetle looks formidable until one discovers the shell is empty.

Most chilling of all was the prospect that the Russians would influence peace negotiations.

With the Soviets in the war and subscribing to the Potsdam declaration, the terms about occupation and free elections in that declaration were absolutely unthinkable. No Japanese would be safe with the Soviets sharing control of the nation. It meant that the Russians would be able to stimulate and support Communist movements in Nippon, that the Reds would attempt to take over and, with Soviet aid, might one day be successful. Then it would be an easy matter to annex Japan as part of the USSR.

Surely the Soviets would do all in their power as occupiers of the land to crush the Japanese under their heels. Most disturbing of all, the Russian occupiers, able to arrest anybody at any time, could arrest even the Emperor himself. Thus they could end the imperial family overnight. In a wink they could snuff out 2600 years of "unbroken" rule, ending the unique national polity of Japan. Either way, to submit to the Potsdam terms and suffer the Allies and/or Soviets on Japanese soil was unthinkable.

In the view of the army officers at Imperial GHQ and the war ministry, there was no alternative to redoubled effort to prevent the horrors of occupation. Thus a fight to the finish, lapsing into scorched-earth tactics and guerrilla warfare in the mountains was the only course. Many of them had served in China and knew that although Japan had fought there for eight years she controlled only the population centers and communication lines, not the country. It would be so in Japan also, with the enemy occupying the key cities, ports, and rail lines, but no occupying force could police all the coastline or control 80,000,000 determined Japanese imbued with the unconquerable spirit of the Yamato race. The Allies could never vanquish Japan.

In the brick-and-stone navy ministry building there was excited discussion also that August 9 morning. Vice-Admiral Zenshiro Hoshina, chief of the Military Affairs Bureau of the ministry, the unit at the fulcrum of navy power, concluded after learning of the Russian attack that the weight of events demanded a final decision for war or peace. Hoshina first called on Vice-Admiral Takajiro Onishi, the navy vice-chief of staff.

Onishi was the fanatical officer credited with perfecting the "special attack" techniques and developing the *kamikaze* (divine wind) planes and boats and their suicide pilots into a formidable instrument. In the Okinawa campaign alone, Onishi's suicide tactics had cost the American navy more ships and lives than any comparable battle in its history.

Beginning with the battles in the Philippines in late 1944, Onishi's deadly brainchild, the Special Attack Corps, had hurled 665 navy officers and 1400 enlisted men at the enemy. Onishi was the focal point if not the active leader of the navy's "bitter-enders."

Hoshina, fully aware of Onishi's inclinations, wanted to verify his current outlook since the Russian entry into the war. "Does the high command still have confidence in the military situation? Whether it has or not is the key to the decision of our policy. If it has no confidence, there is no alternative for Japan but to accept the Potsdam declaration and end the war. What do you think?"

Onishi replied at some length, minimizing the importance of the atom bomb, the Russian participation in the war, the steadily dwindling supply of seaworthy Japanese vessels, oil, and gasoline. He stressed the effectiveness of the special attacks and the suicide weapons now being readied. With the supreme certainty of the self-righteous zealot he stated that there were "ample chances of victory for Japan."

Hoshina then went to the office of Navy Minister Admiral Mitsumasa Yonai. He found the hulking Yonai slouched behind his desk. But before Hoshina could say a word Yonai shifted in his chair and laconically commented "I have given up the war."

Thus the rift was clearly and openly stated for the first time. Certain top officers of the naval high command favored battle to the end; the navy minister wanted to end the conflict. Quite a contrast to the top-to-bottom jingoism in the army. If the war minister had made the same statement as Yonai, he would undoubtedly have been cut down by an assassin.

Chapter 3

The Old New Leader

The leader of Japan at this final hour was a man of unquestioned integrity and loyalty to the Emperor, the seventy-seven-year-old Admiral Baron Kantaro Suzuki. A less likely choice to lead a nation through its severest trials could hardly be imagined.

By the time of the Russian attack, Suzuki had been premier of Japan for four months during which the nation's way of life had literally been destroyed. Still the government had not yet publicly acknowledged this fact, and Suzuki was often to be found reading Laotse in his office while his foreign minister tried frantically to run up a truce flag.

On April 1, 1945, just a week after the fall of Iwo Jima, the Allied landings on Okinawa began in earnest. By the fifth the beachhead, only lightly defended by the Japanese, was firmly established. On that day the Soviet Union renounced the Japan–Soviet Neutrality Pact. Also on the fifth, Japan's premier, General Kuniaki Koiso, resigned.

That evening Koichi Kido, lord keeper of the privy seal, called together the *jushin,* the senior statesmen—the former prime ministers and the president of the privy council.

All but one had served as premier of Japan, and all in a sense had failed at the job. Tojo, for instance, had failed to win the war; Prince Konoye had failed to prevent it. Baron Hiranuma's efforts to effect a Japan-Berlin pact had fizzled; Admiral Okada could not avert a military revolt in 1936; Koki Hirota was unable to control the army; Reijiro Wakatsuki, although he tried, could neither sidetrack nor halt

23

the Japanese army's invasion of Manchuria. The only nonpolitician in the group, the only one not an ex-premier, was the president of the privy council, moss-browed Baron Suzuki.

Kido's purpose in gathering these men was to tap their wisdom for a nominee to succeed the premier who had just resigned. As usual, the privy seal had made discreet prior inquiries so that the results of the meeting would not be unexpected; if he had not rigged the game, he had at least stacked the deck.

The privy seal had set his formidable talents to arranging that Admiral Suzuki be appointed premier. Kido had sent his secretary to fathom the Admiral's views. He then sounded out the Emperor and found no objection to Suzuki for the post. The privy seal had discussed Suzuki with three of the seven *jushin* before the meeting and they agreed to recommend the old man for the job.

When the council settled down in earnest to outline the qualifications for the next premier, Tojo led off, saying that the new cabinet must be the last. Suzuki seconded this, holding that the new government would have to fight out the war at any cost: "The succeeding cabinet leader would be considered incompetent if he did not have this determination."

Over their tea the senior statesmen discussed whether the next premier must be a military man in the active service, as Tojo and Koiso had been. Tojo contended that only a military man could manage both the nation and the war at this stage. Suzuki pointed out that Prince Ito, premier at the time of the Sino-Japanese war in 1894, had not been a serviceman and contended that a military man was not required.

Prince Konoye raised two criteria: the new premier must be worthy of trust; he must be a person unaffected by past circumstances—he must come in with clean hands, untainted by association with past failures. These guideposts were adopted by the group.

Suzuki suggested that the *jushin* take on the task of running the government as a joint effort. "We ought to be prepared to sacrifice ourselves for the state, to assume every responsibility and to die in action for His Majesty. As for the prime minister's office, I should like to ask Prince Konoye, the youngest among us, to assume it as the assignment is physically most strenuous. Beyond that, all of us would do the rest. How about four of us making an effort first?"

This was quashed by Konoye and Hiranuma, who pointed out that this directly contradicted the principles just approved. Hiranuma then nominated Suzuki, and this was seconded by Konoye and Wakatsuki. Suzuki was appalled: "I have always thought that the participation of servicemen in politics would ruin the country. This was the case with the Roman Empire, also with the Kaiser and the end of the Romanoffs. [Believing this, it is impossible] for me to take part in political affairs. Besides, I am hard of hearing and I would like to be excused."

Suzuki could have mentioned other handicaps: He was nearly eighty; he really detested politics; he was guileless; he was a Taoist and devotedly practiced that belief's precept that obscurity is a high virtue. But if the old sailor thought he could sidestep the mantle he was mistaken. He was urged to accept by Kido and all but one of the *jushin:* Tojo. The General warned brusquely: "If you are not very careful it is possible that the army will turn away [withdraw support]. If it should, the cabinet will have to be dissolved."

"It is terribly serious that at such a time as this the army might turn away," Kido replied. "But are there any signs of this?"

"I would say there are," Tojo snapped. This was an unmistakable threat that the military might pull out of any government it could not control. Perhaps only a joint army-navy government would satisfy the military. Perhaps a military *coup d'état* and martial law would be their preference.

The lord keeper of the privy seal called Suzuki aside as the other *jushin* went in to dinner. "You were extremely reluctant a little while ago, but in view of the current situation I implore you to form a cabinet at any cost. I am sorry to trouble you, but will you accept?"

Suzuki, feeling trapped, said "I would like to decline since I have no confidence in myself to do the job."

Kido, knowing that Suzuki was hard of hearing and always spoke ambiguously, pressed him. "The conditions at present are so critical that I must implore you to make a great decision to save our nation."

What Japan required at that desperate moment was a modern-day military and political genius who could turn adversity into advantage, an Oriental Alexander. Instead she had placed at the helm a superannuated naval hero of the wars of 1894 and 1904, a venerable grandfather-figure who for a decade had been major domo for the

Imperial Court, arranging state affairs and directing protocol as grand chamberlain to the Emperor.

Why this choice? Domestically, Suzuki's appointment was a master stroke in many ways. Suzuki was venerated by the public as a genuine war hero. The ancient mariner enjoyed the Emperor's complete confidence. "To Suzuki," Hirohito felt, "I could pour out my heart." His Majesty referred to him informally as *oyaji*—uncle.

There were other subtler reasons for making him premier. Clearly he was not part of the army war clique. Thus to the nation and to the world this was a signal that the army and the all-out-war advocates had been unsaddled. Suzuki was so unworldly regarding political infighting that both the hard-line jingoists and the peace faction believed they would have room to maneuver. With no strong policy of his own, Suzuki, they thought, could be swayed or would assent to decisions developed by others.

The old Admiral did not arouse antagonism, resentment, and jealousy as had premiers General Tojo and General Koiso. Tojo had been highly unpopular because he was so iron-fisted and arbitrary. Koiso stirred up the army, the Court, and the people because he was so clumsy. Suzuki was widely known to be an humble man and, true to his Taoist beliefs, was free of ambition and selfish purpose.

Nevertheless, there were some who had serious reservations about him.

"Army circles were doubtful that at his age he would be able to take prompt and efficient measures to meet the current war situation both at home and abroad," reported the chief of the war ministry's Military Affairs Section. "But at the time there was no strong [official] opposition in army circles to the appointment, since the army knew that Suzuki enjoyed the particularly deep confidence of the Emperor and therefore his premiership would work to the benefit of the army if he accepted army proposals. Further, he was the brother of General Takao Suzuki, in whom the army placed confidence."

As premier-designate, one of Suzuki's first acts was to telephone his friend, former premier Admiral Okada, who had been out of politics for nineteen years and retired from the navy for seven years, and ask him to be the new navy minister. Okada, astonished and apprehensive, immediately rushed to the prime minister's official residence to confer with Suzuki.

The absurdity of Suzuki's idea was blinding: Okada, when he was premier, had been so violently opposed by army extremists that in 1936 they attempted to kill him. He was a retired admiral. The posts of war and navy minister required military men in active service. Obviously Suzuki had not consulted the kingmakers in the navy about this (they would have opposed Okada). But this was an absolute prerequisite if he expected to gain their cooperation.

When Okada arrived at the premier's home his fears were confirmed. He found a group of people "who were not even accustomed to making phone calls," to say nothing of finding their way around the political jungle.

Okada sat down and talked to Suzuki like a Dutch uncle. It was clear that the old man needed somebody with political experience on whom he could rely. Okada recommended a young man he knew to be experienced, Hisatsune Sakomizu. Sakomizu, forty-three, had served as his private secretary when Okada was premier and had continued his interest in politics. In fact, he was now director of banking and insurance in the finance ministry. Okada could vouch for him. And, just incidentally, Sakomizu was his son-in-law. Suzuki appointed Sakomizu to the post of chief cabinet secretary, the wheelhorse spot in the cabinet.

Okada and Sakomizu told the old Admiral the political facts of life in forming a cabinet and the old man heeded their counsel. The first stop on the circuit was the army.

Suzuki, in forming his cabinet, called as was customary on the outgoing war minister, Marshal Sugiyama. He requested the army's recommendation for the post of war minister in his government. Suzuki himself wanted General Korechika Anami, who had been aide-de-camp to the Emperor when the premier was His Majesty's grand chamberlain. He had known Anami intimately in those days fifteen years before, and respected and trusted the General. But the procedure was to request the army to "nominate" a candidate.

In anticipation of this, the army leaders had not only selected a successor but had also, as usual, drawn up a list of conditions. Unless the new premier approved the conditions the army set out, it would withhold a nomination for war minister. And of course a cabinet without a war minister was impossible.

Marshal Sugiyama handed Suzuki the army's list of conditions:

1. Prosecution of the war to the bitter end.
2. Proper settlement of the army-navy unification problem.
3. Organize the nation to carry out the decisive battle in the Homeland.

Each of these points generated considerable heat within the army. There had been speculation that Suzuki would be a Japanese Badoglio and, like the Italian marshal, simply come to power, then sue for peace. Some factions within the army did not oppose a negotiated peace, but all rejected unconditional surrender as tantamount to national suicide. Thus point 1 was meant to put the new premier on record on this score.

Point 2 was a sore one within both services. Following the late thirties there had been increasing friction between army and navy for fair shares of the limited national output. Each wanted more to build up its strength; each fought the other's allocation of industrial output; each attempted to outbid the other for aircraft and armament production, compounding enmity with inevitable inflation.

Unification of the services had been an urgent matter since 1940, but had not advanced significantly. So concerned were the younger officers at GHQ about this that they agitated for it vehemently. Major Hatanaka and Lieutenant Colonel Shiizaki, for example, submitted to their superior officer a petition written in blood demanding the resignation of War Minister Sugiyama "who has been unable to unify the army and navy."

The third point was included because the army thought it inevitable that the enemy would land on the homeland and that in preparation for the battle various laws and ordinances would be needed to build forts and organize militia.

Suzuki read the three points rapidly, nodded his massive head vigorously, and said "I am in agreement with all of these points." Then, and only then, did the army approve Anami as the new war minister.

In general, most Japanese shared the new war minister's opinion of Suzuki. Anami called the old Admiral *teitoku* (great naval man), and told his army associates "the prime minister is not the type of man who would deceive the people and lead them into making peace. He is not the sort who, while planning peace, shouts war."

Suzuki was born in the last year of Japan's feudal era, 1867, the year of the Meiji Restoration that modernized the nation. His father's minor political post was wiped out in that process, and the family of eleven moved first to Tokyo, then to a small provincial town where the boy was educated. He convinced his parents to let him enter a navy prep school and went from that to the naval academy.

He was skipper of a torpedo boat in the China war (1894–1895) and received honors for bravery in action for sinking a Chinese warship, destroying a breakwater, and saving another Japanese vessel and its crew. This brought fame, home leave, the opportunity to marry and enter the Naval War College. Later, the navy sent him to Germany to study naval education and he traveled widely for two years. In the Russo-Japanese war he was in command of a cruiser when the Russian Baltic Fleet finally arrived for its date with doom. Suzuki's ship destroyed two enemy vessels.

Suzuki went on to hold the highest offices in Japan's navy—commander-in-chief, combined fleet; chief of staff; war councilor to His Majesty. In 1929 he was appointed grand chamberlain to the Emperor and his strenuous efforts to convince navy hotheads to comply with His Majesty's wishes during the London Naval Conference made him a marked man. On February 26, 1936, he stood face to face with the blind fury of fanatical young military men. A group of assassins shot him four times almost killing him in the short-lived military revolt known in Japan as the 2–26 Incident.

The old Admiral and the other targets were listed by the rebels as "false counselors" to the Emperor. The grand chamberlain qualified in their eyes because of his support of the 5–5–3 naval ship ratio, his known belief that military men should keep out of politics, and his access to the Emperor.

In 1940 this "former naval person" was named vice-president of the privy council and in August 1944 moved up to its presidency and thereby became one of the *jushin*. When he agreed to be premier, he knew he was putting his head on the block. The alternatives for him and his cabinet were grim: If the Allies didn't get them as war criminals the disgruntled "double-patriots" might; some of Suzuki's associates experienced the wrath of both. And the old man was once again marked as an assassin's target.

The paramount goal of Suzuki's administration was to wind up the war. It had to be. The Emperor wanted it ended quickly. Influential men in business and the aristocracy saw only one alternative to oblivion. Even the masses were sick of incessant, practically unopposed bombing, of starvation rations and sacrifice. The army was another matter. The army acted as if victory was possible, if not inevitable, if the war continued for another decade or two. And the army had five million armed men backing its view.

In these circumstances Suzuki's Taoist vagueness was, at times, an advantage. But it also had grave drawbacks. His belief that one could communicate without words was admirable but frustrating. He was not alone in this approach. For instance, the Emperor, in investing Suzuki with the power of prime minister, said nothing to him on the overriding subject. Nor did Suzuki ask. Why?

"I was aware of Suzuki's sentiments," said Hirohito later, "from the very beginning of his appointment and likewise I was convinced that Suzuki understood my sentiments. Consequently, I was not in a hurry at the time to express to him my desires for peace." That was part of it. Another part was that on every previous occasion when the Emperor revealed his ideas they leaked out in distorted fashion through subordinates and caused embarrassing situations. This time, His Majesty was convinced that such a leak could seriously endanger the chances for peace.

Suzuki apparently read the vibrations accurately. "When I suddenly had to face this unexpected fate," the old man commented later, "my first thought was to end the war as soon as possible because I could read and catch what the Emperor was thinking when I saw him right after the appointment. I could easily understand he sincerely hoped to end the war and recover the peace even though he said nothing about it. However, I could not tell anyone about it, because if anyone knew that I had such an idea, there would have been all kinds of disturbance and riots. So I did not tell my true feelings even to Sakomizu. I was just waiting for a chance to end the war."

So, though his supposed purpose was to arrange a surrender, the new premier's first address to his countrymen was a fiery call to all-out battle to the bitter end. "The war must go forward," he urged, "even if it is over my dead body."

To the Diet he outlined Japan's goals in terms that have a contemporary ring:

The current war is a war for the liberation of Asia aimed at frustrating the design of our enemies, the U.S. and Britain, to turn Asian countries into their slaves. We must bring home to our mind that not only the freedom of the various races in Greater East Asia will be lost forever but also justice in the world will be trampled down completely if we fail in this war. . . .

Japan's fundamental policy for Greater East Asia and the world is to establish an effective system to guarantee the security of the various countries from threats or invasions and to assure them co-existence and co-prosperity in line with the fundamental principle of political equality, economic reciprocity and respect of one another's culture.

He also pinpointed the major roadblock to negotiating a surrender:

The people of Japan are dedicated servants of the Imperial Throne. The Japanese will lose the meaning of their existence if the national polity [the Emperor system] is impaired. An unconditional surrender as proposed by the enemy, therefore, is tantamount to the death of all 100 million people of Japan. We have no alternative but to fight.

Then he outlined the challenge:

If our homeland becomes a battleground, we will have the advantages of position and of personnel working in harmony against the enemy. We will have no difficulty in concentrating huge numbers of troops at any desired position and providing them with matériel. The situation then will be different from the battles fought on isolated islands in the Pacific. We will then be able to annihilate the enemy forces. At this stage of the intensified war, we are not assured of abundant food supplies. Nor is transportation unhindered. Moreover, munitions production will become increasingly difficult. . . . Frankly speaking, we need stepped-up efforts in the future. Judging not only from the trend of the domestic situations in enemy countries and the current delicate international situation, I cannot help feeling that the shortest cut to our victory is to fight this war through.

Suzuki was capable of outlandish sophistry. Speaking of the fall of Iwo Jima, he said:

We can never tell what a fatal blow the unyielding fighting spirit of Japanese soldiers on Iwo Jima and Okinawa has given the enemy mentally. When we compare the magnitude of this shock to the enemy with what we have lost on these islands, we can conclude that we are not losing the war.

The face value of his public statements could only be a vigorous continuation of the war. But this was a superficial reading of his intent. For the former naval person was exercising that Japanese technique known as *haragei* (literally *hara:* stomach—the source of intentions or spirit; *gei:* talk, art or achievement) or "stomach talk." In this communication, the specific words are less significant than the over-all context of the statement. They may be, in fact, diametrically opposed to the true intent of the speaker. This is a historically important fact of talking and listening in Japan, a pattern that stretches back into antiquity.

Theory places its origin in the nature of life in Japan. Families have traditionally crowded into limited space so that privacy, not to mention separate rooms, was practically unknown. A leading contemporary Japanese architect points out that the only sanctuary was the *benjo,* toilet room, and only there could the individual privately release his tears, his despair, his inmost feelings.

In the communal life of the household there were always inevitably two audiences for every word—the intended and the uninvited. Therefore the technique of saying one thing and conveying another was often a practical necessity. Moreover, because of the light construction of many Japanese buildings, with their sliding paper and wood walls and rice-mat floors, voices could be overheard with little difficulty. And one never knew who might be listening. This too was a stimulus to perfection of stomach (real-self) talk, rather than tongue (superficial) talk.

Caught between the necessity to end the war speedily and the adamant opposition of the military, Suzuki employed his *haragei* and hoped for the best.

But temperamentally the rough-and-tumble of political life was not the old Admiral's *metier.* A devoted Taoist—a follower of the Chinese philosopher Lao-tse—he could usually be found reading Taoist works at his desk in the premier's office building. At home Suzuki was fond of playing solitaire with a grubby pack of cards, but at the office his chosen companions were books—history, biography, and Taoist philosophy.

Hisatsune Sakomizu, the chief cabinet secretary, often found the premier at his desk, bushy brows high and chin thrust forward as he avidly read works by such Taoists as Chuang-tzu. Chuang was celebrated for championing the theories that happiness may be achieved only by free development of man's nature and that the best way of governing is through nongovernment.

Suzuki was constantly adding to his library of more than 20,000 volumes and, absorbed in the philosophy that sets a premium on inactivity and believes passivity more potent than action, he spent hours scanning books at his office.

Sometimes, however, Sakomizu would slip into the room and find Suzuki "pacing the quarter deck," shoulders hunched, hands on hips, blowing clouds of cigar smoke as he shuffled in a confined circle like a gray-headed beetle toddling along on its hind legs.

It was a serious problem, as the Court and the cabinet discovered, that from one moment to the next one could never be sure where he stood. While he vacillated, Japan was being reduced to ashes.

Suzuki's field of vision was practically closed out by an obstacle barring the way. The barrier was the simmering opposition of the extremists in the army and navy. Both Privy Seal Kido and Foreign Minister Togo were trying to guide the old man's steps around this explosive hazard. But every time they set him on a path, the war minister and his cohorts took him down a fork in the road. Now that the Russians had attacked it was time to put Lao-tse on the shelf and concentrate on the Potsdam declaration.

Chapter 4

The Big Six

The SCDW—Supreme Council for Direction of the War—was an "inner cabinet" consisting of the premier, the ministers of war, navy, and foreign affairs, and the army and navy chiefs of staff. These men were the "Big Six." The SCDW had no constitutional sanction; theoretically it had power only to consult and advise, not to execute. But with its concentration of power its decisions had major force. When the SCDW met, Japan stood still.

The SCDW was, in effect, a jury of six deciding Japan's fate and affecting the lives of millions in distant areas around the world as well. Not directly, of course, for that would have been un-Japanese. The cabinet, not the SCDW, had the legal power to act for the nation, but the center of gravity was in the SCDW and its decisions inevitably moved the entire cabinet.

By August 9, the SCDW members should have known one another's positions with no voids. They had been meeting more and more frequently, discussing more pointedly as enemy pressure mounted. But though they had spent seemingly endless hours talking about how to end the war, there were still substantial questions about which of these powerful men would opt for what, now that the range of alternatives had narrowed so drastically.

Foreign Minister Shigenori Togo, sixty-two, was Suzuki's second choice for that post. Privy Seal Kido had suggested retaining Mr. Shigemitsu, the foreign minister in the preceding Koiso cabinet. But Koiso had vetoed that.

Admiral Okada recommended Togo. The privy seal endorsed this

34

choice and Kido's private secretary described why: "The war could not be ended in the domestic circumstances then prevailing without a foreign minister who had unusual sincerity as well as superior brilliance and the determination even to risk his life . . . there was no such candidate other than Togo."

Suzuki reached Togo in the resort town of Karuizawa, where he had "rusticated" most of the time since his abrupt resignation as Tojo's foreign minister in September 1942. Togo took the next train for Tokyo and at 10:30 P.M. on the seventh of April met with Suzuki to see if they thought alike about the direction the government should travel.

Togo asked Suzuki for his view of the prospect of the war. The premier replied "I think we can carry on for another two or three years." Togo practically threw up his hands.

"Modern war," he told the old Admiral, "depends mainly on materials and production. Because of this, Japan cannot continue even one more year." Togo felt they would be unable to cooperate effectively with such divergent views. He thanked Suzuki and declined the offer.

But the next day a succession of important callers—Admiral Okada, Sakomizu, Kido's secretary, two of Togo's former seniors in the Foreign Office—pressed Togo to take the post. They said Suzuki could not speak of an early peace because of possible repercussions; that the old man's mind was not decided on the subject and that Togo could and must help him to mold policy on this. Kido confided that the Emperor was considering ending the war and that the privy seal considered it vital that Togo accept.

Togo saw Suzuki once more and this time the old sailor said "So far as the prospect of the war is concerned, your opinion is quite satisfactory to me; and as to diplomacy, you shall have a free hand." On this basis Togo accepted the post.

"Foreign Minister Togo, as a man, was taciturn, expressionless and singularly bereft of anything that could be described as personal charm," wrote his *Gaimusho* (foreign ministry) contemporary Shigeru Yoshida. Blunt, articulate, and determined, he was a Prussian from Satsuma, the province from which the Meiji Restoration's prime movers had come.

Togo's driving, tenacious advocacy and Western-style logic were used by Japan both to start and end the war. It was he, as foreign minister in the Tojo cabinet in 1941, who conducted those final, futile weeks of negotiation that terminated with the Japanese ambassadors arriving an hour late at U.S. Secretary of State Hull's office to deliver a message intended for presentation precisely thirty minutes before Pearl Harbor was attacked.

Formidable was the word that instantly came to mind in describing Togo. His face was pentagonal, capped with a thick shock of steel-gray hair. Beneath his trident-nose was a brush mustache and a mouth poised halfway between a sneer and a grimace. On the large rounded ears were hooked the huge circular black-rimmed glasses that made the job of wartime Allied caricaturists so easy. Behind the glasses the eyes were recumbent commas set above wide, apple-half cheekbones. In dress, Togo was dapper, favoring conservative suits and striped shirts with French cuffs and handkerchiefs that matched his ties. His face carried an expression that pointedly asked "What do you want? Why are you taking up my time? Are you through yet?"

So intimidating was Togo that his subordinates scuttled out of his way when he approached. He was upset, at the end of the war, that there were no suggestions for bringing the fighting to a close from *Gaimusho* personnel. This was in part because of his intimidating nature. But his technique for smoking out proposals and ideas was indicative of his distance from his associates: He asked his daughter Ise to see if her husband (Togo's secretary) and his colleagues at the foreign ministry did not have some thoughts on the subject!

Togo was a career diplomat cut from the classic material. He majored in German literature at Tokyo University, where careers in Japan's foreign service generally began. During World War I he was posted to Switzerland and was a junior member of Japan's delegation to Versailles. He was then sent to Germany to observe conditions and report on the impact of the peace terms. The miseries of war impressed him indelibly.

In the twenties, Togo was first secretary of the Japanese embassy in Washington for four years. After a hitch in Germany he became a bureau chief in the foreign ministry. There he drafted a far-seeing policy paper regarding Japan's relations with Russia, which he considered of paramount importance, second only to relations with China.

The Japanese press credited him as behind-the-scenes strategist for two Japanese foreign ministers of the thirties who swerved away from the liberal foreign policies of the twenties. He was said to be head of the "orthodox current" at *Gaimusho*.

It was ironic that in 1937 he was assigned as His Majesty's ambassador to Nazi Germany. Temperamentally and philosophically opposed to the Nazis, the lover of Schiller and Goethe was a colossal failure in his Berlin tour of duty. He was on bad terms with Ribbentrop, German's foreign minister, and other Nazi officials. "Japan cannot have serious negotiations with an upstart like Hitler," he once stated.

If Togo had ever had illusions about where the signals were being called in Japan, his Berlin experience wiped them out completely. For it was General Oshima, the Japanese military attaché, who was ignoring protocol and carrying on secret negotiations with Ribbentrop to convert the Berlin–Tokyo Anti-Comintern pact into a full-fledged military alliance. Oshima reported to the military in Japan, not to the foreign ministry. The General was purposely bypassing his ambassador and keeping him in the dark about the negotiations. The Nazis went to and through Oshima, not the diplomats, to secure Japan's cooperation. No wonder Japanese newsmen in Berlin occasionally found the ambassador alone, sitting on a sofa, drinking all night and muttering "The Axis persons cannot understand diplomacy."

After ten months in Berlin Togo was transferred to the Soviet Union as Japan's ambassador. General Oshima succeeded him in Berlin and then had a free hand. Togo left the German capital the month after Munich and felt, he said, "as though I was fleeing for my life from a fire."

Although life in Moscow was something like house arrest with diplomatic privileges, Togo thrived.

He handled the spadework and draft of the Japan-Soviet Neutrality pact that was signed in 1940. His stay in Moscow was fruitful and happy and earned the admiration of the Russians. Molotov, not widely known as a bouquet-tosser, toasted Togo: "In my public life of many years I have never known any man who insists so earnestly and so frankly as Mr. Togo on what he believes to be right. I respect

Mr. Togo not only as a distinguished diplomat and statesman, but as a man."

The Matsuoka Hurricane blew Togo out of his Moscow post and onto the shelf, along with dozens of other *Gaimusho* career men. The new foreign minister, Yosuke Matsuoka, simply sacked everyone he considered lacking in fervor for the "new world alignment," the Rome–Berlin–Tokyo Axis. Togo refused to resign because he considered it would be "an endorsement of Matsuoka's policies," and he was kept on the payroll as ambassador without assignment.

When General Hideki Tojo became prime minister of Japan in October 1941, he invited Togo to be his foreign minister. Togo's actions in the prewar countdown still stir acrid controversy. There are those who believe that Togo's determination to end the war in 1945 resulted from a guilt-drive growing out of his part in starting the conflict and his lapse in not following the prescribed form of declaring war.

At any rate, Togo soon crossed swords with Tojo and resigned when the General successfully undercut Togo's power. From that time until the telephone call from Suzuki, Togo pored over the history of defeat; it was almost a morbid preoccupation. He concentrated on the experiences of Germany and Russia after World War I, and reached these conclusions:

The morale of the people is high at the start of a war and while it continues favorable. Dissatisfaction develops as shortages of food, clothing and fuel are felt. Unless dealt with, the conditions lead, when defeat comes, to political and social revolution. With the end of war, the masses experience liberation, whether in victory or defeat. At that stage, surviving remnants of feudalistic customs, institutions and prerogatives are drastically curtailed and the power of the common people enlarged.

Togo considered Japan 1945 comparable to Germany 1918. Thus, to preserve the Emperor system, thought Togo, it is imperative that peace be achieved at the earliest possible moment. It was a monumental challenge.

General Yoshijiro Umezu, sixty-three, was army chief of staff and a member of the SCDW. It was he who actually controlled the five million men in the army fighting machine, who administered the army, issued orders and directives. He was energetic, wedded to his work, and known as the army's leading moderate general.

Umezu was not, in ordinary circumstances, memorable. With his long arms and deliberate movements, his wrinkled uniform hanging loosely on the small, stocky frame, he lacked dash. The only verve was in the darting eyes, set in the deadpan face. His hair was gray, close-cropped; his nose was large and straight. Usually he sat with head tilted back and a slightly bemused curve to his mouth, receiving all wave lengths. His lips were generally ajar, ready to reel out pedestrian, civil-service-type statements that lacked the electricity of Tojo, the emotion of Anami, or the metaphysical inflation of the "double-patriot" extremists. Umezu looked like a smudged photograph of an all-purpose general.

Though Umezu's career began with a citation for gallantry during the siege of Port Arthur in 1905, he was distinguished generally for administrative rather than combat successes. In the twenties he was assigned to GHQ to work on key problems of national defense, ideological preparation of the population for war, and particularly on war plans against Manchuria and China.

After the Manchurian Incident ended with establishment of the dummy state of Manchukuo, Umezu was decorated for his services with the Order of the Double Rays of the Rising Sun and First Class Order of the Sacred Treasure.

It was in 1935 that Umezu next came into public prominence. From 1934 the gray General was commanding officer of Japan's China Garrison Army. The following spring two pro-Japan Chinese journalists were murdered mysteriously in the Japanese concession of Tientsin. Umezu sent his chief of staff to the Chinese commander, General Ho Ying-ch'in, with an ultimatum: These were provocative acts and Japan demanded the commanding officer of the Chinese forces be changed and that police and local political organizations be withdrawn from the province of Hopeh. The Kuomintang satisfied these outrageous demands promptly.

But a week later Umezu sent his errand boy to General Ho again, demanding that "anti-Japanese activities" halt and threatening army action if they did not. To increase the pressure, Umezu cancelled regularly scheduled rotation of troops to Japan in view of "the critical situation."

By June 10 the Chinese had knuckled under completely in what came to be known in Japan as the Umezu–Ho Ying-ch'in Agreement. The Japanese press described the General's action as "directing the movement to grant autonomy to Hopeh Province." In truth, the Japanese had taken over an area of two hundred thousand square kilometers and millions of people. The fact that Umezu had with such economy of time, men, and materials achieved so much made him famous if not popular. The ultras, of course, were dissatisfied that he had not grabbed more. But the contrast with the untidiness and cost of the Manchurian Incident was startling.

The following year when the 2–26 Incident exploded and army and navy extremists killed prominent leaders and seized control of government, Umezu was languishing as commander of the 2d Division in a provincial city. He immediately wired the war minister denouncing the revolt, urging strong discipline and preventive measures to thwart any repeat. This was novel in an army whose leaders tended to treat uniformed assassins as Boy Scouts who had momentarily lost the trail.

Umezu was chosen to help clean house and restore discipline and public confidence. With strong-man General Terauchi as war minister, shake up the army he did. As vice-minister of war Umezu issued orders almost immediately that the army and individual soldiers should keep aloof from politics and concentrate on their assigned duties. This was like trying to change the nature of a lion by taking raw meat out of his diet.

Other measures were more effective. To their astonishment, a clutch of top-ranking officers suspected of condoning if not actually sponsoring the *Putsch* were retired. The vice-minister aborted a plan for rightists to raise funds for widows of army personnel executed for their part in the 2–26 plot. He shocked the ultras by preventing use of the *Hakku Ichiu* slogan in instructions and orders because it would be interpreted as evidence of an aggressive drive for world domination. (See definition of *Hakku Ichiu* on page 86.)

The vice-minister held the purse strings of the army's special funds. These secret resources were not accountable to any other government agency or minister. They were the army's own petty cash. Where the sums came from, where they went were the business of a handful of top officers only. The money had been used freely to finance the press, politicians, demonstrations, pamphleteers, bully-boys, and spies. Umezu cut back drastically on political payments. He reduced the entertainment expenditures, put a check on gifts to right-wing individuals and groups. (Not unexpectedly, he began to come in for attack in the press about this time.) Some scientific studies were continued, but the General slashed total payout by two-thirds. His stated reasons: to prevent misunderstanding of army intentions, particularly in politics; and to ensure that the army would not be drawn into politics. Umezu was about as successful as if he had tried to dry off a swimmer without taking him out of the water.

Among other things, Umezu, with army Chief of Staff General Sugiyama, did succeed in restoring army discipline. He was one of five army leaders who approved the national policy draft that specified war preparation and expansion against China, Great Britain, the Soviet Union, and the United States and full cooperation between Japan and Germany. He was later decorated for his part in bringing about the Anti-Comintern Pact with Germany.

Umezu the moderate was thoroughly committed to the China war that grew out of the Japanese-rigged incident at the Marco Polo Bridge near Peking in 1937. There is strong evidence that Umezu knew all about the China war from conception to execution. But when Japanese troops reverted to beasts in the rape of Nanking, Umezu incensed the expansionists and army ultras by pulling out of China two divisional commanders (one of them a prince) and thousands of reserve troops. An adviser told Prince Konoye, premier at the time, that among the Japanese troops in China, feeling against Umezu was so high that he feared they would try to assassinate the unsympathetic General. Three months later Umezu was in effect exiled—assigned to command the First Army in China, at the front. The civil-servant General was angry at being yanked out of his post and bitterly accused Prince Konoye (the premier) of being blind to his "laborious efforts to bring back military discipline."

During this period Umezu and Sugiyama had given support and encouragement to the chief of staff of the Kwantung army, Lieutenant General Hideki Tojo. (Umezu paid him 700,000 yen from the secret funds on April 13, 1938.) When Prime Minister Konoye wanted to move Sugiyama and Umezu out of their key army positions, they both recommended General Tojo as Umezu's replacement. "The Razor" would look out for their interests until they could return to the center of power. Their recommendation put Tojo on the conveyor belt to the premiership.

In the spring of 1939 the Kwantung army attacked Soviet troops in Outer Mongolia at a desolate outpost called Nomonhan. Over this wind-swept real estate the Japanese lost an estimated 52,000 men and the Soviets about 10,000 before Togo and Molotov in Moscow paved the way for a cease fire. But army GHQ in Tokyo was powerless to shut off the fighting because the honor of the vaunted Kwantung army was at stake, and its commander was taking orders from no one. There was only one way to end it—change the commander.

Normally this prestigious post went to the eldest, or senior, Japanese general. It was a cynosure, a private preserve, run by the army. It included all of Manchuria and several Chinese provinces.

On September 7, 1939, Umezu was named Kwantung army's commanding officer and he immediately clamped down on military action. Hostilities ceased on September 16. The General came to know Togo at long distance during this period, for they worked together on the Nomonhan settlement and establishment of a border commission.

Both countries heaved a sigh of relief—Japan because the cost of the Nomonhan adventure had been too high, and Russia because Hitler had attacked Poland September 1 and Soviet leaders were not confident the Nazis would recognize the Russian border if and when they came to it.

For almost five years Umezu was chief of the Kwantung army and His Majesty's Ambassador to Manchukuo. In effect, Umezu was viceroy of a land of more than 1,000,000 square kilometers, 80 million souls (as many as in Japan itself), and vast natural resources.

This was not a period of sybaritic relaxation for Umezu. He built up the Kwantung army, doubled the number of troops and prepared for the grand assault on the Soviets. Within his headquarters he established a 5th Section under Lieutenant General Sumihisa Ikeda, to plan an occupation regime for the Soviet territory. They trained saboteurs and special combat groups for action beyond Soviet lines, added Russian interpreters and personnel to administer the soon-to-be-conquered land. The invasion was scheduled for mid-1941.

Umezu told his staff officers that year that Japan should not begin a war with the U.S. even under the most extreme conditions. It had not escaped his notice, of course, that the Soviets were locked in mortal combat with the Nazis (Germany attacked Russia June 22, 1941). The time was golden for Japan to strike in Siberia.

Toward the end of 1941, GHQ notified Umezu that the country was preparing for war with the United States and emphasized that the Kwantung army especially was to preserve tranquility with the USSR. When the Pacific War broke out in December, Umezu kissed goodbye any dreams he might have entertained of himself as the Khan of Soviet Siberia and the Maritime Provinces. The invasion plans were put in mothballs.

But there were other accomplishments Umezu could claim. He solved unemployment problems—by initiating compulsory labor service in Manchuria in 1941. He was successful in geopolitics: Japanese immigration to Manchuria was encouraged and the land of the natives was confiscated or taken with token compensation. And the General scored in agriculture and business too: opium-drug revenues hit a high of 110 million yen in 1943, up from a meager 20 million in 1936.

Umezu was going to seed with garrison duty in Manchuria when the order came to report to GHQ as chief of staff in mid-1944. Tojo had not forgotten him. When he got the word, Umezu told General Ikeda "Since from the very beginning I have opposed war against the U.S., I hate to accept this appointment. Moreover, the war conditions are unfavorable. There are no measures which I can take as chief of staff. . . . It is necessary to end this war as soon as possible. For that, diplomacy or other techniques will be required."

Never had the General faced more trying conditions. Though he could not foresee it, his actions now were leading him inexorably to the deck of the battleship USS *Missouri*.

The military teammate of Umezu on the SCDW was a vigorous pinch-hitter, General Korechika Anami, fifty-eight, the minister of war. Unquestionably one of the most popular men in the army, Anami was not an intellectual, not a desk soldier, not a politician. In fact, it was because he had no political ties and was not a leader of an army clique that he was so widely accepted as war minister.

The General was the son of a public procurator in a city of Oita province on the southernmost Japanese home island, Kyushu. He was a product of public education and military training. Anami was the very model of a modern samurai. Single-minded, unswervingly loyal, master of the conventional military virtues and skills, he was erect as a pagoda, with the neck and chest of a *sumo* wrestler. Impeccably groomed, Anami's jackboots gleamed and his curved samurai sword was worn easily, as much a part of him as his left arm.

The oval of Anami's broad face was elongated by the forehead that now stretched without break to the top of his skull. The hair had fled from the wide temple and center of his head. That which remained seemed like lichen holding uncertainly to a rounded mountaintop. His Fuji-shaped mustache was shot through with gray; the eyes were narrow, the nose broad, and the ears pointed, always on the alert.

Ancient records told of Anami's ancestors fighting valiantly against the Mongols in thirteenth-century Japan. Emulating his warrior forebears, the war minister strove to the utmost extent to be a true samurai.

He practiced *kendo* religiously. Anami reached the fifth rank in *kendo;* his brother-in-law Takeshita often took skull-ringing cracks on the head in *kendo* workouts with the agile General, who was twenty years his senior.

Also, until his last day Anami practiced archery with the Japanese bow, that magnificent instrument that often measures more than seven feet from tip to tip. Every morning he stepped into his garden at the war minister's official residence and loosed arrows at a straw target. His object was to calm himself. When he could group five shafts in a clout he considered himself in command of his nerves and went on to the day's business—the inescapable meetings with politicians and statesmen—before his secretary Colonel Hayashi called for him at 7:45 A.M. to go to the war ministry.

His day at the ministry usually ended about 4 P.M. and upon return to his residence Anami would once again take his bow to the garden and "settle himself" with the enforced concentration of the ancient sport. Even when the General was a combat commander in the jungles of New Guinea in 1944, visitors from GHQ were astonished to find him shooting arrows in the tropical wilds, part of the continuing discipline he imposed on himself.

So too was his erect posture. "A straight backbone is good for the health," he used to say. In less demanding times he often attended Zen sessions where a group would meet at a home or in a schoolroom early in the morning or late evening and sit in the prescribed attitude silently meditating for half an hour or so.

As a true samurai, Anami had a highly developed appreciation of poetry. Though his father died when the General was a boy, his mother lived into her ninety-sixth year. Two months after she died in 1943, Anami was promoted to full general. Typically (for him) he wrote a *waka* (a thirty-one-syllable poem) on that occasion:

> A lovely flower blooms at the grave,
>   Too late.
> This blossom I wanted
>   To regale my parents during life.

Anami had the traditional Oriental attitude of the dutiful son toward his parents. But he was unusual in his *laissez faire* attitude toward his own children. "If parents are good to their children," he explained, "they will be dutiful to their elders. It is a case of mutual relations between them. It is the same between senior and junior officers. If an officer gives affection, appropriate duty, and advancement to a junior, naturally he will serve faithfully and work hard."

Gregarious and ebullient, Anami encouraged easy give and take with his juniors. He was warm and gentle, soft-spoken and a good listener. On New Year's Day his junior officers would flock to his home to pay their respects and he would toast the new year individually and consecutively with fifty to sixty of them. He enjoyed bull sessions and drinking and had a reputation as an officer able to hold his liquor. Big reputations and important careers were built on prowess in this department. At parties Anami would sing and dance. He was known as a "happy drunk" and a good yarn-spinner.

His career was full of contradictions. When he was appointed vice-minister of war in 1940, the captive press reported "Anami was a bright person reputed to be a genius from his infancy. . . . In his days at the Military Academy and the Military Staff College he was an honor student."

In actuality, Anami was not considered a mental giant by his colleagues. He flunked the Army War College entrance exams twice before he managed to pass. This was a reverse distinction for which he was well known inside the army. His work at the military schools was satisfactory but showed no indication of genius.

Four years after he received his commission as sublieutenant Anami was assigned to an infantry regiment in which he met a fellow officer from his own Oita province, a meeting that was to affect his destiny. The other man was a rising young chap who was marked as a "comer" by army brass—Lieutenant Yoshijiro Umezu. From then on their careers intertwined. Their ups and downs were parallel, whether by design or coincidence, and at the end their paths converged.

After Anami completed the War College course he was assigned to army GHQ in 1918. Umezu had been on duty at GHQ for about a year and a half at the time, and soon went off to posts in Europe. Anami in 1923 was shipped to cold storage in the Sakhalin Expeditionary Army that occupied the Russian island until 1925. Here he developed a taste for whisky and delighted in its ability to drive off the chill. (Twenty years later, when he dug a bomb shelter in his suburban yard, Anami stashed away bottles of treasured Old Parr Scotch whisky and little else.)

Pulled back to GHQ again in 1925, Anami was joined there the following year by Umezu, who was made a section chief. Anami then received one of those joyride assignments—he was sent to the French army school at Orléans for several months. He came back with a love of things French and a penchant for piling the family in a touring car and driving off for a carefree Sunday outing.

But his assignment when he returned was mark-time duty as commander of a depot unit. About this time Umezu was appointed chief of the powerful Military Affairs Section of the war ministry, and when the annual promotion lists were published the following August, Anami had been dealt an ace: he was named an aide-de-camp to the Emperor of Japan. Here for four years he saw the workings of the core of Japanese life and politics, came to know the Imperial family and the men around the throne.

After this Anami was made commander of the elite 2d Imperial Guards Regiment. Meanwhile, Umezu had been exiled to the China Garrison Army, and when the next promotion lists came out, Anami found himself, after twenty-eight years in the army, superintendent of the Tokyo Military Prep School. Takeshita thought this was the end of the road for his brother-in-law. He fully expected Anami to retire when he completed his thirty years.

But when the army and navy extremists staged their rebellion in February 1936, the reaction brought the army moderates to power and put Umezu in a position in which he could boost his friends. The following August Anami was named chief of the war ministry's Military Administration Bureau and the next year became the powerful chief of personnel. Here Anami issued the orders that made Hideki Tojo chief of staff of the Kwantung army, then vice-minister of war and later inspector general of army aviation.

By then, Umezu had been shipped off to the China front and Anami soon followed him to command a division in China. Shortly afterward the Nomonhan war put Umezu in a position of power again as commander of the Kwantung army. With the next change of government, Anami was in as vice-minister of war. However, it was a period of revolving-door cabinets in Japan, and in 1941 Anami was out. He was shipped to the China front as a division commander again and transferred the following year to Umezu's bailiwick as commander of the Second Area Army in Manchuria, part of the Kwantung army. By late 1943 the Kwantung army's major resources in men and weapons had been sent to the fighting fronts. Anami was assigned to New Guinea and Celebes.

However, when Prime Minister Tojo appointed Umezu army chief of staff in mid-1944, Anami was neither out of mind nor far behind. Six months later Umezu managed to bring him back to Tokyo as chief of army aviation, one of the pinnacles of the military establishment—the same post from which Tojo had moved into the war minister slot and then the premiership just four years before. With the backing of his powerful province-mate Umezu, Anami followed this same path and was installed as war minister in Suzuki's cabinet. There were many who thought he would complete the Tojo circuit shortly after.

Actually, Anami was unhappy with his new assignment as war minister. He had expected a combat command on Okinawa, not a "civilian" administrative post. He considered himself a professional soldier, a samurai, not a politician. He had few illusions about himself in the role of war minister.

How did he operate in this highly sensitive post? Anami's secretary Hayashi reports that the general didn't stick to his desk, didn't spend his time reading cables and studying reports. He had few conferences and did not have meetings with many people outside the army. "He was not a person who thought and thought, examined the data and then arrived at a conclusion. Rather, something would strike his mind and he would make an instant decision. . . . He was a very admirable person, rare among military men. Since he had no political sense, it was unreasonable for him to be war minister. He was artless. . . ."

And yet for all his artlessness, Anami was many things to many people. One is seen in many lights by his colleagues. There were differing views of Umezu, but they were simply variations in shading; concerning Anami the opinions differed absolutely and completely. And such was the nature of the war minister that each of his associates was dogmatically sure that his own view of Anami and his attitudes was the true one.

His brother-in-law saw Anami as a warm-hearted, vital human being who attracted all who met him, particularly his juniors, for they felt real rapport with and love for him. "He was," says Takeshita, "not the brilliant type, not one you would expect to become a general or war minister. He did not belong to what might be called the 'cult of success.' "

Kido, the privy seal, observed that "being intelligent, Anami was not imbued with absurd notions. He had no confidence in the war's prospect. . . . Nonetheless, he used to state that he was desirous of dealing the enemy one big blow before ending the war. His statement presumably resulted from pressure exerted by the army, although I do not believe he deliberately made such an assertion for the specific purpose of deceiving the army. . . ."

To General Yoshizumi, the chief of the Military Affairs Bureau who worked closely with Anami, the war minister was nobody's puppet. "He frankly and definitely expressed his own intentions. . . . It was not his policy to leave political matters to subordinates."

General Kawabe, the vice-chief of staff of the army, noted Anami's "pure and transparent character. . . . I believe that he sincerely desired the war to be continued."

Colonel Hayashi, the omnipresent secretary to the war minister, disagreed with this view completely: "Anami did not have the idea of continuing the war to the bitter end . . . he occasionally confided that if he were to talk about peace the effect would be exceedingly serious."

Anami's chief speech-writer, Colonel Inaba, who had known him since 1940, saw him as "a simple and honest man who did not use tricks. He placed extreme emphasis on spirit and yet frankly submitted to reason."

Yet Togo's aide, Toshikazu Kase, reports that as early as the beginning of 1945 Anami sent word from his command post in the tropics to Shigemitsu, then foreign minister, that Japan must seek a diplomatic settlement of the war.

Contrasting Anami with his superior officer Umezu, General Kawabe, the vice-chief of staff, who knew them both, stated: "Umezu was a very clever man. He did not back continuation of the war until Anami had advocated it first. But Anami was the type to express his views boldly before others."

What could be expected of this man who seemed so indefinable in the welter of contradiction about his nature?

Anami emphasized that the supreme command should be strong, that faith was the greatest fighting power, that unity should be strengthened.

These mottoes were characteristic of the man and reflect Anami's approach:

Morality is a fighting strength!

A road to success will somehow be revealed to us if we carry on with strong determination!

Simplicity represents strength!

If platitudes were firepower, Anami would have been invincible. And if Zen could overcome, Anami, the army and Japan would have been triumphant.

As his secretary pointed out, "Anami was a general at the front, he wasn't a political animal. His attitude was 'in battle we usually cannot get information, we don't know what we should do, but tomorrow we have to attack the enemy!' In such a situation Anami was very good, but to think five or ten years ahead . . . he couldn't do it. General Umezu was outstanding on that score. . . ."

Actually Anami balanced Umezu very well. He was the fatherly division commander who chafes at planning and details and asks only the objective of the mission and a battalion of loyal men who will follow him through blood and mud. To analyze and sift, to tack and run, tack again and close-haul, these were for others—for the chief of staff and the planners—not for the war minister.

It was Anami's nature. It was Zen. It was samurai through and through. The war minister's performance in the final period of the war was Zen philosophy in action in a complex, twentieth-century situation.

Zen Buddhism came to Japan in the twelfth century and rapidly was adopted by the warrior class because of characteristics so akin to the samurai code: strict mental and physical discipline, a Spartan life, antischolasticism. "Having Zen in one's life" meant devotion to work, freedom from arrogant attitudes or egotistical actions, serenity, and much more. Central to Zen is meditation in quest of the flash of sudden enlightenment (*satori*) concerning the oneness of the universe, the nature of Buddha, and so on.

Typically, a Zen master may pose a *koan,* a seemingly irrational problem (What is the sound of one hand clapping?) and his pupils meditate until an answer, perhaps equally irrational, strikes in a flash. Zen did much to give spiritual strength to and toughen the moral fiber of Japan's warriors for hundreds of years. It was admirably suited for the individual hand-to-hand combat of feudal warfare.

Now Anami, facing the impossible problem of winning the war, tested Zen's applicability to the era of mass destruction as he sought the flash of insight that would give a solution. And he sought the answer in the Zen fashion—not through study and analysis and paperwork, but (because the truth is too profound to be found in spoken or written words) through the heart and meditation. In Japan's plight, what more sensible method was possible?

Representing the navy on the SCDW were Admiral Mitsumasa Yonai, sixty-five, the navy minister, and Admiral Soemu Toyoda, sixty, the navy chief of staff. The navy was by now so weak in major weapons as to be nearly nonexistent, except for its carefully hoarded supply of planes and small craft. These it expected to throw into the decisive battle as "special attack weapons"—suicide craft. With this sorry decline all too apparent to many civilians as well as government and military leaders, the navy representatives' political power had declined drastically. Yet the navy had 1,500,000 disciplined armed troops, and any such group at this juncture constituted a force to be reckoned with.

Yonai, the rangy navy minister, was widely known for his good looks, his forcefulness and candor, and his opposition to the Axis alliance. The Admiral was an impressive physical specimen. More than six feet tall, he weighed in at 177 pounds. He was cheerful, gregarious, and popular with his men.

Born into the family of a poor samurai in a small town in northeastern Japan, Yonai managed to enter the Naval Academy. There he steered a middle course, landing at the center of his class in grades and popularity. He advanced through Naval War College, a prerequisite to top rank in the navy, then through posts in Russia, naval GHQ, fleet duty, and administration. He moved up through what the controlled press called "his own special patience and sincerity" and others labeled pushing ahead by alternate rebelliousness and unctiousness.

"The white elephant" was first chosen navy minister in 1937 and survived three cabinets in this post. It was by then 1939 and Japan was being pressed by Germany to convert the Japanese–German Anti-Comintern Pact of 1936 into a full political and military alliance. The fire-eaters in the army were for it and so were the ultranationalists, but the navy, led by Yonai, blocked approval. "The Japanese navy," he said, "belongs to the Emperor. It is not for hire by Hitler or anyone else."

When Hitler and Stalin set their hands to that masterpiece of hypocrisy, the Russo-German Non-Aggression Pact, in August 1939, Yonai and the navy were vindicated and the Hiranuma cabinet was blown out of office.

Yonai was viewed as a liberal by Japanese and Westerners alike for stanchly resisting the enlargement of the Axis pact. This stand earned him the abiding enmity of the army and the lasting suspicion of the ultranationalists. The Emperor and his circle of advisers were pleased to find a champion willing to take a stand. In January 1940 Yonai was named prime minister.

Our American ambassador to Japan, Joseph Grew, saw Yonai's appointment as truly encouraging. In his view, Yonai was a strong and sensible man, likely neither to submit to manipulation or go off the deep end with any extreme policies of his own. *The New York Times* correspondent Hugh Byas thought the Admiral's elevation to premier was "the last desperate effort to confine the war to China."

Yonai's first appearance before the Diet was a great success. It was reported that he "said nothing, said it briefly, elegantly and forcefully." In viewing the problems of the nation in that darkening winter of 1940, the Admiral presented a façade of equanimity and experience. He was, he said, "born to debts, weaned on trouble, schooled in adversity." However, neither he nor Japan was prepared for the developments that followed.

For seven months Yonai steered through the choppy waters of domestic pressures and international maelstroms. The German blitz sent a popular thrill of expectancy through Japan. The ultras and the army avidly looked for a way to share in the coming Nazi victory. Yonai's policies were too slow and too meager for such appetites: they wanted an all-out alliance with the Axis that would assure Japan a share of the spoils.

The dissatisfaction with Yonai and those who held back was intense. In early July the government was tipped off to a plot. The conspirators were a group of fanatics who called themselves *shimpetai,* "soldiers of the gods." They planned to kill leading pro-Anglo-Americans. On their list were premier Yonai, the privy seal, and others of the Court circle. The police struck quickly, gathered up the conspirators and their weapons. The army stayed out of it as the Court held its breath. The army shadow, however, darkened the entire scene.

Within the week, the army had had enough of Yonai and its plans had jelled. Vice-minister of War Korechika Anami called on the new privy seal, Marquis Kido, on July 8. "The military," the General announced, "has been preparing to meet changes in the latest world situation. Unfortunately, the character of the Yonai cabinet is not suitable for negotiating with Germany and Italy and might cause a fatal delay. The military has concluded that a cabinet change is inevitable to 'face the situation.' "

So the army finally pulled the plug on the Yonai cabinet. The war minister resigned and army chiefs declined to nominate a replacement. Yonai was out. For the next four years he was out of the navy and out of power. As a former premier he was automatically one of the senior statesmen, the *jushin,* and was consulted by leaders from time to time.

In 1944 when Saipan fell, Tojo's exit was engineered. He was succeeded by what was intended to be a joint premiership shared by Yonai and General Kuniaki Koiso. The Admiral was to serve as navy minister concurrently. His inclusion in this cabinet was meant to signal a change of policy. But as it worked out, Koiso carried the main load and Yonai confined himself largely to his navy responsibilities. When Koiso's cabinet toppled after the loss of the Philippines, the new premier, Suzuki, insisted that Yonai stay on as navy minister in the new cabinet. Though Yonai protested that his health was poor and he wished to remain out of it, Suzuki would not take no for an answer.

Yonai's general opposition to the war was well known. As he put it later, "I think the turning point of the war was the start. I felt from the very beginning that there was no chance of success. . . ." He also said that the navy high command, if free to decide to terminate the war, first should have taken steps after the wave of early victories at Hawaii, Guam, the Philippines, Singapore, and Rangoon. The second occasion, he said, "would have been after the loss of Saipan; and after that it appeared to be a question of being dragged along, fighting on by inertia, etc."

Admiral Soemu Toyoda was Yonai's navy associate on the SCDW. In appearance he was pie-faced and plodding. Toyoda was the most recent member of the Big Six. On May 29, 1945, he had been appointed navy chief of staff from his previous post as commander in chief of the Naval General Command, the Combined Fleet, and Escort Command. This title was almost as hollow as that of admiral of the Swiss navy, because Toyoda's fleet was nearly nonexistent. Alert and well-informed, the Admiral had no doubt about the final outcome of the war.

Toyoda came from Oita prefecture, as did Anami and Umezu, and this was a factor in Yonai's selection of him for this post. Toyoda's career after the Naval Academy included the Navy War College, duty with the Supreme Military Council during World War I, navy GHQ assignments, and fleet posts. He was primarily an administrative sailor and had held most of the top jobs in the Japanese navy. In May 1944 he was named commander in chief, Combined Fleet, just in time to preside over the catastrophes that destroyed it at Saipan, the Philippines, and Okinawa.

Toyoda thought his transfer to navy chief of staff meant "that I was selected as a companion [to Yonai] to formulate the plan for ending the war. Soon after my appointment Yonai asked me whether the Naval General Staff would quietly consent to end the war. I assured him that I would see to it that it did."

The Admiral was pessimistic about the decisive battle in the homeland, with good reason. His estimate of the situation as of early June 1945:

The navy had lost virtually all of its surface forces and had no heavy oil. Since production of wood turpentine, which constituted the only source of aviation fuel, did not even reach 25 per cent of the expected figure, aviation training of new recruits was suspended after March. The desperate measure of converting training planes into bomb-carrying special attack planes was devised.

The navy intended to maintain some 5000 to 6000 planes in all for June (but this was not possible owing to the unexpectedly great battle losses) and to form *kamikaze* forces composed of surface and underwater special attack weapons—Shinto (crash boats); Koryu and Kairyu (midget subs); Fukuryu (human mines); and Kaiten (human torpedoes)— and to station them at strategic points on the mainland.

Both the army and navy were doing their utmost to prepare for a decisive battle in the homeland because to initiate offensive operations of our own choice was utterly impossible after the beginning of the Okinawa operations. The progress of the army's war preparations was difficult to learn by outsiders, but I always estimated it considerably lower than the official explanations. This is because a person in a responsible position, whether army or otherwise, will tend to be optimistic and will very seldom speak discouragingly when explaining matters in his charge.

Thus Toyoda bared his own attitude toward executive candor. With this skeptical outlook on army strength plus painfully accurate knowledge of the navy's weakness, it was logical that Toyoda would back Yonai in seeking an early end to the war. So the SCDW meeting the morning of August 9, 1945, would have an excellent chance of winding up the matter if Togo, Yonai, Toyoda, and Suzuki could persuade the army representatives to come to terms. And both Anami and Umezu, being reasonable men, could scarcely advocate going on with the hopeless conflict in the face of the atomic bomb and the Soviet avalanche.

There was no use in delaying any further. It was 10:30 A.M. August 9 when the Big Six gathered around the conference table in the air-raid shelter in the premier's office building and Suzuki, fortified with cigar and green tea, officially opened the meeting.

Chapter 5

Hung Jury

In the stifling underground chamber the six members of the Supreme Council for Direction of the War of Japan were seated: the aged Premier Suzuki, Foreign Minister Togo, War Minister Anami, Navy Minister Yonai, Army Chief of Staff Umezu, and Navy Chief of Staff Toyoda.

The Big Six began their discussion with an argument over the bombing of Hiroshima. When they had met last, on the seventh, news of Hiroshima's destruction was confirmed. The army chief of staff had received a message that said starkly "the whole city of Hiroshima was destroyed instantly by a single bomb." Both the army and navy had sent teams to investigate and report, but they had not yet finished and the question of whether it was an atomic bomb had not been settled. That the destruction was colossal was clear and that one or two planes, no more, had done it was unquestionably true. And they pooh-poohed the threat from President Truman to use the atomic bomb on other Japanese cities: "If they do not now accept our terms they may expect a rain of ruin from the air, the like of which has never been seen on this earth. . . ."

Navy Chief of Staff Toyoda argued that no nation, even the United States, had enough radioactive material to mount such attacks as Truman threatened. And world opinion, he predicted, would not stand for use of such an inhuman weapon.

The army leaders said that they did not have precise information about the Russian advances on the ground. Until they did, they rejected the conclusion that Japan was losing the war on yet another front.

The mood of the meeting was grim and contentious. The military men, including Toyoda, far from feeling the urgency of the situation, seemed determined to resist any hasty consideration of enemy terms. Then an aide burst in and shakily handed Suzuki a message.

The premier read to his colleagues the terrifying words: *Nagasaki City was struck this morning by severe attack of Hiroshima type. Damage is extensive.*

The mood of the meeting shifted from grim to grave. This news settled one outstanding question: The enemy did have enough material for more than one bomb. How many more? No one could say, but could they afford to speculate? And world opinion might not be marshaled against the weapon in time to stop the next attack, or the next ten attacks. Even then, would the Allies be swayed by something so fragile as opinion when they were obviously desperate to finish off Japan?

Suzuki, appalled at still another cataclysmic blow, put down his cigar and spoke solemnly. "This, added to the previous barbaric attack on Hiroshima," he said, "compounds the impact of the Russian attack on Japan. I wish the foreign minister to introduce the discussion of the Potsdam terms."

Togo was virtually seething with frustration. He had tried to bring these same men face to face with the Potsdam terms on the seventh, the first SCDW meeting after the Hiroshima bombing. But the army had refused to believe that it had been an atomic weapon and denied that the damage was as severe as the unconfirmed reports indicated. So long as the army would not admit either of these points, there was no way to get the soldiers to agree to a surrender based on the atomic revolution in warfare.

The following day, August eighth, Togo had reported to the Emperor the meager but horrifying news from Japanese observers of the Hiroshima debacle. And he augmented this with information from world capitals that supported the enemy claim of an atomic weapon. When the Emperor told him to convey to Suzuki his wish that the war be ended without delay, Togo had all but run to the prime minister. The foreign minister found that Sakomizu, the cabinet secretary, could not pull together a "Big Six" meeting until the ninth because the chiefs of staff were "unavailable."

Even with the haunting knowledge that scores of thousands in

Nagasaki and hundreds in Korea, Sakhalin, and Manchuria might have been spared if the SCDW had met decisively on the eighth, Togo was outwardly impassive, as usual.

Like a solicitor presenting a brief, the foreign minister said "the war has become more and more hopeless. Since the present situation is so critical as to exclude any hope of victory, we must sue for peace and accept the Potsdam terms immediately. The conditions for acceptance should be limited to those which are absolutely essential for Japan."

Suzuki then proposed that the Potsdam declaration be accepted, thus ending the war.

There was instant silence, a perceptible recoil from the brink of action. The proposal was too much, too abrupt, too un-Japanese in its directness. Though none realized better than these six the desperateness of the war situation, the necessity for immediate action and clear-cut decision was, to these men, an almost paralyzing imperative.

No one ventured an opinion. The silence lengthened, becoming increasingly uncomfortable. Navy Minister Yonai was busily writing on his scratch pad. At length, the focus of all eyes, he broke the stillness. "Silence will lead us nowhere. To lead off our discussion, how about taking up the following questions: If we accept the Potsdam proclamation, should we accept it unconditionally or should we attach certain conditions? If we attach conditions, what should they be? These are merely tentative suggestions, but how about studying the following points:

First, the question of the Emperor system.

Second, disarmament.

Third, war criminals.

And fourth, the occupation of Japan.

"Now, should we attach conditions concerning these or not? If so, in what manner are we going to do so?"

The navy chief of staff, Toyoda, took Yonai's words to mean that he was not saying Japan *should* attach such conditions, but was merely suggesting that these were the main topics raised by the Potsdam declaration.

Togo reacted irritably. "We must act immediately. Since the welfare of the Imperial Family must be guaranteed at all costs, we must obtain a commitment on that point. But the attitude of the Allies indicates they would reject our proposals outright and refuse to negotiate further. If we try to exact more concessions, we should keep our conditions at the bare minimum."

Stirred to action by his responsibility to speak for the army, the war minister contended: "We cannot accept any condition that in any way so much as places a shadow on the national polity. That is without question. Furthermore, the Potsdam item 7 is unacceptable where it reads

points in Japanese territory to be designated by the Allies shall be occupied to secure the achievement of the basic objectives we are here setting forth.

"and item 12

the occupying forces . . . shall be withdrawn from Japan as soon as these objectives have been accomplished. . . .

"We must not surrender our sovereignty in this way. The condition that the Allies occupy Japan would annoy me very much. Try to prevent the Allied occupation," directed Anami, looking at Togo.

Army Chief of Staff Umezu backed Anami on this, and proposed that if unavoidable, occupation be outside Tokyo, in as few places as possible with the minimum troops necessary and for the shortest time required.

Then Umezu brought up item 10 of the Potsdam proclamation:

We do not intend that the Japanese shall be enslaved as a race or destroyed as a nation, but stern justice shall be meted out to all war criminals, including those who have visited cruelties upon our prisoners.

"This does not require that the war criminals be turned over to the Allied forces," said Umezu. "Therefore we should negotiate to enable Japan to dispose of this matter herself. After all, it is unfair to be judged by the enemy."

Anami seconded this idea emphatically.

"I will punish persons responsible for the war," said the war minister. "This is an internal problem so there is no necessity that this be done by foreign countries. If the Allies occupy Japan and arrest those they say are responsible for the war and execute or imprison them, what is to protect the national polity? They can arrest whom they choose and it will be impossible to stop them or to prevent destruction of the nation's character."

Umezu nodded agreement.

Then the navy chief did the unexpected. Instead of coming out for acceptance of the Potsdam terms, Toyoda joined Umezu in backing Anami's opposition. He countered one of the terms, item 9:

The Japanese military forces, after being completely disarmed, shall be permitted to return to their homes with the opportunity to lead peaceful and productive lives.

"We must," Toyoda insisted, "reach an agreement with the Allied powers to have disarmament carried out without coercion. By our own voluntary action we will deliver the arms to the Allied forces at a prearranged time and place. Otherwise the order to cease hostilities will probably cause serious incidents."

No matter how sincere Toyoda's objection, he was putting another hurdle in the path of agreement.

Anami added his own amendment to Toyoda's statement. "Disarmament of our armed forces outside of Japan will be done by me. Japan will do the repatriation of these men overseas by herself. Otherwise millions of our soldiers will be left to die like dogs overseas."

Umezu threw in his own recommendation: Japan's soldiers and sailors could not surrender; the word did not exist in Japanese military annals. The men were indoctrinated with the idea that "if they lost their weapons they should fight with their feet; if they couldn't fight with these, they should bite and if they could not, should cut out their tongues and kill themselves."

With this degree of fanaticism established by nearly fifteen years of indoctrination, it was highly doubtful that the troops would peacefully obey any order to surrender, particularly on the battlefronts overseas where conditions might be more favorable than in the homeland itself. So, if Allied commanders were not forewarned and adequate arrangements were not made in advance, Allied forces might be mowed down when they went to take over areas from Japanese troops. And if this happened the war would be on again in a flash.

To prevent such a calamity, Umezu recommended that at each battlefront there be a designated time and place where both sides would spontaneously stack arms, throw ammunition and weapons. Then these would be gathered at predesignated places and after that, the general said, "we would act just as the enemy told us to." It was important to decide in advance the time and place of surrender of Japanese troops, and additional measures might be necessary to prevent the surrender from breaking down.

Toyoda and Anami immediately seconded the General's points. All of this heartfelt opposition to these conditions in the Potsdam terms was touching, but it did raise questions. For instance, were the army and navy suggesting these points because of valid concern about the safety of a surrender? Or were the military men paving the way for some future moment when they would again pick up the traces and resume battle?

Surrender itself would be for the army and navy the ultimate loss of face. But if demobilization, repatriation, and disarmament were carried out by the Japanese military themselves, would it not appear —domestically, at least—to be instead of defeat a voluntary halt of the war, a truce, a magnanimous humanitarian gesture to save lives and end bloodshed?

The occupation of Japan by foreign troops would damage this pretty picture. Moreover, if war-crimes trials were conducted by the Allies in Japan, it would be apparent to all, within Japan and abroad, just who had won the war. And the dirty brocade that would be publicly laundered in such a circus would tarnish (to say the least) the military's image of selfless devotion to Emperor and country.

There can be no clearcut conclusion that these thoughts were behind the spirited opposition of the army and navy men at the meeting. But it is hard to believe that they did not at least pass through the mind of Umezu, that human calculating machine.

Togo, replying to the military's demands, said coldly that he would make every effort, when opportune, to have the Allies understand the problems concerning occupation, disarmament, and war criminals, but he absolutely refused to include these as conditions for accepting the Potsdam terms.

Heatedly Toyoda argued with him. "The chance to secure conditions will be lost if we wait, because as soon as we notify our intention to accept the Potsdam terms the Allies may send parachute troops to occupy our country and I, for one, cannot guarantee that I can prevent incidents."

Togo once again repeated his earlier stand. "The only condition which we should hold out for is that of inviolability of the Imperial house. Can the military offer any hope of victory in case negotiations on other terms should be undertaken and should fail?"

Anami shot back, "Although I can give no absolute guarantee of ultimate victory, Japan can still fight another battle."

Irritatingly practical as usual, Togo pressed Anami and the chiefs of staff. "Can you say for certain whether you can prevent the enemy from landing on our mainland?"

Umezu, the man responsible for the fighting capabilities of the troops, answered. "We might drive the enemy into the sea if we are lucky . . . though in war we cannot be sure that things will go well . . . but even if some of the enemy's troops succeed in establishing beachheads, I am confident that we can inflict heavy losses on them."

"This would be useless," Togo charged. "According to your explanation, at least some of the attackers might still land even after sustaining serious losses. But though the enemy will follow up with a second assault, we will have sacrificed most of our aircraft and munitions in our efforts to destroy the first wave. With no possibility of replenishing our armaments, we will then be defenseless, even leaving the atomic bomb out of account. We must conclude that we have no alternative to stopping the war at this very moment, and we must therefore attempt to attain peace by limiting our counterdemands to the irreducible minimum."

Yonai readily supported this view. The other military men continued to advocate, at great length, that disarmament, occupation, and war-crimes trials must be under Japanese control.

The meeting was getting more and more out of hand when Yonai's big voice cut in: "It is past the time to take this stand. We have to accept the terms. We have to follow the foreign minister's recommendation." His remarks were pointed not only at the army men, but directly at Admiral Toyoda, who blandly gazed off into space. The balance, instead of being four to two in favor of the peace faction, was three to three because of Toyoda's defection. Or was it? Just where did Suzuki stand?

The premier had been sitting silently, sipping his green tea and smoking his cigar. He seemed to have missed details of the discussion. As the debate progressed, he had grown increasingly nervous. At Yonai's words he became visibly agitated. Now he broke in, shouting at the military men: "You are putting in too many conditions. You are deliberately opposing my opinion in order to break up the peace negotiations!"

Anami, Umezu, and Toyoda chorused that this was not so, but Suzuki's anger was unabated.

"The discussion," Togo noted later in typical diplomatic understatement, "became rather impassioned, but remained inconclusive." In fact, Togo became more and more exasperated as he rebutted the arguments.

The two chiefs of staff and the war minister evidently were frozen in their positions. They offset Togo, Yonai, and Suzuki. Thus there was no hope for action in the SCDW. To resolve it, the question would have to be put to a different panel. As in Western jury trials, the agreement had to be unanimous—or else.

The prime minister was still visibly upset. He noted that the Potsdam declaration would have to be considered by the cabinet anyway, and announced that the cabinet meeting scheduled for noon would be convened at two o'clock. It was 1 P.M. when Suzuki adjourned the SCDW meeting and the Big Six emerged from the insulated, artificial safety of the bomb shelter into the reassuring blaze of the midday sun. The heat stung and the humidity suffocated. But the sun had been there yesterday, last week, last year, and for eons before. It would be there tomorrow and next week and for ages after they were gone.

War minister Anami returned to the ministry building from the SCDW meeting with buoyed spirits. It was evident from his manner, from his jaunty stride and confident grin, that he was in control of the situation. None who saw the war minister at that moment, sweeping down the hallway to his office with a retinue of high-ranking officers, could doubt that Anami was master of his fate and that of the nation.

Word that he had returned from the meeting raced through the ministry grapevine. Within minutes, his adoring junior officers flocked to his office, boisterous and full of renewed confidence, wanting to share his report on the Russian invasion and status of the effort to thwart the peace faction's defeatism.

As relaxed as a lion in the safety of his lair, the war minister glanced from face to face, impressed by the eager trust evident there, and spoke in generalities about the continuing discussion of the current situation by the Big Six. The questions of his colleagues were not to be satisfied by such broad responses, Anami realized. He told them that the Russian invasion, the Potsdam terms, and the bombing of Nagasaki had been discussed, that he and Umezu had taken a strong stand in defense of national interests, but that naturally he could not say more.

Disappointed, but aware that Anami could not discuss the meeting openly, the young tigers stood and talked with the war minister good-naturedly. He was relaxed among these disciples, and the conversation skirted the SCDW meeting and its subject matter. The visitors tossed out gratuitous comments and speculative statements, fishing for hints of the secret discussions. Anami's brother-in-law flung at him, as an absurd suggestion, "If you are going to accept the Potsdam declaration, you had better commit harakiri." Unwittingly Takeshita had touched a sensitive nerve.

After the young men had poured out of his office, Anami summoned Colonel Hayashi and they drove to the war minister's residence. In the car, Anami seemed tired and deflated. He told Hayashi about Takeshita's remark. "Takeshita said such a cruel thing to me. Since I am nearly sixty years old, I do not think it would be difficult for me to die. Perhaps it is not easy for a young man like you, Hayashi."

Though he was not on the inside and did not know precisely what was being discussed or said at the Big Six meetings, Hayashi was observant enough to realize the drift of events. To Anami, his private secretary said "I believe that the nation has been steered gradually in the direction of peace. Great numbers of troops, millions of men, are scattered in various parts of the Pacific and your greatest duty is carefully to disarm and repatriate them. I believe it would be advisable for you to commit suicide, if you intend to do so, after you have accomplished that task. There is no reason why you should take your life rashly."

Resting both hands on the butt of his sword, obviously concerned, Anami mulled Hayashi's words, weighing them against Takeshita's gibe and its implications. He gazed far out the window, his face clouded, and he sat silently with lips pursed. Without looking at Hayashi, the war minister said softly "I believe you are right."

The secretary's look of perpetual surprise softened and he permitted himself to believe that he had given sound counsel at a critical moment for his chief.

They arrived at the vice-minister's official residence, across the street from the ashes of what had been the minister's residence. Anami's things had been moved in the morning after the fire and his vice-minister, Wakamatsu, had moved into the Peers Club, about a third of a mile away. Anami stepped from the car very deliberately, Hayashi noticed, not with his usual *élan*. The war minister hurried inside, sought his aide, and immediately set his target in the garden. Not until he shot the seventeenth arrow had he grouped five to his satisfaction. Then he went in to lunch.

Chapter 6

Another Hearing

Shortly after two P.M. August 9, 1945, fifteen perspiring men gladly took refuge from the stark August sun in the prime minister's residence. They were the premier's official family, his cabinet, and the heat was on them wherever they might be. Of the fifteen, ten were civilians, thus the balance on the paramount question of peace conceivably might have changed. The degree of change was soon to be tested.

Premier Suzuki, outwardly calm, called the meeting to order and asked the foreign minister to outline the current situation.

Togo reported on the SCDW's pulling and hauling over the Potsdam declaration. "The Big Six agreed that there was one indispensable condition: the Emperor system must be maintained. However," he emphasized, "there was disagreement as to whether other conditions need be added relating to occupation, disarmament, and war criminals."

Slouched in his chair, the reticent navy minister Admiral Yonai said "there is no chance whatsoever of victory; therefore I agree with the foreign minister that the Potsdam declaration should be accepted at once, with only that one condition about retaining the Emperor."

Like a defiant fortress commanding a sector of the green terrain of the conference table, General Anami angrily rejected Yonai's pessimistic view as if it had been a personal attack aimed at him. "The army," Anami insisted, "is confident that it can inflict a telling blow on the Allied forces in the inevitable decisive battle of the homeland." Although the war minister did not pretend that victory was absolutely certain, he advised that defeat was not inevitable either. "If we put everything into our all-out efforts in the decisive battle, an unexpected turn of events in our favor is possible."

Yonai leaned forward and derisively rejected this. "We have reached the end of our resources, both spiritual and material. To continue is out of the question!"

General Anami denied that the nation was defeated, citing its millions of armed forces in the homeland eager to meet the foe under favorable conditions for the first time. With command of the countryside, with shortened supply and communications lines, with no need to rely on long overseas transporting of troops and material, conditions would be vastly different. The decisive homeland battle could be a toss-up, he contended. And Japan could at least for a time repulse the enemy and might thereafter "find life out of death," even though there was no certainty of victory. Anyway, he said, there was no way to demobilize Japan's forces overseas, so the nation would have to fight on.

Suzuki cut in on this exchange and, to cool it off, called on the other ministers to report.

The rice harvest would be the worst in fifteen years, according to the agriculture minister, and might even be the worst in half a century, depending on conditions.

Maintaining contact with Korea and Manchuria for supplies of materials and food was in doubt, said the transportation minister. In fact, there was even serious difficulty shipping to and from the outer home islands, Hokkaido and Kyushu, because of mines, enemy planes, and hostile warships.

War production was dropping, reported the munitions minister, because of lack of raw materials, parts, subassemblies, and absenteeism, not to mention the destruction from air raids.

Home Minister Abe brought up the probability of internal revolt if the nation accepted the Potsdam declaration unconditionally.

"The morale of the people has already been destroyed to a considerable extent," Abe said. "However, the majority do not think Japan has been defeated so badly because of the propaganda of the military, in which the battle results announced by Imperial GHQ have always been 'Japan won the battle.' Therefore, if Japan should accept the Potsdam terms at this moment, it is likely that a considerable public outburst might result."

At this stage everyone needed respite from the smoke, clinging heat, and stale arguments—particularly those who had been wrestling with the same questions since ten thirty that morning. The premier called a short recess.

Suzuki rose and sought Cabinet Secretary Sakomizu. Acutely aware that the cabinet meeting was going the same way as the SCDW session, the premier was glumly convinced that no consensus was possible. Only because the cabinet was the body that must approve decisions of state was there any use in continuing the meeting. If only a majority instead of unanimity had been necessary the matter could have been settled hours before. But Anami, far from weakening in his insistence on the four conditions, was actually wearing down the others with his boundless vitality.

If the erasing of Hiroshima and Nagasaki and the tidal wave of Soviet attack could not convince the ministers to surrender, what logical argument could? Now, the old premier decided wearily, the time had come for the plan first discussed weeks ago with Kido and with Togo just before the meeting.

Kido had assured Suzuki that the Emperor would state his will at a full-dress, Imperial Conference. The military chiefs would be there and would not be likely to ignore the Emperor's desires. They could, of course, reject his wishes, for legally the Emperor was not in a position to command—his advice could be accepted or rejected by the conference and, in any case, would have to be acted upon by the cabinet. The fact was that there was no sure way of knowing what the result would be, for it had never in history been done.

The unvarying practice was for the SCDW or cabinet to decide a matter, then present it to the Throne for ratification. If the conferees could not agree unanimously on a matter of importance, the government was expected to resign and be replaced by a regime that could decide the question. This practice was followed to keep the Emperor's skirts clean of responsibility in case a decision backfired. True, he gave his sanction to the decisions of cabinet and SCDW, but this was automatic and he was expected to do so whether he personally approved or not. To put an undecided question to His Majesty and ask for *his* view was absolutely unprecedented.

Having found his man, Suzuki instructed Sakomizu to prepare for an Imperial Conference. Sakomizu raised a few points. "For this," he said, "we need a formal petition to the Emperor."

"Fine," replied Suzuki, waving him on, "go ahead and prepare it." He was about to leave. The old man had a natural aversion to technicalities.

"But for an Imperial Conference," the cabinet secretary continued, catching the premier's sleeve, "the petition must have the signatures of the premier and the two chiefs of staff."

Suzuki sucked in his breath. General Umezu and Admiral Toyoda were not likely to agree to such a conference. They had stalled to avoid conferences ever since the Hiroshima bombing. Their fundamental strategy seemed to be to prevent a decision and to continue to fight. Toyoda appeared to be just as adamant as Umezu on this.

However, Sakomizu, for all his relative youth, had been in politics and government for more than a decade. He was skilled in manipulation, and now he would have to demonstrate it. Suzuki signed the petition and left to reconvene the cabinet meeting. Sakomizu set off to "hustle" the chiefs of staff.

He located Toyoda at the navy ministry building and Umezu at IGHQ. To both he gave a plausible, matter-of-fact explanation: The premier had asked the cabinet secretary to get the signatures of the chiefs of staff on a petition for an Imperial Conference in order to save time and trouble later. "After all, it is certain that an Imperial Conference must be held sooner or later to take care of crucial issues such as a declaration of war against the Soviets. And with conditions now so unpredictable, the meeting might be called on very short notice —even in the middle of the night. When that time comes I will have to start looking for you to sign the petition and it will only mean additional trouble for you and for me and the loss of precious time. Of course I will be sure to call you beforehand to let you know if and when the petition will have to be used. In order to be ready for such an emergency please sign these papers."

Both the General and the Admiral could see the validity of Sakomizu's request. An Imperial Conference would be mandatory before an imperial rescript declaring war. Already half a day had passed since the Russian attack and Japan had not yet made any formal response. Of course, any other matter to be placed before His Majesty, they thought, would be thoroughly prepared by the Supreme Council secretaries—one a navy admiral and another an army general. These men would naturally keep the chiefs of staff informed. And no matters that had not been fully prepared, discussed and agreed upon by the cabinet or SCDW would ever be taken into the August Presence in an Imperial Conference. After all, Imperial Conferences were meant to secure Imperial endorsement. The Emperor did not participate in deliberation or debate; he signed on the dotted line, as he was supposed to. Umezu and Toyoda both questioned Sakomizu sharply on one point: "You will let us know in advance if the petition is to be used?" The cabinet secretary assured them both that he would. The two chiefs of staff, confident that they would receive plenty of preliminary notice of the conference business, took out their brushes and signed as the cabinet secretary had requested. Sakomizu streaked back to his office with the priceless petition.

At the palace that afternoon the Emperor's ear, Marquis Kido, was busily receiving information. At two o'clock the Emperor's chief aide-de-camp came to report to Kido the latest word on the Russian invasion of Manchuria—the Reds were rolling ahead on all fronts.

At four, the privy seal welcomed his good friend Mamoru Shigemitsu, the former foreign minister. Shigemitsu limped in, rested his cane, and unburdened his mind. (Shigemitsu's left leg was buried in Shanghai, where a bomb had blown it off in an assassination attempt in the thirties.) In 1944 the two men had concluded that only the intervention of the Emperor in an Imperial Conference could bring the military to heel. Shigemitsu now urged this again, saying that if Japan insisted on the four conditions under discussion a rupture of negotiations was inevitable. Kido promptly relayed these views to the Emperor and talked with him about the current situation.

While the cabinet scudded along toward its inevitable split on the peace question, another meeting a mile and a half north of the palace was reaching unanimity on war. At Imperial General Headquarters the supreme military commanders were in session. The army chief of staff and the top brass of the army were assembled to agree on a policy toward Russia. The direction was obvious: Japan had been attacked. It would therefore do what any nation does when attacked —fight back.

While their superiors were focusing on the Russian question, the junior officers at GHQ were at the boiling point about the Soviet invasion and the persistent rumors that the peace faction was making headway. The hotheads were convinced that the time had come to sweep the peacemongers away and bring the Emperor back to his senses. Their thoughts and their talk and their actions began to coalesce around the perennially popular Japanese technique of the *coup d'état.*

The prime minister, now determined to see the drama played out to the last act, reconvened the cabinet meeting. He knew it would be a futile exercise, but it had to run its course.

The split appeared to be about two to one in favor of accepting the Potsdam terms as Togo recommended. Still not enough support for action when unanimity was the only acceptable criterion.

Then education minister Ota chilled the peace advocates to the marrow by uttering the words that the rest of them feared even to think. Replying to Suzuki, Ota said, "I will not express my opinion on this problem, for this is a serious matter. I insist the cabinet should tender its resignation because it has failed in its responsibility."

In normal times this would have been normal procedure, but not now. Angered and afraid that Ota's words would start an avalanche that would sweep the government out of office, Premier Suzuki commented acidly: "I am fully aware of our responsibility, but this is no time for the cabinet to argue about responsibility. We must, rather, take steps to remedy the matter."

For a harrowing moment the fate of millions depended on the minute fibers and tiny electrochemical currents in the brain of the war minister. The general brushed Ota's suggestion aside.

Here was an open test of the military's intentions: If the war minister had been dead-set on all-out battle, he had the opportunity at this point to destroy the cabinet. A military cabinet would surely be the only alternative to Suzuki's limping government, and a bitter-end fight to the death using scorched-earth tactics and guerrilla warfare in the mountains loomed as the inevitable consequence. Was it possible that Anami had missed the significance of Ota's suggestion?

Suzuki wiped his brow and informally polled the group. It was no surprise to find the cabinet hopelessly split. The premier announced that he wished to report the situation to the Emperor. He instructed the cabinet to continue its deliberations and signaled Togo to accompany him.

They drove straight to the *Gobunko,* the Emperor's library set in
the Fukiage gardens, and went in to see Hirohito.

Togo pointed out that it was obviously hopeless to expect any consensus in either the SCDW or cabinet. Suzuki then urged the Emperor
to convene as soon as possible—*that very night*—an Imperial Conference in his presence. Hirohito instantly agreed. This Imperial Conference, all three of them recognized, would be the final chance. It
had to succeed. It was the last workable brake lever available.

As Togo and Suzuki re-entered the conference room the heat,
smoke, and stifling air signaled that nothing had changed. They found
that though the words had flowed like water, the factions had moved
not one millimeter; the debate was still deadlocked. While others
flagged and faltered, Anami seemed to grow in confidence and vitality.
The premier wearily adjourned the meeting about 10 P.M.

Sakomizu, the ever-efficient cabinet secretary had meanwhile prepared the necessary Imperial Conference notices. By the time the
cabinet meeting broke up, the notices were ready to send. Suzuki read
one through, signed, and directed Sakomizu to send them out.

All but Togo and the premier were surprised to receive the conference call; the military men were not merely surprised, they were
rocked to their roots. Of course Toyoda and Umezu had signed the
petition, but they expected no such event as this until the SCDW had
arrived at a meeting of minds—and nothing, as they well knew, was
more remote! What could Suzuki be thinking of? What crafty plot
had Sakomizu set in motion? The cabinet secretary had specifically
promised to notify them in advance if and when the prime minister
decided to use the petition they had signed to call an Imperial Conference. But Sakomizu had not called them. He had notified no one. He
had tricked them shamelessly.

Umezu, Anami, and Toyoda were immediately incensed. They suspected something was up, but they could not foresee what. What
galled them most was the fact that the supposedly passive Taoist
premier had taken the initiative. They had fully expected to drag their
heels and postpone further SCDW meetings, delaying as long as possible the ultimate time of reckoning.

Within half an hour the chief cabinet secretary was the center of a
violent reaction. The army and navy men assigned to cabinet liaison

bitterly accused Sakomizu of breaking his "promise" to the chiefs of staff. They protested that they had not been consulted, that the agenda and conclusions had not been drawn. Sakomizu could not deny that he had failed to notify the chiefs of staff. Nor could he tell the military men the real reason why. It was because, he says, "I was afraid that if they were notified both chiefs of staff would cancel the validity of the petition by withdrawing their names." And if they killed the Conference in this way the stalemate would continue—with destruction of the Suzuki cabinet almost certain.

Therefore Sakomizu minimized the importance of the Conference by telling the angry officers that the meeting had been called simply so that the Emperor could hear the views of the Big Six and the privy council president.

In his "national uniform," the simple olive-drab jacket prescribed for all business and social wear now that new clothing was unobtainable, Sakomizu was conspicuous among the army and navy khakis and samurai swords. The atmosphere in the cabinet secretary's office grew increasingly ugly as more and more officers from the war ministry arrived.

Sakomizu's mind flashed back to the slaughter on that snowy February 26 in 1936 when rebel troops had shot down key government leaders. The cabinet secretary had been in this very building when the rebels had stormed the residence for his father-in-law, Admiral Okada, who was then premier. As Okada's private secretary, Sakomizu had come face to face with the rebels, but by good fortune both he and the premier had managed to elude them.

By eleven thirty Sakomizu's nervousness had increased tenfold, with good reason. He was surrounded by men from GHQ and the war ministry. They pressed in upon him, their long samurai swords at their sides and their hands on the hilts in the traditional threatening gestures of the samurai, as they muttered about his perfidy in calling this hasty conference without the knowledge of the military.

Afraid that the tempers might reach the flash point at any moment and that some zealot might do more than merely threaten, Sakomizu decided he had to make a move to escape, do it quickly and without arousing his visitors. Marshaling all his self-control, he rose from his chair and called out resolutely "let us go to the Imperial Palace—

time is pressing." With that, he pushed his way to the hallway and out to the reception foyer of the *kantei,* determinedly threading through the angry, muttering young officers. His outer assurance barely hid his inner alarm.

Sakomizu found the secretariat chamber buzzing with army officers who were almost literally gnashing their teeth. Like a tank wheeling up to crush a thicket, War Minister Anami strode up to the cabinet secretary and asked how matters stood. Though Sakomizu knew full well that the Emperor was to be asked for his imperial decision, he bluffed glibly. He assured the skeptical war minister as he had the junior officers that the conference had been called to present the Big Six's views to the Emperor, not to reach conclusions. The grumbling among the officers continued threateningly.

The conference was to be in the palace air-raid shelter under the Fukiage gardens. In this classic oriental garden with its lotus pools, ponds, artfully conceived paths, and traditional bridges, peacocks and cranes had once wandered serene and secure. From the high point, the view included forest giants as well as dwarfed trees. It had been a lavishly tended arboretum of hundreds of plant species from the mainland set artfully in graceful bowers.

As the hour closed on midnight the conferees entered the narrow door in the concrete scar on the side of the hill. The pines near the entrance were silhouetted against the moon. The men descended single-file down the mat-covered steps of the palace air-raid shelter. Fifty feet down and sixty feet laterally into the hill they advanced into the musty, hot shelter, past the steel door to the machine room, and into the anteroom. And then it was time to move into the conference room. Down the hall they went through the first door of foot-thick steel into a passageway, then through another steel door, and finally the double wooden doors to the conference room itself.

Each conferee received three sheets of paper. One paper carried the Potsdam declaration in full. The second was headed *Proposition A* and listed Togo's single condition for acceptance of the Potsdam terms. The third was headed *Proposition B* and gave the three additional conditions favored by Anami, Umezu, and Toyoda.

Now in the conference room and finding their seats at the large table were the Big Six: Premier Suzuki, Foreign Minister Togo, War

Minister Anami, Navy Minister Yonai, and the army and navy chiefs of staff, General Umezu and Admiral Toyoda. Also taking their places were the directors of the army and navy Military Affairs Bureaus, Lieutenant General Yoshizumi and Vice-Admiral Hoshina; Lieutenant General Ikeda, chief of the Combined Planning Board; Baron Kiichiro Hiranuma, president of the privy council; and Sakomizu, the cabinet secretary.

Suzuki had purposely brought Hiranuma to the conference. It was strategically important to have the privy council represented. The council was a group of twenty-seven leading statesmen appointed by the Emperor; on paper and in theory it was a powerful panel. However, since it would be as divided as the cabinet (and twice as unruly) on this question, the old Admiral had at Sakomizu's suggestion, decided to finesse the privy council by including its president in this conference. Thus the privy council would be informed and would participate, technically, in the proceedings.

The army saw Hiranuma's inclusion in the conference as additional proof of a dark plot. The privy council president was not supposed to attend Imperial Conferences of the SCDW, they contended. This notion riled them. Actually, Sakomizu had carefully checked this point and had found that there was ample precedent going back fifty years for inviting the president of the privy council.

All were now seated. All were tense and tormented by heat and the lively inhabitants of the shelter—savage mosquitoes who welcomed the arrival of fresh meat. The etiquette of the Imperial Conference dictated that participants endure stoically and silently, hands on knees, sitting rigidly at attention, so the mosquitoes had easy pickings. All waited breathlessly for the arrival of the Emperor.

Chapter 7

Ultimate Appeal

The setting for this Imperial Conference, this convergence of destinies, was grim and graceless. It would have made an excellent root cellar.

In spite of the carpeted floor, the drapes, the brocaded tables, it was unmistakably a concrete bunker and it was as ugly as the necessity that required it. But it fulfilled its primary purpose, protection. The rooms were surrounded by up to twenty-one feet of reinforced concrete above and on all sides and were buried in the hill under an additional forty-five feet of earth. The passageways were moist with seepage and the ceilings and walls of the rooms were clammy with condensation.

In addition to the conference room, the complex included a telephone-switchboard chamber, the machine room for air and water supply, the anteroom from which the conferees had just come, and the Emperor's underground living room. The conferees had filed in through the garden entrance to the shelter. The Emperor would enter through the door and stairway from his library.

Eleven leaders of Japan were now seated around two parallel tables. At one end and at right angles to them was a smaller table covered with gold-lined brocade. Behind it as the throne for this occasion was a simple wooden chair with plain wooden arms. As a backdrop for the imperial presence, an elegant six-fold gold screen had been placed in back of the chair.

At precisely 11:55 P.M. (after twelve minutes of final counseling by Privy Seal Kido), the Emperor in his army uniform appeared from behind the screen with Lieutenant General Hasunuma, his chief

76

military aide-de-camp. As his loyal subjects scrambled to their feet and bowed rigidly, he took his place and the historic conference began.

Suzuki, tight-lipped and painfully aware of the gravity of the moment, asked the chief cabinet secretary to read the Potsdam declaration. Afterward the aged premier slowly rose and addressed the Throne.

"The Supreme Council for Direction of the War met today to discuss the Potsdam terms. Although no decision has been reached, the following conditions were discussed:

"1. A guarantee that the imperial family will continue to reign.

"2. Disarmament of the armed forces by Japan herself.

"3. Trial of war criminals by Japan herself.

"4. Occupation of Japan to be limited to the minimum time and places.

"It was suggested that these conditions be preliminary to our acceptance of the Potsdam terms.

"The foreign minister has put forward the following proposal, Proposition A:

The government will accept the Potsdam Declaration with the understanding that it does not include any demand for changes in the Emperor's status, as provided for in the national laws.

"An emergency cabinet meeting was held today and the following results were recorded after deliberating on this matter:

"Favoring the foreign minister's proposal: 6

"Favoring the proposal with the four conditions: 3

"Those who were neutral, but with opinions to decrease the number of conditions: 5."

The Admiral paused, glanced at Togo, and continued.

"Now I shall have the foreign minister explain the reasons for his proposal."

The heat and humidity made the room a veritable pressure cooker. Togo, his face drawn, rose and spoke directly to the small man behind the brocaded table.

"It is both humiliating and terribly difficult for Japan to accept the Potsdam terms," he said, to make clear his personal view of the document. "However, present circumstances compel us to accept.

The atomic bomb and Russia's participation in the war have suddenly changed the situation and have strengthened the enemy's position. It is no longer possible to rely upon negotiations for further developments or better conditions. Especially now that the Soviet Union has resorted to arms, negotiations have become impossible.

"In view of this, there is danger that if too many conditions are presented they may all be rejected entirely. I think it better to present only one condition: that the maintenance and security of the imperial family be guaranteed. As for the other conditions, the disarmament issue should be considered at the time of the armistice negotiations. I think we cannot help but accept the occupation of Japan and the prosecution of war criminals. The Japanese race would endure and work for rehabilitation in the future if the imperial family is left in peace. It is my opinion, therefore, that we should concentrate upon this one thing: the continuation of the imperial family."

Suzuki then called on the navy minister. Yonai stood and, with typical brevity, said "I agree fully with the opinion of the foreign minister."

It was then Anami's turn. The war minister was obviously under great strain. He spoke in an unnaturally high voice, choked with emotion. "My opinion is quite the contrary. First of all, the Cairo declaration calls for relinquishing Manchukuo. It would cease to exist as an independent nation." He hesitated, then launched into what by now were familiar arguments to all present.

"Even if the Japanese government accepted the Potsdam terms it should set forth at least four conditions. In case it is impossible to include all four conditions we should continue the war. If we can give a great blow to the enemy in a decisive last battle on the homeland we can win better terms. It is true that we may not expect certain victory in that decisive battle but defeat is not always certain, either. I am convinced that unity is strength and the battle would cause the Allies to suffer greatly. If we cannot halt the enemy, a hundred million Japanese would gladly prefer death to the dishonor of surrender and they would thus leave the Japanese people's mark on history.

"We must recognize," Anami concluded, "that Japanese troops overseas will never accept unconditional surrender. Moreover, in Japan itself, there are many who are determined to fight at all costs. If Japan surrenders, internal chaos will result!"

Was this a threat, an informed prediction, a bargaining ploy? The war minister sat down heavily; his cheeks were wet with tears and he shuddered with quiet sobs.

There was a moment of painful silence. Then the premier nodded to General Umezu, the army chief of staff. Though his face was impassive as usual, Umezu's voice quavered with strain.

"I am of the same opinion as the war minister. Preparations for the decisive battle of the homeland are already completed and we are confident of victory. Although Russian attack has made the situation unfavorable, I do not think we need abandon the opportunity to deliver one last blow to America and England. The war has already continued for several years and many comrades have gladly fought and died for the Emperor. Therefore, if we surrender unconditionally now, it will be inexcusable to these dead heroes. Although I have no objection to accepting the Potsdam declaration, I think the four conditions are the minimum concessionary request."

Further down the table, General Sumihisa Ikeda, who had served under Umezu for years, looked at his former commander sharply. He observed that Umezu's heart was not in the statement. The General's argument, Ikeda thought, lacked his usual force.

Premier Suzuki skipped Admiral Toyoda and called on the privy council president, Baron Kiichiro Hiranuma. Xenophobic and ultra-nationalistic, Hiranuma at eighty was of Suzuki's vintage, but he had a completely different orientation. In the thirties Hiranuma had founded one of the largest reactionary societies. It favored fascism, armed might, and rule by the military. Even so, he had a distinguished record as president of the Supreme Court and former minister of justice and was recognized as one of Japan's foremost experts on constitutional law. Gaunt and horse-faced, Hiranuma had been prime minister briefly in 1939. His government had been wracked by dissension over the question of enlarging the Berlin–Tokyo Anti-Comintern Pact into a full military alliance between Japan and Germany.

Before the conference Hiranuma had been briefed thoroughly, it was thought. He had been told of the urgency of ending the war at all costs. Time was of the essence. The midnight conference illustrated the exigency. In spite of all this, Hiranuma arose, cleared his throat and proceeded like a coroner at an inquest. "Before I express my opinion," he rasped, "I should like to ask the foreign minister about progress of negotiations with Russia."

Togo, taken aback at the intrusion of a subject now made irrelevant by Russia's war declaration, managed to contain himself. Patiently he related the sequence: "On July 12 we transmitted to the Soviet government the will of His Majesty requesting arbitration to terminate the war as soon as possible and notice that a special envoy was to be dispatched. Thereafter, despite repeated inquiries, no answer was received. On 7 August a telegram came from our Ambassador Sato in Moscow with notice of a conference appointment with Foreign Commissar Molotov on 8 August at 5 P.M. Last night Molotov rejected the Japanese proposal for mediation and the Soviets declared war on Japan."

The octogenarian pressed for details. "Have you ever made proposals to the USSR on concrete matters?"

All but gritting his teeth, Togo replied "Though I notified the Soviets that concrete matters would be explained by the special envoy, I did not make such proposals."

"Then," persisted Hiranuma, "what is the reason for the USSR's declaration of war against Japan?"

Togo recapitulated the gist of the Soviet war declaration as stated in the Tass broadcast from Moscow.

Hiranuma plodded stoically on with his examination: "Is it true that, as quoted in the Soviet statement, Japan formally rejected the three-power ultimatum?"

"No steps," said Togo tersely, "were taken to reject the ultimatum."

"Then what," asked Hiranuma, "is the basis for the Soviet claim of rejection?"

Impatiently Togo shot back. "It's in their imagination."

Finally turning his attention to the matters at hand, the conditions named in the Potsdam declaration, Hiranuma mused "Exactly what is meant by the cruelties inflicted on Allied prisoners and the surrender of all war criminals, as set forth in the Potsdam declaration? Can we interpret this to mean that we can punish war criminals ourselves?"

"In the past, war criminals have always been turned over to the victors," Togo said.

Apparently startled by this, Hiranuma queried "Mr. Foreign Minister, are you thinking of handing them over to the enemy?"

A study in controlled exasperation, Togo replied. "Depending on the situation, I think it may be unavoidable."

The old jurist continued. "Do you think that they may not agree to our request that Japan be allowed to disarm its troops independently?"

"I do," Togo snapped.

Unruffled, Hiranuma then tested his lance on the military: "I should like to ask the war minister and chief of army general staff the following. Do you have the confidence to continue the war in the future?"

Umezu, starting to rise to answer, halted as Hiranuma wheezed on.

"I am afraid this is very doubtful. Although it was explained that victory in the decisive battle on the homeland is possible, there are successive air raids daily and we are even being bombarded from warships. Above all, the atomic bomb has displayed a dreadful effectiveness. Is a defense against these bombs possible? In most cases the Japanese do not retaliate in any way against enemy air raids, and the enemy do as they please. There are absolutely no counterattacks against enemy air raids over medium and small cities and towns."

Once again there was a pause and all present hopefully watched Umezu get to his feet. But once again Hiranuma's cracked voice continued its ambulating journey over familiar terrain.

"I think the enemy air raids on the homeland will hereafter become more intense; more than half of Tokyo will probably be demolished, and medium and small cities and towns will be completely destroyed. Then all facilities will stop. Are there any counterplans against the atom bomb?"

Another pause as Hiranuma sought to pin down another thought; another expectant wait by the conferees confined in this damp oven.

"Today the uncertainty of the people has increased greatly, and their fighting spirit is lost. Transport facilities are destroyed and food is scarce. As in the case of Tokyo, food sent from other places has all been exhausted. The import of cereals from Manchuria has become difficult. I feel very uneasy about these matters. Also, I want an explanation of the extent of air-raid damage on the homeland transportation facilities."

This time Umezu stood and spoke before the old man could continue. The General's shaved head gleamed like a polished stone. "The Supreme Command will exert our utmost efforts in the future," he promised, spinning out a typically bureaucratic answer. "Although it is difficult to avert disaster from the special bomb totally, it might be checked to a certain degree if proper antiaircraft measures are taken. I think the intensification of air raids in the future will be inevitable. However, I believe that if we have the firm resolution to withstand the damage and difficulties caused by air raids, they will not bring about the conclusion of the war. I am sure the people will lose fighting spirit, due to the unrest in their daily lives and from the destruction of transportation facilities. It is difficult to avoid damages completely, but the Supreme Command will exert our utmost efforts. You may count on us hereafter since a change in policy has been effected. We will never surrender to the enemy because of air raids alone."

Hiranuma then prodded the navy. "Does the navy have any countermeasures against the enemy task forces?"

Having practically no navigable capital ships left to use for the purpose, Toyoda made the only possible response: "Air force should be used to cope with the task forces. Task forces not escorting transports are highly maneuverable. Therefore it is difficult to detect them without a great air force. Heretofore our air force has been concentrated and stationed in readiness for the decisive battle in the homeland, and its strength has been preserved for future use. Therefore we have only used surprise counterattack by small forces. However, we expect to counterattack hereafter, using considerable strength."

Turning to still another area, Hiranuma's inventory of Japan's tribulations continued. His audience silently fumed and sweated. None dared interrupt or brush off the venerable judge. "Maintenance of public peace in the homeland is important, but what measures are you going to take hereafter? If the government's policy is not appropriate, internal disorder will be aggravated. How about the food situation?"—another rhetorical question. His colleagues waited morosely for him to run down. "It is getting worse day by day. Although there is no doubt that the people are loyal at heart, the present conditions are extremely dangerous, a situation requiring much concern. In view of the present deterioration of the general situation in Japan, we can suppose that continuation of the war will create greater domestic disturbances than would ending the war. . . ."

Finally Suzuki, agitated almost beyond endurance by the seemingly endless flow of questions from Hiranuma, broke in, in an attempt to end the ramble. "I fully agree and am worried. Under the present situation the progress of the war is unfavorable for us. Thus the people are uneasy. They cannot withstand the air raids any longer. If the war is continued under conditions such that our nation cannot be defended no matter how much we try, the path will be extremely difficult and dangerous."

Aware now that the examination period was over, Hiranuma launched his summation. "Although I have not had time for thorough consideration, I shall express my opinion because of the urgent situation." (At last, thought more than one of the conferees.)

"In substance, the foreign minister's draft condition is as it should be. Its objective is solely the defense of the national polity and I concur. However, the wording is undesirable and unjustifiable. The sovereignty of the Emperor is not derived through state law, nor is it provided for by the Constitution. It is only referred to in the Constitution. If the wording is changed to read 'the said declaration does not comprise any demand which prejudices the prerogatives of His Majesty as a sovereign ruler,' I would then have no objection."

Togo nodded assent at this seemingly minor adjustment of language in his proposed condition. After all, Hiranuma was an authority on constitutional law.

"As to conditions 2, 3, and 4," Hiranuma droned on, "although the foreign minister said the enemy would refuse to negotiate, I think that the statements by the war minister and army chief of staff are quite right. I think we should disarm ourselves. Since there is no demand for handing over the war criminals, this condition may or may not be added. . . . The occupation is also an important matter concerning the honor of an independent country. . . ."

While the ancient barrister catalogued the points in his brief in excruciating detail, Suzuki was suppressing his impatience as best he could. Hiranuma had held center stage for more than half an hour. That was sufficient time for Allied bombers to obliterate another city, for Russian columns to advance five or ten miles, for another atomic bomb to be put aloft, while they sat chewing over cold cabbage. At any moment some incident might destroy the whole tenuous climate of acceptance within the nation. And still Hiranuma talked on.

". . . if the war must be continued due to the enemy's refusal to accept the conditions, a feeling of unrest will prevail in the country. We must cope with this after making a thorough study of the situation. . . ."

It was difficult to judge which was more oppressive, the heat in the bunker or Hiranuma's marathon review. "Will he never finish?" thought Togo.

"We cannot wage war with military strength alone. Since we have national mobilization, the people's spirit, production conditions, and daily necessities must be considered. Can the present situation be classified as satisfactory? How is the food situation?"

The old man was repeating his repetitions. His audience was now fidgeting openly.

"The welfare of the people is the secret of politics. In addition, if there is any uneasiness, no matter how strong the army and navy may be, it is impossible to continue the war. . . ."

Hiranuma was also president of Nihon University, and it began to appear that he was including elements of several commencement addresses.

"As for the other conditions, the authorities should make the decision after thorough deliberation. Since this is a very important matter, I think this should be left to the decision of the Emperor. . . ."

What was this? Suzuki, Togo, and Sakomizu were presumably the only ones present who knew that the Emperor was to be asked for his decision. Had one of them leaked this to Hiranuma? Was he going to botch things so near the crucial moment? He was speaking directly to the Emperor now.

"In order to fulfill the heritage of the imperial forefathers, Your Majesty also has a responsibility to prevent uncertainty in the nation. I ask Your Imperial Majesty to make a decision with this point in mind."

At last the garrulous old man ceased talking, folded, and sat down.

Before the audience had time to react to this request, Admiral Toyoda, perhaps dizzied by the Hiranuma labyrinth, perhaps concerned that the premier had skipped him earlier, felt compelled to speak. Suzuki recognized him.

"As the naval supreme commander, I agree with the opinions of the war minister and chief of the army general staff. In considering the prospects of victory or defeat in this war, I cannot say that the probability of victory is certain, but do not think that we will be positively defeated. The naval supreme command is concerned over the negotiations merely with one condition: that of preserving the national polity. The fighting spirit still prevails among the people. Soldiers at the front are doing their best, and they are full of the spirit of self-sacrifice. I think it is possible to restore the fighting spirit of the people through future leadership even though some of them have already lost it."

This left Toyoda in an ambiguous position—was he withdrawing support for the other three conditions or was he not?

The count at that point was three and three: Anami, Umezu, and Toyoda(?) ranged against Togo, Yonai, and Hiranuma. Suzuki, seeing (as expected) that consensus was no closer, rose. It was two in the morning, August 10. The room was torrid and the mosquitoes were merciless.

"Gentlemen," the premier said, outwardly calm, "for hours we have discussed these matters and come to no decision. Even now agreement is not in sight. We cannot afford to waste even a minute at this time. So, though it is unprecedented and awe-inspiring, I propose to seek the Imperial guidance and to decide the conference's conclusion on that basis. His Majesty's wish should settle the issue, and the government should follow it."

Suzuki, without a pause, stepped forward to the Imperial Throne. There was a gasp at the effrontery of this move. "Mr. Prime Minister," choked Anami in stunned disbelief. The aged Admiral advanced and addressed the Emperor. The silence was as oppressive as the heat.

"Your Imperial decision is requested as to which proposal should be adopted, the foreign minister's or the one with the four conditions."

Not in recorded time had the Emperor been so called upon for the expression of his own will to decide an important issue. Almost never did he take an active part—or even speak—at these ritualistic, prearranged shadow plays. To actually put the question to him was absolutely unheard-of. The military had expected that the conference would simply be for discussion and then would disperse into the night. What now, from the living god whose every command they had sworn to uphold?

This was not the finale intended. It was not the end predicted. In those thundering days before the Pacific War, during the military reviews, the victory celebrations, and the ceremonial observances, the man-god in his trim uniform had taken the salute seated on his favorite charger, First Snow. Far from the thoughts and never on the lips of those military leaders who had pressed for empire were visions such as this sweating concrete cubicle and the ignominious question at hand.

Imperial destiny, carrying enlightenment to the barbarians, *Kodo* (the Imperial Way), and *Hakku Ichiu* (the eight corners of the world under one roof)—those were the talismans of the thirties. And to these had been added self-defense against strangulation by the democracies. Japanese conquest became holy war.

Certainly during the victory-drunk period in 1942, when Japan held sway over one-sixth of the earth, none of the military leaders breathed even a word of caution. Those were the times of heady predictions and rotund schemes for carving up the world-melon with the Nazis—magnanimously leaving to them everything from the Indian border westward. For the time being.

Those were the days of delirious celebrations, as after the victories at Pearl Harbor, at Hong Kong, in the Philippines, and following the fall of Singapore. Then the Emperor appeared on the bridge overlooking the wide palace plaza to accept the *banzais* of thousands of gloriously joyful subjects. In military uniform and astride First Snow, Hirohito rode out repeatedly before the jubilant multitudes below.

Nowhere on the horizon did the military leaders report even a man's-hand-size cloud. But then into the communiqués crept a newly coined term: *tenshin,* "to march elsewhere." It was first used after the Supreme Command had committed all its prestige and presumably its uttermost efforts to hold Guadalcanal. Soon the term became familiar. All too familiar.

The navy had its semantic peculiarities also. There were the "victories" at Formosa, the Solomons and Gilberts, and Midway—fictions on which the military solemnly required the Imperial signature.

Then the talk increasingly turned to a war of ten to twenty years' duration, one that would require killing 100 million Japanese in order to defeat the sacred nation.

The military leaders' dream of a vast victory parade, with the Emperor on the white charger prancing buoyantly at the head of his conquering troops, had evaporated. More aptly, it had condensed to this—this debate over whether to sacrifice additional millions or stop the carnage by taking the unthinkable step.

Which required the greater courage? To fight on from the lower depths, wasting away like trapped moles in the army's newly built mid-mountain vault in remote Matsushiro? With the enemy ruling the skies and chasing everything that moved, was it certain even that the special bulletproof car could deliver the imperial family safely to the "impregnable" hideaway in the mountain fastnesses of that remote northwestern area?

And then what? An end like Hitler's? Wipe out the dynasty as the loyal subjects obediently pitted their flesh and feeble weapons against the unleashed atomic power of the universe in *gyokusai*—Armageddon? The Japanese, as descendants of the Sun Goddess, now faced the titanic power of the sun itself, turned against its offspring. The supernatural racial-superiority legend that spawned and strengthened the samurai spirit now faced the altogether real, demonstrable, and scientifically predictable destroyer derived from the same sun. How would that fit into the Shinto cosmology?

Surrender? What could be expected then? *If* the army obeyed and *if* the people followed the Emperor's orders, the destruction and mass slaughter at least would end. Could the victors be trusted to maintain the Emperor system? Would they allow Hirohito to remain? Would they banish him or turn him over to the Chinese for trial and punishment, as influential voices had urged? Would the nation be divided and ruled, like conquered Germany and Austria? Would Japan be reduced to a truck garden, forbidden to use native industriousness in manufacturing and trading? Would the country be sacked, raped, and looted? Would it be decimated by relentless war-crimes reprisals? Would it cease to exist? These were the possibilities that haunted the Showa Emperor on this August 10 in the twentieth year of his reign.

Having repeatedly communed with his spirit ancestors ceremonially from his accession to the throne and through the annual rituals and special observances, Hirohito was sworn and committed to the laws and traditions of his forebears and, above all, to the continuation of the line, the survival of the imperial descendants of Amaterasu, the Sun Goddess.

But the line could not continue if the Yamato race were extinguished in continued warfare. It could not continue if the imperial family were forcibly removed from reign—eliminated in some vicious reprisal by the victorious enemy.

Such was Hirohito's choice.

Faced with such a decision, what does a man think? Each man's conclusion may be as valid as the next's, but the decision was not put to an ordinary man; it was placed before Hirohito, 124th reigning Emperor of the Yamato race, descendant of Amaterasu Omikami, the Sun Goddess, and therefore Son of Heaven.

Though the corporeal form was that of a man, this being was to his countrymen a god, the embodiment of all that was good. He was the loving, vigilant, earthly as well as heavenly ruler. He was also head of the family—the divine father of all Japanese. To him was due, obviously, the unquestioning loyalty and obedience of each member of the family.

For twenty-six hundred years the emperors of Japan had been gods to their loyal subjects. And so the Emperor still was to them all at 2 A.M. on the tenth of August 1945. It was time for the god to speak at last.

Chapter 8

The Emperor-God

Charlie and Emma was what the foreign press corps in Tokyo irreverently called them during the thirties. God or not, the Emperor and his Empress seemed depressingly, blatantly middle-class in appearance, attitude, and actions. They were rather like a respectable couple passionately dedicated to tea parties, gardening, and water-color painting, to conservative gowns and suits devoid of any hint of personality in plumage.

Determined to do the *right* things, they could be pictured playing golf for the exercise, never for fun; patting the heads of the royal children but never bouncing them on their knees or setting them on their shoulders; going through the motions at the imperial carp-netting and duck hunts. They looked like the Japanese Everyman and his wife. Their Western dress and actions seemed inelegant and *déclassée*. Even in his military uniform as Marshal Commander in Chief of the Armed Forces of Japan, Hirohito in the thirties appeared as ill at ease as a sophomore at a prom in his first rented tux.

But he was not Mr. Everyman. He was the Emperor of Japan, head of the Heavenly House, his Solar Dignity, Hirohito, *Tenno* of Nippon, directly descended from the Sun Goddess herself in a lineage so ancient that its members had no family names. In his imperial robes for state and religious occasions, there could be no more regal monarch in any region of the globe. He was thoroughly Japanese. He was the epitome of Japanese eternal verities—culture, religion, ethics, and mores. It was a large order to fill, even for a god.

Hirohito was of moderate size and slight build; five feet six inches tall, he normally weighed about 140 pounds. Worry and distraction about the war had brought on insomnia and nervous afflictions that had eroded his weight to 123 pounds and etched deep lines extending from the corners of his eyes, nose, and mouth. His thick black hair was graying and thinning somewhat in his forty-fourth year, but it still was rebellious. There were glints of gray in the wide mustache that graced his slightly pursed full lips like an Oriental umbrella. The face was oval, the widely separated, heavy brows were sable and the brown eyes were heavy-lidded. His ears were prominent and rounded. The cheeks were flaccid now; there were pouches beneath the eyes, and a double chin was noticeable. Hirohito's skin was dark, as though it had been exposed to the wind and sun, and contrasted vividly with his white teeth. Thick-lensed, circular glasses reinforced the symmetry of his head.

His round shoulders and short legs were evident in Western dress, but hidden in the ancestral robes of ceremonial occasions. The Son of Heaven's head appeared slightly outsized in relation to his body, although no more so than for millions of his subjects.

Hirohito's tastes were not regal. His preferences, in fact, were for the simple and ostentation was not so much eschewed as uncontemplated. It was not because of incapacity—he was one of the world's richest persons—although his forebears at the time of Columbus' voyage had lived in penury. His ancestor Emperor Go-Tsuchi had rotted for forty days beside the palace gates because at that time the imperial family lacked money to bury him. (The funeral costs were finally borrowed by the heir-apparent from Buddhist priests.) Then came the problem of enthronement of his successor, a costly business that had to be postponed for twenty years as a result of a shortage of cash and credit.

History tells of past Japanese emperors who found it necessary to go to extremes to sustain themselves. It is not recorded that any of them emulated Caligula, but they pursued various unregal projects. One begged. One copied poems in his elegant brushwork. Another peddled autographs. Still another depended for his robes and food on a friendly noble. In 1690, men and women of the Court actually made baskets of straw and sold them. Though conditions had improved immeasurably by his time, Hirohito's great-grandfather the

Emperor Komei reportedly loved wine "but was too poor to afford any except that of the watery kind."

By 1945 the change had been phenomenal. The Emperor's Imperial Household Ministry required 5000 employees to administer the affairs of the family. His salary was $1,600,000 annually (tax exempt!) and his holdings included land (6000 square miles—25 per cent larger than the state of Connecticut), thousands of shares of stock in leading enterprises with a healthy concentration in banking equities. (The prime minister's salary was $2250 and generals and admirals were paid $1520 annually.)

But, seemingly oblivious of his vast fortune, Hirohito demanded utmost frugality to share the austerity imposed on his people. He insisted on using both sides of scraps of paper and wearing pencils and erasers down to the stubs. He restricted himself to a Spartan diet and it was said that even his underwear was patched. He was reported to be relieved when the palace building burned in May 1945. As he put it, the people now could see that he shared the misfortune of the thousands who had been burned out.

Though quiet, His Majesty was known to have a biting temper. It was his lot, however, to suppress completely his emotions in public. After all, until 1868 it had been a crime punishable by death to set eyes on the face of the ruler. Hirohito's grandfather, Emperor Meiji actually had to issue an edict that people *should* look at him. Even now, when Hirohito went among his subjects the upper stories of buildings were cleared and the blinds lowered, in order that none might look down on the sacred personage.

This concern was sometimes carried to absurd lengths. It was a popular belief that even the Emperor's picture was too sacred to be viewed by profane eyes. In 1936, *Time* Magazine printed Hirohito's portrait on its cover. The Japanese Embassy in Washington swiftly called the editors and asked them to make a special appeal to *Time* readers not to desecrate the holy likeness by placing things on the magazine or handling it so that the portrait was down!

Rigidity and impassivity were the prescribed public façades for the imperial bearing. Yet when running up the bank of his summer place, picnicking, swimming, wading, and stuffing specimens of sea life into his jacket pockets, Hirohito's expression was relaxed and his body as poised and lithe as that of an amateur athlete. It was said that he was so adept a swimmer that he could shade himself with an umbrella held in his toes while swimming backstroke! And there was no doubt that he was in his element when he was diving from a small boat for marine specimens at his summer place in Sagami Bay, just outside the entrance to Tokyo Bay.

The Sun Goddess' descendant delighted in natural history, to the annoyance of the militarists and fundamentalists who saw this study of biology undermining the supernatural underpinnings of his own godship. Nevertheless, Hirohito had a small laboratory built on the palace grounds where he and an aged professor pored over microscopes studying specimens. In the late thirties he published a work on mushrooms (under his tutor's name), and his work in marine microbiology earned him the respect of the international scientific community.

In his lab he kept the busts of Darwin, Lincoln, and Napoleon. He had bought Bonaparte's bust on his great adventure, an incognito shopping spree in Paris during his European trip as Crown Prince.

The Emperor's taste ran to Japanese and Western classical music, a taste he indulged for the most part with phonograph records. There were few command performances and when internationally known musical stars performed in Tokyo it was the sadly circumscribed lot of the Emperor to hear them via recordings rather than at the theater. That would have been too ostentatious . . . particularly in the increasingly austere thirties when Japanese soldiers were dying in Manchuria and China for His Imperial Majesty.

In the liberal twenties, Hirohito had hung the walls of his summer place with Western paintings. Later these were put in storage and the severity of the Japanese tradition reintroduced: bare walls, except for the *tokonoma*—the one place of honor where a scroll, vase, and flower arrangement would satisfy dramatically and simply.

His abstemiousness extended to his personal life. His great-great-great-grandfathers were allowed one empress, three consorts, nine wives of high rank and twenty-seven of lower, and eighty-one concubines. There were, in addition, ladies-in-waiting without special limit. His grandfather Meiji had a modest covey of twelve court ladies, one of whom was Hirohito's grandmother. But His Majesty had limited himself to only one—Princess Nagako Kuni, his Empress.

There had been a time, however, when the army and the ultras had been upset about this self-denial and had suggested in no uncertain terms that the Emperor should bed down with concubines. This was after his second daughter, then the third and—good heavens!—the fourth. But the Emperor sired a fifth offspring and—*mirabile dictu!* —it was a boy. The arrival of the Crown Prince was announced by two blasts of every whistle in Japan. Thus at least one crisis was averted. (This performance was clinched later with the birth of a second boy-child.)

No such pressure had built up around Hirohito's father. In the first place, Hirohito was born a year after his father Yoshihito's marriage And nobody had to encourage Yoshihito to interest himself in concubines. It was a hobby that came naturally.

Just three months after his birth in 1901, Hirohito was removed from his family in the traditional way. Until four he lived in the house of an old Court noble, Viscount Kawamura, whose happy family life and good character qualified him for the honor of rearing the future Emperor.

Then the toddler was put in charge of General Nogi, the hero of the Russo-Japanese War, captor of Mukden and Port Arthur. Nogi was an old-school samurai whose two sons had been sacrificed in the bloody siege of Port Arthur. He was severe, unsparing, and gravely aware of his responsibility in guiding his young charge. As a true samurai, Nogi also was adept at such cultivated pursuits as the tea ceremony, flower arrangement, *bonsai,* and calligraphy. A strong bond grew between the two; it was as close to a filial relationship as the young prince was to know, for his father was seen infrequently.

But when the great Emperor Meiji died in 1912, General Nogi, as one of the close, loyal retainers, committed ceremonial *seppuku* with his wife. Young Hirohito then became the charge of Admiral Togo, the other great hero of the Russo-Japanese War. Hirohito's father ascended the throne and took the reign-name *Taisho*—Great Peace. (Taisho was the son of Meiji and a favorite Court lady, as has been mentioned. Meiji's Empress bore him fourteen children, but none of her four boys survived childhood.)

Taisho had been on the throne only a few years when it became obvious beyond the Court circle that he was not well—mentally or physically. The occasion when he came to the Diet to read an imperial speech and used the scroll as a would-be telescope, scanning the legislators' faces, scandalized the nation and the diplomatic corps, causing Japan to lose face internationally. Taisho soon was removed from public view and Hirohito became Prince Regent.

As Crown Prince, Hirohito showed evidence of a mind of his own. He made an unprecedented and thoroughly exhilarating grand tour to Europe in 1922. He traveled on the Japanese battleship *Katori* and had a fabulous trip. In Cairo he was feted by Field Marshal Allenby; at Malta he witnessed Western opera for the first time (Verdi's *Otello*); at Gibraltar he was taken to the horse races. In Britain he was the guest of the royal family and went hither and yon with the Prince of Wales, visited Scotland, and in Glasgow had a taste of what democracy does to common people when shipyard workers refused to bow to him and insisted on shaking his hand.

In France Marshal Pétain took him on tour of the battlefields of the Western Front and he was entertained by the President. Most wonderful of all, he was able to go incognito and shop, ride the Metro, and visit a restaurant without the overwhelming handicap of an entourage.

By the time the *Katori* finally sailed for Yokohama, Hirohito had visited five European countries, met eight heads of state (including the Pope), and absorbed an abiding admiration for constitutional monarchy of the kind he observed in Britain. These impressions were to affect his actions ever after.

In 1926 Taisho finally expired and Hirohito succeeded him. The new ruler was said to have independent ideas. For instance, he had kicked over the traces when he decided to marry. He supposedly insisted on marrying the girl he wanted rather than be bound by the blind arranged-marriage sequence. And, upon his return from Europe, he had a golf course built on the palace grounds. Furthermore, he brought back Western music and a keg of whisky, and went so far as to give a very select, very proper, very private party for his former schoolmates to share these exotic treasures. More upsetting to the Court advisers and the reactionaries, however, were Hirohito's words of admiration for constitutional monarchy.

The new ruler's interest in things Western was characteristic of the twenties in Japan. The nation was one of the Big Five in the world, had shared the fruits of victory with the Western democracies in World War I, and was imbibing the heady concoction of *dem-mok-ra-*

sie, with its universal manhood suffrage and politics for the people as well as the aristocrats. The city folk took to Western music, dance, clothing, food, frivolity, and even a few fundamentals. The breeze of liberalism was felt in the land, from the Court on down.

The young monarch was serious about ruling, and adopted the reign-name *Showa.* A more ironic label for his reign could scarcely have been selected: Showa means Enlightened Peace. But the imperial rescript issued when he ascended the throne December 28, 1926, was his own statement of his own thoughts, and in it he said:

With Our limited gifts, We are mindful of the difficulty of proving Ourselves equal to the great task which has devolved upon Us. The world is now in a process of evolution. A new chapter is being opened in the history of human civilization. This nation's settled policy always stands for progress and improvement. Simplicity instead of vain display, originality instead of blind imitation, progress in view of this period of evolution, improvement to keep pace with the advancement of civilization, national harmony in purpose and in action, beneficence to all classes of people, and friendship to all the nations of the earth: These are the cardinal aims to which Our most profound and abiding solicitude is directed.

But any thoughts Hirohito may have had about ruling as a constitutional monarch were foredoomed. The Meiji Constitution, "given" by that ruler to the Japanese people in 1889, starts out:

The Empire of Japan shall be reigned over and governed by a line of Emperors unbroken for ages eternal. . . . The Emperor is sacred and inviolable . . . is head of the Empire, combining in Himself the rights of sovereignty, and exercises them, according to the provisions of the present Constitutions. . . . The Emperor exercises the legislative power with the consent of the Imperial Diet . . . gives sanction to laws and orders them to be promulgated and executed . . . determines the organization of . . . the administration, and salaries of all civil and military officers, and appoints and dismisses the same . . . has the supreme command of the army and navy . . . declares war, makes peace and concludes treaties. . . .

All these grandiose powers and perquisites were but window-dressing for the real wielders of power. The Meiji Constitution, like the Meiji Restoration, was a creation of dedicated, vigorous men intent on consolidating their own power while they brought Japan into the modern world. The Emperor was a convenient rallying point.

His existence gave them leverage to carry out their (at the time) unpopular reforms—reforms that extended from cutting off queues to reorganization of the government. This veritable revolution modernized the nation, created a conscripted army and navy, dumped the samurai system, and overturned the feudal lords—compensating them according to set formulas and helping them convert to the capitalist system.

But the real power was not neatly tied in a package and presented to the restored monarch; far from it. The clan chiefs created the illusion of a constitutional monarchy without the substance. Every action that was taken officially was taken in the Emperor's name and presumably with his sanction. A popularly elected legislature (the Diet) was established, but it had little control over the cabinet. The prime minister was appointed by the Emperor, who invariably followed the advice and selection of his close advisers, the *genro* (elder statesmen) and later the lord keeper of the privy seal.

Unlike constitutional monarchies in the Western democracies, the prime minister after the twenties was usually not the head of a political party representing the majority in parliament. He was the man the Emperor's advisers thought best able to contend with the opposing forces and issues uppermost at the moment. The premier appointed his cabinet ministers to represent those various forces.

Major decisions were made by the cabinet and presented to the Emperor for sanction before promulgation. Other major decisions, such as war in Manchuria, China, and border incidents in Siberia, were made by the military—who moved first, then forced cabinet acceptance and imperial sanction for these *faits accomplis*. The Emperor was in no position to countermand or contradict. He could question, his advisers told him, but not change. His function was to listen, look, and approve but not criticize, modify, or veto.

For example, it was understood that Hirohito had not clamored for war with America in 1941. Yet the events and the men in control of them were beyond his reach. At the crucial Imperial Conference of September 6, 1941, when the official, formal decision to war on the United States was made, the Emperor was present—of course—and silently observed the proceedings. This was customary. But this time the Emperor unexpectedly spoke up. He reached into his pocket and drew out a paper. From it he read a brief poem written by his grand-father, Emperor Meiji:

> When I regard all the world
> As my own brothers
> Why is it that its tranquility
> Should be so thoughtlessly disturbed?

"This is a poem which has always been one of my favorites," said the Emperor. "It expresses my heartfelt thoughts and those of my grandfather when he wrote it, about his great love for peace."

The conclusion that the militarists were to draw was that the Emperor disapproved the war. The rest of the world may wonder that this was the strongest opposition of which he and the system were capable. Though the military realized that this was a reproach, it had scarcely more effect on them than if the Emperor had pulled a fan from his pocket.

Many people find that their lives are living fictions; many live fictions all their lives. Some select theirs, some fall into them, some are forced into them. Others are born into theirs. Hirohito was one of the latter, and his was one of the supremely paradoxical fictions of all.

Because the Emperor was head of the "national family" and all Japanese (except naturalized ones) were related by blood to him, unblinking, wholehearted belief was given such slogans as *Emperor and People Are One*. Through ages eternal, past and future, each Japanese had a place in the supreme scheme of things. And the Emperor was the pole star by which he could orient himself and to which he could direct his devotion. It was the combination of three things deriving from this that made the Japanese character distinctly Japanese: unswerving loyalty to the Emperor system, deep conviction of their mission on earth, and belief that their inherited, divinely given qualities were superior.

As head of the state Shinto religion and a major object of veneration, the Emperor was chief priest at the twenty-one key ceremonies during the year. And he played the central part in the semiannual rites at the Yasukuni shrine, where the spirits of fallen heroes were deified.

"The Emperor," said the Meiji Constitution, "is Heaven-descended, divine and sacred; he is preeminent above His subjects. He must be reverenced and is inviolable."

Because he was simultaneously the most important god in the Shinto pantheon and supreme commander of the armed forces, Hirohito's orders to the troops had all the impact of holy writ and lent to military actions the moral force of a crusade. His imperial rescript declaring war in 1941 had, to the Japanese, all the impact of Pope Urban II's call in 1095 to liberate the Holy Sepulchre from the infidels. To work, to sacrifice, to die for the Emperor were the highest callings open to Japanese citizens.

The military had evangelically promoted the Emperor's exalted power and sublimity and exacted the unquestioning cooperation of every citizen as his duty to His Majesty. And yet the same military leaders saw no hypocrisy in their practice of ignoring the Emperor's wishes.

When the Emperor's thoughts coincided with theirs the military were pleased and carried their plans forward. When his wishes conflicted with theirs, the military said he was being misled by hostile counselors, whispered darkly that the false advisers should be swept away from the Throne, and carried their plans forward.

His Majesty was like a brilliant maple leaf on the crest of an autumn torrent: the focus of all eyes, the most dazzling object in sight, but unable to control the pace or direction of the current under him.

It was a fiction that he was supreme commander of the army and navy. True, he held the title, but when he attempted to exercise control he was hamstrung or his wishes were politely ignored. Of course it was nothing personal. The mechanism was so rigged that the military could easily block efforts they disapproved.

The emptiness of the Emperor's title as commander-in-chief was evident when the army created an "incident" in Manchuria. Efforts of the Emperor, through *Gaimusho,* the Japanese foreign office, and the foreign minister to halt the army were fruitless. The cabinet and prime minister took no action. Cabinets and premiers came and went, but the army stayed on and flourished. The army took over all of Manchuria and ran it as a fief under the Kwantung army. An "independent nation," Manchukuo, was established, and the commanding officer of the Kwantung army was Japan's "ambassador" to it. But when the ambassador whistled, Manchukuo danced to his tempo. And then there was the China Incident. Again the army had acted first, then informed the cabinet and the Emperor after the fact that it had taken retaliatory action for "Chinese hostility" near Peking. His Majesty was told by the war minister that it would take a month to finish the retaliation. That was eight years before and still no end to the Chinese struggle was in sight. (A sixteenth-century Korean sage had aptly written that the idea of Japan conquering China was like "a bee trying to sting a tortoise through his armor.")

Another fiction was that of mission: bringing *Kodo,* the Imperial Way of Showa's enlightened peace to the backward barbarians of Manchuria, China, and the conquered lands of the south was the "Japanese destiny." And yet there were noisy rumblings that hinted something less than benevolence in this. The aroma emanating from the pacification of Nanking—referred to rather differently by Chinese and Western observers as the rape of Nanking—was a pungent example of the emptiness of the beneficent mission. There had been other examples reported from abroad, but all had been discounted by the army as enemy propaganda.

The man-god seated in the steamy concrete bunker that August night in 1945 was in the vortex of a whirlwind. His memory that night might have flicked back through time to more than one of the occasions when he had told his advisers and the military his wishes, with precious little effect.

There was the day in September 1931 when he personally warned General Minami, the war minister, "to take extra precautions regarding the actions of the army in Manchuria and Mongolia." His meaning, typically circumspect, was "restrain the army." But there was no restraint. Instead, the army staged the Manchurian Incident on September 18, and overran four provinces of China.

In December that same year, Hirohito cautioned the new premier, Ki Inukai, "on the matter of the mismanagement and high-handedness of the army. The army's meddling in domestic and foreign politics, trying to get its own way, is a state of affairs which, for the good of the nation, we must view with apprehension. Be mindful of my anxiety."

Inukai made out his own death warrant by being mindful and

sincerely trying to bring the army to heel. The consolidation of the Manchurian campaign and establishment of the Japanese puppet state of Manchukuo were monuments to his failure and the army's contempt. For his efforts, on May 15, 1932, Inukai was slaughtered in the premier's residence by a group of young fanatics, army cadets and navy officers.

One time the imperial temper stung the army was in 1938. In July that year, Japanese forces attacked Russian troops and tried to eject them from a hilly position at Changkufeng. Army leaders were pressing for war with the Soviets at the time. The foreign and navy ministers had agreed to precautionary troop dispositions but strongly opposed any aggressive steps against the Russians.

The war minister and army chief of staff requested an imperial audience to get the Emperor's endorsement for attacking the Soviets. Through his chief aide-de-camp, an army man, the Emperor notified the military that on no account would he consent to the use of force.

The war minister and chief of staff insisted on seeing the Emperor. When the audience was held, Hirohito asked if they had conferred with the foreign and navy ministers. They said they had, and that these men had agreed to the use of force. Recognizing deceit, the Emperor tore into the army:

The actions of the army in the past have been abominable. Speaking of the Manchurian Incident and the actions at the Marco Polo Bridge at the beginning of this [China] Incident, there was absolutely no obedience to central orders. There have been instances when the methods used have been arbitrary and underhanded, things altogether improper in my army. I feel it is disgraceful. Nothing like that must happen this time. . . . Hereafter you may not move one soldier without my command.

Stunned at the unexpected vehemence of the Emperor's attack, the war minister and chief of staff withdrew and the army pulled back. Its leaders were infuriated. Whose imperial army was it, anyhow?

The following year, when the army was pressing relentlessly for an alliance with the Axis and was even threatening cabinet members, Hirohito's comment to his close advisers was prescient: "I am perplexed with the present army. They will never understand unless Japan is forced by other nations to return Korea and Manchukuo to their original status." That same month his brother addressed junior officers at army headquarters about the dangers to Japan of alliance with Germany in a war against England. Next to a statement from Hirohito's own lips, this was as authoritative a reflection of their Emperor's wishes as the soldiers were likely ever to hear. The Prince's words went unheeded. The army continued its pressure on the government to conclude the Axis pact.

The Emperor called in his chief aide-de-camp, Lieutenant General Usami, and gave him an order to transmit to the army chiefs in strictest secrecy. Hirohito's message was that the cabinet would collapse if the army continued its coercion to bring about the Axis pact. Therefore both General Headquarters and the war ministry were to conduct a fundamental review of the entire issue. The Emperor stressed the urgency and secrecy of this order—to no avail. Usami betrayed his sovereign's wishes: the message was not kept secret. The army flouted Hirohito's order: They acted—not to review and revise their attitude toward the Axis pact but to redouble their efforts to hasten it.

There was a time in those somber days of late 1941 when Hirohito asked his prime minister almost wistfully "If peace should be decided upon will the army submit to regulations?"

The premier in turn asked the war minister, General Tojo. And that single-minded expansionist replied as expected, that he could not guarantee that the army would. In the situation then existing, Tojo said, only an imperial prince would be able to suppress the army. He had in mind Prince Higashikuni, an army officer on active duty and the Empress' uncle. This suggestion was flatly rejected by the Emperor and his advisers. They did not want the imperial family involved in politics particularly in a manner which might place on its shoulders the responsibility for a war decision, whether pro or con.

Nearly at the zero hour, when Tojo received his appointment as premier, the Emperor, through the privy seal Kido, told "Razor Brain" that the September 6, 1941, decision to go to war was, in effect, rescinded. Tojo and the navy minister were instructed that "as regards the fundamental line of national policy . . . careful consideration be taken by studying both the internal and external situation more comprehensively and more profoundly than ever, regardless of the Resolution of the September 6 Imperial Conference."

Tojo called his a clean-slate cabinet, but in the next two weeks followed the philosophy "rather than await extinction it is better to face death by breaking through the encircling ring to find a way for existence." This argument effectively nullified any incipient opposition and by November 2 Tojo had the military and civilian leaders' agreement that no course was open but war if the United States rejected the last two notes that would then be sent. But they were stale notes, offering nothing that had not been rejected previously.

Tojo frequently used the term "the chance of one thousand years for Japan" to describe the opportunity before her. Now the chance had played out.

It was now, this August 10, 1945, just three weeks short of four years from the day that, in the same palace compound but above ground, another Imperial Conference had made the decision for war. Only one of that group was in the current conference. And he was, ironically, the only one who had spoken out against war—Hirohito. Even the building in which that 1941 conference took place was gone, burned to the ground last May.

Thus the supreme commander of the armed forces, the all-powerful god-ruler whose slightest desire was said to be incontrovertible command, could not be certain—judging from past experience—that at this critical point in the nation's history his words would be obeyed. Late as the hour was, in this twentieth year of his reign, his words would carry only the force of an advisory, not an imperative, for by custom and constitution, government action had to be taken by the cabinet. But the key to peace was held by the military.

Now the soft vault of blue above ground was washed clean by the sparkling light of the near-full moon. Mercifully, there was no air raid this night. The Emperor could have looked far over the city from the palace ramparts.

Perhaps his ancient ancestor Emperor Nintoku may have come to his mind. Nintoku once climbed a tower and viewed his country. In whatever direction he looked he noticed that no smoke was to be seen coming from his subjects' houses. The old Emperor deduced that his people were so poor they could not afford rice to cook. He therefore ordered the abolition of forced labor for three years. However, his own fortunes depended on the fruits of such labor and so his palace soon became shabby and poor. For Nintoku, though, it was sufficient that "the people had plenty, the praise of his virtues filled the land, and the smoke of cooking was also thick."

Certainly wherever Hirohito might have looked this glassy summer night devastation and malnutrition were the rule.

In the early days of Japan, the death of a prince demanded that his retainers be buried alive with him. This practice was changed when some man of genius devised the much more civilized custom of substituting clay dolls called *haniwa* to be buried with the royal remains.

In August 1945 it was impossible to propitiate the savage flames and explosives with clay figures. On the contrary, instead of the live retainers being buried with the dead prince, the reverse seemed likely unless a decision was reached quickly. And now the decision was put to the prince.

Chapter 9

God's Will

At 2 A.M. on August 10, 1945, the military leaders were shocked when Prime Minister Suzuki called on the Emperor to speak. In fact, all but three men (and one god) in the room were surprised by the audacious move. Togo, Suzuki, and the Emperor had planned it and Sakomizu knew that His Majesty was to be called upon. They were convinced it was the last desperate throw of the dice and that on it depended the lives of millions, the fate of the imperial family and the Yamato race, and the shape of the Far East and the world for decades, perhaps a century, to come.

There, in his simple wooden chair, wearing the uniform of Marshal Commander of the Armed Forces, Hirohito had sat frozen during the Imperial Conference discussion, his white-gloved hands knotted on his knees. His face had been as impassive as a *Noh* mask, but never before in his life had he followed a debate with such intensity. His mind was like a bird of prey swooping on each statement made, but, like a character in a *Noh* drama, though he vibrated inwardly with a momentous struggle of conflicting emotions at this moment, no outward evidence of human sentiment was allowed to breach the barrier of imperial will power. Those in the claustrophobic conference room had no doubt that all the powers of imperial heredity and training were being brought to bear to maintain the composure of the Emperor-god.

Now Hirohito leaned forward, gripped the arms of his chair and rose. If anyone present had thought he would be inhibited by his muffled role in the past or reluctant to speak because of habit, training, fear, or indecision, they underrated their Emperor. Slowly, but with no indication of uncertainty, the voice that had so often inspired tens of thousands of subjects in the palace plaza now spoke in anguish to this handful of chief ministers.

"Then I will state my opinion," he said, in his high, slightly metallic delivery. His audience scarcely breathed, waiting for his words.

"I agree with the foreign minister." The war minister, General Anami, shuddered as though he had received a body blow. General Umezu's expression did not flicker. "My reasons are as follows."

The words came now in an agonized flow, phrase by phrase, sometimes a mere syllable, punctuated with irregular, uncontrollable pauses as Hirohito spoke from the depths of his soul.

"After serious consideration of conditions facing Japan both at home and abroad, I have concluded that to continue this war can mean only destruction for the homeland and more bloodshed and cruelty in the world." Sakomizu suddenly realized that he was crying. A glance around the table showed that most of his fellow conferees also were wet-cheeked.

"I cannot bear to have my innocent people suffer further. Ending the war is the only way to restore world peace and relieve the nation from the terrible suffering it is undergoing." Heavy breathing and signs from his listeners had become an audible murmur. The anguish was catching. The Emperor swallowed several times and narrowly maintained his composure.

He was too wise a god and too experienced a man to believe that the military would accept this unadorned statement and abide by it alone. Besides, he had some reckoning to do with the leaders of the armed forces, particularly the army. He was not about to let them dodge their culpability:

"I was told by the army chief of staff that in June the coastline defenses at Kujukuri-hama would be complete, with new divisions installed in fortifications ready to repel the invaders' landing operations. But the report of my aide-de-camp, who made an on-the-spot inspection of the area, is completely contrary. It is now August and the fortifications still have not been completed."

(The chief of staff, Umezu, was more candid with his Emperor on Japanese troop capability farther from home. When he returned from a flying visit to commanders of troops in China, Manchuria, and Korea in June 1945, General Umezu reported to Hirohito that the prospects for continuing the war were dim. He then said, among other things, that Japanese forces in China and Manchuria equaled about eight U.S. divisions and had ammunition enough for a single battle only. They could not hold out longer than a month, he judged, if sizable American forces landed.)

There was fire in the Emperor's words now. "It was officially reported to me that equipping of a newly created division had been completed. But I know that in reality these soldiers have not yet been supplied even with bayonets! I understand it will be after mid-September before the required equipment is delivered." The heat in the bunker had not increased, but the military men were beginning to feel a touch of sunstroke from the Son of Heaven.

The Emperor lashed out again. "Furthermore, the scheduled increase in aircraft production has not materialized as promised. Air raids are becoming more intense day by day."

(Both in anticipation of a day of reckoning such as this and from suspicion that he was not getting all the facts, the Emperor had appointed in February 1945 a Special Inspector of Navy War Potential, Admiral Kiyoshi Hasegawa. A former governor-general of Formosa, Hasegawa reported directly to the Emperor and was ruthlessly honest. For three months he inspected arsenals, naval districts, and attack units. On June 12 he stood before Hirohito and his aide-de-camp, General Hasunuma, and read a blunt, hair-raising report of navy weakness.

(When the formal report was finished, Hasunuma left the room and Hirohito offered the Admiral a chair. He wanted further information. In his inspection of special attack units, Hasegawa found that "makeshift small vessels fitted with used auto engines were being prepared as weapons for special attack. Whereas such a state of affairs was already sufficient to move anyone to pity, the members of the special attack units who operated such simple machinery were sorely lacking in training. The bulk of the other weapons for special-attack use were incomplete and I considered [inadequate] the hurried and shortened training of the personnel."

(Hasegawa cited actual instances of navy incapacity to finish plans and pointed out that the mobilization program was not realistic; it caused waste and duplication. "Operational strength and transport capability were decreasing with each bombing, deteriorating war potential tremendously."

(The Emperor listened attentively and looked greatly worried. "Even his hair," said the Admiral, "was a little untidy." When the icy water of Hasegawa's findings had thoroughly awakened him, His Majesty said, mournfully, "I suspected so; your explanation is quite understandable."

(The only conclusion possible from Hasegawa's information was that Japan could not continue the war. "For the Emperor," said Kido's secretary, "this [report] provided the necessary facts.")

"Some advocate a decisive battle in the homeland as the way to survival," continued the Emperor. "In past experience, however, there has always been a discrepancy between the fighting services' plans and the results. If, in conditions such as these Japan should be rushed into a decisive battle in the homeland, how could an enemy be repulsed? What would become of Japan? I do not want to see our people continue to suffer any longer. Also, I do not desire any further destruction of our culture, nor any additional misfortune for the peoples of the world."

Once more a pause, while will power mastered emotion. "I am afraid that faced with a situation such as this the Japanese people are doomed, one and all. But in order to hand the country of Japan to posterity, I want as many of our people to survive as possible and rise again in the future." Under his voice, the sobs of the leaders of the empire were audible. Even the most stoic of his listeners by now was weeping unashamedly, not attempting to restrain his tears. Hirohito's gloved hands touched his glasses and cheeks lightly, sweeping away his own tears.

"I feel great pain when I think of those who have served me so faithfully—the soldiers and sailors who have been killed or wounded in distant battles, destitute families who have lost all their possessions—and often their lives as well—in air raids in the homeland. Indeed, disarmament of my brave and loyal military is excruciating to me. It is equally unbearable that those who have rendered me devoted service should be considered war criminals. However, for the sake of the country it cannot be helped. To relieve the people and to maintain the nation we must bear the unbearable. When I recall the fortitude of my Imperial Grandsire the Emperor Meiji at the time of the Triple Intervention, I swallow my own tears."

The voice faltered fleetingly. "All of you, I think, will worry about me in this situation. But it does not matter what will become of me. Determined, as I have stated, I have decided to bring the war to an end immediately. For this reason I agree with the foreign minister's proposal."

There it was. He had heard all the arguments. The military demanded death before dishonor for Japan. Hirohito, God-sent Ruler of the Great Japanese Empire (his official title) favored dishonor, if need be, as the price of life for his countrymen and survival of Japan. What kind of Japan could survive the near-annihilation of *gyokusai?* The embodiment of twenty-six hundred years of tradition and considerable common sense, how could the Emperor conceivably endorse any alternative that might hazard the disappearance of the people to continue that tradition?

In this, the longest public speech of his life, the Emperor ended the conference, an epoch, and—presumably—the war.

But of course, it was not so. Like any fine Oriental mechanism, there were wheels within wheels within wheels. Hirohito's statement was legally only an advisory opinion to the Imperial Conference of the Supreme Council for Direction of the War. But the Imperial Conference was not legally constituted to decide the future of the nation. Only the cabinet could do that. The Emperor could make his recommendation to the Imperial Conference and the conference could advise the cabinet, but it was that body that would have to take action. Having taken action, the cabinet decision would then have to be presented to the Emperor for his sanction, to make it official, legal, and binding.

At this point Premier Suzuki (who, in spite of his semi-deafness had missed not a word) pulled himself from his chair and addressed the conferees. "The Imperial decision has been expressed," he said hoarsely, "and as such it should be the conclusion of this conference. The conference," he went on briskly, turning back to the Emperor, "is adjourned." Such decisiveness and dispatch on Suzuki's part were phenomenal.

It was now 2:30 A.M., August 10. The Emperor's composure had returned. The face was once again a *Noh* mask, though it was wet with tears. Hirohito rose from the simple wooden chair. His aide General Hasunuma brought himself to attention and the conferees struggled to their feet and approximated bows. Their eyes were red, their faces flushed and streaked. All were racked with sobs. Several leaned heavily on the table for support. With Hasunuma at his heels, Hirohito moved out of sight behind the gold screen.

The men of might, in the wake of the Emperor, pulled themselves together and began their climb toward the world of reality.

Leaving the conference room close behind Suzuki came his Jack-of-all-trades, Sakomizu. Having been a participant in this momentous event, the cabinet secretary was shaken. He was still wavering as to "whether it was good for Japan or whether we should not have held out longer. There was no end to my indecision. But, at length, I persuaded myself that His Majesty could not be wrong."

He did not have long for such personal turmoil. As the premier and he came into the anteroom, Lieutenant General Yoshizumi, the chief of the Military Affairs Bureau, stalked up to the old Admiral and blocked his way. Belligerently he accused Suzuki. "Isn't this false to your word, Prime Minister?"

Suzuki was caught up short. Before he could reply, War Minister Anami stepped between them, pulling Yoshizumi aside. Trying to calm the obviously distraught officer, Anami said "Be quiet, please. I understand you, Yoshizumi." The premier pushed on by with Sakomizu, stepped into his waiting limousine, and drove to the official residence. The cabinet secretary immediately began rounding up the ministers for an extraordinary cabinet session to act on the Emperor's decision.

Yoshizumi's reaction was the first indication of the army's attitude, a glimmer of the trouble still ahead.

Foreign Minister Togo, ashen from fatigue and strain, looked about for his foreign ministry associate, Toshikazu Kase. Driven from the anteroom of the conference chamber by unbearable heat and insatiable mosquitoes, Kase had fled long before and waited now in the foreign minister's limousine. His concern stretched to the breaking point, the Amherst-trained Kase searched Togo's face for the answer to his unasked question. Togo's characteristically terse statement that the Emperor had directed that the peace terms be accepted was like sweet fresh air to Kase and gave him the first solid feeling he had had in months that Japan would be saved. For this sensitive soul it was endorsement and reward for two years of incessant intrigue with others of the peace faction who had worked behind the curtain. For Togo, the occasion brought the vivid recollection of that December night in 1941 when he had told the Emperor that all alternatives had been exhausted, that war was to begin:

Retiring from my audience, deeply moved by looking upon the countenance of the Emperor and there reading his noble feeling of brotherhood with all peoples, but seeing also his unflinching attitude even when receiving me on the very brink of war, I passed solemnly, guided by a Court official, down several hundred yards of corridors, stretching serene and tranquil, of the midnight Palace. Emerging at the Sakashita Gate, I gazed up at the brightly shining stars, and felt bathed in a sacred spirit. Through the Palace plaza in utter silence, hearing no sound of the sleeping capital but only the crunching of the gravel beneath the wheels of my car, I pondered that in a few short hours would dawn one of the eventful days in the history of the world . . . having labored with heart and soul through the preceding month and a half for the sake of mankind and my country, I felt the conviction that our course, taken only when it had become a certainty that there could be no alternative, must find approval in the ultimate judgment of Heaven . . . on my return home from the Imperial Palace on the verge of war . . . I was filled with the assurance that, having participated in a momentous event, I had exhausted all my powers and my abilities in the conviction that Heaven knows a heart true to country and to mankind.

Heaven's "judgment" had been rendered—the stars remained; those corridors and palace buildings, along with the "chance of a thousand years," had vanished in flames. Now, at long last, the Emperor had spoken.

Togo drove to the prime minister's residence for the cabinet meeting and Kase went on to the foreign ministry, where senior staff officials had been waiting impatiently for hours. In the dim room with its heavily shaded lights Kase told them the decision. Profoundly relieved, they began work on the messages that would notify the outside world of Japan's choice.

As the deflated conferees climbed one by one up the dank, narrow stairs into the astringent moonlight amid the pines outside the air-raid shelter, still another conference was in session.

At precisely 2:33 A.M., noted Marquis Kido, the privy seal, the Emperor summoned him to an audience in the *gobunko*. With tears in his eyes, Hirohito told his chief adviser the gist of the conference and his statement that concluded it and, hopefully, the war.

Kido had met with the Emperor six times during the day August 9, for a total of two hours. Not only had Kido helped engineer the moment, he had also coached the star performer. He had spent the last twelve minutes with him before his moment of truth. Now that the irrevocable move had been made, he listened dumbstruck as his Emperor, still choked with emotion, replayed key points and phrases. It was one of the few times in his life that the voluble privy seal had been speechless.

Kido hung his head, with its sparse wisps of tousled gray hair, and lowered his gaze. He could not bring himself to watch his sovereign in this agony. Perhaps through his mind flashed a pang of guilt; perhaps it was no more than an unvoiced sigh for his five and a half years of counseling His Majesty. His prewar advice had advanced the extremists and diminished the power of the pacifists, promoted Konoye and Tojo; his counsel had gagged his royal master until now.

At precisely 2:38 A.M. Kido bowed his way out of the Imperial Presence and headed for his home. His thoughts traveled back nearly four years, to December 8, 1941. At the same hour of the morning he had trekked in the reverse direction, traveling from his home to his office to meet Foreign Minister Togo, hoping to jubilate but prepared to commiserate depending on the results of the whiplash of Japanese fury unleashed that morning. Now, through his mind, his thoughts of that distant morning recurred:

When I was climbing up the Akasaka slope [he had written in his diary December 8, 1941] I saw the rising sun above a building over there. I thought it was symbolic of the destiny of the country that had now entered the war with the United States and England, the two greatest powers in the world. I closed my eyes and prayed for the victory of our Navy planes making an attack on Pearl Harbor by that time. [News of the "glorious" success of the attack arrived shortly after 4 A.M.]

It was 3 A.M. when the privy seal dropped into bed for long-overdue sleep. He drifted off into blissful slumber for the first time in months. But it was not to be. Before daylight enemy bombers routed Kido and hundreds of thousands of Tokyoites from their fitful rest in yet another air raid. Thrust forcefully face to face with grim reality once more, Kido realized there was still a slippery path ahead before he would have earned his rest.

While the privy seal was settling himself into his *futons* to begin his brief sleep, Suzuki convened the cabinet meeting in the premier's official residence. The old Admiral announced to the fifteen ministers that the Imperial Conference just ended had adopted a resolution accepting the Potsdam declaration with the single proviso that the Emperor system be maintained intact. This had been the Emperor's own decision, said Suzuki. The SCDW had made this its own decision and proposed that the cabinet follow suit.

More than twelve hours had trickled by since this group of statesmen had met on this same subject on August 9. It had been twenty-three hours since the Russians had thrown their weight into the scales. Those hours had been dissipated largely in verbiage and vacillation, during which Nagasaki and seventy-four thousand human beings of the Yamato strain had been erased from the earth.

Togo, now haggard and nearly voiceless but still determined, reported on the Imperial Conference. Since the "decision" had been rendered by His Majesty, Togo proposed that the government accept the Potsdam terms with the single condition agreed upon. The foreign minister stressed the urgency of deciding (as he had all the preceding day) and explained that Hiranuma, the president of the privy council, had participated in the conference, so the privy council had been technically informed.

For once the cabinet actually agreed and did so without debate. Even Anami acquiesced without a murmur. Only the prickly home minister, Abe, quarreled with the decision and, though he grudgingly voted for acceptance, he balked at signing the formal document. As one who throughout his career had been a police chief and hatchet man for the extremists, he still feared a revolt. Furthermore, he was all too familiar with the techniques of the bully-boys in whipping up opposition, intimidating and assassinating those who opposed them. He could foresee that those who signed this document approving surrender were very likely putting their names to their own death warrant.

"I fail to see the necessity of signing," Abe said contentiously.

The education minister, Ota, a close associate of Hiranuma and a dedicated rightist, patiently explained. "The procedure is necessary, since the decision of the Imperial Conference cannot take effect unless all the cabinet members hold themselves responsible for it." He advised Abe to sign and, with the other cabinet members standing by, fuming at the delay, the home minister reluctantly put his name to the document, making it complete and official.

The cabinet found itself in a dilemma. It recognized the essential truth of Abe's contention that an uprising might take place if the people suddenly were told, without warning, that the war was over, and the country was to be occupied by enemy troops. After all, the masses for a decade had heard that defeat and surrender were impossible for Japanese troops. A completely captive audience, they knew only what the press and radio reported. And these government-controlled sources told them even now that Japan was still winning the war.

To prevent the masses from rebelling at the sudden announcement of defeat, the cabinet agreed that there should be no word of the acceptance of the Potsdam terms until the official statement from the Emperor was made public. That, of course, would be after the conditions had been agreed upon with the Allies. So to "lead the people into the atmosphere of the war's end," the minister of information, Shimomura, was to consult with Anami, Yonai, and Togo and issue whatever was appropriate in the way of newspaper and radio reports.

Having dispensed with the essential matters, Premier Suzuki promptly adjourned the meeting. With mixed feelings of triumph and despair, Sakomizu placed the cabinet resolution in his maximum-security file.

As Togo hurried from the premier's residence to *Gaimusho,* darkness was lifting. The silhouette of the Diet building loomed like a huge tombstone. Completely spent, Togo reviewed the message drafted by foreign ministry officials. Approving the epochal words, he directed that telegrams be sent to the Japanese ministers in Switzerland and Sweden, to be delivered to the U.S., China, Britain, the USSR.

Leaving the details to Vice-minister Matsumoto and Kase, Togo sank back against the cushions of his 1938 Buick sedan and drove to his home, almost more dead than alive.

By 7 A.M. the *Gaimusho* code clerk reported to Kase and Matsumoto that the wires had been dispatched. The notes were identical.

In obedience to the gracious command of His Majesty the Emperor who, ever anxious to enhance the cause of world peace, desires earnestly to bring about a speedy termination of hostilities with a view to saving mankind from the calamities to be imposed upon them by further continuation of the war, the Japanese Government several weeks ago asked the Soviet Government, with which neutral relations then prevailed, to render good offices in restoring peace vis-à-vis the enemy Powers. Unfortunately, these efforts in the interest of peace having failed, the Japanese Government in conformity with the august wish of His Majesty to restore the general peace and desiring to put an end to the untold sufferings entailed by war as quickly as possible, have decided upon the following.

The Japanese Government sincerely hope that this understanding is the joint declaration which was issued at Potsdam on July 26th, 1945, by the heads of the Governments of the United States, Great Britain and China, and later subscribed by the Soviet Government, with the understanding that the said declaration does not comprise any demand which prejudices the prerogatives of His Majesty as a Sovereign Ruler.

The Japanese Government sincerely hope that this understanding is warranted and desire keenly that an explicit indication to that effect will be speedily forthcoming.

August 10th, the 20th year of Showa.

The foreign ministry officials had been on duty more than twenty-four hours and were exhausted. They left for their homes. Kase, in his book *Journey to the Missouri,* describes his feelings: "What a night it was! A night of endless anguish and anxiety. . . . Also it seemed that the fatigue of previous sleepless nights now began to tell heavily upon me. I still recall the deserted streets of Tokyo. . . . As I got on a passing tramcar, the shrill air-raid sirens started their banshee howling. . . . I saw the few passengers look up startled. They appeared frightened, shifting uneasily on their seats. After all, they did not know that just a short while before their government had sued for peace."

And Kase did not know that the pendulum had begun to swing in the opposite direction. Even as Kase rode home on the trolley, Lieutenant General Yoshizumi, the indefatigable head of the Military Affairs Bureau, was attempting to block sending the messages accepting the Allied terms.

Chapter 10

Tiptoeing after Peace

Most of the world's people sincerely desire peace—and are willing to annihilate everyone in their path to secure it. The Japanese were no exception.

But by mid-1944, Japan was a beaten nation. Navy leaders knew there was no hope after their crushing defeat at Midway in June 1942. Certain army leaders suspected this as early as Guadalcanal's loss, in January 1943. They were convinced when imperial Japanese troops *tenshin* (marched elsewhere) from Saipan in mid-1944. Government leaders knew that all was lost when Leyte fell in late 1944: some, of course, thought the war should have been ended long before that climactic blow.

Why didn't they try to end the war earlier? Some of them did. There were men in and out of government and in the upper reaches of both navy and army who tried to move Japan toward peace. But they were disorganized, out of power, hamstrung, or cowed. The reasons for their ineffectiveness were many.

The Allied declaration at Cairo in December 1943 was one reason; it was a major stumblingblock. There Chiang Kai-shek, Churchill, and Roosevelt set out the war aims against Japan: Japan will be reduced to the main islands, her territorial entity before she set out on her conquests in 1894, and "the three Allies . . . will continue to persevere in the serious and prolonged operations necessary to procure the unconditional surrender of Japan."

Nippon's leaders could understand the Allied demand that all conquered lands must be returned. This was a point that could be bargained when the negotiations for peace became serious. But the other point—*unconditional surrender*—was out of the question. It was tantamount to a blank check.

No one unconditionally surrenders an entire nation. Armed forces, yes. But surrendering *everything* and *everybody* unconditionally meant, literally, that the conquerors could dispose as they pleased of the defeated. They could even end the existence of the beaten nation! No self-respecting Japanese could do anything but reject this possibility. Even Premier Tojo, on the defensive because of the succession of defeats beginning with Guadalcanal, justified his dictatorial methods by stating: "We have no choice but to fight since they demand unconditional surrender." Any peace discussion, no matter how tentative, was considered subversive.

Tojo's iron grip on Japan included complete censorship of news information and education so that only a handful of Japanese had any idea of what was really going on. Further, Tojo had beefed up the *kempeitai,* the military police, and he used them mercilessly to ensnare the unwary, suppress the discontented, and control the unpredictable. He increased the conventional police authority over citizens and made it dangerous for known liberals and "peace-mongers" to get together. The masses thought Japan was still winning the war. There was therefore no public opinion pressing for peace—until the savage bombing of the homeland.

Leadership was squelched before it began. Partially because of the aggressiveness of the *kempeitai* and other police and partially because they had splintered into tiny powerless groups, loyal opponents of government policy were submerged, considered subversive, or simply silent. The sad fact was that there were few of them, and if any of them was to exert open leadership or question government policy he could expect a prompt call from the secret thought police.

There was no safe rallying point. Even the Emperor, on the advice of his closest counselors, was unable to exert his will. He was victimized, even as his subjects were, by the military. Striking examples of the way in which he was duped and used by his "loyal" military leaders are the imperial rescripts issued over his name celebrating in glowing terms the fictitious victories over the enemy in the Solomons and the Gilbert Islands.

Hirohito could not simply issue the order "stack arms." He did not have the power. His army and navy were running the show, not he. The Emperor could appropriately have uttered Kaiser Wilhelm's complaint of a generation before: "If people in Germany think I am the Supreme Commander, they are grossly mistaken. The General Staff tells me nothing and never asks my advice." There were no brilliant recipes for peace in Japan's serious condition. And there were no men of genius coming forward with proposals and suggestions that could possibly have some effect, for the reasons just mentioned. Achieving peace was like an intricate chemical formula in which each element and compound had to be first identified and then carefully removed from or fitted into the complex, interlocking construction. It was extremely delicate. It had to be done without disturbing the over-all equilibrium and thus destroying the whole thing.

The element of paramount importance—one which had worn out its usefulness—was a man: General Hideki Tojo. Tojo was premier of Japan from 1941 to mid-1944 and concurrently minister of war (so he could run the war machine) and home minister (so he could control the nation's civilian police force). From time to time he served concurrently as minister of foreign affairs, of education, of commerce, and created a ministry of munitions (with himself as head) to mobilize all industry under his control. When he took over the army as chief of staff in addition to his other posts in February 1944, even his army colleagues grumbled that he had bitten off far too much. The pressure against him began to be felt.

Another key element in the formula was the Emperor. This man, the life force of the nation, was hemmed in by his constitutional and traditional limitations. He saw his role as one of acting as a constitutional monarch and approving measures passed on to him by the cabinet and military leaders. And his advisers encouraged him to remain passive. Yet his was potentially the most powerful influence in the country—if it could be brought to bear.

Unfortunately, his closest advisers—the privy seal, household minister, and grand chamberlain—miscalculated his strength. Their timid or purposeful reining-in of the Emperor was done, they said, because they feared that Tojo was so powerful that if the Emperor opposed him and the war, His Majesty would be put under house arrest. If he did not cooperate then he would be forced to abdicate in favor of the Crown Prince and a regency would be established. Of course the military would control the regency.

So, instead of a steady, dependable source of encouragement and activity pressing toward an end to the war, the Throne was a cipher, checkmated by the combination of Tojo's power and Hirohito's faint-hearted counselors.

One of those counselors and a factor of incalculable value in the formula was the Marquis Koichi Kido, lord keeper of the privy seal. The nominal job of this extraordinary man was to guard the Emperor's signature seals and produce them when needed to make official state documents and imperial rescripts. But his real function was vastly more important.

Kido had the Emperor's ear at almost any and all times. He was the chief counselor and adviser to the Throne; he was the Emperor's closest and most trusted confidant. He was in a very real sense the turnkey, the keeper of his imperial master. Most of the men allowed the rare privilege of a private audience with the Emperor had been carefully screened by Kido before they were permitted such an honor. This power over access to the Throne was a vital control. Kido could, for instance, cut His Majesty off from people whose opinions the privy seal thought inconsequential or untimely. And he did.

There was no rule book setting out the privy seal's functions. They had simply accumulated and were exercised without question. Perhaps his most crucial responsibility was arranging the orderly, peaceful transfer of power by nominating the prime minister when a change of cabinet occurred. It was Kido who had advocated General Tojo to the Emperor in October 1941, and Prince Konoye before Tojo. Kido would have to recommend a successor to Tojo when, inevitably, Tojo stepped down. Compact and kinetic, the privy seal seemed alive with intense energy. Socially prominent but quiet and retiring, Kido found time to participate in an occasional *Noh* presentation and met regularly with his "Eleven Club" cronies to discuss the way of the world and Japan.

Through his round glasses Kido's wide eyes snapped up much; his active mind and network of friends and acquaintances sifted much more. He had few illusions. Kido knew where the aggregate of power was—and he knew how much, how fast, in what directions and into what hands it was shifting at any given moment. He had to know, for it was he who guided the Emperor's actions and responses. He had the answers to all questions—or had to get them. He was expected to plan ahead and to have or make plans to take into account all eventualities, to deal with all situations.

Kido's background had prepared him well for such service. His grandfather was one of the wise young men who successfully engineered the peaceful overthrow of feudal Japan in 1867–1868 and brought the nation into the modern world. As one of the top three men in Japan at that time, the elder Kido was immensely influential. The same statement held true for his grandson, in 1945.

Born in 1889, schooled with princes, he plunged into the bureaucratic world as auxiliary secretary of the minister of agriculture and commerce in 1915. His route was upward through various government units and ministries until he became the chief secretary to the lord keeper of the privy seal in October 1930. For more than five years Kido served as secretary to the privy seal, learning more than he ever imagined possible about the way in which the Emperor and the Throne operated and were manipulated.

When Kido's boyhood chum and schoolmate Prince Konoye became premier in 1937, he appointed Kido his minister of education. The new minister used the opportunity to "reform" the educational system so that it worked in support of the military and fostered war spirit in youth. Kido's ministry also worked closely with the *kempeitai* and the police to root out teachers suspected of unpatriotic teaching or thoughts and to keep the others in line.

Two years later, when Konoye's cabinet fell, Kido was appointed home minister in the succeeding government of Baron Hiranuma. The most important function of this ministry was the civil policing of the entire country, down to the local precinct cop on the beat. All the police in the nation reported to the superintendent of police, who reported to the home minister. Kido used this powerful office to support zealously the continuation of the China war.

He also initiated repressive motion-picture censorship and religious-organization laws. He directed the police to step in and muzzle the Asahi newspapers, the nation's largest, for being too outspoken. This intimidated the rest.

And Kido carefully helped stage-manage, with army assistance and financing, the 850 anti-British demonstrations that "broke out" in various parts of Japan that summer. The purpose was to whip up anti-British feeling so that the climate of opinion would force the government to enlarge the Anti-Comintern Pact with the Nazis and Fascists into a full-fledged military alliance against the English and other democracies.

Kido continued his political activity with his schoolmate Prince Konoye and helped pull a most ambitious fraud when they arranged for the peaceful suicide of all political parties in Japan—save one. That one was their own newly launched party, a super-colossus supposedly encompassing every shade of political opinion. This party had the impressive title Imperial Rule Assistance Association and was a monolithic fascist setup. Konoye was its president. Kido was scheduled to be vice-president, but he received a better offer. The post of lord keeper of the privy seal suddenly became open and he was invited to take it. He accepted.

As the eyes and ears of the Emperor as well as his warden, Kido was from that moment on a major influence on Hirohito's actions and Japan's history. He neglected to encourage the Emperor to take a stand against war either at the last moment or earlier, when it might have been more effective. A number of examples can be cited.

In those darkening days of 1941, Kido counseled his increasingly anxious sovereign about peace and war prospects. The privy seal wrote in his diary on July 31 that the navy chief of staff told the Emperor Japan should avoid war, that he had opposed making the Triple Alliance a full-fledged military pact because it would hinder friendship between Japan and the U.S. The Admiral said that if diplomatic relations were not restored between the two, Japan would be cut off from oil supplies, that her present reserves would run out in two years at the present rate, or in eighteen months if Japan went to war with America.

Kido reports: "The Emperor showed anxiety that war with the U.S. would be hopeless." But the privy seal had answers: "The navy chief of staff's opinion is too simple; the U.S. recognizes the existence of the Tripartite Alliance and to annul that pact would not increase U.S. confidence in Japan but would bring contempt of Japan. We have not yet exhausted the possibilities of restoring U.S.–Japanese friendship. We must deliberate on the matter constructively." And so the matter was left unconstructively hanging in midair.

Kido was not squeamish about hurling Japan into war. In fact, he was consistent on this point. In 1937 he confided to his diary that a Mr. Matsui came to see him after the Japanese engineered the outbreak of war with China. Kido reported that he "became furious over Matsui's talk of halting the dispatch of the Imperial Japanese Army to north China."

With his long record of cooperation with the military, Kido's recommendation for premier to succeed Konoye in late 1941 should have been no great surprise. The privy seal nominated an army man. He was General Hideki Tojo, the gourd-headed, mangy-scalped general dubbed "Razor Brain" by his associates. Kido suggested Tojo "as a preventive of a rush to war, after a thoughtful consideration of the situation." He told Hirohito that Tojo, as an army man, could control the army as a civilian could not and that a military man was needed at the helm at this time. "The Emperor approved my answers, saying 'nothing ventured, nothing gained.'"

Kido's actions did not always promote war. He tells us that "as early as the audience with the Emperor on February 5, 1942, I advised him of the necessity of ending the war speedily by taking advantage of the capture of Singapore." (Having just witnessed a month of dazzling Nipponese military successes throughout the Pacific, the Emperor, says Kido, looked at him as though the privy seal were daft.)

A workable scheme to end the war became more and more essential as the slaughter increased. There were plenty of schemes, but the operative word *workable* disqualified most of them.

There were, for instance, the proposals of General Seizo Arisue, chief of G-2—army intelligence. In January 1943 he advocated building a broadcasting station at Bandung, Indonesia, and beaming a special broadcast to the U.S. It was to include General Tojo as master of ceremonies, Japanese foreign minister Tani, Count Ciano of Italy, Ribbentrop of Germany, and the puppet heads of Manchukuo, occupied China, the Philippines, Burma, and Indonesia. The message was to be "Japan has no territorial ambitions . . . this is a war to free the people." The plan was not accepted.

In February 1944, Arisue proposed building a radio station on

Saipan. "It would be used," he counseled, "to negotiate directly for peace. Of course, the U.S. might say 'What is the idea of talking about the peace at this stage?' If so, the Japanese would say 'In spite of our plea, the U.S. would not listen. Then we will fight to the last.' When I proposed this to Tojo, I was flatly rejected with the remark 'What nonsense.' " The wonder of this is not the particular proposal but that Arisue continued as intelligence chief throughout the war.

There were, however, sounder suggestions. One was advanced by Shigeru Yoshida, who became Japan's outstanding prime minister after the war. Yoshida and his circle of influential fellow aristocrats and intellectuals thought that the fall of Singapore was an excellent opportunity to make a peace overture and bring the war to an early and advantageous end. One of Yoshida's friends, Marquis Yasumasa Matsudaira, was Kido's chief secretary and told him that the privy seal felt the same way.

It was Yoshida's idea that a bona-fide, responsible, top-rank Japanese should go to Switzerland to put forth peace feelers. He had in mind Prince Konoye and, when he heard that Kido had told the Emperor the war must be ended, Yoshida spoke to the Prince about this project. Konoye, though surprised, seemed willing. He asked if Yoshida really thought the mission could succeed. Yoshida told him that even if it only demonstrated to the Allies that Japan seriously desired to make peace, the trip would be worthwhile. Konoye suggested that the plan be discussed with Kido.

Yoshida saw Kido—who, he says, "refrained from giving a straight answer on the matter." Matsudaira, Kido's secretary, had told Yoshida that General Tojo was constantly harping to the privy seal that Konoye should be muzzled, and Yoshida guessed that the close surveillance of Konoye was probably behind Kido's cool reception of the plan. At that point the matter died, filed away in one of Kido's myriad pigeonholes.

There were other rudimentary moves in the direction of peace. The army even had a planning unit charged with long-range studies. Called Group 20, it was small and its work was top-secret. Led by Colonel Makoto Matsutani, Group 20 officers put together in early 1944 a realistic paper: "Measures for the Termination of the Greater East Asia War." This document was stamped *State Secret* and circulated only to the heads of both army and navy.

Matsutani and his fellows correctly foresaw the approaching destruction of Germany and advocated that Japan make a major effort to end the war when the Nazis collapsed. It was clear that for Japan the war could only become more costly when the Allies had crushed Germany and turned their full power against Japan. And with that situation would come still harsher terms. Group 20 had worked out several alternative plans with the terms to be sought varying according to the conditions at the time of negotiation.

The Third Plan was the absolute, final line beyond which Japan could not afford to concede an inch. This "ultimate" alternative simply held that when and if the situation came down to a choice between surrender or annihilation, Japan should hold out for only one thing: an Allied guarantee that the national structure (the Emperor system) would continue and the Japanese nation would be preserved. Face, conquered lands, everything else would have to be sacrificed.

When Matsutani explained his analysis to Premier–War Minister–Munitions Minister–army Chief of Staff Tojo, he found out in short order what "Razor Brains" thought of his ideas.

The Colonel said he could not understand why the nation had no over-all peace plan and presented the Group 20 memorandum. As Matsutani explained the necessity for seeking peace before it became necessary to beg for mercy, Tojo exploded and ordered him to duty on the China front. He left the next day. He was lucky. Others were turned over to the *kempeitai* and imprisoned indefinitely for less.

By spring 1944, various leaders were cautiously, tentatively extending hands to bring themselves together and bring down Tojo. Guarded discussions and secret consultations were held by the secretaries and close associates of key men. Thus Colonel Matsutani (before he was sent to China) and Admiral Takagi met with Kido's secretary Matsudaira, and with Toshikazu Kase, the English-language expert at the foreign ministry, and a young man who was a bureau director in the finance ministry, Hisatsune Sakomizu. These men got together frequently and compared notes, exchanged news, and passed along to their influential friends accurate though fragmentary information about what was going on. This dangerous function was extremely important to unlocking the "peace puzzle."

At one point in 1944, when dissatisfaction with Tojo and the war situation had fermented for some time, there was a serious effort to bring Umezu back from the mainland to head a new Japanese government. According to Umezu's son, the conspirators included several members of the Diet and a Mr. Egami. One of the planners flew to the General's headquarters to persuade him to come to Tokyo and take over in a *coup d'état*. The next step would be to suppress the young officers so that a peace move could be made. It was to consist of a special envoy to the Soviet Union to negotiate through the USSR for an end to the Pacific War.

But the General, says his son, was "so cautious that he would not cross a bridge without sounding its stones with a stick before taking a step." He would not think of leading such a *coup*.

Another key element in the solution was Japan's foreign minister. From 1942–1945 he was Mamoru Shigemitsu, a man who had broad background as ambassador to the Soviet Union, Britain, and China. He worked toward peace, influencing the elder statesmen, cabinet ministers, members of the Diet and, most significant of all, his friend Privy Seal Kido.

Shigemitsu was convinced that "nothing but practically unconditional surrender could save the country." Working from this basic premise, he discussed with Kido the possible approaches to ending the war. He concluded that with the power weighted so heavily in favor of the army, no method was so likely to work as invoking the prestige of the Emperor at an appropriate moment—perhaps at an Imperial Conference.

The *jushin*—the elder statesmen who had been premiers of Japan —had potential as a factor in bringing about peace. By the spring of 1944 they had decided individually that Tojo's policies were disastrous. Included in this group were Baron Reijiro Wakatsuki, who had been premier in 1926 and again in 1931; Admiral Keisuke Okada, whose ship of state was torpedoed in the infamous February 26, 1936, rebellion; Koki Hirota, who succeeded Okada; Prince Fumimaro Konoye, premier from 1937 to 1939 and again in 1940 and 1941; Baron Kiichiro Hiranuma, the old bureaucrat whose government was paralyzed by discussion of the Axis pact; and Admiral Mitsumasa Yonai, the man who blocked Japan's signing the Tripartite Axis alliance for six months in 1940.

The *jushin* had, in earlier times, been a panel consulted by the Emperor and his prime ministers. Since Tojo's takeover, it had been quite clear that the dictator distrusted the *jushin* and wanted no interference from it or its members in running Japan. By May 1944, however, the elder statesmen gathered up their courage and met surreptitiously. They agreed as a group for the first time that Tojo was mismanaging both the war and the nation.

Admiral Okada was designated by the group to have a talk with Tojo to let him know their concern about the way things were going. Okada called on the short-fused dictator, but before he had fairly begun his exposition the temperamental dictator flew into a rage and accused the *jushin* of trying to oust his cabinet. He didn't want to hear, much less profit by, the *jushin's* suggestions.

In another quarter, Prince Takamatsu, Hirohito's younger brother, was a rallying point of the opposition to Tojo and the war's continuation. As a captain in the navy he was well aware of the bitter feud between the two services on strategy, tactics, allocation of materials, share of munitions and annual budget—in fact, on almost every matter of substance. Takamatsu believed that a negotiated peace must come and that the foreign ministry must be strengthened for this purpose at the same time that Tojo and the army must somehow be circumvented.

The prince told Shigemitsu at the end of June 1944 that the Japanese navy had practically been put out of action in its debacle in the Marianas. In three days it had lost 450 aircraft, three carriers, and two tankers and suffered severe damage to four more carriers, one battleship, one cruiser, and one tanker. (The U.S. lost twenty planes in the air and suffered negligible damage to ships.) Furthermore, when Saipan was captured—which would be any day—the war was as good as lost. If the Emperor system could be guaranteed, said Takamatsu, Japan should try immediately to negotiate a peace.

Meanwhile, Shigemitsu and other cabinet members had become increasingly outspoken about Tojo's running of the country. In June they had threatened to resign and Tojo had tried to patch together a satisfactory compromise by new appointments to the cabinet. However, as Japanese strongholds in Burma crumbled and Saipan was invaded by the enemy, the opposition to Tojo became adamant. It was to be satisfied with nothing short of his scalp.

With the fall of Saipan, Tojo tried desperately to rearrange his government to satisfy the ever-more numerous and outspoken critics. He told Kido his plans. Kido advised him that the army and navy ministers and chiefs of staff must be separated (Tojo was serving as both war minister and chief of staff of the army), that "spare-time strategy cannot reassure the nation." He also advised that Navy Minister Shimada (an out-and-out Tojo tool, and increasingly disliked because of his subordination of navy interests) must go. Furthermore, said Kido, a better means of involving and using the elder statesmen and national leaders would have to be found.

But by now the elder statesmen, the *jushin,* had had enough. After Saipan fell on July 9 they met at the home of Baron Hiranuma. This time they decided to take their case to the Throne—or the next best place, to the lord keeper of the privy seal. And this time they agreed definitely that Tojo must go. A statement was prepared and delivered to Kido by Admiral Okada:

New life must be injected into the minds and hearts of the people if the nation is to surmount the difficulties besetting it. . . . A partial reorganization of the cabinet will serve no purpose whatsoever. A strong National Cabinet that will move forward unswervingly must be formed.

By the time Tojo and his cabinet resigned in a bloc on July 18, Kido had already moved to find a successor. He had called the *jushin* together to hear their advice on the next premier. Kido narrowed the field by saying "The only solution is to get a person from the army, judging from the necessity of improving the defense forces, increasing the army's strength on the mainland and that of the *kempeitai* in order to prevent civilian revolt."

The *jushin* finally recommended Generals Terauchi, Koiso, and Hata for premier. Kido presented the names to the Emperor, who asked General Tojo about them. The outgoing premier immediately rejected Terauchi saying the man was needed at his command post in the Southern Region every moment with the enemy pressing as it was. Thus the choice went to General Kuniaki Koiso, sixty-five, governor-general of Korea, former head of the powerful Military Affairs Bureau of the army, and plotter of a March 1931 attempt to bring down the government.

That same evening, Prince Konoye called on Kido with the suggestion that instead of another army man as premier alone, it would be better to make it a joint army-navy cabinet by including Admiral Mitsumasa Yonai as vice-premier. (Furthermore, Konoye, Okada, Kido, and others believed that Yonai could be counted on to press toward peace; they were not so sure about Koiso.) Kido agreed and sent his secretary to sound out the *jushin* on the idea. They approved.

Koiso flew back from Korea and presented himself at the palace for installation as premier. The scene that followed (as Koiso later described it) was straight out of Gilbert and Sullivan:

I unexpectedly met Yonai in the same waiting room. I asked him what business brought him there and he replied that he had been summoned also. That made me think that perhaps Yonai was going to receive the Imperial command to form a cabinet and I was going to receive orders about something else. Then the privy seal informed us that we were to go together before the Emperor. When asked "who should lead?" Kido said "It is, of course, Koiso." So I took the lead and appeared before the Emperor.

At that time the Emperor did not say who was to become the premier, but told us "the two of you, in cooperation with each other, will form a cabinet. . . ." When we returned to the waiting room Kido was there. Yonai asked him "Now which of us is to be the premier?" Kido replied "Of course Koiso is." At the time I thought to myself, "What a strange conversation," however, later it occurred to me that Yonai, who no doubt took part in the conference of the *jushin* to select the next premier, must have known that I had been named. . . . So I then asked Yonai "Now what office are you going to fill? Is it the office of navy minister?" To this Yonai replied "I am incapable of filling any other office than that."

With this curious launching, the Koiso–Yonai cabinet began. Koiso had been in Korea for two years and was unfamiliar with the home front and the political infighting that had taken place in his absence. Furthermore, he was saddled with a mandate that seemed to him impossible.

As he put it, "It was my belief that the fall of Saipan meant our defeat in the war. Such being the case, I did not think there was anyone—if he was at all informed of this grave situation—who felt that Japan could still win the war. Generally speaking, such hopelessness would persuade a man of common sense to decline an Imperial mandate to assume the reins of government. However, in Japan, when one is summoned before the Emperor and given a mandate that is absolute and final, one cannot, as a subject, follow the dictates of common sense. Now, when I heard the Imperial words (particularly 'put forth efforts to attain the objective of the Greater East Asia War. Further, you must be careful not to irritate the Soviet Union.') I thought it an absolute command and felt awe-stricken."

What about peace? As Koiso saw it, if the government had then sued for peace "it would have been compelled to surrender under merciless terms and therefore would have given rise to a revolt because the people, who had been led only to believe that the war was being won, would probably have become indignant over such a peace move." Besides, Saipan had fallen.

Now, he decided, "if there is another battle, let's throw our entire strength into it to win. Let's make peace overtures only after such a victory, for then if we ride on the wave of victory and sue for peace, the terms certainly will be somewhat lighter and [more] favorable."

On August 19, 1944, Premier Koiso convened the SCDW and the conferees threshed out a new and revised basic policy for the war. In spite of Japan's mortally weakened condition, the policy was as bellicose as if written at the height of her fortunes. Stressed was the absolute determination to fight to the end. But in the fine print there was mention of dispatching a suitable man to the Soviet Union with the unstated aim of negotiating with and through the Soviets.

Koiso, the premier who thought the war hopeless, found himself mousetrapped by the belligerent basic policy adopted by the SCDW and by the Supreme Command at GHQ.

He checked with the high command, which told him it planned a final decisive battle in the Philippines. Its strategy would be "to inflict a vital blow upon the enemy at the cost of equally vital sacrifice on Japan's part." When MacArthur's invasion of Leyte began on October 20, Koiso double-checked with the high command to verify that the plan was, as had been agreed upon August 19, to fight the decisive battle on Leyte.

The term *decisive battle* had special meaning to the Japanese military. It was by definition an all-out effort in which an offensive would be launched. It was not and could not be simply a defensive operation, for taking the initiative was inherent in the term. So Koiso, armed with the assurances of the high command, went on radio and broadcast to the Japanese nation that the Leyte battle was the war's turning point. It was, he said, a modern-day Tennozan. (Tennozan was a small mountain on which in 1582 one of the crucial battles of Japanese history was fought. There a young samurai named Hideyoshi defeated his enemies in what proved the decisive move that made him supreme ruler of Japan.) Known to all Japanese, the battle of Tennozan was, therefore, a crucial undertaking and they fully believed Koiso when he said "If Japan wins on Leyte, she wins the war!" On the other hand, defeat in this battle would mean that a strategically contested battleground, comparable to Waterloo, had been given up. Defeat in this battle would mean the downfall of Japan, because—according to the premier—the nation was going to pour everything into this fight. Presumably there would be nothing left for future battles.

On December 20, 1944, Koiso called at the palace for an audience with his sovereign. He was in the anteroom when quite coincidentally the war minister General Sugiyama came in and whispered to him "Prime Minister, the high command has abandoned plans for a decisive battle on Leyte in favor of a decisive battle on Luzon."

"Stunned," as he put it, Koiso had no time to question further; he had to go in to see the Emperor immediately. He made his prepared report on the state of things without mention of the Leyte decision. Hirohito, listening to this routine recitation, must have been nonplused. When Koiso finished, the Emperor asked about the overriding question of the day: did Koiso know the high command had abandoned Leyte in favor of Luzon? The premier told him that he learned it only as he came in the door and Hirohito then asked the question that all of Japan would ask soon: "Have you thought of a way to justify your statement that the Leyte battle was a Tennozan?"

Confused and incensed, Koiso sputtered that he had to think of a way to make the best of the situation, and withdrew. Then he called together the SCDW and angrily accused the army and navy chiefs of staff of doublecrossing him. He realized then that unless he knew from the inside what the high command was planning he and the government could never run the nation as was required. Defeat followed upon defeat; Leyte fell to the Americans, then Manila, and finally Luzon and all of the Philippines.

Meanwhile, Koiso made a curious attempt to bring about peace with China through a renegade from the Kuomintang. This man, Miao Pin, convinced Koiso's representative that he was in contact with the Chungking government of Chiang Kai-shek by radio and could negotiate on his behalf with the Japanese. To the annoyance of Foreign Minister Shigemitsu, Koiso arranged with the army to fly Miao with his radio and operator, a cryptographer, and another liaison man from Japanese-controlled China to Tokyo. But as the group was about to take off, the *kempeitai* stopped everyone but Miao.

"When we discovered that Miao had come alone," says Koiso, "we were thunderstruck . . . with even his radio gone, Miao was helpless." (After the war, Miao was one of the first persons executed by Chiang Kai-shek as a traitor.)

This fiasco on top of the Philippine gaffe, destroyed the Emperor's confidence in Koiso. When the Allies invaded Okinawa April 1, 1945, this penetration of Japan's inner defense perimeter finished him. As if that were not enough, the Russians denounced the Soviet-Japanese Neutrality Pact on April 5, indicating that they would not renew it when it expired the following year. On April 5 Koiso and his cabinet resigned, but remained on duty until Admiral Baron Kantaro Suzuki was installed on April 7 as the new premier.

There were other peace moves during General Koiso's regime. One significant one began in September 1944, when Navy Minister Yonai ordered Admiral Sokichi Takagi to carry out further secret studies. The topics included how to get army agreement to end the war; public opinion and morale in the event of peace; how to reach the Emperor and work through him to achieve peace. Study results were reported periodically to such key leaders as Kido, Prince Konoye, Tsuneo Matsudaira (the imperial household minister), Admiral Okada, and certain army men.

Perhaps the major conclusion from these studies and discussions was that the Emperor would be the key to control the public and prevent a military *coup* when peace was decided.

When Koiso stepped down he handed in a letter of resignation recommending a drastic change in government. He called for establishing an Imperial GHQ cabinet.

To Kido this immediately suggested that the army wanted to take over the reins of government and that the high command was stepping in. Filled with apprehension, he rushed to confer with the war and navy ministers and the two chiefs of staff. He found that this was not their idea, but merely a parting brainstorm of Koiso's. The military men opposed such a cabinet.

The Emperor, sorely troubled by the course of the war, was deeply disturbed by late 1944 by the suffering of innocent civilians in the devastating fire raids. When the enemy invaded Luzon in January 1945 it shook him out of his torpor. He talked to Kido and initiated his own careful moves toward peace. He told Kido that he wished to see the *jushin*.

Kido had purposely kept the *jushin* away from the Throne. It was known that most of them were in favor of ending the war and were anti-army. (They had good reason to be—most of them had tangled with the army as prime ministers and lost.) For the Emperor to see them would be a subtle outward display of his belief in and support of moving toward peace. Seemingly insignificant, this delicate move by the Emperor was a clear signal to the contending factions that His Majesty now favored action to end the war.

Another example of initiative was the Emperor's appointment of Admiral Hasegawa to inspect war preparations throughout the nation. Though he received regular briefings from both army and navy chiefs about war conditions and could ask them for any specific information he needed, Hirohito decided to send his own man out to check up—a clear slap at both services. The report, which was made June 12 to His Majesty personally, was honest, blunt, and dismal, as noted earlier. The facts were invaluable, however, when the Emperor was called on to speak his mind at the Imperial Conference on August 10.

When Admiral Baron Kantaro Suzuki was installed as premier April 7, 1945, one of his first acts was to assign the new chief cabinet secretary, black-thatched Hisatsune Sakomizu, to report on the nation's fighting capabilities. Suzuki wanted a trustworthy estimate of Japan's ability to wage war. Sakomizu produced evidence within a month documenting that Japan could not continue. Tremendous shipping losses, declining aircraft production, a critical food situation, and increasing antiwar feeling on the part of the people were the main points cited by his report.

Suzuki accepted the findings and presented the study to the Emperor, for whom it was further confirmation of the nation's desperate situation.

It was only shortly before this that two Japanese peace moves had been attempted abroad. The first came about through the initiative of Japan's assistant naval attaché in Berlin, Commander Yoshiro Fujimura. He was transferred to Berne, Switzerland, at the end of March 1945, just before the breakup of Germany, but he had seen enough of the Nazi disintegration. And he had heard of a special U.S. intelligence unit in Switzerland, headed by a man named Allen Dulles. Fujimura, literally taking his life in his hands, approached the Dulles organization—the U.S. Office of Strategic Services—to find out what terms Japan could obtain.

Dulles' associates told Fujimura that they hoped for an early settlement of the war and would spare no effort toward that end. Fujimura, elated, conferred in utmost secrecy with his colleagues and sent a coded, urgent cable directly to the navy minister and navy chief of staff in Tokyo on May 8, the day of Germany's surrender.

Fujimura attributed the initiative to the OSS. He had to. Otherwise he would have been open to charges of treason. But in his Urgent, Personal, Secret, Code Operational Dispatch the commander said he had received a proposal from the Dulles organization. He described Dulles as head of American political warfare for Europe, said the U.S. agent was willing to tell Washington if Japan wished to end the war and would exert himself to that end. The offer, said Fujimura, was addressed only to the Japanese navy.

Back in Tokyo, the decoded cable was brought to Rear Admiral Tomioka, chief of naval operations, by his diplomatic affairs assistant, who was grinning happily at the unexpected news. Though both recognized that it might be a trick or a trap, they believed it might give a clue to America's minimum terms for ending the war. They decided to advise their superiors to cooperate in the negotiations.

Tomioka knew, however, that his superior, Vice-Admiral Onishi, the vice-chief of staff, was adamant about continuing the war. If he showed the cable to Onishi, it would die on his desk—or in his wastebasket. So Tomioka sidestepped the chain of command and took it directly to Chief of Staff Admiral Toyoda and gave his opinion in favor of it. Expecting Toyoda to agree, Tomioka was disheartened when the chief of staff said "All you have to do is to devote your heart and soul exclusively to military operations. You should not concern yourself about the problem of peace."

Tomioka followed orders. He all but forgot the message. Meanwhile, Fujimura sent a barrage of cables to Tokyo trying to blast loose some action on the proposal. He cabled on May 10, 13, 14, 16,

18, and 20, urging action and including brief essays on such inspiring topics as Germany's "tragic end," moving of Allied and Soviet troops to the Far East, and the Dulles organization's part in Italy's separate truce.

Then, two weeks after his first cable, Fujimura received a reply: the proposed negotiations sounded like an enemy effort to drive a wedge between the Japanese navy and army; take utmost care. The truth was that in Tokyo no one knew who Dulles was and they could not understand why any sincere peace feeler would be entrusted to a mere naval commander.

At one point Navy Minister Yonai asked Foreign Minister Togo about Dulles and told him of the cables. Togo didn't recognize Dulles' name, but recommended replying to Fujimura that Japan must have some conditions—she could not accept unconditional surrender. He asked Yonai to cable this response. Togo learned weeks afterward that Yonai had not sent a reply.

Fujimura stalled the Americans and sent another cable. This time he pleaded that navy GHQ accept his word, that their suspicions of a plot were unfounded, and give him authorization to open negotiations at once to save Japan from Germany's fate. No answer. Four more cables from Fujimura to Tokyo and still no reply.

Desperate, Fujimura and his associates considered whether the commander should fly back and present his case in person. They discussed it with Dulles' adviser on Japanese affairs, who came up with a better idea: Ask Tokyo to send a substantial person—admiral, general, cabinet minister—to Switzerland. If they would do so, the U.S. would guarantee safe conduct for the mission. Fujimura immediately sent this word to Yonai.

This was an echo of Yoshida's proposal to send Konoye to Switzerland. It also mirrored an earlier proposal made by Admiral Takagi to Yonai in which he urged the navy minister to take this route to approach the U.S. directly and that he, Takagi, be sent to open negotiations. Navy GHQ killed both suggestions.

A cable was sent to Fujimura telling him that the navy ministry had referred the matter to the foreign ministry and advised him to work henceforth with Japan's minister to Switzerland, Shunichi Kase. That ended the effort so far as the OSS was concerned, for (it was revealed after the war) the codes of Japan's foreign office were known to all the Allies. Therefore the negotiations could not be kept secret and would stir up serious problems.

Simultaneously and independently of Fujimura's effort, the Japanese military attaché to Switzerland, Lieutenant General Seigo Okamoto, moved to similar action. With two Japanese officials of the Bank for International Settlements in Basel, Okamoto decided that contact with the U.S. should be made directly through the OSS. This was discussed with Japan's Minister Shunichi Kase. A Swedish banker named Jacobsson was known to the Japanese bankers and he was asked to be an intermediary. He agreed.

Given the Japanese basic points for discussion, he was picked up by an auto especially dispatched for him, taken to Wiesbaden, Germany, where Dulles met him. Thirty-six hours later Jacobsson came back to Basel and spelled out the particulars of the OSS chief's reply. Washington, he reported, did not object to continuing the Emperor system in Japan, but many objections had been raised in the past by other nations among the Allies. Therefore no firm commitment on that point. However, the U.S. would state that it was its "understanding" that the Emperor system would be continued "if Japan surrendered." Other points: Japan's Constitution would have to go; it was in part responsible for the ascendancy of the warlords (Okamoto had specified that the Constitution not be revised). And as for internationalization of Manchuria and allowing Japan to keep Formosa and Korea, Dulles said "no comment."

He warned, however, that if the Japanese didn't begin negotiations before the Soviets' possible entry into the war their effort was doomed. But Jacobsson's information was delivered to the Japanese a scant three weeks before the Allies' Potsdam meeting. Okamoto cabled the gist of this report to Tokyo and a week later Minister Kase did likewise. Okamoto received no reply; Kase heard from the foreign minister—a cool, guarded request for more information. And so the matter rested. Stuck on dead center.

One other peace feeler is worth noting. Its roots went back to September 1944, when the managing director of the Asahi newspaper, Bunshiro Suzuki (not related to Premier Kantaro Suzuki) called on the Swedish Minister to Japan, Widar Bagge. Suzuki had a peace proposal. He was, he said, representing Prince Konoye and a group of Japanese who wanted to end the war even if it meant giving up all conquered territories—perhaps even Manchuria.

Suzuki asked Bagge to forward the request to the Swedish government and that a discreet query be made to Great Britain through Swedish channels. The Suzuki–Konoye group believed that such a plan might be better received by Britain than by the U.S. Bagge reported all this to his home base in Stockholm and over a period of months had numerous discussions of peace with Suzuki. But the time dragged on and Japan's fortunes sank. There was no real progress.

Finally, after twenty years in Japan, Bagge was about to return to Sweden. It was near the end of March 1945, and he decided to offer his good offices to the Japanese government formally. The Swede met with Japan's former minister to Finland and told him that he felt sure the Allies would not insist on unconditional surrender if Japan would initiate a peace move. He believed also that if Japan made the first move the Allies would leave the Emperor system intact.

Bagge's views were immediately relayed to Foreign Minister Shigemitsu, who arranged to meet with the Swede. Shigemitsu asked Bagge "very earnestly" to do his utmost to find out the chances of a negotiated peace.

But the Koiso government fell before Bagge left for Stockholm. Shigemitsu was out. However, the same Japanese diplomat who had arranged for Bagge to see Shigemitsu reported to his successor, Togo, the Swedish minister's words. Here, however, a kink entered the communications pipeline. Togo misunderstood. He thought Bagge intended on his own initiative to determine U.S. attitudes toward Japan's desires. Togo was enthusiastic, said he would like to talk with the minister. But Bagge's plane was due to leave at any moment and he was unable to meet Togo.

The Swedish diplomat flew to Manchuria and took the train via Siberia. He did not arrive home until early May, and not until May 10 did he call on the Japanese minister to Sweden, Suemasa Okamoto. There he found that Okamoto was completely in the dark about the possibility of negotiations and had no word from Tokyo on this subject. Puzzled, Bagge urged Okamoto to fire off a cable to Togo requesting instructions.

When Okamoto's wire hit Togo's desk, it was the foreign minister's turn to be surprised. Having thought Bagge was going to push the inquiry on his own, Togo now had before him a statement that the Swedish government would gladly explore the peace question with the Americans if the Japanese formally asked it. Togo, puzzled, wired back that the matter would have to be investigated thoroughly before the Japanese government could act. Thus this effort ground to a standstill until Togo could find out the background. But by this time—mid-May—Togo's attention was focused on other activities centering around the Soviet Union.

By May 1945 the few doors to peace so tantalizingly open were closing quickly. Efforts via Dulles and the OSS in Switzerland were sputtering to a close; the Swedish channel was waiting. But Togo was not keen about going through either of these routes. He knew in advance, he told those who asked, that through these avenues Japan would get back only the same old answer—the Allies demand unconditional surrender.

The Vatican? Togo saw the Pope as lukewarm on the peacemaking role and believed that the result would be no different than through Switzerland or Sweden.

Direct approaches to the Allied nations (as some influential Japanese encouraged) through responsible Japanese who had friends in the upper strata of the U.S. or Britain? Too dangerous—the military might even step in immediately and arrest all concerned; furthermore, the chances of success were remote.

Negotiate through China? With the bitterness and mistrust that existed between Japan and China any negotiations would be difficult. There were the added complications of the Japanese puppet government of China and the Chinese Communist regime, neither of which recognized either the other or the Kuomintang of Chiang Kai-shek. Just where to begin negotiations in such a situation would be a knotty problem in itself.

Again and again the Japanese looked at their situation and saw looming ever larger and more important in their future their traditional enemy, Russia. By going to the Soviets for help in negotiating an end to the war not only would Japan be spared annihilation by the Allies; a Soviet attack would be forestalled as well, for, as the old Japanese proverb says, "even an ogre will not eat you if you throw yourself on his mercy."

As Japan was to learn, the truth of this depends on the ogre.

Chapter 11

Floundering toward a Finish

When a thoroughly crushed Nazi Germany finally capitulated on May 6, 1945, Japan's foreign minister Shigenori Togo received a formal visit from the German ambassador, Herr Stahmer. Stahmer explained in painful detail how and why Germany had been forced to surrender, overwhelmed by the enemy's superior equipment, superior numbers, and superiority on land and sea and in the air. Germany was prostrate. Even the Führer was reported to be dead.

Togo responded, punctilious as ever. "I reminded him that surrender constituted a violation of Germany's treaty obligations." Germany had quit, as had Italy, even though there was a no-separate-peace clause in the Axis pact!

Germany's surrender was one of the times flagged in the army Group 20 study on ending the war. It was a moment for Japan to act to save herself. With Okinawa practically gone and Germany and Italy knocked out, on May 11, 12, and 14 the SCDW met in strictest secrecy. Their central subject was Russia—how to use her, how to keep her out of the war, how to get her to mediate for Japan, how to wring vital supplies out of her. The discussion stirred up violent reactions. Admiral Yonai was insulted by Togo, who all but called him stupid for believing Japan could wheedle oil and airplanes from the USSR to use against the Allies.

The talk ranged onward to peace in general and even the military, for the first time, did not object to the general idea. The argument began when concrete terms for a truce were discussed. War Minister

Anami heatedly insisted "We should remember above all that Japan still retains a large block of enemy territory. We have not lost the war so long as this is so, and we should negotiate from this basis." Togo threw back at him "Although Okinawa is the only sizable piece of our territory we have lost, it is future developments on the war front that will count and it is impossible to visualize peace conditions merely on the basis of captured or lost territory." The two debated this until Navy Minister Yonai whispered to Togo that the conference would break up if he pressed this point. Premier Suzuki meanwhile suggested that this decision be postponed until the Soviet attitude was plumbed.

The official conference précis reads, in part:

. . . It is absolutely necessary, regardless of how the war against Britain and America may develop, that our Empire make supreme efforts to prevent the USSR from participating in the war against us because this will be a fatal blow to our Empire at a time we are fighting so desperately against Britain and America. Furthermore . . . [we should] induce the Soviets to observe a benevolent neutrality toward us . . . and mediate for the purpose of terminating the war. With these ends in view, we should begin negotiations with the USSR at once. In the negotiations, we should induce Russia to agree by convincing her that her victory over Germany was made possible by our remaining neutral; that it is to her advantage for Japan to retain a fairly important international position since the USSR is bound to be confronted with America in the future; and that it is necessary for Japan, the USSR, and China to stand hand-in-hand against Britain and the U.S. However, at the same time, we must be prepared for the heavy demands which the USSR will, in all probability, make. . . . Though it is natural that we should try to lower her demands, the abrogation of the Portsmouth Treaty and the Russo-Japanese Basic Treaty should not be avoided if we are to make the intended negotiations successful. Namely, we shall have to: (1) return So. Sakhalin; (2) relinquish our fisheries rights; (3) open Tsugaru Strait [between the Japanese home islands of Honshu and Hokkaido]; (4) transfer railways in No. Manchuria; (5) recognize the sphere of influence of the Soviets in Inner Mongolia; (6) lease Port Arthur and Dairen.

In addition, the northern half of the Kuriles may have to be given to the Soviets if circumstances demand. However, Korea must remain in our hands and the independence of Manchukuo must be maintained as far as possible through such means as maintaining a neutral zone in So. Manchuria. As for China, it is most desirable to establish a cooperative system among Japan, Soviet, and China.

It is significant how much Japan's leaders were willing to give at this point, and how clear-eyed their vision was in general. It was surprising, in view of some of the naive statements during these meetings. War Minister Anami said that "as the USSR will be in confrontation with the U.S. after the war and therefore will not desire to see Japan too much weakened, the Soviet attitude toward us may not be severe." And to Suzuki Stalin seemed like Saigo Nanshu (a paragon of sincerity and trustworthiness in Japanese history). The premier believed therefore that Stalin would act fairly with Japan. Togo pointed out the danger of setting a course on the basis of the Japanese way of thinking, but could not suggest any other country than Russia likely to promote a favorable peace with the Allies.

After the Big Six meetings, Togo immediately sought out Koki Hirota, his chief at the Foreign Office in earlier days, and pressed him into service to contact the Soviet ambassador in Japan. Hirota was to sound him out on basic problems between the two nations, keeping in mind the kind of negotiations the SCDW had discussed. Hirota, a former envoy to Russia, foreign minister, and premier of Japan, agreed.

Beginning June 3 he met informally for two days at a spa near Tokyo with Jacob Malik, the Russian ambassador. Hirota reported a favorable reception, but nothing substantial was accomplished.

Suddenly on June 5 Togo received word that there was to be a formal meeting of the full Supreme Council for Direction of the War on June 6. It was to include the secretaries, the nonvoting members (the chiefs of the military affairs bureaus of army and navy, the head of the cabinet coordinating bureau, and the chief cabinet secretary), plus the ministers of agriculture and munitions. The agenda was short: "The Fundamental Policy to be Followed Henceforth in the Conduct of the War."

The foreign minister glanced through the document and was shocked. It was a fire-and-brimstone call to fight to the death, mobilizing the entire nation to die in the attempt to repel the invaders. Obviously the army and navy zealots had prepared this even as their chiefs had been discussing Russian mediation to end the war and Hirota had been attempting to soften Mr. Malik! This was the first word that Togo had received of this matter and he was understandably upset.

Meanwhile, a meeting of the Diet had been set for June 9. The navy, particularly Admiral Yonai, thought that bringing the debating society together at this time was a mistake. The army saw it as an opportunity to whip up popular support for their battle-in-the-homeland principle and to ram through necessary laws to expedite mobilization of all civilians. Premier Suzuki went along with the army.

Obviously, the SCDW meeting was intended to spell out the policy for the nation and make it the platform from which the Diet session would operate. To Togo, this was a dangerous procedure, for to come out now with a blatant fight-to-the-death manifesto would complicate the delicate negotiations he hoped to carry on. The only breath of reality in the agenda material consisted of two background reports: "Estimate of the World Situation" and "The Present State of National Power."

Oddly enough, these contained data that were sober and relatively accurate pictures of the actual state of affairs. The second was the report prepared by Sakomizu for Premier Suzuki in April and May. But the conclusions drawn from the data by the army and navy planners were hallucinations.

Sakomizu's study opened:

The ominous turn of the war, coupled with increasing tempo of air raids, is bringing about great disruption of land and sea communications and essential war production. The food situation has worsened. It has become increasingly difficult to meet the requirements of total war. Moreover, it has become necessary to pay careful attention to the trends in public sentiment [a drastic change; among the docile Japanese slave-labor conditions in the nation and the bombings had finally aroused rumblings of discontent]. Morale is high, but there is dissatisfaction with the present regime. Criticism of the government and the military is increasing. The people are losing confidence in their leaders, and the gloomy omen of deterioration of public morale is present . . . among leading intellectuals there are some who advocate peace negotiations as a way out.

The report continued, with statistics about the inefficient use of manpower, declining birthrate, and increased infant mortality, as well as the chilling statements that "shipping is faced with insurmountable difficulties" and that shortages of materials would practically end coal, synthetic-oil, explosive, and light-metals production. It also noted that aircraft production was dropping steadily and living conditions had worsened to the point that a crisis would occur before the end of the year. Starvation symptoms had been noted in several remote parts of the nation.

Presumably drawing upon the research reports, the "Fundamental Policy" was full of patriotic exhortation and rhetorical bombast. Its central message was:

With a faith born of eternal loyalty as our inspiration, we shall—through the unity of our nation and the advantages of our terrain—prosecute the war to the bitter end in order to uphold the national polity, protect the imperial land, and assure a basis for the future development of the nation.

In outline, its four points were:

1. The army and navy will immediately prepare for a decisive battle on the homeland and will annihilate the attacking enemy forces at points where the attack will be directed.
2. Thoroughgoing diplomatic steps toward the Soviet Union will be promptly taken in order to facilitate the prosecution of the war.
3. Internal preparations will be strengthened speedily so as to have them meet the decisive battle on the homeland.
4. In putting into effect the various measures which accompany the above-mentioned items, special effort will be made for their speedy and reliable execution.

When the SCDW meeting began, Togo found himself the only person in the room willing to criticize the contents of the policy. As the presentations progressed through the morning and into the afternoon, Togo alone took issue with them.

He stuck a pin in the army and navy contention that Japan would have greater advantages as the battlefield moved closer to home. "Not so," said Togo, "when we do not have air superiority."

When Sakomizu suggested that Japan's situation might be saved by diplomacy, bringing up the horsetrade with the Soviets again, the foreign minister scored the idea. This is daydreaming, he cried. Japan's diplomacy is up against a blank wall. The Soviets are not and will not become Japan's ally.

With only silence from those who disagreed (such as Yonai) and overwhelming support from the rest of those present, the Fundamental Policy was adopted. To Togo, as to anyone with the knowledge that the Big Six had agreed three weeks before to ask the Soviets to help end the war, this result seemed like incredible hypocrisy.

Hypocrisy is a highly charged, negative term for what in positive terms is called diplomacy, tact, or, in the West, bluffing. In Japan it is called *haragei* and is perfectly acceptable. In fact, the man who employs *haragei* successfully is admired much as the man in the West who wins out in the face of huge obstacles by sheer guts. There is a certain affinity here, allowing for cultural differences.

It was perhaps *haragei* that moved Premier Suzuki to accept the Fundamental Policy with as much enthusiasm as he had shown in mid-May for peace talks with the Soviets.

It was certainly *haragei* that caused Yonai laconically to agree to the policy. He later admitted that "by early June I felt that there was absolutely no sense in continuing this [war] any longer."

And navy Chief of Staff Toyoda's report at this conference was a clear-cut example of *haragei*. He spoke to the meeting about expected enemy losses in the invasion. The first draft prepared for him by navy experts estimated Allied casualties at 20 per cent in July or 25 per cent if the invasion was in September. Toyoda, with a stroke of the pen, simply changed these figures to 30 per cent and 40 per cent; when it came his turn to speak at the SCDW he raised the figure to 50 per cent.

He explained (later):

Once the conference was underway, I suppose I must have felt like giving a round figure like "about one-half" instead of a sharp estimate like 30 per cent or 40 per cent. I may have said 50 per cent because I thought that the proposal to continue the war at all costs was as good as passed beyond reversal and that the use of pessimistic figures would not be in harmony with such a resolution. . . . The fact is that the conference decision was contrary to our true intentions. . . . Furthermore . . . there was such a crowd present that frank discussion was completely out of the question. And, as was the usual case at such meetings, there was for us no other way than to concur with extremely militant resolutions.

And to cap the militancy of the discussion, it was decided that Japan's capital should not be moved to the underground fortress in the mountains of Nagano Prefecture. The government and the Court would fight and die in Tokyo!

The following day Suzuki took the SCDW resolution into the cabinet and described the "secret weapon" Japan would use in the final battle. The weapon was to be suicide—suicide planes, suicide submarines, crash boats, human torpedoes, mines, and antitank bombs. He asked his cabinet to endorse the Fundamental Policy paper, and rubber-stamp it they did.

To put the ultimate seal on the policy, the Emperor's approval was necessary, and Suzuki chaired the Imperial Conference on June 8 for that purpose. The Big Six ran through their parts as they had on June 6, but in the presence of the Emperor their words took on heightened importance. And, though the Emperor sat attentively throughout without a word, the fact that he was there and heard all constituted the sanction of the Son of Heaven. Only matters of extreme gravity required such stratospheric endorsement.

As the fire-eating statements and wild exaggerations (Toyoda repeated his performance, too) flew from the previous participants, they were endorsed by additional conferees such as Baron Hiranuma, president of the privy council. This old extremist pressed his fellows to stamp out any and all pro-peace moves among the people.

With the background studies spelling out Japan's weakness before him, "the Emperor appeared quite disconcerted with it all," Toyoda reports. "Of course, he did not say a word, but discontent was written all over him. Under the circumstances, I could not take the discussions seriously. . . ."

Premier Suzuki, the man Hirohito and Kido had chosen to lead Japan out of the war, declared the policy adopted. Though Togo, Toyoda, and Yonai saw the impossibility of such a policy, the tragedy was that others took it absolutely seriously: the army and navy hotheads who had drafted it and the vast masses of loyal subjects of His Imperial Majesty, both in and out of uniform.

But this was not to be the last word on the Fundamental Policy.

The Emperor, telling Lord Keeper of the Privy Seal Kido about the conference afterward, showed him the research papers and the conference decisions. He was perplexed, if such a word can apply to a god, that the facts were so grave and the decision so obviously suicidal. Kido went over the papers and realized that he could no longer sit by and expect Premier Suzuki to close out the war. In his hand the privy seal held the papers that proved the old Admiral, after marking time for two months, had now set sail 180 degrees off course. He was steering the nation not to peace but into certain death. This was too much. How could apparently rational men fly in the face of the evidence this way?

Even at that moment at the premier's office building, there was a special display of weapons to be used by national service corps volunteers to repel the barbarian invaders. Featured in the exhibit were bamboo spears, bows and arrows, crossbows, knives, and farm implements. These primitive weapons were on view for the legislators, cabinet members, and bureaucrats; there could have been no more graphic illustration of how Japan's warmaking potential had regressed. While Japan's leaders seriously planned to use bamboo weapons, enemy planes floated seven miles above them almost undisturbed.

Only two weeks before, 130 B-29 bombers had set a blaze that made the hills of Tokyo flare like the head of a torch. Even the main buildings of the palace had gone up in the wind-driven flames—the pavilions of the Empress Dowager, the Emperor, the Crown Prince. And the palaces of princes Chichibu, Mikasa, Kanin, Higashikuni, Fushimi, Riken, Hashimoto, Riou, and the Aoyama palace were destroyed also. When even princes were homeless, what commoner could expect a roof and four walls?

Kido could not allow the situation to be propelled along by the ultras without counterweight. Resolved to act, he left his sovereign and trotted down the palace pathway to the household ministry building and his office. Through his mind flew these thoughts:

If the matter is left in the hands of the cabinet in the existing circumstances the war cannot be ended unless some drastic measure is taken to give the government a foothold on which to work toward peace. My policy has been to let the cabinet function as much as possible in its own right and not trouble the Emperor with governmental affairs. But since the cabinet is powerless even in this urgent situation, there is no alternative but to take action.

Though the military situation is grave, even more important is the decline of our over-all fighting strength. And two months ago the army and navy chiefs said they expected such a decline! . . . In short, our operations are a total failure. The Japanese people, therefore, have lost hope.

The privy seal then set to work and sketched out a "Tentative Plan to Cope with the Situation." In this remarkable document Marquis Kido bluntly analyzed what was to come and recommended, in all but the taboo word itself, that Japan surrender. He began by saying that the Okinawa battle was "destined to be a miserable fiasco." Reading the reports of national strength, he said, indicated that "in the latter part of this year we actually would be all but disqualified in the conduct of war on all sides."

Kido avoided any analysis of tactics or military strategy, but judged "from his air force at present and the tremendous effectiveness of his mass incendiary bombing, it would be easy [for the enemy] to sweep away by fire, one after another, all the nation's cities and towns down to the villages. He would not require much time for it, either."

If this was generally accurate, he noted, "with the cold season approaching, extreme shortages of provisions and food throughout the country during the latter part of this year and thereafter would cause serious unrest among the people at large. And, in consequence, the situation would be really past saving. Therefore, I believe it urgently called for that resolute steps should be taken under the present circumstances."

Facing up to the truly difficult questions, Kido went on:

It is well nigh certain that the enemy looks upon overthrowing the so-called "militarist clique" as his chief objective. Although I believe it is a proper course to start negotiations after the military proposes peace—and the government then drafts a formula for it—this is not only almost impossible in the present stage, considering our current condition, but, also, we are most likely to lose a good chance should we wait until the opportunity matures. As a result, we can't be sure that we won't share Germany's fate and be reduced to such circumstances that we could not even safeguard the Imperial Household and preserve the national structure.

The privy seal then swept the path in front of the Big Decision:

Although it might be very much unprecedented and it is extremely regrettable to ask for His Majesty's approval to this proposal, for which we are filled with trepidation, I believe we have no alternative but to ask the Imperial resolution for the sake of all the people and to exert our wholehearted efforts to save the war situation according to the following policy:

1. To negotiate with a mediating country with His Majesty's personal message.
2. Gist of the message: The Throne, always interested in peace, citing the Declaration of War, has decided to bring the war to a close on reasonable and realistic terms, bearing the impossible in view of heavy war damages sustained by us to date.
3. Limit of terms:
   a. Honorable peace (we could not help but restrict our demands to the minimum level).
   strong demands to be forced on us. There will be no other choice in the true sense, Japan would give up areas occupied or administered in the Pacific inasmuch as, respecting our occupied areas, it would be enough if we could help various nations and races achieve independence in their respective countries.
   c. The army and navy forces in occupied areas will evacuate on their own initiative. (It is possible that they may be forced to give up their arms on the spot; for this we will have to depend on negotiations.)
   d. Regarding armaments reduction, we must be prepared for pretty strong demands to be forced on us. There will be no other choice for us but to be contented with a minimum defense.

That was it. Kido had crossed the Rubicon, and for him there was no backward glance. Now his problem was to set his hands on the right levers and start the whole dilapidated, misdirected Japanese machine moving toward the goal of peace. His first stop was the top. As Premier Suzuki, War Minister Anami, and Navy Minister Yonai opened the emergency Diet session with more exhortations to do and die in the holy war, Kido placed his plan to surrender before the Emperor.

Hirohito was by now sick of the war and its blood-price. He foresaw annihilation for his people and a Japan drawn and quartered out of existence as a nation if she followed the military's "Fundamental Policy." He felt the direct approach was the best approach and favored going directly to the U.S. and Britain, but he thought this impossible. His advisers assured him it was. The situation in the nation and particularly the radical beliefs of his military men prevented it. These diehards looked at the Allies as enemies unto death and believed that since the Soviets were neutral it was best to negotiate through them. Hirohito knew that risking the future in the hands of the Soviets was dangerous, but he saw no alternative in the circumstances. Kido's scheme therefore, received his blessing. He was willing to issue the personal message. He told the privy seal to put the plan into effect—hoping against hope that Kido would succeed.

Kido next called Prime Minister Suzuki, but the old man was the center of a storm in the Diet and could not be reached. In his address opening the Diet session the premier had called for a volunteer service corps and said the expected: "The Japanese people have to sacrifice themselves for the sake of the Emperor." But he had also included a reference to his 1918 navy visit to the U.S. and a quotation from his San Francisco speech that if Japan and America warred they would both incur the wrath of the gods. This caused an uproar from Diet members, who considered the remarks a slur on Japan's holy war and rejected any hint that war guilt rested anywhere but with the U.S. A vigorous attack on Suzuki was whipped up, but just as quickly cooled when the war minister passed the word through his military–Diet liaison officers to cease.

After the Diet approved the new mobilization act and was set to adjourn, Suzuki flapped into the palace to obtain the Emperor's approval of the imperial message officially closing the parliamentary session. Kido saw the premier briefly and tried to tell him of his new plan, but Suzuki postponed the meeting until later that afternoon and rushed off, trailing cigar smoke.

Navy Minister Yonai called on His Majesty in the afternoon, and Kido cornered him afterward in the imperial library. Discussing ways to "save the situation," Yonai quickly and bluntly made it plain that he thought surrender was urgent. Reassured, Kido put before him the plan he had worked out and explained it. A wry expression on his face, Yonai cocked his head and asked Kido "Is that all there is to the plan?" The privy seal assured him that this was the basic outline and the Admiral said he would give it serious consideration. "But what does the prime minister think of this?" Yonai queried. "I believe that he is very strongly in favor of continuing the war."

Kido replied that he was going to discuss the plan with Suzuki later that day and would find out then.

An hour later the premier dropped anchor in Kido's office. "What business do you have with me, Mr. Lord Keeper?"

Kido explained his plan to the old navigator. Suzuki filled the room with a cloud of cigar smoke as he listened, agreed with Kido in general, then remarked "It is all very well, but I would like to think it over." As an afterthought he said "You know, it seems that the navy minister strongly favors continuing the war."

The privy seal was struck by the ludicrousness of the situation. "That is strange," he said, "since the navy minister said that you favor continuing the war and you say he is in favor of doing so. Have you ever discussed the matter between you?"

Suzuki tapped himself on the head and admitted "We have not gotten around to discussing the subject."

The following day Yonai again visited Kido. The privy seal told him Suzuki's statement. Yonai shook his head. "From what you say, it seems the premier is willing to accept your plan. Then I will talk to him personally." And he left.

On June fifteenth Foreign Minister Togo saw Kido and went over the privy seal's plan for the first time. To Togo it seemed a great hurdle had been cleared. Here was a fusing of the Emperor's sanction, Kido's energy and dedication—in short, the entire imperial establishment behind a coherent goal. "From the time I joined the cabinet I have wanted to work toward an early peace but the pro-war faction has been too powerful," sighed Togo. "And since it was decided at the Imperial Conference to war to the bitter end, I as foreign minister am powerless to do anything. I will study the points in the plan."

"Do everything in your power to speed peace and carry out a study of what type of plan is best for attaining it," Kido urged. "The Emperor's desire to end the war as early as possible is absolute and determined."

Yonai visited Kido on the sixteenth and reported that he had talked with the premier and discovered that he was generally of the opinion that the war should be ended soon. Suzuki was going to the Grand Shrine at Ise that evening to report on the Diet session and all other governmental matters to the imperial ancestors, from Emperor Taisho back to the legendary Sun Goddess Amaterasu. Yonai had urged Suzuki to concentrate on the question of ending the war and to seek from Amaterasu spiritual strength to carry it through—somewhat like Agamemnon going to the Oracle at Delphi, twentieth-century style.

On June 18 War Minister Anami came to see Kido. The General's star was clearly in the ascendant. He was universally popular in the army, and the new mobilization law would increase his importance vis-à-vis the chief of staff and army GHQ because the law would be coordinated through the war ministry. He would be in charge of mobilizing all of Japan's adult population to repel the invaders.

Resplendent in a spotless full-dress uniform, with decorations and ceremonial sword, Anami all but bounded into Kido's room, beaming and bursting with news. Joviality was his tone, and he ticked off the items on his agenda like a man in full command of his world.

There was no question about continuing the war—of course it would be fought to the last.

Though the work on the huge underground command center in the mountains of Matsushiro was on schedule, Imperial GHQ would probably not move there, since the decision to fight it out in Tokyo had been taken.

The Diet session had gone according to plan, and the new mobilization law would be pressed with all haste.

The policy toward China should be modified and a new approach to the Yenan (Communist) government must be tried. One approach to withdrawing from the Chinese fronts would be, he suggested, local truces and disengagements arranged between Japanese and Chinese commanders in the various specific areas. (This was revolutionary, for it tacitly endorsed relinquishment of Japan's conquests in China. Following the truces and disengagement, the Chinese could be expected to resume control of the areas.)

Anami had heard, he said, rumors that the lord keeper of the privy seal was thinking of resigning in the near future. Was this so?

Kido had planned to discuss with the war minister the plan he had drawn up. But Anami had forcefully taken the initiative in calling on him, in the subjects presented, and now, in this bold—or was it ingenuous?—suggestion that Kido resign, he knocked the wind out of the privy seal. But before Kido could ruminate on the matter, the war minister was back on the offensive again.

"If the present domestic situation is left alone," he warned, "the peace movement will grow strong and cause trouble."

Catching his breath, Kido made up his mind to beard the lion. "I was just about to mention the peace movement," he said. Then he explained the background of his plan, went over the points in the outline, and wound up saying "There is absolutely no hope of our winning the war."

Slowed but by no means halted, Anami puffed on a cigarette as Kido's explanation floated through the air like some gossamer creation that had as much chance of halting the war machine as a geisha's kimono flung in front of a tank. Nevertheless, the war minister recognized Kido's determination and power.

"In general, Kido-san, I agree with you. In your position it is only natural that you take this stand. We military men, however, strongly desire to execute a decisive battle on the homeland. Wouldn't it be to our advantage if peace was negotiated after we gave the enemy a terrible beating in the decisive battle?"

Kido had a house outside Tokyo near the shore, a location that was sure to be in the path of the invading armies when they made their thrust to take Tokyo. He had seen the primitive preparations for the onslaught and had received word from others who had witnessed the slow and pitiful buildup of Japanese defenses elsewhere. The privy seal was convinced that these preparations would be completed too late for the Allied strike.

"Anami," he replied, the decisive battle is hopeless. Although you may wish to fight this one last time, the Emperor is anxious because he believes it futile even to continue the war up to the point of that decisive battle. If your homeland battle is fought it will lead ultimately to scorched-earth operations and will destroy the nation."

Now pensive, Anami regarded Kido coolly. "I understand your position, Mr. Lord Keeper. Of course I will give careful consideration to your views [this could have been as much threat as promise, but Kido believed he knew the war minister's character well enough to trust him.] You know, the prime minister has called a meeting of the SCDW for 1700 hours today. My guess is that the subject of discussion will be ending the war."

"Do your best to lead the discussion to a successful conclusion," Kido entreated. Anami rose briskly, threw a token salute at the privy seal, and marched off.

The meeting of the Big Six that afternoon was significant. Just ten days after the Imperial Conference had decided there was no alternative to a back-to-the-wall fight to the death, these six key men consciously opened the door to a negotiated peace. Though Anami and the two chiefs of staff had said they wanted to smash the enemy invasion and then negotiate from a position of enhanced strength, they did not balk at starting the ball rolling. They ruled out direct talks until the decisive battle began but agreed that the time had come to approach the Soviets to mediate. And they snipped the strings they had attached earlier: they would not hold out for a Soviet nonaggression treaty or for a renewed neutrality pact. The minimum basis for peace was the preservation of the national structure—the Emperor system—and all six agreed that the target time for ending the war should be by late September. Therefore, they estimated, the USSR should be sounded out by early July.

Premier Suzuki took the news of the Big Six conference to Kido the following day. The privy seal had been preparing a report to the Emperor about the problems affecting peace negotiations, but he now went a step further. Recalling Togo's complaint that the Imperial Conference decision hamstrung him in negotiating, Kido counseled the Emperor to act. He was certain that if the Emperor merely said indirectly that he wanted peace it would run off the diehards like summer dew. Therefore, he told Hirohito, nothing would do but an Imperial Conference summoned by His Majesty in which he directly and definitely told the Supreme Council for Direction of the War that he wanted them to accelerate action for peace.

And so, on June 22, the day the enemy announced Okinawa won, the Emperor did just that. He gave his six key ministers a dose of strong medicine. "Both domestically and internationally a critical stage has been reached," Hirohito stated. "The war situation is extremely ominous, and our difficulties will become all the greater with increased air attacks. It is therefore my desire that, even though the recent decision of the Imperial Conference may be left unchanged, you exert every effort to make an end to the war with the greatest expedition. The war has already been waged for three and a half years and its havoc is becoming more severe day after day. Although it has always been important for those engaged in battle to exert their utmost, I feel that we as a nation must do something to terminate the war. Do you have any plans?"

Premier Suzuki replied. "We members of the Council have already conferred. I hereby wish to have Navy Minister Yonai explain."

But Yonai passed the ball to the foreign minister and Togo, though he had reported to His Majesty in detail just two days before on this subject, explained again. (Togo had discovered from Kido that the Emperor knew nothing about the May 11–14 Big Six discussions [nor did Kido], for Premier Suzuki had said not a word about them. This had upset Togo considerably, for it aroused suspicions that Suzuki had some unrevealed purpose. Could it be that the premier was playing some complicated stratagem? But when faced with the question, Suzuki said he simply had not gotten to it and asked Togo to explain all to the Emperor.)

Now Togo recounted the Big Six discussions and the Hirota–Malik talks, "Moreover," he said, "Ambassador Sato in Moscow has been instructed on this matter and our plans to dispatch a special envoy to Moscow are under way. However, no definite progress has yet been made."

"What have you scheduled as the date of the diplomatic settlement?" asked Hirohito. "Is there any concrete plan?"

Togo estimated that the Potsdam conference would be held in mid-July, after the British elections. "Therefore," he reported, "I am hoping to see agreement reached in early July—that is, before the Soviet leaders leave for Potsdam."

"What is the navy minister's opinion?" queried the Emperor.

Yonai endorsed Togo's report: "I believe we should push the plans in accordance with the foreign minister's report."

The Emperor asked for the war minister's opinion and Anami said "Although I have no objection to starting the effort to terminate the war, I could not approve of the plan unconditionally. I believe it is necessary to give careful consideration so as not to seem too eager for it and thus reveal our weakness."

Army Chief of Staff Umezu was called next. "The proposal to make peace," he reckoned, "being one which would have a profound impact at home and abroad, should be advanced only after thorough deliberation and should be treated with utmost caution."

Hirohito picked him up on this immediately. "Does 'treating the proposal with the utmost caution' imply acting only after having struck another blow at the enemy?" Umezu denied this, and the Emperor asked if there were any other opinions. Toyoda, the navy chief of staff, kept silent because he agreed with Yonai's statement and had nothing special to offer.

"Seeing that there is no other opinion," the Emperor said with finality, "even though the recent decision of the Imperial Conference may be left unchanged, I desire that the negotiations under the present plan be pushed."

"We shall comply with the Imperial wishes and do our utmost," Premier Suzuki responded. It was an important turning point.

Togo, however, was having trouble catching the ear of the Soviets. It was an ear that had been made deaf to Japan when Stalin, Roosevelt, and Churchill had met at Yalta and Russia had agreed to join the war against Japan three months after Germany's defeat. Of course Japan did not know of this decision, and the Soviets took great pains to deny that Japan had even been discussed at meetings of the Allied leaders.

The foreign minister prodded Koki Hirota to go after Soviet ambassador Malik again to try to get the negotiations moving. Hirota met with Malik on June 24 and tried several ploys: Japan wanted to sign a new, stronger pact with Russia to replace the neutrality pact. Malik stifled a yawn and said it was unnecessary because the neutrality pact held good until April 1946. Hirota then offered the Reds rubber, tin, lead, and tungsten in exchange for oil. The only catch was that the Russians would have to pick up the cargo in their own ships at ports in Japanese-occupied southern regions. Malik apparently showed no flicker of interest, saying simply that Russia could not help because her own supplies of oil were small.

The Japanese negotiator then proposed "If the Soviet army and the Japanese navy were to join forces, Japan and the Soviet Union together would become the strongest powers in the world." At this empty boast the Russian yawned again and said that Japan's army men might have a different opinion. Unmoved by anything Hirota said, Malik suggested that there was no future in such talks unless he had some "concrete plan" from Japan. That ended that.

On June 29 Hirota, armed with written proposals, called again on the Soviet ambassador. The *quid pro quo* was spelled out. In exchange for a new nonaggression treaty with Japan, she would free Manchuria, drop her fishing rights in Soviet waters in exchange for Soviet oil, and discuss anything else Russia wished to bring up. Malik asked if it was true that Japan and the U.S. were negotiating for peace through Sweden. Taken aback, Hirota gasped "That's impossible! Japan would consult Russia before attempting negotiations anywhere else." To Hirota's relief, Malik agreed to forward the proposals to Moscow and continue talks when the reply came back.

But when Togo found out, the next day, that the Soviet ambassador had sent the proposal by a courier (who would take days to deliver the message) instead of by cable, he gave up hope of negotiations through Malik. Now he turned to the only practical possibility left: dispatch of a special envoy to Moscow.

Time was now closing in. The Potsdam conference of the Allies was expected in the third week of July, and it was now the end of June. There is no satisfactory explanation for the delay that followed. Togo on July 2 called on Prince Takamatsu and reported that Japan's desperate military situation meant an early peace was necessary. He told the Prince that both army and navy were strongly in favor and that there appeared no alternative to Russian mediation, for which a special envoy was necessary. Takamatsu was not surprised. Admiral Yonai had told him the same things. Togo suggested Prince Konoye for the mission, and Takamatsu approved. The foreign minister then talked to Suzuki about Konoye for the mission and Suzuki also agreed.

Meanwhile, as Japan's cities were converted to ashes in the wake of the enemy bombers day and night, the Emperor became more and more apprehensive. On July 7 he summoned the prime minister and asked him about negotiations with the Soviets. Suzuki reported the Hirota–Malik stalemate, and His Majesty pushed him beyond that. The agreement had been that Japan would first sound out Soviet intentions before asking her good offices. Now the Emperor told Suzuki he thought it was timely to call directly on Russia to act as intermediary, without going through Malik. "Therefore," he said, "we had better arrange to dispatch an envoy with the imperial message." The old Admiral told the Emperor that Togo was even then on his way to sound out Prince Konoye about this very thing.

In Togo's assessment of it, the man who took this assignment would be taking his life in his hands. It couldn't be kept secret from the military, for the envoy and his party would have to travel by air to Moscow, and that would mean using a Japanese military plane and landing in Korea, China, or Manchuria before crossing to Soviet soil.

So from takeoff until they arrived in the USSR, the peacemakers would be easy targets for military extremists.

Togo thought it only fair to discuss the mission and its perils with the man he had decided to nominate, Prince Fumimaro Konoye. Sad-eyed and shrewd, effete and articulate, Konoye had served as prime minister three times before the Pacific War began.

On July 8, 1945, Foreign Minister Togo went to the Prince's summer place in the mountain resort of Karuizawa and sounded him out on the mission. Captivated, Konoye accepted, with a typical proviso: that he would be embarrassed if limited by too rigid instructions. "Try for anything short of unconditional surrender," replied the foreign minister. Konoye agreed.

On July 10 the SCDW met and Premier Suzuki and Foreign Minister Togo briefed them about the developments. But not until the twelfth did the Emperor receive Konoye and ask him officially to head the mission.

At about the time this *tête-a-tête* was taking place, Japan's ambassador to the USSR, Naotake Sato, was reading a cable sent by Togo that morning. It was perhaps the most important Japanese message of the war. The foreign minister bluntly stated:

His Majesty is extremely anxious to terminate the war as soon as possible, being deeply concerned that the further continuation of hostilities will only aggravate the untold miseries of the teeming millions, innocent men and women, of the countries at war. Should, however, the United States and Great Britain insist on unconditional surrender, Japan would be forced to fight to the bitter end with all her might in order to vindicate her honor and safeguard her national existence, which, to our intense regret, would entail further bloodshed. Our government therefore desires to negotiate for a speedy restoration of peace, prompted as we sincerely are by solicitude for the welfare of mankind. For this purpose Prince Konoye will proceed to Moscow with the personal message of the Emperor and it is requested that the Soviet government be good enough to accord travel facilities to him.

For months Sato had been cabling Tokyo reports on the Allied crushing of Germany and the shift of Soviet troops to Siberia. He had sent reasoned, sober dispatches describing the inevitable doom Japan faced unless she sought peace before it was too late. For his trouble, Sato was thought an appeaser and labeled unreliable by the extremists. Togo, who was pressed to replace Sato, resisted. He trusted the man and was able to fend off the military's demands by telling them that no one else who was experienced could be sent (Togo had asked Hirota to go, but he refused) and the post was too important to leave vacant for even a short time.

On the desk of the Secretary of State in Washington, D.C., a few hours later, the black folder of top-secret war and foreign information was placed. In it was the translation of Togo's note to Sato. The U.S. had broken the Japanese code before the war, and from the pre-Pearl Harbor negotiations down to the surrender messages, the highest echelon of American officials had an inside view of what the Japanese were telling and hearing from their overseas representatives.

At this critical time, just five days before the Potsdam conference was to begin, American leaders were given this flash of insight into the major hurdles holding off Japan's surrender on the authority of the Emperor himself, as transmitted by his foreign minister. This should have been sufficient to bring about a crash program by the U.S. to end the war. Instead, plans and preparations for the Potsdam conference proceeded as scheduled and other efforts went ahead on a "war as usual" basis.

In Moscow, Stalin and Molotov were preparing for their triumphal trip to Berlin. They were already anticipating the spoils, and were moving with all haste to prepare their attack on Japan's Manchurian and Korean territories. Thus when Ambassador Sato tried to deliver Togo's message he was shunted to the vice-commissar for foreign affairs, Lozovsky.

On July 13 Sato called on Lozovsky and asked permission for a special envoy to be received. Sato stated that a letter from the Emperor would be presented and asked Soviet cooperation in picking up the Prince in an aircraft sent to Manchouli or Tsitsihar in China. Only one thing was omitted by Sato—the most important point—that Japan was seeking Soviet mediation of the war's end.

Lozovsky was polite. He listened carefully and took notes. And he assured the Japanese ambassador that it was impossible to give an aye or nay even in principle to the request since both Molotov and Stalin were about to leave for Germany. He promised to reach the two leaders at their Berlin headquarters when they arrived. Sato requested a reply with all possible speed so that arrangements could be made for the mission. Lozovsky agreed, he would give Molotov the papers the ambassador handed him. These were the Russian translation of the Emperor's wishes, as Togo had relayed them, and a letter from Sato to Molotov explaining the special mission. With that, Sato left, hoping against logic that the response would be quick and favorable.

But it was not until July 18, the day after Churchill, Truman, and Stalin met at Potsdam, that word came to Sato. It was a letter from Molotov's deputy, a put-off: There were no concrete proposals in Togo's message and the purpose of the special mission was not clear to the Soviets. Just what was its aim? The USSR could not really say yes, no, or maybe to either the message or the request to receive a special envoy.

Sato cabled this reply to Togo, and on July 24 was told to inform the Russians that Prince Konoye would be the Emperor's special representative and would ask the Soviets to mediate to end the war. The specifics would be outlined by the Prince himself. Later that day Togo sent a postscript to Sato: above all, Japan could not accept unconditional surrender. The Yamato race would be forced to fight on as one man if this enemy demand remained. Because the Emperor wished it, Japan wanted to enlist Soviet aid to end the war on better terms. And a rapprochement with Russia was desired, giving due consideration to her needs and requirements in the Far East.

Togo was hamstrung by the military. He could not spell out specific conditions which, if met by the enemy, would end the war. The military would not hear of this, nor would it suffer any hint that mediation was requested because Japan's armed forces were defeated. The best the foreign minister could do was to identify Konoye, make sure the Soviets understood he was the spokesman of the Emperor and would be empowered to negotiate an end to the war.

Sato called on Lozovsky the next day, July 25. The Big Three were still in session at Potsdam, and Sato pressed on the commissar the importance of procuring a quick reply from Molotov on the Konoye mission as newly defined. Lozovsky promised immediate action. Instead, the next word received by Tokyo—and the world—was the proclamation issued on July 26 by the United States, Britain, and China.

At 6 A.M. on the twenty-sixth Japanese listening posts picked up the San Francisco broadcast of the Potsdam declaration. The historic document, whose opening paragraphs included many phrases written by movie-actor-in-uniform Douglas Fairbanks, Jr., had been largely prepared by Secretary of War Stimson and Eugene Dooman, Joseph Grew, and James Byrnes of the State Department. It had almost been issued in May. Now, dusted off and refurbished, it was to Japanese peace advocates a new and hopeful element in the steadily worsening war picture:

We—the President of the United States, the President of the National Government of the Republic of China, and the Prime Minister of Great Britain, representing the hundreds of millions of our countrymen, have conferred and agree that Japan shall be given an opportunity to end this war.

The prodigious land, sea and air forces of the United States, the British Empire and of China, many times reinforced by their armies and air fleets from the west, are poised to strike the final blows upon Japan. This military power is sustained and inspired by the determination of all the Allied Nations to prosecute the war against Japan until she ceases to resist.

The result of the futile and senseless German resistance to the might of the aroused free peoples of the world stands forth in awful clarity as an example to the people of Japan. The might that now converges on Japan is immeasurably greater than that which, when applied to the resisting Nazis, necessarily laid waste to the lands, the industry and the method of life of the whole German people. The full application of our military power, backed by our resolve, *will* mean the inevitable and complete destruction of the Japanese armed forces and just as inevitably the utter devastation of the Japanese homeland.

The time has come for Japan to decide whether she will continue to be controlled by those self-willed militaristic advisers whose unintelligent calculations have brought the Empire of Japan to the threshold of annihilation, or whether she will follow the path of reason.

Following are our terms. We will not deviate from them. There are no alternatives. We shall brook no delay.

There must be eliminated for all time the authority and influence of those who have deceived and misled the people of Japan into embarking on world conquest, for we insist that a new order of peace, security and justice will be impossible until irresponsible militarism is driven from the world.

Until such a new order is established *and* until there is convincing proof that Japan's war-making power is destroyed, points in Japanese territory to be designated by the Allies shall be occupied to secure the achievement of the basic objectives we are here setting forth.

The terms of the Cairo Declaration shall be carried out and Japanese sovereignty shall be limited to the islands of Honshu, Hokkaido, Kyushu, Shikoku and such minor islands as we determine.

The Japanese military forces, after being completely disarmed, shall be permitted to return to their homes with the opportunity to lead peaceful and productive lives.

We do not intend that the Japanese shall be enslaved as a race or destroyed as a nation, but stern justice shall be meted out to all war criminals, including those who have visited cruelties upon our prisoners. The Japanese Government shall remove all obstacles to the revival and strengthening of democratic tendencies among the Japanese people. Freedom of speech, of religion, and of thought, as well as respect for the fundamental human rights, shall be established.

Japan shall be permitted to maintain such industries as will sustain her economy and permit the exaction of just reparations in kind, but not those which would enable her to rearm for war. To this end, access to, as distinguished from control of, raw materials shall be permitted. Eventual Japanese participation in world trade relations shall be permitted.

The occupying forces of the Allies shall be withdrawn from Japan as soon as these objectives have been accomplished and there has been established in accordance with the freely expressed will of the Japanese people a peacefully inclined and responsible government.

We call upon the government of Japan to proclaim now the unconditional surrender of all Japanese armed forces, and to provide proper and adequate assurances of their good faith in such action. The alternative for Japan is prompt and utter destruction.

Chapter 12

Extravagant Fumble

Japan's morning papers on Saturday, July 28, carried the Potsdam declaration as expurgated by the Information Board. They also quoted Premier Suzuki as saying that Japan would *"mokusatsu"* the Allied demands.

The prime minister had said this in the cabinet meeting the day before. An argument had developed between the military and Foreign Minister Togo over releasing the Potsdam proclamation to the public. General Anami had urged that the government promptly denounce the Allied ultimatum and reject it as unacceptable. Togo jumped on this, saying it would be a dangerous mistake.

Suzuki had put aside his cigar long enough to agree with Togo and say "the government should simply *mokusatsu* the declaration." By this he meant to shelve it, or "take no notice of it." The somewhat archaic term that he chose can be interpreted as "ignore by keeping silence," "take no notice of," or "treat with silent contempt." Suzuki was trying to forestall further demands by the military for an official denunciation of the Potsdam terms.

The cabinet had finally agreed that the people should be told the contents of the Potsdam declaration before they heard about them in distorted fashion from other sources. Of course, the ministers insisted, certain judicious deletions would be necessary to prevent damage to morale. So, in the Information Board's trimming of the declaration, the most threatening portions were dropped out. Gone, for instance, were the words about "utter destruction of the Japanese homeland," the "stern justice" for war criminals, and such phrases as "self-willed militaristic advisers." The net effect was a more moderate and attractive enemy statement than the original! To this the peace advocates, Togo, and the Court obviously had no objections. But Togo was incensed when he discovered that War Minister Anami was pressing the Information Board to have newspapers interpret Suzuki's statement as "reject by ignoring" and had even induced the head of the Board, Dr. Shimomura, to speak on the radio interpreting the Potsdam terms negatively and Suzuki's statement as a rejection. The foreign minister tried to stop Anami's activities, with only partial success.

Somehow Premier Suzuki's words about the Potsdam declaration wound up in the hands of news editors that evening of July 27. We do not know to this day exactly by what route—whether cabinet secretary Sakomizu or Information Board chief Shimomura released them, whether Suzuki himself approved the release after the cabinet meeting adjourned, or whether the cabinet as an afterthought decided to approve release of Suzuki's statement.

In any event, the morning papers on Saturday July 28 carried the expurgated version of the Potsdam declaration and also quoted the premier, that Japan would *mokusatsu* the Allied demands. *Asahi Shimbun* that day spelled out its interpretation: "Since the joint declaration of America, Britain, and Chungking is a thing of no great value it will only serve to re-enhance the government's resolve to carry the war forward unfalteringly to a successful conclusion!" *Mainichi* put the heading LAUGHABLE MATTER over the proclamation, though it refrained from excoriating the ultimatum. Other newspapers treated it similarly, discounting it but running the full censored text.

The regular weekly meeting of government leaders and the Supreme Command at the palace that Saturday morning revolved around this issue. Togo was not present—he had urgent business back at *Gaimusho*—and when the premier sat down with the army and navy chiefs and their top political officers, the military demanded that the Potsdam declaration be rejected publicly, promptly, and powerfully. Caught in the middle, Suzuki couldn't say yes, couldn't say no. If he agreed to reject the Allied terms it might cause some unforeseen retaliation by the enemy—the declaration threatened overwhelming force if the terms were not accepted quickly. And it might push the Soviets off the fence and into the war against Japan. Yet if Suzuki refused to reject the Potsdam terms, the army and navy hotheads would be incensed and might decide to take the law and the government into their own hands.

To deal with this quandary, Suzuki called the leaders into another room to grapple with this hot potato. The absence of Togo gave the warhawks a decided edge over the malleable Suzuki. They pressed the premier to disavow the Potsdam proclamation specifically and unequivocally, but the old man held back. Sakomizu threw a compromise suggestion into the hopper: Since a news conference was scheduled that day, it gave an opportunity for the premier to respond to a question about the Potsdam terms without making a formal government pronouncement. This device was agreed upon, leaving only one crucial question: What should Suzuki say when the "planted" question was tossed at him?

Sakomizu and the political affairs chiefs of the army and navy, Lieutenant General Yoshizumi and Vice-Admiral Hoshina, were instructed to come up with the requisite statement. Sakomizu found it a nightmare. He fashioned first one comment, then another. But no matter what he wrote, he "was compelled to revise it over and over again by the stout opposition of the chiefs, especially Yoshizumi, the Bureau of Military Affairs chief. Every correction gave birth to a stronger expression."

There was more pulling and hauling over this matter, but finally, in haste and desperation, they agreed on a response that would tell the Japanese people and the world at large that the Potsdam declaration was being neither clasped to the bosom nor spurned. The statement Sakomizu and his army and navy co-authors wrote said "The Potsdam declaration is only an adaptation of the Cairo declaration and our government will place no importance on it. In short, we will *mokusatsu* that."

"The last point of our dispute," says Sakomizu, "was whether 'much' should be placed before 'importance' or whether 'for the present' should be after *mokusatsu*. In the end, I was argued down and I could not help but agree that these words should not be added." History might have been different if Sakomizu and his chief, Suzuki, had not been so amenable. The addition of "for the present" after the word *mokusatsu* would have clarified it and would have made it apparent that the Potsdam terms were still under consideration—not rejected.

But the nub of the statement was the word *mokusatsu*, and it was on this that Sakomizu should have spent more effort. "As to the use of *mokusatsu*," the cabinet secretary tells us, "I intended to mean 'no comment.' "

Back at the premier's *kantei*, the statement was put into Admiral Suzuki's hands and at 4 P.M. the scheduled press conference began. There were questions about government measures to counter enemy air raids and bombardment from enemy warships and a query about the recent 10-per-cent cut in food rations. Suzuki's reply in each case amounted to a plea to his people to "endure what is otherwise unendurable." Then, as planned, this exchange took place:

Question: Recently the enemy powers have been making various kinds of propaganda about terminating the war. What is your opinion about this?

Answer: I think that the joint declaration by the three powers is nothing but a repetition of the Cairo declaration. The government does not see much value in it. All we have to do is *mokusatsu* it. What we should do is devote ourselves to the prosecution of the war.

Suzuki's use of *mokusatsu* and the handling of it by the Japanese press closed the hinge of doom on scores of thousands of his countrymen. This one ill-chosen word provided the enemy the needed excuse to unleash all possible power against Nippon.

When the premier's statement reached editorial desks at Japan's newspapers the crucial word *mokusatsu* was rendered "ignore." At the news editors' desk at Domei, the overseas voice of Japan, it was translated into foreign languages and broadcast "ignore." Domei's broadcast in English was picked up and quoted within hours by American radio and newspapers which headlined the news JAPAN REJECTS POTSDAM DECLARATION. It was this "rejection" that President Harry Truman cited when he said: "It was to spare the Japanese from utter destruction that the ultimatum of July 26 was issued at Potsdam. Their leaders promptly rejected that ultimatum."

Thus the pressure of the military and Suzuki's clumsy handling of the Potsdam declaration gave the Allies their justification for sending the B–29 Enola Gay on its fateful atomic-bomb mission August 6. And it was *mokusatsu* that gave the Soviets their technical excuse for smashing into Manchuria on August 9.

In Tokyo, the early hours of July 28 were typically summery—there was a high haze and the promise of another hot, sultry day.

Some astute sections of the public spotted the significance of the Potsdam declaration. The Japanese stock exchange was moribund because there was so little activity. Now, after the Potsdam terms appeared in the press, there suddenly was trading in the long-dormant stocks of such consumer products as textiles, tobacco, paper, and beer. On August 2 the exchange kicked up an average rise of three points. Apparently some businessmen were betting that peace was approaching.

Now in Japan a lull began, a curious period of inaction during which all eyes were focused on the USSR. Togo cabled Sato but otherwise marked time. Kido explained:

Even though the Potsdam declaration was announced, a request had been made to the Soviet Union to mediate. We expected the Soviets would give us a reply when Molotov and Stalin returned to Moscow. Moreover, the Soviets were not signatory to the Potsdam declaration and therefore questions were pending, such as what kind of reply would be given by the Soviet government, what sort of mediation action the Soviets would take, and what the outcome would be. Since the whole nation was awaiting the Soviet Union's reply we just could not rush and accept the Potsdam declaration. Accordingly, there was no move to accept it. The Imperial court left the matter to the cabinet.

At Court there was an other-worldliness during the days following the Potsdam declaration. On the last day of July, for instance, Hirohito talked at length with Privy Seal Kido about moving the sacred treasures from the Atsuta Shrine to a safer place.

Togo pressed Sato in Moscow to pry a reply from the Soviets about the Konoye mission. Sato did his best, urging Lozovsky to request action on the matter. But the Russian dawdled, stating that it would have to wait until Molotov returned from Potsdam. Not until August 5 was Sato given a firm appointment with Molotov, who just that day had arrived back in Moscow. The appointment was set for 11 P.M. (Japan time) August 8.

Numb with speculation about the Soviet response, Japan prepared for the expected Allied invasion while her cities went up in flames. So helpless was she that the enemy boldly began "advance-notice" bombing. Leaflets were dropped on cities that were destined to be targets days before they were scheduled to be hit. The leaflets urged civilians to evacuate before the fire-bomb deluge. As threatened, the Allied bombers followed up with inexorable efficiency, day or night, storm or shine, proving to even the most unschooled observer that Japan's military power was incapable of protecting her people at home and at work.

When one or two enemy planes kited high above a city, the Japanese ignored them. Terror came with the flocks of fire-bombers, not with the occasional observation and photography aircraft.

In Hiroshima there was an early air-raid warning on August 6. But the bombers were destined elsewhere and the "charmed city" went back to its business even before the all-clear that morning. The city was one of the largest that remained relatively unscathed by war. Rumors had it that Hiroshima had been spared because so many of its citizens had relatives in the States. By 8:15 A.M. on the sixth the townspeople were busy with their chores, with breakfast, or hustling to their factory work. And on the huge parade ground in the center of the city, Western District Army soldiers were doing their morning calisthenics.

At eight fifteen the brilliant flash, the fireball, the smashing concussion, incinerating heat, and engulfing whirlwind of the first atomic bomb obliterated the city of Hiroshima on Japan's Inland Sea. The industrial metropolis of 400,000 population became instantly a Stone Age crematorium for 80,000 persons. Some 37,000 additional civilians were injured and 90 per cent of the buildings in the area were destroyed. The atomic age burst on the world as an all-consuming dragon of fire.

Faced now with a revolution in warfare that made their inadequate, outmoded conventional weapons even more hopeless, by every application of Western logic, the Japanese should have thrown in the towel and surrendered immediately. They did not. Why?

Some of the leaders, for various reasons, were not willing to admit the Hiroshima bombing was atomic. The army, for instance, resisted this conclusion and insisted that an investigation was necessary to determine the nature of the bomb. But the investigation was conducted in such a haphazard, lethargic manner that it was not completed until after Nagasaki was blasted three days later. Army leaders preferred to fight a bloody final battle with the enemy on the homeland rather than admit the Allies had a weapon unheard of in the annals of warfare.

The navy response was, at the lower echelons and among the diehards, almost identical to the army's. The navy investigation did not even begin until two days after the Hiroshima bombing and was not completed until August 12. But at the top, the navy knew and admitted the nature of the bomb. Sometime on August 6 Admiral Yonai, the navy minister, scrawled an ultra-top-secret memo that read "Hiroshima destroyed by atomic weapon. This war is lost." The Japanese reaction to the bomb is a study in confusion, distraction, and obfuscation.

General Seizo Arisue, chief of army intelligence, tells what Tokyo observed at that time: "At 0816 the Tokyo control operator of the Japan Broadcasting Corporation noticed that the Hiroshima station had gone off the air. About twenty minutes later the Tokyo railway telegraph center realized that the main telegraph had stopped working just north of Hiroshima. From some railway stops within ten miles of the city there came unofficial and confused reports of a terrible explosion in Hiroshima. . . ."

Military headquarters repeatedly tried to call the army control station at Hiroshima, but the complete silence from the city puzzled the men at GHQ. They knew that no large enemy raid could have occurred, and they knew that no sizable store of explosives was in Hiroshima at that time.

"A young officer of the Japanese General Staff was instructed to fly immediately to Hiroshima, to land, survey the damage, and return to Tokyo with reliable information. It was generally felt at headquarters that nothing serious had taken place, that it was all a terrible rumor starting from a few sparks of truth.

"The staff officer took off . . . and after flying for about three hours, while still nearly 100 miles from Hiroshima, he and his pilot saw a great cloud of smoke. In the bright afternoon, the remains of Hiroshima were burning. They landed their plane south of the city and the staff officer after reporting to Tokyo immediately began to organize relief measures."

About this time Togo's lieutenants reached him with word of an American broadcast announcing that an atomic bomb had been dropped on Hiroshima. The Allied leaders were threatening to use this weapon until Japan was annihilated if she did not surrender quickly. Togo immediately demanded the facts from the army leaders. It was, he believed, a violation of the international laws of warfare, if true. The foreign minister's concern was to fire off a protest against use of this devastating weapon.

The army authorities replied that an investigation was under way, but at the moment they knew only that there had been a bomb dropped and it had been highly effective. They said it might actually have been an extraordinarily destructive conventional bomb, and that the evidence must be examined more closely. Togo prodded them to hurry because, as he put it, "foreign countries are attaching great importance to the new development."

A report had come in about noon from the Domei correspondent near Hiroshima, but the degree of destruction was unclear.

Kempeitai headquarters through its own communications network had received word the afternoon of August 6 that a small number of bombers had turned Hiroshima into a sea of flame. This word was passed on to the war ministry chiefs, who sat on it. Later in the day a district official reported that the city had suffered incredible damage in an attack by "a small number of enemy planes" and something that might be "an entirely new-type bomb." However, the most terrifying notice was one that roused General Kawabe, the army vice-chief of staff, at dawn the following day: "The whole city of Hiroshima was destroyed instantly by a single bomb."

Kawabe was one of the few Japanese army men familiar with Japanese atomic research. Actually, the military had ridiculed a request for 50,000 yen for atomic research some years before and accused the scientists of wild-eyed dreaming. They changed their minds, Saburo Hayashi says in his book *Kogun,* "only when Dr. Odan and two buildings, including his laboratory, exploded before their very eyes." But then it was too late: at that stage Japan had neither the money, the resources, nor the technological ability to gamble on an atomic weapon.

General Kawabe sent an officer from the army's Aeronautical Department to call on Japan's leading physicist, Dr. Yoshio Nishina. The officer told the professor that a bomb had been dropped on

Hiroshima causing heavy damage and there was speculation that it was an atomic bomb. Would Nishina go to Hiroshima with an army investigation group? The professor, director of the Science Research Institute, agreed and as the two men were about to leave a Domei news reporter arrived. He wanted Nishina's comment on President Truman's announcement that the Hiroshima bomb had been atomic and had the destructive power of twenty thousand tons of TNT. This coincided with calculations that Nishina had worked out years before when he was doing theoretical work on atomic energy. It tended to corroborate the claim.

Nishina and the army officer drove to Ichigaya Heights, the army GHQ, and were briefed on the mission, then went by car to the airfield at Tokorozawa, where a band of army technical experts and the physicist boarded two planes and took off for the bombed city. Engine trouble forced Nishina's plane to turn back, but the other, carrying General Arisue, arrived after a detour around an enemy bombing raid on Osaka en route. Arisue found "the entire city was practically leveled . . . there was but one black dead tree, as if a crow was perched on it. There was nothing but for that tree. . . . As we landed at the airport all the grass was red . . . as if toasted. The officer in charge came toward us. His face was burned on one side but not the other. He told us 'everything which is exposed gets burned, but anything which is covered even slightly can escape burns. Therefore it cannot be said that there are no countermeasures.' "

Hiroshima's transportation system was wiped out, so Arisue went by boat to the Ujina Shipping Command, where he wrote his report to GHQ by candlelight. It had three main conclusions: (1) A special bomb was used; (2) burns can be prevented by covering the body; (3) rumor has it that the same kind of bomb will be dropped on Tokyo August 12. Arisue handed the report to the local commander and asked that it be sent immediately. The following morning after breakfast he discovered that his dispatch was still there, unsent. He raised hell and the message was sent over the radio, so it was the morning of August 8 that GHQ had its first on-the-spot confirmation of the catastrophe.

Not until Professor Nishina and his group arrived at four that afternoon had an expert eye assessed the Hiroshima landscape. The physicist looked at the city from the air and decided at a glance that "nothing but an atomic bomb could have done such damage." His on-the-ground investigation calculated from melted roof tiles that ground heat reached 2000 degrees centigrade—unheard of from conventional bombs. Other observations confirmed the atomic nature of the blast and Nishina reported this to army GHQ.

On the eighth Marshal Hata, the commander of the Western District Army, with headquarters in Hiroshima, sent in his report on the devastation. The burns suffered by those wearing white clothing were light and those in shelters had relatively light burns. Most important, said Hata, the bomb exploded about 8 A.M., a time when many households were using fire to prepare breakfast. This, he concluded, probably accounted for the widespread fire and burns reported.

It was also on the eighth that the navy sent the chief of its Osaka garrison to call on Osaka University physicist Professor Asada. The professor lived in nearby Kobe and had narrowly escaped death the morning of August 6 when a conventional air raid struck that area at 2 A.M. His house was completely burned. About noon he was standing in the smoking ruins, absent-mindedly picking at the debris when a man carrying a portable radio stopped and told him that some special-type bomb had been dropped on Hiroshima, damaging it severely. The admiral who called on Asada two days later told him the enemy claimed it was an atomic bomb and asked him to investigate the blast for the navy.

Dr. Asada agreed, and because his clothes had gone up in flames, he was issued shoes, baggy pants, and knapsack as his navy "uniform." He built a Geiger counter and other technical equipment to test radioactivity in the city, and with three navy officers and a crew of ten seamen carrying instruments and food set out for the lost city at 10:30 P.M. on the ninth. They traveled by night purposely, to avoid the bombing and strafing that struck most trains by day. Even so, they were delayed three hours en route by an air raid on a town.

Privy Seal Kido hurried to Hirohito on August 6 with word of the new calamity. He was received by the Emperor within an hour after the attack, and, at Kido's word that Hiroshima had been struck with a new-type weapon that had wiped out scores of thousands of men, women, and children and laid waste the city, the god reacted as a man. "He was," says Kido, "overwhelmed with grief for the innocent civilians who were victims."

"Under these circumstances," said Hirohito gravely, "we must bow to the inevitable. No matter what happens to my safety, we must put an end to this war as speedily as possible so that this tragedy will not be repeated."

The sketchy information that arrived August 7 merely increased the horror. The enemy continued to broadcast news about the atom bomb and Japan's leaders were almost persuaded that it was not propaganda but the truth. Kido heard that 130,000 had been killed or injured. The army and navy still contended officially that the matter was being investigated.

When the cabinet met that same afternoon, Togo took the initiative and quoted American radio reports that Hiroshima was destroyed by an atomic bomb, that this new weapon would revolutionize warfare, and that more bombs would be used on Japan unless she sued for peace. Discounting the propaganda exaggeration, Togo told his cabinet colleagues that this weapon "drastically alters the whole military situation and offers the military ample grounds for ending the war."

Togo meant that with the introduction of this "ultimate" weapon the military leaders had a face-saving device that would allow them to quit. Pointing at the atomic bomb they could say that "against this revolutionary power further resistance was impossible and foolhardy, and so, though they were willing as always to sacrifice their lives, for the survival of the nation they were forced to recommend ending the war." But the military were not willing to follow this path.

The foreign minister prodded the cabinet to consider a peace move based on the Potsdam declaration. Not only did the other ministers not support the idea, War Minister Anami rejected it outright. "Any such move is uncalled for," he persisted. "Furthermore, we do not yet know if the bomb was atomic. Until the investigation reports are received, we must not take any impetuous action." Togo instantly deduced that the army planned to minimize the effects of the bombing and deny that it now faced an atomic weapon.

Home Minister Abe, to whom all the nation's civilian policemen reported, outlined the meager information so far available from Hiroshima through the police organization. "In short," he said, "an unknown type of bomb, completely different from known types, hit Hiroshima. It killed a tremendous number of citizens and destroyed almost all buildings. Hiroshima was completely devastated."

In spite of the growing evidence that drastic action was required, the cabinet adjourned without meeting the challenge. The leaders of Japan decided to do nothing.

Wednesday, August 8, began with "fine weather," according to Privy Seal Kido's diary. At 10:20 Shigemitsu, the former foreign minister, called on his friend in the imperial household building. Kido welcomed the call, for he needed to talk to a solid-thinking citizen at this point. They discussed the atom bombing and its implications, and Shigemitsu again returned to his perennial theme: the Emperor must now order an end to the war. How to do so and make it stick was the question.

Togo had an audience with Hirohito that afternoon, after an air-raid alarm had sent the palace staff and the Emperor himself scurrying into the bomb shelters. In the shelter Togo brought his sovereign up to date on enemy announcements about the atomic bomb, and counseled that it was absolutely imperative now that the war be ended. Hirohito, weary of the floundering, ineffectual efforts toward peace that had so far netted nothing but increasing misery, endorsed Togo's view.

"Furthermore," Hirohito warned, "since the nation can no longer continue the struggle with this weapon opposing it, Japan should not miss the chance for peace by vain efforts to secure better terms. There is little hope of bargaining for more favorable conditions now; therefore all efforts should be concentrated on ending the fighting quickly. Tell the prime minister my thinking," he concluded.

Togo stopped in to see Kido and summarize the Emperor's statement, then hurried on to corner the premier. Admiral Suzuki was "pacing the quarter deck" in his official office. Suzuki listened attentively to Togo's recitation of the Emperor's thoughts. He called cabinet secretary Sakomizu in when Togo demanded an immediate meeting of the Supreme Council for Direction of the War. Sakomizu telephoned the rest of the Big Six, only to find that not all of the military leaders would be available until the following morning. A meeting was set for 10:30 A.M. in the bomb shelter of the premier's office building.

As time trickled on, Ambassador Sato in Moscow at long last received his appointment with Foreign Commissar Molotov. Finally, he believed, the Soviets were ready to respond to the Emperor's request for the Konoye mission to be admitted to Russia. Dapper and smiling, Sato advanced into Molotov's office precisely at the appointed time. Drawing on his limited Russian vocabulary, Sato greeted Molotov warmly on his return from Potsdam. But Molotov cut him short and waved him to a chair. Then he told Sato that he had an important communiqué to deliver to him, and read a proclamation of war, to begin at midnight that night.

The Japanese ambassador suppressed his immediate reactions and calmly pointed out that the neutrality pact between the two nations was still alive and, supposedly, effective. Sato asked Molotov's assurance that during the next six hours, before war commenced, he would be able to use his diplomatic privileges to cable Tokyo about the communiqué. "Naturally," Molotov replied, "you have liberty to do so. Not only that but you can wire in code."

Sato, a gentleman and diplomat to the last, stood. "I have been ambassador to your country for the past three years in the midst of war. . . . I am grateful for the goodwill and hospitality of your government which has enabled me to stay in Moscow during this difficult time. It is indeed a sad thing that we shall have to part as enemies. But this cannot be helped. I wish to part with you after a handshake, which may be the last one."

Grasping Sato's hand, Molotov responded "I, as well as my government . . . especially appreciate your efforts which have enabled us to maintain the good, friendly relations between our countries until today. Now I wish to say goodbye." They parted.

How much of this touching scene was cynical irony on Molotov's part cannot be accurately judged. One indication is the fact that Sato's cable to Tokyo, with its message of the Soviet declaration of war, never arrived in Japan. In fact, Tokyo's last word from its ambassador was an earlier message that he was to see Molotov and discuss the Konoye mission at 6 P.M. Moscow time.

Japan's next word from Moscow was delivered in unmistakable language across the Manchurian–Siberian border from the muzzles of countless Soviet guns.

Chapter 13

The Tigers Learn the Truth

By the morning of August 10 career diplomat Shunichi Matsumoto, Togo's second in command in the foreign ministry, had been on deck more than twenty-four hours. He had just supervised sending the surrender messages to Japan's ministers in Switzerland and Sweden for transmission to the Allies. Matsumoto, who had been Japan's ambassador to Indochina until Togo had pulled him back to Tokyo to be vice-minister, was convinced that Japan's war prospects were hopeless and was inexpressibly relieved that at last the holocaust was going to end.

Stocky, gregarious, effervescent, and energetic, he was all the things Togo was not: personable, humorous, colloquial, open, and friendly. But his thinking mirrored Togo's; they agreed completely on the necessity of surrender, and quickly. The telegrams just sent would, Matsumoto thought, end the war in short order.

Wearily he chugged out of the *Gaimusho* offices, hopped into his limousine, and was driven to his temporary official residence at Reinanzaka near the old U.S. Embassy and not far from Kido's place in Akasaka. As he swung through the door into the Western-style house there was only one thing on his mind: sleep. Completely fatigued, he tossed jacket and tie onto a chair and hurled himself onto his bed. Still wearing his shoes, he was just on the threshold of sleep when the maid came to the door.

"General Yoshizumi is here to see you."

Starting from his presleep reverie, the vice-minister thought crossly, "Why did that nuisance come here?" He put on his tie and went to the parlor, where the army's political hatchetman was waiting for him. Yoshizumi looked mild enough, and in private life was known to be a gentle and pleasant person. But officially he was chief of the Military Affairs Bureau, the unit that was the accelerator, navigator, and bulldozer for the army juggernaut in domestic affairs.

Yoshizumi cut short the pleasantries. "Did our overture go out yet?"

Matsumoto nodded and said that it had been sent.

"I thought there were several other conditions to be attached to the overture." The General frowned. Then the army's traditional weapon, intimidation, was unsheathed: "It places us in an awkward position because you've dispatched it without consulting with us first."

But the vice-minister was not accepting this onus. "I understood that, besides the decision made at the Conference, this affair had been entrusted entirely to the foreign minister. Moreover, time was of the essence." In fact, Matsumoto did not know what had happened to the other three conditions the military favored, for Togo had been too tired to tell him. However, the vice-minister was firmly convinced that adding any more conditions would sink the surrender negotiations, and he had stressed this with Togo on every possible occasion. Matsumoto was placed in an uncomfortable spot. But he told Yoshizumi the contents of the note and acted as though the three additional conditions had been left out at Togo's direction.

Yoshizumi, seeing that he was too late to halt the surrender message, moved on to the next point on his agenda: "It would never do to let this news reach our front-line troops or the public here at home. The troops would be uncontrollable and might take some action that would endanger the negotiations." (His concern did not impress Matsumoto.) "And," the army politician predicted, "if the Japanese people found out, they would tear the existing government to bits."

Matsumoto was not sure of Yoshizumi's real purpose. On the surface, the army's political strategist was telling him that Japan should not broadcast to the world or her own people any hint that surrender was being considered. Such broadcasts were the responsibility of the Foreign Office. Yoshizumi was saying, in effect, "Don't put this news on short-wave radio and don't let it out via either radio or newspaper in Japan itself." Why? Was it really solicitude for soldier morale and public order? Or was the army looking to the future?

If the army was going to resist the surrender, it would be far easier to do so if neither troops nor public had any inkling of the negotiations, the Emperor's part in them, nor the fact that the army had acquiesced. If there was to be an army move, it would stand a far greater chance of success if all news of negotiation was withheld until the army was ready to strike. At that point, it would not matter whether the news came out or not. And apparently the army was not, at this moment, ready to strike.

Of course, it was also possible that the army simply wanted to rig appearances so that it would seem that the military, still mighty, had been sold out by traitorous advisers to the Throne. The Nazis had used a similar canard in the twenties with great success in Germany; why not Japan now?

Togo's deputy took the General's statement at face value and brushed it aside. "After all, this is a matter which the Allies will broadcast to the entire world. To have everyone on earth know and then to have the Japanese people learn of it at the very last is an upside-down procedure. Therefore the government should take positive steps to inform them about this vital matter."

But Yoshizumi saw no paradox in this. He was not amused. "That approach," he insisted sternly, "would place the army in an awkward position. It must not be done."

The discussion went back and forth and Matsumoto became convinced that the General would not or could not yield on this. Aching for some rest, the vice-minister finally gave in. "Very well. We may as well cancel the broadcast of the news to the East Asia area."

This seemed to satisfy Yoshizumi, and he stalked out. Matsumoto, with singleness of purpose, headed immediately back to his bed. He knew that he had given the military a hollow victory. Canceling the East Asia broadcast was meaningless, because the broadcasts from other parts of the world would obviously not keep the news secret.

As for the domestic news, that was not Matsumoto's department; that was up to the Cabinet Information Bureau.

There was one bit of unfinished business on Foreign Minister Togo's docket August 10. For a man of such punctiliousness, it was a matter that was mandatory. Since the morning of the ninth pudgy Jacob Malik, the Soviet ambassador, had been trying to see Togo. His purpose was no secret—it was to serve the USSR's formal declaration of war on Japan.

Togo had put him off because of the interminable meetings all day on the ninth. He had suggested that if Malik's business was urgent he should take it up with the vice-minister. But the Soviet ambassador calmly replied that the following day would do just as well.

So, on the morning of the tenth in the foreign minister's makeshift office Togo acted out a performance that paralleled Cordell Hull's demonstration of controlled outrage on December 7, 1941, when the Japanese envoys called on him after the Pearl Harbor attack.

Malik, spruce in a dark business suit, blandly told Togo that at the instruction of his government he was now to serve the formal declaration of war. He handed over the note that had been broadcast the preceding morning when Soviet troops jumped off in Manchuria. By now they had advanced 105 miles in some sectors. Togo, because of the shutdown of communications with Moscow, did not know that the Japanese ambassador to the USSR had received the notice the evening of the eighth. Of course that technicality did not really matter, since the note had never been transmitted to Tokyo.

Togo, fixing the Soviet ambassador with that cold-fish eye for which he was famous, reminded Malik that Russia had attacked while the neutrality pact between the two nations was still in effect. Further, Togo charged, the Soviets had most nefariously begun the war without answering Japan's request to act as peacemaker. The USSR had given as its reason for attacking, that Japan had rejected the Potsdam terms, but the Soviets had made no effort to find out what Japan's actual position was on this matter.

Drawing himself up, Togo delivered an echo of Cordell Hull's pronouncement. "The USSR's act," he flung at Malik, "will incur the condemnation of history."

Malik was unperturbed. He replied in generalities and claimed there was nothing in the Soviets' actions for which they could be faulted.

Now Tokyo shook and reverberated as B–29s hit the city in waves. It was a fitting background as Togo gave Malik a copy of the message sent that morning to Sweden and Switzerland and asked him to notify his government that Japan accepted the Potsdam declaration. Malik accepted the note. Mission accomplished, he left speedily.

At the war ministry the word went out that General Anami and Lieutenant General Yoshizumi wanted to see all senior section members of the ministry at 9:15 A.M. Men with the rank of lieutenant colonel or above assembled in the ministry's air-raid shelter amid a rising tide of conjecture and rumor.

There was the usual barrage of scuttlebutt, but the consensus was that Anami was going to report on the Imperial Conference just past and the measures decided against the Soviet attack. Some suggested that a new policy to cope with the atomic bomb might be the heart of the war minister's message. A few speculated that the long-discussed army-navy merger was now going to be effected by directive of the Emperor. Someone even jokingly suggested that the Emperor had decided to end the war.

The men snapped to as General Anami strode in with Vice-minister General Wakamatsu and Lieutenant General Yoshizumi. There were deep circles under Yoshizumi's eyes but Anami looked fresh and rested. The Military Affairs Bureau chief put the men at ease and stated briefly that, as they knew, there had been an Imperial Conference during the night, and that he, the war minister, and the chief of staff had attended. General Anami would now report on that conference.

The war minister stood, scanned the faces of his subordinates, and then—speaking quietly, reining in his emotions—he stunned them with these words:

"In compliance with the Imperial will, it has been decided to accept the Potsdam declaration . . ." There was an outburst of *no*'s from the men as they started, then stared at the General in disbelief. Anami continued ". . . on condition that the national polity be preserved." His face was taut, and the officers closest to him could see that Anami was desperately striving to keep his self-control.

He did not look at them now, as he explained that Japan had already sent a note of acceptance to the Allies. Nor could he look into their eyes as he said firmly that there was no alternative to complying with the imperial decision.

"I can offer no excuse to you," he continued, "but since it is the decision of the Emperor that the Potsdam terms be accepted there is nothing to be done. I am sorry that I could not live up to your expectations. My powers simply were not great enough. I believe I have had your trust and I have tried to represent you faithfully. At the Imperial Conference I insisted unswervingly upon a fight to the finish to protect our national polity. But now we have to follow the Emperor's will. I wish to emphasize something about that: Under the strict military code it is supremely important that the army act in unison at this time. Do not misbehave now, when the nation is facing the most critical hour in its history. You must disregard your personal feelings and those of the men serving under you. If even one soldier goes against the military code it could be an act that would destroy the nation."

The war minister glanced at the contorted features of his men and warned them to keep steady. "The Emperor's decision is based on one condition—that the Allies guarantee to preserve our national polity. Until we know that this point is accepted it is too soon to say that the war has ended. Therefore, the army must be ready for either peace or war."

Anami stopped short, then said emphatically "If anyone here is dissatisfied and thinks of acting against His Majesty's decision, he will have to do so over my dead body!" The war minister sat down heavily and fixed his eyes on a point in space. The rumble of discontent swelled in a crescendo until General Yoshizumi began to speak. He recapitulated the conference highlights, stressing the arguments advanced by Anami, Umezu, and Toyoda to continue the war, and the Emperor's statement.

But the weight of Anami's announcement had struck his chief lieutenants like a roundhouse punch to the head. The young tigers finally had learned the truth. "News of the Imperial decision grilled our brains severely," Takeshita agonized. And in his mind, as in those of others, the determination to act surged to the fore. His rationale was widely shared, and it was simple:

Disbanding the Japanese armed forces and occupying the homeland by foreign troops would mean that we would be compelled to change in whatever way the occupation forces desired. Since our unique national polity was beyond the understanding of foreign nations, there was little doubt that the occupiers would eventually compel us to change it as they wished. So the four conditions insisted upon by the war minister and chief of staff would be absolutely necessary to preserve the national polity. It would be useless for the people to survive the war if the structure of the nation itself was destroyed.

The Emperor had stated that a time would surely come when the state could be restored if only its roots remained alive. But was that a proper view? The Emperor's statement was not thought to be consistent with the ideas of Meiji and the Imperial Ancestors. Although the result would be temporary disobedience of the present Emperor—a situation certainly to be avoided—to act in compliance with the wishes of his Imperial Ancestors would constitute a wider and truer loyalty to the Throne in the final analysis. Eastern concepts hold that it is not enough to obey strictly an Imperial edict. Remonstrance and expostulation are, on the other hand, part of true loyalty.

(The form of Takeshita's "remonstrance and expostulation" took sinister shape when he talked with his fellow members of the Military Affairs Bureau after this meeting, as we shall see.)

The navy also was something less than tranquil on this day after the "unbearable" decision. Key staff members of the navy ministry and GHQ had, as Admiral Toyoda put it, "learned of the general situation and the atmosphere gradually started showing signs of tenseness." Rumors flew around the old brick-and-stone navy ministry building. Fearing the effects of the grapevine reports on navy personnel, Toyoda and Navy Minister Yonai jointly sent out an instruction to all naval officers.

The navy chiefs reminded the sailors of their eternal duty to the Empire and candidly stated that on August 10 the imperial government had begun diplomatic negotiations to terminate the war, with the condition that the national polity be preserved. Toyoda and Yonai warned their men not to be led astray by false propaganda and ordered them to exercise strict discipline and control.

Admiral Toyoda, moreover, got wind of an assassination plot aimed at "the white elephant," Admiral Yonai. The navy minister's longstanding opposition to the army, the Axis pact, and the war were well known. It was easy for extremists to jump to the conclusion that he had been the chief engineer and architect in the peace negotiations. Therefore he was a prominent target for those who wanted to fight to the finish.

Admiral Toyoda knew where to find the number one ultra in the navy. He was in the next room, and he was Toyoda's deputy, vice-chief of staff, Takajiro Onishi. As "father" of the ultimate weapon, the *kamikaze* attack, Onishi was consistent to the last. He favored the final battle; he welcomed guerrilla warfare; he urged all-out "special attack." The man who had sent more than 2,000 Japanese navy officers and men on one-way missions was the focal point of fanaticism in the service.

The chief of staff went next door and spoke to the vice-chief of staff. He warned Onishi specifically not to "resort to indiscreet actions." And he told him that as chief of staff he would assuredly do his utmost to protect the nation and the honor of the navy. Toyoda repeated his words to his key subordinates. They all nodded agreement and on the surface discipline seemed firm. But at the *kamikaze* training station, Atsugi Air Base, just outside Tokyo, the bull sessions of outrage and recalcitrance began in earnest. And they were led by the commandant.

The special duty of Hirohito's official wizard, Marquis Kido, on this day after the "insufferable" decision was unmistakable: to rally and solidify Japanese leadership behind the Emperor's extraordinary action and prevent reaction from wiping out the peace negotiations. Kido threw himself into the effort like a whirlwind.

His day began with an unusually long audience with Hirohito that lasted from 9:30 to 11:10 A.M. and covered a wide range of subjects, including the fateful conference and setting out the plans for the period immediately ahead. Kido reassured His Majesty that it had been the only possible move, and then the two of them turned their attention to the future.

The rest of the day was enlivened if not enlightened by meetings with two admirals, one former privy seal, and seven senior statesmen and former premiers—the *jushin*. They were leaders whose influence it was important to have in back of the surrender effort (referred to euphemistically as "the termination of hostilities").

At 2:30 P.M. the senior statesmen met with Foreign Minister Togo at the premier's residence for a briefing preliminary to meeting the Emperor in private audiences. The foreign minister set out the facts in his usual dry, workmanlike fashion to open the discussion.

General Kuniaki Koiso asked how the Potsdam declaration would affect Japan's armed forces. Togo said that it would mean severe limitation, even though it did not specifically spell out disarmament. There were in the document the phrases "driving militarism from the world" and preventing "rearming for war." Koiso, who at parties fancied himself "champion baldhead of Japan," protested that this would never do. By divine will from ages eternal, he pontificated, Japanese had carried weapons. Without adequate arms it would be impossible to maintain the national polity! He was outraged and rebelled at the possibility.

General Hideki Tojo agreed with Koiso and took the floor to argue that this acceptance of the Potsdam terms meant suicide for Japan. He hotly rejected Togo's reassurances that the condition preserving the national polity would protect the nation. Finally, still shaking his close-cropped head Tojo subsided, saying that if accepting the Potsdam terms was His Majesty's wish, nothing could be done and he had nothing further to say.

The other *jushin,* Okada, Hiranuma, Abe, Wakatsuki, and Konoye favored the surrender. The meeting then adjourned and the *jushin* drove to the palace.

The seven men heard from his own lips that their Emperor had requested that the war be terminated. They then said their pieces and departed. The whole process took only fifty-five minutes. Kido and Hirohito conferred for ten minutes afterward and Kido caromed off to direct his staff in the next arrangements.

The B–29s were still flying over Tokyo in early afternoon when suave Kainan Shimomura, president of the Cabinet Information Bureau, placed before the war, navy and foreign ministers sheets of paper on which were drafts of a statement. The painfully prepared announcement had been threshed out by Shimomura and his staff using the impossible formula set by the cabinet in its last session.

To any practical mind it was obvious that news of the Japanese surrender offer would soon be flashed around the world by radio from Allied nations. Japanese overseas, with easier access to short-wave, would quickly learn of the impending surrender. Even within Japan, where listening to foreign broadcasts was outlawed, the Soviet war declaration had been heard and its telltale statement about "Japan's request for mediation" was a certain tipoff that some negotiations had been going on behind the scenes.

But the cabinet had skirted a solid decision on how to inform the people. Too many ministers opposed telling the public. They feared an explosion of popular resentment, perhaps a revolt. And as for the army! Who could contain the soldiers' fury when they heard?

The cabinet's compromise was unwieldy: first, there would be no immediate announcement or mention of the imperial decision. Second, if the Allied reply approved Japan's condition, a formal rescript would then be issued over the Emperor's signature. Third, the cabinet authorized Shimomura, with his background as editor of *Asahi,* Japan's leading newspaper, to work out suitable statements to inform the people gradually of the changed conditions. These releases were to condition the public for what might be an almost instant reversal of policy, if and when. . . .

Shimomura was convinced that this first statement should be subtle, not a drastic break with the past. Therefore the release he now presented to the three ministers, Anami, Togo, and Yonai, had the usual bombast. But he was satisfied that it gave a clear hint that the end was approaching and that it was not necessarily to be a victorious one for Japan.

Anami, Yonai, Togo, and Shimomura settled down with the draft and began worrying and bedeviling each word and phrase. All four men know that the people had to be informed of the situation sooner or later. Yonai was all for a clear and direct statement now. Anami favored a cautious, slow revelation by stages. Shimomura was the arbiter—trying, as he put it, "to deviate the people's 'fight-until-victory' line of thought to one of terminating-the-war."

The war minister took an enthusiastic lead in suggesting amendments and polishing the statement. During the conference, Shimomura was interrupted time after time by calls from his Information Bureau staff, asking him to rush back to the office immediately. He stuck with the other conferees, however, until the release was finished to the satisfaction of all four and dispatched to newspapers and radio. As the first song of a new quartet their effort had an all too familiar melody.

In the opening paragraphs of the statement the enemy efforts were being destroyed everywhere by the unflinching spirit of the Japanese fighting forces. It called the enemy diabolical for using a "new-type bomb" that "spreads death and destruction unprecedented . . . in ruthlessness and barbarity." The release warned that the enemy was preparing to invade the homeland. But then, in its summary paragraph, the release referred to Japan's multiple afflictions and said

> In truth, we cannot but recognize that we are now beset with the worst possible situation. Just as the government is exerting its utmost efforts to defend the homeland, safeguard the polity, and preserve the honor of the nation so too must the people rise to the occasion and overcome all manner of difficulties in order to protect the polity of their Empire.

It was nearly 5 P.M. when the president of the Information Board arrived at his office after leaving Togo, Anami, and Yonai. A serious crisis had developed.

Shimomura's Information Bureau associates had been besieged by telephone calls from newspapers. Editors had received a bellicose statement over the war minister's signature and wanted Information Bureau guidance on how to handle it. No wonder! The army message was a rousing all-out exhortation to yield no quarter and battle to the death:

Instruction to the Troops

I declare to all officers and men of the Army:
The Soviet Union, directing its armed might in the wrong direction, has invaded Japan. It is obvious that it aims to invade Greater Asia although it tries to justify its aims. Things having come to this pass, words do not avail any more. All that remains to be done is to carry through to its end the holy war for the protection of the Land of the Gods.

We are determined to fight resolutely although we may have to chew grass, eat dirt, and sleep in the fields. It is our belief that there is life in death. This is the spirit of the great Nanko who wanted to be reborn seven times in order to serve the country, or the indomitable spirit of Tokimune who refused to be swayed and pressed on vigorously with the work of crushing the Mongolian horde.

All officers and men of the entire Army without exception should realize the spirit of Nanko and Tokimune and march forward to encounter the mortal enemy.

—War Minister Korechika Anami

Something had gone awry. The intent of this message would be clear to the most obtuse—and it was directly contradictory to the painfully labored release Shimomura had sent out only minutes before with the full approval of both Anami and Navy Minister Yonai. Shimomura's release was intended to hint that surrender was a distasteful but almost inevitable possibility.

The newspaper editors couldn't reconcile it with Anami's bloodthirsty proclamation. Was the army planning to fight on even though the government might surrender? Did this statement of Anami's have Information Bureau sanction? Or was the army about to take over? The editors wanted to know.

Shimomura called Anami to get the truth of the matter. The scene had its comic overtones—as Shimomura waited for the war minister to come to the telephone he was surrounded by his deputy chief, Hisatoni, navy Captain Takase, and others who were arguing angrily that if the army could issue such a statement and have it printed the navy would have to do likewise!

When Anami answered, his replies to Shimomura's questions about the "Instruction to the Troops" were vague and distant. He didn't know what the information minister was talking about. Shimomura caught a few words from another voice in Anami's office and surmised that the war minister, distracted, was hearing from his staff. Then, suddenly catching himself, Anami said "Ah, ah! Are you referring to *that?* Well, now I understand. Please push it through somehow and have it published."

Slowly the information minister put down the phone. He had known that Anami was hemmed in between the stubborn opinions of his unruly junior officers and the official government position. "The minister of war certainly is in a tight spot," Shimomura said to himself. It occurred to him that Anami might actually be in physical danger if he did not go along with this action of his subordinates. Shimomura decided that to drive the war minister to the wall would play into the hands of the ultras, possibly destroy him, and eliminate any effective control over the extremists. Therefore he gave orders to the newspapers to publish the Anami Proclamation as well as the statement issued by the Information Board.

The whole incident was a classic example of *gekokujo*—rule by juniors—typical of the young tigers in the military. It had begun when a deadpan dynamo, Lieutenant Colonel Masao Inaba, left Anami's morning meeting with his officers with one big idea absorbing him.

Inaba thought that the imperial decision would become known to the whole nation immediately (neither Anami nor Yoshizumi had explained that it would not). But, since the war was still on until the surrender was final, Inaba believed the troops should immediately receive a strong dose of encouragement "so that unrest would not develop." Already Inaba "could discern a tendency toward unrest even within the war ministry and the office of General Staff." Since he was one of the leaders of it, this was not a spectacular insight.

But Inaba had a second, very genuine concern. Japan's army in China and Manchuria was a sitting duck. "The Kwantung army had to be encouraged . . . a formal decision of the government had not yet been made as to the nation's course. . . . No new orders from the Supreme Command had been issued. The Kwantung army was performing peacetime duties. In other words, in opposing the enemy attack, it did not go beyond its guard duties. The war ministry and army GHQ were busy drafting the 'Outline of War Policy' and nothing was done about new orders while they waited for the nation to reach a decision . . . some sort of inspiration from the central authorities was needed as a stopgap measure."

This officer, fired with enthusiasm for what he believed to be a sorely needed action, collared his superior, Colonel Arao, and explained it to him. Arao thought it had merit and gave him his approval to discuss it with the war minister. The budget chief unrolled his idea before General Anami. Without hesitation Anami ordered that an "instruction to the troops" be prepared, calling for a firm stand and unconquerable determination and that it should be issued immediately. Inaba rushed out of Anami's office and in an instant began drafting the instruction while possessed by the muse of patriotic exhortation, brass-tongued Diana.

By the time Inaba finished his recall to arms, it was nearly 2 P.M. and the war minister had gone off to a cabinet meeting at the prime minister's residence. Inaba showed his draft to Colonel Arao, who read it through, said it was too long, but in the interests of expediency approved it. Inaba hand-carried it to Lieutenant General Yoshizumi, who wrote in minor changes and put his seal on it. The budget expert then hurried along to the vice-minister of war, General Wakamatsu, who also made some changes and affixed his seal.

At this point nothing more could be done until Anami's approval was obtained, but he was still at that meeting. Colonel Arao was to see Anami at his residence that evening; Inaba therefore gave the draft to Arao who would get the war minister's seal of approval.

The budget chief felt, a bit smugly, that he had made a real contribution thus far. He had no idea what a ruckus he was about to touch off.

At three o'clock Lieutenant Colonel Oyadomari of the Military Information Bureau came to the Military Affairs Section of the war ministry. Lieutenant Colonel Takeshita and Major Hatanaka were on duty.

Oyadomari reminded Takeshita that the afternoon radio announcement was due to be broadcast at four. He suggested that the "Instruction to the Troops" that Colonel Inaba had drafted be used in the newscast. Major Hatanaka enthusiastically seconded the idea.

With Oyadomari, Takeshita went to Inaba's bailiwick and discovered that the "Instruction" had been completed and was ready to go. Moreover, it had been approved by all but the war minister. Even though the document lacked his seal, it had been drafted along lines he suggested. The broadcast deadline was approaching. Takeshita checked quickly and found that both his superiors were out and could not be reached. He arbitrarily decided to release the statement on his own responsibility.

There was a minor hitch. Colonel Arao was not to be found, and he had the final draft with him—the only one with all the approved changes. What to do? Inaba had a solution. He and his friends ransacked his wastebasket until they found the first draft, then Inaba carefully went over it, changing it so that it corresponded, as best he could remember, with the draft in Arao's pocket.

The inflammatory style and the incendiary content of the instruction should have given all of them second thoughts about releasing it without Anami's approval, particularly during a period of delicate negotiations. But they forged ahead. After all, said Inaba, they knew that "its purpose was merely to encourage a greater war effort and that it had been approved already by the minister in principle. . . ."

So, with Inaba's help, Takeshita, Oyadomari, and Hatanaka put together their fiery version of the "Instruction to the Troops" and distributed it to the radio stations and newspapers. It went out over the air on the 4 P.M. broadcast and stirred the editors to immediate reaction.

Back at his office in the premier's office building, cabinet secretary Sakomizu found one of his newspaper friends waiting for him when he returned late that afternoon. He found also that there was a list of repeated telephone calls from editors who requested urgent response. His reporter friend handed him a copy of a fresh "Instruction to the Troops" over General Anami's signature and asked if the cabinet had approved it.

Sakomizu scanned the paper and, shaken, immediately rang up Lieutenant General Yoshizumi and quizzed him about the release. The Military Affairs Bureau chief had just returned to his room at the war ministry building and knew nothing of what had transpired while he was out. As Sakomizu read the text of the statement to him Yoshizumi thought from the flavor of the words and the action as well as his knowledge of the man's habits that the so-called "Instruction" appeared to be the work of one person—the young firebrand Major Kenji Hatanaka.

The General called Hatanaka in and questioned him about the release. Yoshizumi's guess seemed confirmed and Hatanaka became the scapegoat for the incident. The General ordered Hatanaka to retrieve the error. "Make the rounds of the newspaper offices and withdraw the information. Use my car." In the era of the telephone, this was akin to sending Mercury to deliver a message by elephant express. Hatanaka did as instructed. He drove off to the offices of all of the newspapers in a staff car.

Hibiya Public Hall was and is one of Japan's great theater buildings. Located in block-square Hibiya Park across the street from the Imperial Hotel on one side and the palace moat on another, the brown brick walls of the Hall also hold offices. Here Domei, the official Japanese news agency, was housed. And in the traditional squalor typical of newsrooms all over the world, the Domei offices were fully equipped. The battered desks were dirty but sturdy, the floors dark and littered, the walls a perpetually changing collage of admonitions to accuracy, calendars, pinups of newsphotos and recent stories. The clutter of typewriters and telephones, desk lights, ash trays, and coffee cups made the place one in which a reporter from any newspaper in the world might have felt immediately at home.

At this particular moment in time Saiji Hasegawa, foreign editor of Domei, was one on whom fate's thread fell. It was his duty to co-ordinate Japan's foreign broadcasts. Since Japan's most rapid contact with the outside world was this channel, Hasegawa became, for this fleeting moment, one of the important actors in the tragedy. The day before he had been alerted by friends in the Foreign Office that the Imperial Conference was to be held, and, believing that there might be some important news as a result, he had slept on his desk in the Domei office. It was harder but no hotter than his bed at the Imperial Hotel.

So when the imperial decision was made, a Domei reporter brought Hasegawa word about 6:30 A.M. that the Emperor had called for peace and the cabinet had followed this "advice." Hasegawa immediately telephoned Domei's president, then went back to his job of organizing the news for overseas broadcast. He was filled to bursting with excitement about the report of the tentative surrender, and hovered at the telephone for further word, *any* word, for instructions to send word. . . . But nothing came, and Hasegawa's tension eased into a dull numbness that existed and continued but was thrust aside as other news flowed across his desk.

Then, about 4 P.M. he had a call from the Information Ministry. A special statement from the minister of information was on the way. "Now," thought Hasegawa, "the nation and the world are going to learn the momentous truth."

He read through the statement when it arrived with impatience, irritation, and finally disgust. "It is so vague," he thought, "that you really can't tell what it means." It was totally inadequate, he believed, to do anything but confuse the people of Japan or the outside world. Hasegawa did a rare thing. As a government employee, it was his job to transmit official statements by the nation's leaders, and this was such a one. If he had not known of the Emperor's decision, he would have sent it on to the translators for English broadcast. But, he thought, it wouldn't help end the war. He held off; he put the statement aside.

While he was sitting on Shimomura's statement, along came a release from the army. It was the Anami Proclamation. Hasegawa read it and was shocked. "This could not be sent out in English," he thought. "It surely would damage negotiations. And besides, no American could understand those references to Nanko and Toki-mune. Nor would the Allies appreciate the call to 'press on vigor-ously' to crush the modern equivalent of the Mongolian horde."

But this was a matter of a different stripe. An Information Ministry release might be forgotten and excused, but a statement from the war minister! Not likely. "I'm not a very wise man," mused Hasegawa, "but I think it is wise for me not to send these two statements." He had sufficient wisdom to realize that he had to have some authority to back his nonaction. So he called Matsumoto, the vice-minister of foreign affairs.

"There are two important statements that have come from the Ministry of Information and the army just now; do you know about them?" Matsumoto did not, so Hasegawa read the texts of the two messages. "I have not yet sent these to foreign countries," he said slowly. "I'd like to ask your permission to hold them up, not send them."

Matsumoto was still very much on edge, fearing that some incident might explode without warning and destroy the fragile negotiations. Thank goodness Hasegawa had had sense enough to call before send-ing these! "All right," the diplomat agreed, "hold them until you hear from me."

The vice-minister hastily put in a telephone call for Togo. The for-eign minister could not be located. Matsumoto pulled his chief lieu-tenants into his office to discuss how to deal with the war minister's announcement.

Even before this, there had been ugly reports from abroad that caused consternation in the foreign ministry. Matsumoto and his col-leagues were studying one such response. It was an article from a Chinese newspaper flatly labeling a hoax the "rumors" of impending surrender coming from Japan.

Although *Gaimusho* officials as well as many Tokyo editors sus-pected the army statement to be a fraud, the fact remained that the army refused to withdraw it. At this point there was only one way to prevent its circulation: halt distribution of the already-printed papers. Togo, thought his lieutenants, might just be able to stop them in time.

Finally, Togo was reached and told of the Anami Proclamation. But in weighing the alternatives and the dangers, the foreign minister decided that the domestic situation was too volatile and that an arbitrary move to suppress the statement now would cause the nation to be drenched in a "rain of blood." He turned down suggestions that he act to stop the newspapers.

In late afternoon General Yoshizumi heard again from Sakomizu. "The newspapers have already completed their press setup," the cabinet secretary reported. "Therefore, to prevent the war minister's instruction from being published we would have to suppress publication of the newspapers themselves. Such a drastic measure would be too extreme, so let's leave the matter as it is."

Thus, when Major Hatanaka returned breathlessly some time later, Yoshizumi was not surprised at the hotspur's words: "The newspaper offices complained about the untimely withdrawal of the information." Perhaps he was secretly pleased. The General dismissed the Major and all concerned sat back to wait.

In Japan the captive press did what it was told. The hand that operated the levers was discreetly hidden behind a fan, but was nonetheless effective in enforcing its wants. All newsprint was dispensed by the Information Bureau, and newsprint, of course, was the lifeblood of the papers. Yet in a conflict between Information Bureau and army, a newspaper could be whipsawed. The choice, essentially, was one between losing newsprint or personnel and machines. If the Information Bureau didn't cut off the paper supply the extremist thugs in and out of uniform were perfectly capable of putting the newspaper out of business by damaging men or presses.

Thus it was that Japan's newspapers on August 11 published side by side on page one the two diametrically opposed statements. (Only one paper, the English-language Nippon *Times,* showed courage and editorial integrity enough to reject the Anami Proclamation. It printed only the cabinet statement. The following day, however, even the *Times* was forced to run the army release.)

As a result, fresh shivers of fright assailed the peace-minded when they read their morning newspapers. Read together, the government statement and Anami's call to arms added up to an official admission that the worst had come and that suicidal defense of the country was imminent.

The statement handcrafted by Shimomura, Togo, Anami, and Yonai as a hint of approaching surrender turned out to be a near-total failure in that respect. The editors of one newspaper even ran it under the headlines:

TOTAL WARTIME EFFORT ASKED JAPANESE NATION—

*Overcoming of Present Crisis to Defend
National Polity Urged by Shimomura*

Most Japanese read the official statement as another flagwaving call to all-out effort. The subtlety of Shimomura's insinuation that the war would be over if "the polity" could be guaranteed was largely lost in the welter of bombast.

But beyond that, the army instructions seemed to indicate that the military had no thought of ending the war whatsoever, and furthermore, that the warhawks were strong enough to nullify the government attempt to prepare the nation for surrender. All this was bad enough, but in addition there was the international aspect to think about. What effect would this Anami Proclamation have on the peace negotiations when the Allies read it? Was it a deliberate military effort to sabotage the government's offer to accept the Potsdam terms?

The incident had one immediate effect. Togo changed his mind about radio. He had opposed broadcasting any mention of Japan's acceptance of the Potsdam terms until the formal note reached the Allied governments through conventional channels. Now, with this jolt from the extremists, Togo reversed his stand and gave Matsumoto the green light to broadcast the information.

In the make-do offices of the foreign ministry, crowded into space made available in the finance building, Togo's assistants at *Gaimusho* worried themselves about the tenuous situation. Japan had sent official word to the Allies through Switzerland and Sweden that she would surrender if the Emperor system could be retained. Yet the war was still on, and the fighting services might just upset the applecart with some military action or diplomatic mistake. The Allies had given no official sign that they had received Japan's note. And at home the Japanese people still thought Nippon was winning the war, as did Japanese troops overseas.

It was essential to give some sign to the Allies that the country was willing to surrender. If only it had been possible to run up a white flag with a small streamer below it: *if the Emperor system is retained!* A straight voice broadcast would be the speediest, most direct method. But the military would not allow that and since they monitored incoming as well as outgoing broadcasts, it would be foolish to try it.

Who it was who thought of it is now lost to the record. But one of the men around Togo and Matsumoto had a sudden bright idea: perhaps, just perhaps, the military may not be monitoring Morse-code transmissions. Why not have Domei send the text of the message to the Allies as a news item in English, in Morse? At least there was a good chance it would clear before the military monitors decoded and translated it. Matsumoto okayed the plan. The vice-minister immediately telephoned Hasegawa at Domei.

"I am sending you another document by hand. Wait until that reaches you and do as instructed by the courier."

Within ten minutes the chief of the foreign ministry's information section, Saburo Ota, appeared at Hasegawa's desk. He took an envelope from his brief case and handed it to the news chief. Hasegawa's hands trembled as he unfolded the paper, on which was the message sent that morning to Switzerland and Sweden. His eyes clouded as he scanned the text.

Ota conferred with the news chief and Hasegawa summoned his English expert Mr. Yaso and one other Domei man, Mr. Alta. With Ota they went to the second floor where they could have privacy. There, behind locked doors, Hasegawa instructed Yaso to translate the message into English, then convert it into code so that Mr. Alta could transmit it.

By 8 P.M. the message was ready to go, and Hasegawa put it on the transmitters, aimed at America first, then on the beam to Europe. Now the real suspense began for the Domei man. The primary concern of the foreign ministry was that word of Japan's willingness to accept the Potsdam terms reach the outside world. Togo and Matsumoto wanted to finesse the army in this way. They aimed to forestall further A-bombs. And they also figured very shrewdly that once the victory celebrations began in Allied nations their very force would compel their governments to accept Japan's one condition without delay.

Within fifteen minutes Hasegawa had confirmation that the message had gone through. From Domei's monitoring station he had a telephone call. The English-language monitor reported an Associated Press story via shortwave from San Francisco. President Truman had just finished his breakfast when a paper with the Domei announcement was brought to him. Mr. Truman, said AP, summoned Admiral Leahy, General Marshall, and Secretaries Stimson, Forrestal, and Byrnes to confer on Japan's surrender offer.

Shortly afterward came a Reuters dispatch from London. There, at just after 1 P.M., word that "the war is over" was flashed. In the noonday sun staid Londoners started dancing in Piccadilly Circus, celebrating the coming of peace.

Hasegawa was pleased. The transmission had succeeded. The war, he thought, was indeed over now. It was not until 5 A.M. the following morning that he found out that the armed forces had a different idea.

Meanwhile, Privy Seal Marquis Koichi Kido received a summons from the Emperor's brother, Prince Mikasa. Kido hastily went to Mikasa's palace and reported to him on developments. He took pains to go into detail with Mikasa, because the Prince was an army officer and it was possible that the army might conceive some plan to depose Hirohito and substitute Mikasa—if the Prince would cooperate with them. But Kido counted on Mikasa's basic loyalty to his brother and the true facts of the situation to prevent him from any such course.

Following this Kido made his way home through the scorched and pockmarked streets of the bedraggled city. Waiting at his house he found Prince Konoye, full of apprehension because of the Anami Proclamation, steeped in dark expectations of a combined army-Communist uprising. As so often in the past, Kido and his closest political confidant talked and talked about the current developments and the "measures for coping with the situation." Konoye had repeatedly proved a poor prophet in the past. Now Kido was holding the lantern and leading the way through the twilight.

On the night of the tenth the government finally had its first scientific confirmation of the nature of the Hiroshima bomb, from a tiny physicist in baggy navy pants. Professor Asada of Osaka University had at last returned with his navy team to the Kure naval base. They reviewed their findings at Hiroshima: the electrometer and Geiger counter both showed intense radioactivity in the city; and white blood counts of people exposed to the bomb were abnormally low; the photographic plates specially prepared to determine radioactivity were exposed, showing graphically that radiation was still present. From this evidence Professor Asada concluded that the "special bomb" was undoubtedly atomic.

The professor was impatient to send this information to Osaka, to the navy man who had chosen him for this mission, and to Tokyo, to the government. But land communication wiped out by the A-bomb had not yet been restored. There was, however, one destroyer anchored in Kure's port, and Asada was determined to send his message by means of its facilities. He wrote out a cable and asked the navy to transmit it. It was sent and, he later learned, was the first direct information received by the government in Tokyo that the bomb was atomic.

The army had sent its team to Hiroshima on the seventh and eighth and had received word from it, but had not shared this information. Asada's message arrived late on the tenth and said:

The bomb dropped on Hiroshima unquestionably was an atomic bomb. We have determined this scientifically. The damage was tremendous. There are no means to cope with such weapons. Japan is facing a major crisis. It is necessary to prepare ourselves for the worst.

According to rumors then circulating, Tokyo was next in line for an A-bomb, and it was reported that an Allied short-wave broadcast had given August 17 as the target date for the drop on Tokyo, the twenty-first for one on Osaka. Asada thought the U.S. probably had five or six A-bombs and could make good on the threat. Furthermore, he had seen enough destruction in his two days of travel to convince him that surrender was the only alternative. The ambiguous last sentence of his cable was meant to convey both meanings, but particularly *Quit now*. His words went through, but his meaning did not reach all those who read them.

Chapter 14

Banzai! Then Die, Empire!

In his dingy news office at Domei in Hibiya Hall, foreign news editor Saiji Hasegawa was curled up on his desk, sleeping fitfully. It was 5 A.M., Saturday, August 11. He was in shirtsleeves and his collar was open. Through the haze of sleep he heard his name called.

"*Hasegawa!*" The wiry, middle-aged man twitched. There was a hand on his shoulder, a shake.

"Hasegawa!" the voice commanded. The editor opened his eyes and found a navy captain in full uniform shaking him.

He recognized the man. It was Captain Arima of the operations section, navy GHQ. Scrambling to his feet, Hasegawa experienced a flash of apprehension. He knew this man was in favor of peace. He also knew that Arima held an important post in the navy and therefore could not indicate his personal feelings. The sleep-dimmed corners of the editor's mind cleared instantly as Arima sat down and said quietly: "Our monitors have picked up propaganda broadcasts from foreign countries this morning. They say that Japan has accepted the Potsdam terms."

Arima casually glanced around the grimy office, then looked into Hasegawa's eyes. "The broadcasts mention Domei as the source of this information."

Hasegawa was frozen to the spot, expecting the worst.

"Of course," smiled Arima, examining the editor's face, "I myself do not believe such propaganda broadcasts, but for confirmation, to settle the matter, I agreed to come and ask you if it is true that Domei has sent such information."

At that moment, Hasegawa found out what sort of man he was. If he had been braver he would have owned that he had sent this news; but he was not that brave. Discretion dictated a different answer. "Please ask Sakomizu and Matsumoto about that," he replied. "I can say nothing."

The Captain eyed him thoughtfully, rose to his feet. "I see," he said. "Well, we will have a talk with them." He put on his cap and walked briskly out of the office to his staff car outside.

Filled with foreboding, the editor reckoned that in the navy there must have been considerable discussion before someone as high up the ladder as Arima was sent to talk to him. Normally an inquiry would come by telephone from one of the section chiefs in the information bureau of the navy. Hasegawa now steeled himself for a similar visit from the army. And he wondered what action the military men would take when the cabinet secretary or vice-minister of foreign affairs confirmed that the Domei message had been sent.

General Yoshizumi, the army's political strong arm, didn't bother to call Hasegawa. He had the same monitored broadcasts from British, Indian, and American stations, and he knew where to complain. He went directly to Sakomizu and Matsumoto. And his protests were full-blast tirades: Why did you allow such a story to be sent? There are many millions of Japanese soldiers still at the front. This news from Domei will discourage them and may endanger the nation. The war must actually be ended before such information is released. How can you allow such an irresponsible action as this? He barked on and on.

Matsumoto's response was unassailable: "Why do you object to releasing the information approved in His Majesty's own words? Do you dispute the Emperor's decision to end the war? The war will end sooner if the Emperor's decision reaches the Allies earlier. We merely broadcast what had already been approved by the cabinet and sent to the Allies via neutral nations."

Deflated by the foreign ministry official, Yoshizumi charged off to yelp at Sakomizu.

But the cabinet secretary had his responses ready: "If you have any complaint about our action, please ask your representative, the war minister, to bring the matter up at a cabinet meeting."

Completely rebuffed, Yoshizumi trotted to GHQ to lick his

wounds. He did not make a formal complaint to the war minister, and Anami did not bring the matter up at any meeting of government leaders.

Hasegawa learned of Matsumoto's and Sakomizu's defensive actions and breathed easier . . . for the moment.

On this bright, hazy summer morning, General Anami stepped into the garden of his official residence, samurai bow in hand. In shirtsleeves, the war minister hung a quiver of arrows on a peg and, flexing the bowstring, settled down to test his nerves. The magnificent seven-foot Japanese bow requires muscle as well as nerve, and Anami was well equipped with both.

General Anami was head of an organization that had failed in its mission and was torn by dissension. His troops were being chased like jackrabbits across the Manchurian plains by Soviet planes and armor. His air force was watching helplessly as B–29s blanketed the sky and inflamed the earth. His planes were sniffed out and destroyed by wolfpacks of enemy deck planes. His soldiers were being pushed back on fronts in Burma and China. In Japan his forces were digging in for the doomed last-ditch, suicide effort. And while he was being pressed by the volatile, vigorous young tigers around him to take over the nation and fight to the death, his Emperor and the government had said surrender.

It was a measure of the man that though he felt the pressures converging on him he was as fit and energetic as a *sumo* wrestler preparing for a match. Now, bringing to bear his Zen control of self and submerging himself in the act of archery, Anami let fly at the target. On this quiet morning he had managed to group five arrows in the clout by the eleventh shot.

Satisfied, he pulled the arrows from the target, carefully ran them back into the quiver, padded back to the house, and put the gear away. Then he donned his uniform and, with Colonel Hayashi, drove to his office at the war ministry.

"I begin to wonder about the prime minister. Admiral Suzuki has been acting suspiciously ever since August 9," Anami told Hayashi. Later, in his office, Anami repeated his suspicions to the younger officers, including Takeshita and Inaba. The flap over the war minister's "Instruction to the Troops" was glossed over. Though General

Yoshizumi had severely reprimanded Takeshita for releasing the statement, the war minister said nothing about it now, thus confirming the belief in the young tigers that he condoned their extreme behavior and was in reality dead-set against the Potsdam terms.

Anami's words to the young firebrands in his office that morning strengthened this notion:

"I felt somehow that I was deceived at the Imperial Conference," he confided. "There I was, thinking it only proper that both the Togo plan and our plan containing the three additional conditions be presented. But only the Togo plan was proposed. I whispered to General Umezu 'Perhaps there is a plot in completely disregarding our plan. Maybe we should take up the argument not on the question of conditions but on the basic point of whether to accept the Potsdam declaration or not—that is, whether to continue the war or accept peace.' "

(Umezu had dourly turned thumbs down on Anami's suggestion and neither of them pursued this line. The other point, about presenting only Togo's plan, did not hold water. Both "plans" had been printed and passed to the conferees. But the premier shut off extended debate and referred the question to His Majesty after the Big Six and Baron Hiranuma had had their say. True, he did not bring up the soldiers' plan separately, but the basic discussion covered its points. Anami conveniently neglected to mention this.)

The General told his protégés that Baron Hiranuma's inclusion in the conference was another suspicious act. The military had not been informed that the president of the privy council was to attend, and it was, he said, illegal to include him. Obviously, he implied, this was part of the plot—Hiranuma had been included so that the military would be outnumbered and outvoted. (Actually, the military had welcomed Hiranuma's presence until he opened his mouth, as we have seen. The old man had for forty years consistently led the right-wing and was a self-appointed defender of the "national polity." The military leaders were sure he could be counted on to back the fight to the death and oppose surrender to the very end.) As for the legality of Hiranuma's attendance, Sakomizu had checked that point carefully and found plenty of precedent for the privy council president's attendance.

Nevertheless, Anami continued to pour explosive thoughts into the ears of his junior officers. Several times he divulged to Takeshita and

Inaba his deep-rooted suspicion: "We were caught in a trap by a trick of the conspirators who are betraying the country. They are keeping in contact with the enemy through some secret channel."

Takeshita was full of opinions and self-confidence. His assignment was national affairs liaison and he frequently called on the war minister for decisions and guidance. His special relationship as brother-in-law gave him almost unlimited access to Anami. Anami's secretary, Colonel Hayashi, observed "Anami confided his personal thoughts to Takeshita without my knowing them. I believe Takeshita transmitted to his colleagues many of the war minister's views. . . . Although I do not know what Takeshita told his colleagues, I believe his words excited the young officers and that, as a result, the war minister began to fear that he might become another Saigo."

The posturing and defiance of the young officers were part of the fanaticism ingrained by their military training and education, by the position of the warrior in Japanese history and their concept of *Bushido*—the "way of the samurai."

For seven centuries the samurai, the Japanese warriors, had been the hereditary class empowered to carry arms and to defend their lords and masters. In feudal times they wore their two-handed swords proudly as badges of rank and power.

Though they swore devotion to their liege lord and to a Spartan life, were determined to uphold duty and fight to the death, in truth they often found themselves living well, if not luxuriously, transferring allegiance without disabling qualms, and surviving in spite of the demands of duty. Their oversensitive devotion to highly-perfumed concepts of "honor" was frequently a morbid obsession. Restless and mercurial, most of them did not work (it was beneath their dignity) and they avoided the contamination of workaday affairs. Thus they shunned such mundane matters as money and arithmetic and avoided the common people . . . farmers and tradesmen.

The samurai were the ruling class and they ruled by the sword. They did not hesitate to split the skull of any commoner who displeased them—perhaps by failing to touch forehead to earth with sufficient alacrity. One of the great rulers of Japan decreed "common people who behave unbecomingly to the samurai or do not show respect to their superiors may be cut down on the spot." The commoners had no recourse.

Sword-swinging was not the only activity of the samurai. Especially in recent centuries more and more of them developed the administrative skills needed to run their overlord's estates. In times of peace they whiled away the days in practicing fencing, archery and swordsmanship, in Japanese chess, in poetry contests, calligraphy and tea ceremonies. Some painted, some wrote, but many were bully-boys who swaggered and flattered the vanity of their masters, upon whom they depended utterly.

The samurai had enjoyed for seven hundred years the enforced homage of the nation and were considered the carriers of the highest ideals of national life. Many of these ideals are embodied in the classical tale of "The Forty-seven Ronin." Based on an actual incident, it tells of a provincial lord who is tricked into a gauche act at court. Publicly embarrassed and infuriated, he pulls his sword on the lord who tricked him. Though he manages to nick the man's pate, he is prevented from killing him and forced to commit *seppuku*, ceremonial suicide, for the unforgivable act of drawing his sword in the court precincts.

The lord's death leaves his samurai masterless (ronin) and 47 of them dissemble and plot, undergo every privation and sacrifice to avenge their master's humiliation. For two years they pursue their task. One sells a daughter into prostitution, another sells his wife to finance the project. A third gives his sister to the target of the vendetta as a concubine; a fourth kills his father-in-law. Others sink into drunken debauchery. In the end the ronin succeed in killing the lord who tricked their master. They place his head on their lord's grave and all 47 of them commit ceremonial suicide. Such were the ancient ways of the samurai.

But in 1873 the Meiji Restoration wiped out the samurai traditions and instituted compulsory western-style military training overnight. Emperor Meiji announced "the era of freedom is now gradually dawning upon the people. The hereditary distinction between the soldier and the farmer will be done away with." The new, democratic army in which peasant boy, prince and samurai's son served side by side was revolutionary. It captured the support of the people, replacing the samurai class as an object of homage.

To be a soldier, therefore, was to be in an honored and privileged group. To be an officer was to be of the elite. And to be assigned to the war ministry or Imperial General Headquarters was to be in the stratosphere of the elite. There were other key assignments, such as the major army commands and military government posts, but the headquarter slots were at the apex.

The samurai's devotion to his lord and master was transformed in the Meiji era to dedicated service to the god-Emperor and complete obedience to his wishes as conveyed by the officers to the rank and file. Loyalty of the soldier to the Emperor was his duty and the voice of the army officer was the "voice" of the Emperor. The soldier's highest calling was to die for the Emperor, thus to become a guarding deity of the nation honored and revered at the shrine of heroes, Yasukuni, in Tokyo.

The Japanese soldier lived a Spartan life. During World War II food and lodging were minimal, pay was infinitesimal ($1.26 per month for a private; $126.50 for a general), but the frugality not only inured, it worked to build puritanical *esprit* and a belief in superiority.

Trained in the military prep schools, the army officer began his military education at age 13 or 14. Those who progressed through the *Shikwan Gakko*—the Japanese West Point—were trained in the conventional military subjects. The curriculum purposely excluded economics, comparative government, international law and international relations. Most emphasized was the officer spirit with its unflinching self-denial, devotion to duty and self-sacrifice for the Emperor.

In the Emperor's army it was expected that the officers would fraternize with the enlisted men, and the superior officers with their subordinates. Such practices were meant to build strong bonds and to substitute the army circle for the family circle. In the palmy days, drinking with fellow-officers was a popular activity. A modest soiree —dinner with sake and geishas—might be an occasional treat. Officers won kudos for their ability to hold their liquor and built reputations for their prowess.

But the modern samurais, the officers, faced uncertain futures. Every year 800 entered the military academy. Seven out of eight could expect retirement, after thirty years service, as majors or colonels on a pension of about $50 a month. This they considered grossly unjust. The officer sacrificed half his life serving his Emperor and his nation and ended up in seedy gentility. His contemporaries who went into business became wealthy, enjoyed luxurious living, complete with clubs, vacation homes at beach and mountain, and perhaps a tender geisha set up in a cozy, quiet nest. Other peers started out as ward-heeling political errand boys and clawed their way to power. Once arrived, they were appointed to prestigious cabinet posts and received honors from the government and Emperor. Obviously, the officers believed, the military men were not getting their fair share.

To obtain their due the officers went more and more into politics. There were hundreds of societies to which the military men belonged; most of these organizations were distinctly political, usually reactionary and ultra-nationalistic. Each generally was convinced that it had the true vision of national greatness. Most of them were of little consequence in themselves and were ephemeral. But there were perhaps two dozen that had thousands of members and considerable power. Their names were poetic—Cherry Blossom Society; Purple Cloud Villa; Society of the White Wolf; Black Dragon Society—but their purposes were often bloody. Beginning about 1930 their members moved into politics for the top stakes by pulling strings and triggers or passing ammunition to assassinate leading Japanese they considered to be anti-military.

It was all done with the purest of motives, naturally. The purpose usually was to bring about "the Showa Restoration." This catch-all rallying cry became loudest when the military was hurt most in budget cutbacks, in reduction of forces, and when unpopular treaties were signed. At such times the superpatriotic societies (some of them completely, some only partially composed of military men) prattled and plotted darkly to do away with the Emperor's false counselors and let the Imperial goodness shine forth. When one skimmed away the metaphors the meaning was actually "get rid of the present government and its key backers and replace them with a military or pro-military regime." And this they attempted all too often, as the zooming assassination rate in high government and business circles proved.

The army was an organization with a holy mission. General Sadao Araki, with his pointed mustachios and spellbinding oratory, was one *eminence grise* behind many army plots and coups in the thirties. He trained the young officers when he was president of the Staff College and later as war minister. He souped up thousands of these impressionable young men with doctrines such as "our Ancestress (the Sun Goddess) commanded her Emperor descendants to organize expeditions against those who would not submit to good rule." Another: "Japan's mission is to glorify the Imperial way to the end of the four seas." This was the "imperial century" and at its end Japan's Emperor would rule the world.

In his searchlight on Japan in the thirties, "Government by Assassination," Hugh Byas calls the young officers "the active militant members of a party permanently in power." This they certainly were. And it was typical of conditions in large Japanese organizations, whether army, government or business, that the men in the middle—manager-supervisor layer—called the shots. This was *gekokujo*—"rule by juniors" or "good staff work": the middle ranks developed the plans and pressed their chiefs to push them through. On the other hand, they had sense enough not to propose plans that their chiefs could not nor would not endorse.

By cultivating their subordinates the chiefs made known their positions on issues, involved the energetic, driving elements of the army in supporting their positions and working out plans to further them. The result was a regenerative cycle in which the young officers then presented the plans and demanded action. This pressure was generally felt at upper echelons or by other military or governmental units who then learned that if the plan was not endorsed, financed or executed, the chief "would find it difficult to control the young officers." This statement, which became a cliche in Japanese politics, was an all-but-naked threat.

The young officers were like tigers. They were the creatures of their chiefs. But once nourished and encouraged by the chiefs, they had to be ridden or curbed, and the belief was fostered that curbing was impossible.

Now, as Japan's horizons contracted and the end drew near, there was frenzy among the young tigers. They had seen their wildest dreams and most daring schemes come to fruition in the early successes of World War II. At its zenith Nippon was overlord of more than 600,000,000 human beings and territories half again as large as the U.S. The military had carved out an empire and had ignored the early protests of the Foreign Ministry, then progressively coerced the succession of cabinets and premiers. They had, reportedly, ignored even the Emperor when the army had, on its own initiative, taken Manchuria in 1931 and created a "China Incident" in 1937. They saw the empire and the power slipping through their clutches. They saw control of the government going too. And looming before them was defeat—something Japan had never experienced as a modern nation. Even worse was the specter it raised: humiliation. In *giri* to the army's name, the young officers could not accept surrender.

(*Giri* is part of that peculiar Japanese system of obligations and reciprocals of infinite complexity that we lump together as "face." This system motivates and determines much of Japanese action and is a force of extraordinary strength. *"Giri* to one's name" includes the individual's duty to admit no failure and the duty to clear one's reputation of insult or imputation of failure.)

No, clearly, the *giri* of the young army officers such as Takeshita, Inaba, Arao, Hatanaka, Ida and Shiizaki and their comrades would not allow surrender. They slapped the hilts of their samurai swords belligerently and swore to crush the Russians and all the rest of the Allies.

The young tigers prepared to shout their Banzais! and die for Emperor and Empire. The rejected truth was that the Empire was doomed; they were doomed. Their chant might have been more accurately "Banzai! then die, Empire!"

Many of the officers in the Military Affairs Bureau were under the influence of Professor Hiraizumi of Tokyo Imperial University, Colonel Hayashi reminds us. "Anami also had interest in Dr. Hiraizumi's historical interpretations. I believe Hiraizumi greatly influenced army officers spiritually. He gave special lectures on Japanese history at the Military Academy and the Army General Staff College. Whenever he spoke he always referred to the Shokyu Civil War and the like to stress the fact that when the Emperor was placed in extremely adverse circumstances the people helped him regain his sovereignty out of their great respect for him."

Hiraizumi was a mythologist who held a chair in history and had built up a sizable following for his extreme doctrines. Essentially, he taught the divinity of the Emperor and his brilliant heredity stretching

Hirohito and family in cozy domestic scene in the air-raid shelter beneath Fukiage garden, 1945.

A January 1945 aerial photo of Kojimachi-ku, *the Imperial Palace in Tokyo.*
1. Palace buildings (destroyed by fire); 2. Imperial household ministry
building and Sakashita gate; 3. Imperial Plaza; 5. Nijubashi (twin bridge);
6. Seimon (main gate); 7. Sakuradamon gate; 9. Metropolitan police headquarters;
13. Fukiage garden; 16. Imperial Guards Division; 17. Guards headquarters;
22. Palace police department; 25. Privy council; 28. Miyakezaka, site of
war minister's official residence; 29. Diet building; 30. Premier's official
residence; 31. Road to Ichigaya Heights, site of war ministry and army GHQ.

Sakuradamon (cherry blossom village gate), site of the signing in 1854 of the treaty between the United States and Japan; on the right, the Imperial Plaza and business district beyond.

Ruins òf the Imperial Palace buildings after the bomb raid and fire in May 1945; the Imperial household ministry (upper center) and Sakashita gate (right) survived.

Imperial Guards Division barracks and parade grounds; General Mori was murdered in his quarters above the central entrance to the square at upper center of picture.

No. 1 Nagata-cho, the kantei, *or official residence of the prime minister; (strange shapes in front of entrance are trees bound with straw to withstand winter).*

KYODO

The Suzuki cabinet: Admiral Baron Kantaro Suzuki, premier, front row center; Navy Minister Admiral Mitsumasa Yonai at his left; Foreign Minister Shigenori Togo, third row second from left; Chief Cabinet Secretary Hisatsune Sakomizu, last row center; to his right, General Anami, war minister.

Marquis Koichi Kido, after his arrest for war crimes in 1945.
He was close adviser to the Emperor.

War Minister General
Korechika Anami, holding the
samurai sword, symbol
of Japan's hereditary ruling class.

*Shigenori Togo, foreign minister, at
the beginning and end of the
Pacific War, as he looked in 1946.*

*Navy Minister Admiral Mitsumasa
Yonai in 1947, while
testifying at the Tokyo Trials.*

*Admiral Soemu Toyoda,
navy chief of staff.*

*Army Chief of Staff General Yoshijiro
Umezu, who signed for the Japanese
·military at the surrender ceremonies
on the battleship* Missouri.

*An artist's conception of the Imperial
Conference of August 10, 1945;
Hirohito sits at center; Premier
Suzuki stands at right; next to him is
General Anami, war minister, flanked
by General Umezu, army chief of staff.
On the far right sits Chief Cabinet
Secretary Sakomizu; on the left, nearest
Hirohito, is privy council president
Hiranuma, and to his right is Navy
Minister Yonai, then Foreign Minister
Togo, and Navy Chief of Staff Toyoda.*

back to the Emperor Jimmu, out of an alligator by Amaterasu's grandson, in 660 B.C. Hiraizumi's heady message was that the Imperial Way was as natural and inevitable as sunrise. The momentum of Japan's destiny was, he taught, impossible to block. When misguided or evil counselors to the Throne failed to realize this, it might be necessary to remove them so that their poison would not affect the Emperor.

Further, the Emperor himself, as the bearer of the Imperial House and Nipponese destiny, might, in extraordinary circumstances, be incapable of determining and directing the nation toward that destiny. (Hadn't Emperor Taisho, Hirohito's father, been such a one?) In such cases, unusual measures would be required and should be used. For instance, it might be necessary to go so far as to put the Emperor *himself* under protection for his own good, for the sake of the nation and its future.

Hiraizumi carefully outlawed drawing the sword *against* the Emperor, and endorsed using weapons only on the Emperor's behalf. This was a fine line indeed, difficult to recognize and open to interpretation. To the Professor the 2–26 Incident of February 26, 1936, was directed against the Emperor and was, therefore, an outlaw action even though the plotters said they were acting, as their manifesto put it, "to safeguard the Fatherland by killing all those responsible for impeding the Showa Restoration and slurring Imperial prestige." But surely there could be no doubt that protecting the Emperor from the ignominy of surrender was acting on his behalf. Such was the Professor's view and that of the passionate young tigers.

With Anami's suspicions to fuel their vivid imaginations, the young tigers closest to the war minister decided to act. They gathered in the war ministry air-raid shelter to contrive a "way out of the situation." Hot-tempered Takeshita was the senior officer present and so led the plotters. Gathered around the table were Lieutenant Colonel Inaba and Kiyoshi Minami, classmates of Takeshita's at the Military Academy, plus Lieutenant Colonel Shiizaki and Major Hatanaka, Takeshita's two subordinates.

"We decided," Takeshita relates, that the "peace faction should be overruled and a *coup* staged in order to prevail upon the Emperor to change his decision." The purpose of the *coup?* "Separate the Emperor from his peace-seeking advisers and persuade him to change his mind and continue the war. We did not consider it essential to kill the members of the peace faction. All we wanted was a military government with all political power concentrated in the hands of the war minister."

That was all. The Colonel and his cohorts wanted to turn the clock back to the situation pre-1867 when the military leader, the Shogun, controlled the country and the Emperor was kept as an inconvenient but necessary appurtenance, sequestered with his effete, stuffy court in the ancient city of Kyoto. The new Shogun would, of course, be Anami, and the young tigers, as his closest associates, would help him lead the nation in the final battle and protracted guerrilla warfare that would follow.

"We did not believe that the Japanese people would be completely annihilated through fighting to the finish. Even if a crucial battle was fought in the homeland and the Imperial forces were confined to the mountains, the number of Japanese killed by enemy forces would be small. Despite the constant victories of Japanese troops in the China Incident, relatively few Chinese were killed. Almost all the strategic points in China were occupied, but the Chungking government in Szechuan could not be defeated. Even if the whole [Japanese] race was all but wiped out, its determination to preserve the national polity would be forever recorded in the annals of history, but a people who sacrificed will on the altar of physical existence could never rise again as a nation."

Outside of their own Military Affairs Bureau, the conspirators included only three men, Colonels Minami, Hosoda, and Hara. The latter two were members of G-2, GHQ. The plotters concluded that they would not contact other units within the ministry. "Nor did we plan to effect deliberate liaison," Takeshita reveals, "with such outside offices as the inspector general of army education, although some personal contacts were made voluntarily by younger participants with their intimate friends."

Above all, the plotters were concerned that the *coup* must be more than just a local attempt. "We wanted to gain allegiance of all the army units stationed even in remote sections of the country. We intended to avoid a situation where individual forces here and there would be holding out against us. The first prerequisite, therefore, was to secure the approval of the war minister and the chief of staff. Before we could act we also had to obtain the consent of the commanders of the 12th Area Army [better known as the Eastern District Army, in charge of Tokyo defense] and the 1st Imperial Guards Division [the 2d Imperial Guards Divison was overseas and the 3d was assigned to the 12th Area Army]."

How to go about this? Anami's brother-in-law and his friends had a simple method, and the beauty of it was that it was perfectly legal. "We decided to utilize the war minister's emergency authority to employ troops in maintaining peace and order. The war minister was already empowered to resort to emergency use of armed forces for local security purposes at his own discretion. We planned to rely chiefly on the 12th Area Army but also to employ the Imperial Guards Division because the plan also concerned the Imperial Palace."

Takeshita and his colleagues enthusiastically threw themselves into working out a foolproof plan. Of course the Colonel's very participation in the plot gave it more status and kinetic energy than other plots, by the fact of Takeshita's special family relationship to the war minister alone. It could easily be inferred—and was—by others that the *coup* had Anami's knowledge and tacit approval.

While his brother-in-law presided over the budding cabal to override the Emperor's decision to surrender, Anami was closeted with Hirohito, giving him his regular report on military conditions. His Majesty, like his subjects, had read Anami's Proclamation to the troops that morning and had been impressed by its grim tone and its implications. It was, of course, diametrically opposed to his peace decision. The Emperor had summoned his chief aide-de-camp, General Hasunuma, to investigate the background of this announcement and report to him.

We do not know specifically what was said when Hirohito was called on that same morning by his one-time aide-de-camp, current war minister, and presumably loyal subject, General Korechika Anami. For all his dissatisfaction with the Imperial Conference decision and the acceptance of the Potsdam declaration, Anami may not even have referred to either. Nor can we be sure that he entreated the Emperor to change his mind, however much he may have wished it. We do know that he reported to His Majesty the dry bones of the war communiqués, embellished somewhat by official statements describing the devotion to duty of Nippon's beleaguered troops in Manchuria, China, and the Southern Regions. It was all very polite and very formal. But was it strictly routine?

From his home on the slope of Akasaka hill, Marquis Kido, the peripatetic Pooh-bah of the Showa Emperor looked out at the mild morning sunshine and recorded in his diary "Saturday; fine." It was unquestionably Saturday; the sun was indubitably beginning another slow-roast of Nippon through a slight haze. The temperature was already eighty and it promised to climb high and quickly. And Kido was feeling fine. He was at the top of his form, with the victory in the recent Imperial Conference inspiring him with confidence that peace was within reach. Today, as yesterday, he would spend his efforts on consolidating support behind the Emperor's decision.

Kido stopped briefly at the tomb of his father in Somei cemetery, meditated fleetingly on the greatness of his grandfather, one of the key men in the Meiji Restoration, and hurried on to his office in the palace. There he buzzed about, arranging that the great and near-great, the leaders of factions and wielders of influence receive indisputable evidence of His Majesty's own decision to surrender.

After a short audience with Hirohito in the *Gobunko* at 9:55 A.M., the Marquis went forward with telephone calls and arrangements. At eleven o'clock Foreign Minister Togo called on him and reported the reactions from world capitals to news of Japan's peace move. In the midst of the world-wide jubilation Nippon was a blacked-out spot on the globe where the Anami Proclamation was an anachronistic rallying cry to return to the Stone Age.

But, Togo told Kido, there was no official news from the Allies. Kido brought the foreign minister up to date on efforts to consolidate the leaders behind the peace decision and asked him to address the princes of the blood that afternoon.

At noon Premier Suzuki came in to see Kido with no news of overriding importance. The privy seal gave him a verbal injection of encouragement and sent him back across the moat.

Shimomura, the president of the Information Board, followed. He went into detail with Kido about the whys and wherefores of the Information Board and Anami statements in the morning papers. This confirmed Kido's belief that decisive, rapid action would be required to overwhelm the anti-peace factions when the surrender was final. As Kido viewed the situation, the second atomic bomb on Nagasaki and the Russian attack had given "sudden powerful stimulus to moves and countermoves between the peace and anti-peace groups. Surveying the situation, I foresaw difficulty and thought it could only be overcome by a broadcast by the Emperor." Shimomura and Kido several times had discussed using radio to get the Emperor's own peace message to his people in his own voice. It was, they agreed, the quickest way to beat the recalcitrants to the people.

Shimomura, in his capacity as president of the Information Board, had the Japan Broadcasting Corporation, NHK, as well as the newspapers and periodicals, under his wing. He would assign a special crew to prepare for such a broadcast. For convenience to the Emperor as well as maximum security, the two men favored recording the message in the palace precincts. Kido would make those arrangements.

The privy seal then went in to talk with Hirohito in the *Gobunko* and broached the subject of a broadcast to the people when the acceptance was final. The Emperor had committed himself at the Imperial Conference to broadcast if necessary. Kido told him it was necessary and he agreed wholeheartedly.

They went over the mechanics of the recording process and the broadcast itself. The two men discussed the actual content of the message, Kido suggesting wording and phrases. He recommended that the message specifically state that the national polity (the Emperor system) would continue. This would reassure the doubters and quiet the extremists.

It was this statement of the war's end from the Emperor-god himself that the privy seal counted on to convince the people. The army would not be able to claim that the Emperor's will heard by millions of his subjects, had been misinterpreted by "false advisers" or government usurpers. The wheels were now in motion to bring the "Voice of the Sacred Crane" to the Japanese. In Japanese life throughout the centuries the unseen Emperor was considered to be ever-present and his words, like the cry of a high-flying bird hidden by clouds, were referred to as the Voice of the Sacred Crane. Kido would now make this mythical phenomenon a reality.

At the mansion of Prince Takamatsu, Hirohito's second brother, the princes of the blood assembled at 1 P.M.. Foreign Minister Togo outlined the current situation and answered questions. Takamatsu, the navy captain, had consistently been for peace; Mikasa, the Emperor's third brother, was an army officer; and Kanin had served as army chief of staff before the war. Higashikuni, the Empress' uncle, was perennially mentioned as a candidate for premier, particularly by the military. It was vitally important, therefore, that these men know the facts and support Hirohito's efforts at this critical time.

After two hours with them, Togo felt that "the princes fully understood the situation when I left them."

Like a yo-yo, Kido bounced back and forth. He went over broadcasting details with Household Minister Ishiwata. He called on General Hasunuma, the chief aide-de-camp, and told him the plans. He met with Machimura, the Tokyo chief of police, who reviewed the peace-and-order situation in the capital. The chief had formerly been a provincial governor. When Home Minister Abe had said he doubted that peace and order could be maintained if surrender occurred, Machimura had volunteered to make sure that there was no outbreak of violence. Suzuki appointed him chief of Tokyo police and was counting on him. There had been serious consideration of replacing Abe. The possibility that such a move might trigger a reaction from the military prevented such action.

Now the police chief implored Kido to bring the end swiftly. He reported that leaflets were being distributed in the streets denouncing the "Badoglios"—Kido, Sakomizu, Suzuki—and calling for death to "traitors." "So far," Machimura said, "the activity is sporadic and apparently without coordination. But hurry the end," he urged.

Back at Domei's offices, about 4 P.M. Hasegawa received a telegram from the Domei representative in Nanking. It said that the *kempeitai* had summoned him to its headquarters and grilled him.

Had Domei broadcast a story about accepting the Potsdam terms? Was it true or not? The Nanking man (and later the Domei bureau men in each major city overseas) had wired to ask Hasegawa if such a story was sent.

The foreign editor read the cable and with great care, crushed it into a tiny ball and dropped it in his wastebasket. He gave those that followed the same treatment.

At 6 P.M. Premier Suzuki arrived once again to see Kido. He reported that still no message had been received from the Allies, that enemy bombers were not flying, apparently grounded by directive of President Truman, and that rumors of army unrest were rampant. Having given his information, the old sea gull headed home for the evening.

Not until 8 P.M. had the bureaucratic wheels revolved to the point where Hasegawa's earlier actions came under scrutiny of responsible government officials. At that time a telephone call came from the Information Bureau asking Hasegawa to report immediately. Full of dread, he told his assistant to take over, climbed aboard his battered bicycle, and pedaled to the Information Bureau offices.

Convinced that his career as foreign editor was over and apprehensive that he might be arrested for not sending Anami's Proclamation or the Information Bureau release over Shimomura's signature the day before, Hasegawa slowly opened the door to the office of the official who had called him. One look and the editor smiled broadly. The man behind the desk had been his junior at college. In Japan old school ties are thicker than water and nearly as strong as blood. Hasegawa relaxed.

His schoolmate was very kind. He explained that he himself in his heart and mind agreed with Hasegawa's action in sending the text of Japan's note abroad, but the army was very angry. Therefore, he wanted the truth of the story behind it. Hasegawa told him the whole history of the event. His friend said candidly that a report would have to be submitted and that he hoped Hasegawa would not suffer any consequences, but he could not promise. That, of course, was up to his superiors.

Hasegawa mounted his bicycle and set off down the hill to Hibiya Park, praying that the reply from the Allies would come quickly, before the military had a chance to claim his scalp. He had another four hours to wait.

While the Domei editor was coasting downhill to his office, Lieutenant Colonel Takeshita was entering the war minister's official residence. He found Anami just finishing dinner. Takeshita had come to apologize for the newspaper announcement and his part in it. For the Colonel this was an unpleasant but not a difficult chore.

Anami waved away Takeshita's concern. "It's all right. Don't worry about it. I was asked by Shimomura at the cabinet meeting about the statement and I explained that I had given my approval to the purport of the message." Far more serious, however, was the war minister's next report. "The Emperor rebuked me about this. He asked 'Isn't this contrary to the cabinet policies?' But I explained 'The army will have to stand against the enemy to the very end, therefore the issuance of instructions to the forces was necessary.' " The war minister assured his brother-in-law that everything was now all right, and by so doing in effect condoned still another breach of discipline in the long and sorry history of *gekokujo*. Furthermore, he gave encouragement by his permissive attitude to the belief that he was "with" the conspirators in fact as well as sympathy.

At GHQ the top echelon was worried that Japan's soldiers overseas would not lay down their arms even if commanded to do so. They were anxious, said Lieutenant General Kawabe, the deputy chief of staff, as to whether the reasons Japan was forced to surrender would be understood by the troops at the front overseas.

After all, they were cut off from Japan; they were receiving only the controlled press reports and broadcasts from home, and these carried few of the dismal facts about Nippon's prostration and destruction. The troops overseas still had substantial supplies of arms and ammunition. They were, by comparison, adequately fed and housed and capable of carrying out a war of attrition or guerrilla warfare for some time. They had no idea that their families were starving and homeless.

General Kawabe believed that the China Expeditionary Army would be the most difficult to control. As GHQ saw it, no part of the China theater was in danger of collapse. In fact, the psychological set of the CEA was that of victors. The commanding officers of the CEA were confident that they could carry on independent operations in China even though faced with increasing numbers of American-equipped units and disruption of their roads, railways, and telephone lines by enemy aircraft. Even the fact that they could now expect no further supplies from Japan did not seem to affect their morale. And the CEA commanders knew they could expect to divert troops from central and south China to the Manchurian front, now that the Russians had attacked.

But, Kawabe noted, "Even assuming increased American aerial activity to be a prelude to American landings in central China in the near future, the feeling in the CEA seemed to be that they would be satisfied if they could divert even one U.S. soldier or one American plane from the Japanese homeland. Because of this high morale, we feared that when an Imperial order for cessation of hostilities was issued, there still might be instances of disobedience within the CEA, bringing disgrace that would be difficult to overcome."

During the morning of the eleventh proof arrived that this analysis was reasonably accurate. A cable came from General Okamura, commanding officer of the CEA, to the war minister and chief of staff. It encouraged continued resistance. Okamura had picked up foreign news broadcasts about a Japanese surrender. From these suspect sources, the CEA commandant surmised that the atmosphere in Tokyo must be in a state of upheaval. He urged Anami and Umezu to continue the fight. To surrender unconditionally to China and the other enemy powers, Okamura said, would be insufferable and "would plunge the land of our ancestors into utter ruin." Okamura was confident that the central authorities, by exertion would take "the proper measures." GHQ responded by rapping out instructions to armies in the field to check unrest and restrain agitation. But at home, in Tokyo, the unrest and agitation continued.

Chapter 15

Unacceptable Answer

Half an hour after midnight August 12, Domei's foreign editor Saiji Hasegawa was once again routed from his sleep atop his office desk. This time it was a telephone call from the Domei monitoring station in the countryside. A newsflash from a San Francisco short-wave station said U.S. Secretary of State James Byrnes had just announced the Allied reply to Japan's acceptance of the Potsdam declaration. The flash was followed by the full text of the U.S. reply.

Hasegawa directed a trusted aide to copy the text while he called government officials to tell them that the critical moment was at hand. His first call was to the foreign ministry. Then the foreign editor called Sakomizu and army and navy headquarters to report the incoming message.

More than a dozen officials from *Gaimusho* arrived, led by Okazaki, the chief of information for the ministry, and including Toshikazu Kase, the English-language expert. The *Gaimusho* delegation feverishly copied the reply and Kase and Okazaki pored over its phrases, preparing to translate it into Japanese. The Associated Press quoted Byrnes as saying:

With regard to the Japanese Government's message accepting the terms of the Potsdam proclamation but containing the statement, "with the understanding that the said declaration does not comprise any demand which prejudices the prerogatives of His Majesty as a sovereign ruler," our position is as follows:

From the moment of surrender the authority of the Emperor and the Japanese Government to rule the state shall be subject to the Supreme

Commander of the Allied Powers, who will take such steps as he deems proper to effectuate the surrender terms.

The Emperor will be required to authorize and ensure the signature by the Government of Japan and the Japanese Imperial General Headquarters of the surrender terms necessary to carry out the provisions of the Potsdam declaration, and shall issue his commands to all the Japanese military, naval and air authorities and to all the forces under their control wherever located to cease active operations and to surrender their arms, and to issue such other orders as the Supreme Commander may require to give effect to the surrender terms.

Immediately upon the surrender the Japanese Government shall transport prisoners of war and civilian internees to places of safety, as directed, where they can quickly be placed aboard Allied transports.

The ultimate form of government of Japan shall, in accordance with the Potsdam declaration, be established by the freely expressed will of the Japanese people.

The armed forces of the Allied Powers will remain in Japan until the purposes set forth in the Potsdam declaration are achieved.

As the Foreign Office specialists read and reread the message a pall settled on them. This was not the answer they had asked for or expected. They wanted a clear-cut "Yes, the Emperor system will be maintained." Instead, the reply brought it into question even more and its provisions about occupation and surrender would surely inflame the military.

It was shortly after 1 A.M. that Shunichi Matsumoto's sleep was ended abruptly by a telephone call from Sakomizu. The cabinet secretary told him Domei had picked up the Allies' reply. Throwing on his clothes, the vice-minister of foreign affairs called for his car and sped to the premier's residence to meet with Sakomizu.

By the time Matsumoto arrived Kase and Adachi, a Domei reporter, were with Sakomizu. They were morose. Sakomizu handed Matsumoto the message and, after reading it, Togo's deputy joined their gloom. On first reading they agreed that it was probably impossible for Japan to accept the terms. Analyzing the message, they were sure that the public would focus on the phrase "shall be subject to the Supreme Commander of the Allied Powers." But to the diplomats the most important part of the note was the statement that "the ultimate form of government . . . shall . . . be established by the freely expressed will of the Japanese people." Did this mean that some form of republic was to emerge? Certainly it did not guarantee that the Emperor system would be retained.

Considering the rumors of unrest in the military and the constant grapevine reports of plots to riot, to assassinate leaders, to take over in a *coup d'état* and the likelihood that a move to have the Allies change the terms would either fail or take so long that the government would collapse, Matsumoto and his colleagues decided the terms had to be "swallowed without chewing." "Let's push it through in its present form," urged the vice-minister.

Matsumoto drove off to confer with Togo. He stopped to pick up two *Gaimusho* specialists—Ando, chief of the Political Affairs Bureau, and Shibusawa, head of the Treaties Bureau—then putted along to Togo's house in Hiroo-cho, on the heights of the Azabu section of Tokyo. About 5:30 A.M. Matsumoto handed the kimono-clad foreign minister the monitored text of the AP release.

Togo was silent until he had read the entire message. Then he put his finger on the paragraph concerning the ultimate form of government.

"This is the key provision, and the most difficult to accept," he said. Matsumoto had discussed this with Ando and Shibusawa in the car. "It would be better if you did not bring up this subject," the vice-minister advised. "If this is made an issue the military services will use it to oppose acceptance." He pointed out the strategy of focusing discussion on the phrase "subject to"; Togo, impressed, agreed to it.

Back at Domei, Captain Arima, the navy man who had shaken up Hasegawa the morning before, arrived to pick up a copy of the Byrnes note. Finding it was in English, as monitored, Arima asked that Domei translate it into Japanese because, he said, the navy men were not very good in the other language.

Though he doubted this, Hasegawa was in no position to argue the matter, so he called his secretary over and wearily dictated a word-for-word translation to her. In the first paragraph, when he came to the crucial phrase "subject to," the foreign editor used the Japanese word, *reizoku,* meaning "subordinate to." When the secretary had typed up the dictation, Arima took a copy with him back to navy

GHQ and an army representative took one to army GHQ. Hasegawa sent a copy to Sakomizu by messenger.

When Sakomizu received Hasegawa's translation he erupted. He called immediately to protest because Hasegawa had used strong Japanese words that would fortify the military's opposition to the note. He asked the foreign editor to find some softer words for the "subject to" phrase and amend his translation.

The Foreign Office experts had been racking their brains and sifting frantically through their English–Japanese dictionaries and phrase books for suitable, more acceptable interpretations of the phrase. After interminable discussion, they came up with the translation "the Emperor . . . will be under the limitation of the Supreme Commander. . . ." This became the official *Gaimusho* version of Byrnes' note. And over the distance between this phrase and "subordinate to" the next battles in the intramural war were waged.

At army headquarters on Ichigaya Heights the chief of staff, General Umezu, and his staff officer met at 8:20 A.M. to assess the Allied reply and concluded that the enemy terms were absolutely unacceptable.

Fired with vehement opposition, the army and navy chiefs of staff called at the palace for an audience with His Majesty. In the small room off his library, Hirohito—with General Hasunuma—met with Umezu and Toyoda. The army chief of staff, the senior in years and service, was the spokesman.

They had come to the Emperor, the General intoned solemnly, to deliver their joint analysis of the newly received Allied terms. He then outlined to Hirohito a harrowing picture of the results to be expected if the note were accepted. His report was frightening enough to shatter a brass idol into a splintered heap of metal.

Without question there was but one alternative: reject the impertinent terms and fight to the very last. With great pleasure the armed forces would die for the Emperor and their country. For to make peace on these terms would cut off the expeditionary forces without support and would lead not only to invasion by foreign troops but to internal destruction of the country as well. Millions of soldiers and sailors would be lost in the last-ditch defense, but there was no other way. The Allied terms were impossible.

General Hasunuma, who by custom was always present when military representatives called on the Emperor, had long years of observation of the army leaders' presentations to His Majesty. Furthermore, he knew many of the top army men personally. Watching and listening to Umezu and Toyoda, Hasunuma thought their performance rang false.

"Both chiefs of staff," he observed, "seemed to be making their recommendations unwillingly, on the request of their subordinates." Hasunuma's deduction was related also to the fact that he had received a call earlier that morning from an army GHQ section chief. This officer had sought out the aide-de-camp to go over the Allied reply with him and object to its "unsatisfactory" contents.

Hirohito listened to the harrowing predictions of the chiefs of staff and was not reduced to splinters or to hysteria. He absorbed the pleas of his two top warriors and said "No *formal* Allied answer has come yet. We will be sure to study it well after it arrives. We can probably make another inquiry about those points still in doubt." In the Emperor's face Hasunuma detected that Hirohito sensed the General and the Admiral were merely going through a required formality demanded by the intransigence of their subordinates. Hirohito, his aide noted, "displayed no strong reaction."

Umezu and Toyoda, having received His Majesty's response, withdrew. The Emperor, in the loneliness of his circumscribed existence, sadly realized that they had not really heard him when he said, in the Imperial Conference on the tenth, that he wished the war ended immediately.

At the foreign minister's home Togo and his lieutenants settled on their strategy. *Gaimusho* would take an aggressive stance, maintaining that the Allied reply was acceptable. It would go full speed ahead to bring about surrender before the opposition coalesced sufficiently to block it. Matsumoto and his colleagues departed for the foreign ministry leaving Togo to tackle the leaders.

Outwardly as granitic as ever, Togo at this moment heaved a sigh. His task was formidable: he had to carry the cabinet along with him in approving the Allied reply. This was one of those moments Togo most missed his beloved Turkish cigarettes. One or two would have been a real comfort at a time such as this. But his heart specialist had said no to tobacco and alcohol when Togo was in Moscow five years ago, and, typically, the steel-willed diplomat had overnight cut his ration of cigarettes from sixty a day to zero. On the alcohol he was not so extreme, indulging in an occasional bracer. The doctor's prognosis was that he could probably live to ninety years or more if he took it easy and cared for his health. He could scarcely have said more plainly "Change your work or prepare for an early end." But who had the right to refuse his country's call?

After donning his suit, Togo gave his Sealyham an affectionate head-rub and plunged into the cavernous back seat of the Buick limo. "To the *kantei*," he ordered, and settled back to put his thoughts in order. "My task," he reflected, "is to win over the military leaders . . . my strategy must be to gain my point by persuading a majority of the cabinet, including the premier, to agree with me. If the PM changes his mind, I will be checkmated, and to insist on my point in the face of growing support for continuing the war will result in forced resignation of the cabinet. This, in turn, may well mean not only loss of the present opportunity, but increased agitation against ending the war . . . and an end to all hope of peace."

But if he *could* bring the cabinet around, today, he thought, could be the turning point to wind up the whole bloody war.

At the premier's official residence Togo found Suzuki in his office "pacing the quarter deck" amid a fog of cigar smoke. The foreign minister took the Admiral to a table and over green tea went through the Byrnes note item by item. Suzuki nodded his massive head as Togo explained, and the foreign minister believed that most if not all of his counsel was getting through to the old man. (He was over-optimistic, as it turned out.)

Togo drove to the palace, stopped briefly at Kido's office and discussed the note with him. Then he was ushered into the Imperial Presence at 11 A.M. Togo noted that His Majesty's hair was a trifle disheveled and there were circles under his eyes, accentuated by pallor and loss of weight.

The foreign minister analyzed the Allied reply with Hirohito, pulling no punches. It was true that the terms meant depending on the Allies' good intentions for the Emperor's safety and the continuation of the imperial line. Togo pointed out that the Allies were not fools, and would not be likely to do anything to His Majesty or the imperial family that would cause the Japanese people to resist them. So it was to their interest, from the standpoint of peace and order if nothing else, that the Emperor continue as ruler.

At the worst, Togo advised, the occupation would keep the Emperor until a plebescite was conducted. But in any free and uncontrolled referendum the people would favor continuation of the Emperor system. Any other alternative simply was inconsistent with Japanese character. Togo had no fear on this point and counseled the Emperor to trust his subjects on it. He warned that the military, however, might react strongly against this provision of the reply.

Hirohito was clear-eyed as he told Togo that he considered the reply satisfactory and said that it should be accepted as it stood. He instructed the foreign minister to tell the premier his wishes in this matter. In effect, the Emperor said, "I understand the dangers but to me the prime matter is ending the war now. Get a move on."

Togo climbed back into the Buick and rode back to the *kantei*. He slipped into the old Admiral's office and relayed the Emperor's directive that the Allied terms be accepted forthwith. Suzuki had heard variations of this ever since June 22, when the Emperor had openly announced his intention of ending the war. In the premier's mind, as always, was the unspoken question "How?"

Now Baron Hiranuma unexpectedly came in. He had been reviewing the note (the military had generously furnished him a copy) with great care. Bringing his prodigious legal talent to bear on the document, the privy council president had dissected it completely and found it wanting. From his lookout point as self-appointed number-one defender of the national polity, the ancient barrister spied doom in paragraphs two and five.

Togo left to prepare for the upcoming cabinet meeting, and the two old men continued their discussion, Hiranuma's fear of Allied intentions acting on Suzuki without antidote.

"Reduced to its simplest elements," said Hiranuma, "Japan agreed to accept the Potsdam terms on condition that the Emperor's prerogatives to rule the nation would be safeguarded. Does the U.S. reply contain such safeguards? No. This is the vital matter. This point must be fully confirmed before we give our final reply. The foreign minister believes it unnecessary to get further confirmation on this. What about you?"

Suzuki, eyes rolling like a stag at bay, sucked on his cigar and admitted that he had to agree with Hiranuma on that particular point. "It is not that the Allied reply could not be accepted in its present form, but that we should ask for confirmation of this one point once again since it is such a key matter."

Encouraged by the Admiral's response, Hiranuma left him hidden by a cloud of tobacco smoke and indecision and trundled off to the palace to work on the lord keeper of the privy seal. Kido sandwiched him in between Household Minister Ishiwata (concerning questions about the Korean royal family) and another audience with His Majesty. The privy seal was not surprised that Hiranuma had decided the Allied note was unacceptable. This was in character for him; the uncharacteristic action had been his coming out at the Imperial Conference in favor of accepting the Potsdam terms.

Sakomizu's informers reported that Hiranuma's house was a regular command post of the opposition, with military officers running in and out all day as though a campaign were in full swing and the officer in charge was situated there. Adjoining Hiranuma's house was the building that housed an ultrapatriotic society founded years before by the old man. It was a rallying point for extremists and now served as a convenient way station on the route to rejecting the surrender. Sakomizu thought it looked now like the "headquarters of the resistance."

Fundamentally Hiranuma objected to the phrase "subject to" the Supreme Commander of the Allied Powers, holding that it invaded the Emperor's sovereign rights and prerogatives. He violently rejected the paragraph calling for the people of Japan to decide their own form of government by their "freely expressed will." Into this the solicitor's eye read dark hints of submerged plans to overthrow the imperial system of government.

Though no such plots ever surfaced, the wording of paragraph five was intentionally framed to serve not only the needs of the Japanese, but the clamor of Allies as diverse as the USSR and Britain on the final type of government for Japan. It answered the demands of those who wanted to uproot the Emperor system as well as those who wished to preserve it: the decision would be up to the Japanese people, as the Potsdam proclamation had promised.

It was almost noon when Navy Minister Yonai heard that Admiral Toyoda had called on the Emperor and had recommended rejection of Byrnes' note. The navy minister ordered Vice-admiral Zenshiro Hoshina, chief of the Naval Affairs Bureau, to summon both Toyoda and the vice-chief of staff, Onishi, at once. When Hoshina returned, Yonai pointed to a spot alongside his desk, ordering "You too, stand here as a witness to this." Hoshina stood by as Toyoda and Onishi came in. Yonai was behind his desk, drawn up to his full six feet in icy fury. "Never," says Hoshina, "have I seen him greet any man with such dignity and indignation as he did at this moment."

(At the last SCDW meeting, Onishi had suddenly appeared in the conference room without warning or advance notice to either Toyoda or Yonai. Saying not a word to his two navy superiors, Admiral Onishi called the war minister out of the room. There, in the hallway, in front of several military men and secretariat officials, Onishi had passionately addressed Anami. "The navy minister is weak-kneed. He is of no use, so you military people must insist strongly on the continuation of the war." He implored Anami to reject the Allied terms and told him that many in the navy were depending on his leadership in this.

(Anami had told his confidants his view of Yonai: "Yonai is so timid"; "The navy minister does not have strong will." In general, Anami agreed with Onishi. But to make a public announcement of disloyalty to one's superior officer was more than the war minister could stomach. He summarily thanked Onishi for his confidence and returned to the conference. Onishi's words, of course, were relayed to Yonai shortly after the end of the meeting. They had sent the "white elephant's" blood pressure skyrocketing; with word of the Toyoda–Umezu delegation to the Emperor, Yonai boiled over.) Now, eyes blazing, the navy minister lacerated Toyoda and Onishi verbally.

"The behavior of the Naval General Staff is execrable. If you have anything to say about me, why don't you come to me and tell me about it personally? Such impudent behavior as walking into the meeting of the SCDW uninvited is unforgivable."

Admiral Yonai then turned to the chief of staff. "And what is the idea of recommending to the Emperor such momentous action as rejecting the Allied note without even consulting me? The spirit of the instructions issued yesterday to all naval personnel, in substance was to warn against such action as this. To have behaved as you have, despite the warning, is inexcusable."

Toyoda remained rigid. He said nothing, but his eyes sought out Hoshina, and Hoshina thought his expression meant "I am really very sorry."

Onishi, tears rolling down his cheeks, apologized to Yonai. As the navy minister sat down behind his desk he curtly dismissed the three men.

The atmosphere in navy GHQ, says Hoshina, had been so bad that for a while the Admiral worried that Onishi's fanatical followers might even threaten Yonai's life. But after the navy minister put the vice-chief of staff in his place, Hoshina's worries were relieved, "at least partially," though he still sensed that some trouble was brewing.

At two thirty in the afternoon the Military Affairs Bureau conspirators, led by the war minister's brother-in-law Colonel Takeshita and his close friend Colonel Inaba, had decided it was time to secure the kingpin in their plot. They knew that they must win Anami's cooperation in the *coup*. So a delegation headed by Takeshita and Inaba went to the war minister's office.

Takeshita explains: "Before seeing Anami I thought it best to talk to the vice-minister, Wakamatsu. So I went to his office and reported that, under the circumstances, the troops would probably have to be used to maintain the peace and order in the country. The vice-minister wrote what I had said on a small slip of paper and handed it to secretary Hayashi with orders to deliver it to the war minister.

"Seeing little hope of getting their way at that rate, my colleagues, who had been waiting in the hall, immediately entered the war minister's office. Wakamatsu, Colonel Inaba, Colonel Arao, Major Hatanaka, Colonel Hayashi, and Lieutenant Colonel Hirose [private secretary to the vice-minister] also hurried in." They caught Anami as he was buckling on his sword, with his hat in hand, ready to dash out to the cabinet meeting.

"Representing my comrades, I stated to the minister our view that it was utterly inadvisable to end the war under the present conditions and the the Eastern District Army should be alerted to furnish troops to maintain order inasmuch as circumstances might well require such action." Anami reacted typically: instant action without reflection. "The minister," continues Takeshita, "immediately directed Waka- matsu to take necessary steps in accordance with our advice."

At this point Colonel Hiroo Sato, the War Preparations Section chief, accidentally came into the room, caught the drift of the situa- tion and, with tears in his eyes, pleaded that the officers not act hastily. "Thereupon," Takeshita reports, "Hatanaka made a remark about 'Badoglios' in the Japanese army which was pointedly directed at Colonel Sato. The war minister said sternly 'Military men must trust one another,' producing a solemn effect in the room where con- fusion had reigned a moment before.

"Then Lieutenant Colonel Hirose tugged at my sleeve and whis- pered 'Tell the minister that all the young officers have faith in him and are willing to follow him without question.' I felt awkward, but relayed this to the war minister. Since Anami had to hurry away to his appointment, the meeting ended there."

"Though still unable to determine the war minister's real attitude, we secretly went ahead with the necessary preparations," recalls Takeshita.

"Contact with the Imperial Guards Division was particularly im- portant. Therefore on the same day we sounded the view of Lieu- tenant General Mori, the Division Commander, and found out he was absolutely opposed to the *coup*. Since he had been charged with guarding the Emperor and the Imperial Palace he would, he stated, perform the duty in direct accord with the Imperial wishes regardless of the orders from the war minister or chief of staff to the contrary. Since we had independently won over the regimental and subordinate commanders of the division, we decided that when the time for the *coup* arrived we would call Mori to the war ministry, try once more to persuade him to join us and, if he resisted, confine him in the min- ister's office and use the Imperial Guard Division's troops as planned."

The plot was simmering along, but the key elements were yet to be nailed down. Time was growing short. The plotters had arbitrarily set midnight August 13 as jump-off time. Their major concern was whether they would get to Anami in time to enlist him in the plot before then.

At 3 P.M. the Japanese cabinet met in special session at the *kantei* to review the contents of the Allied note. It was now up to Togo to demonstrate his powers.

He was candid. "The Allied response," he admitted, "is not entirely reassuring. Japan had raised one condition—that the Emperor's sovereignty would be continued. The Allies replied in effect that His Majesty's powers would not be unlimited during the occupation, but that the Supreme Commander's authority would be paramount in order to make sure the Potsdam terms were carried out. Naturally the state and the ruler would be limited to this extent, until the terms were executed and the occupation ended. The Emperor's position was not destroyed, nor changed in principle."

Paragraphs three, four, and six, were understandable and acceptable, said Togo. But paragraph five, about the "free will of the Japanese people," needed examination.

"Establishing the form of government in this way was one of the most important points in the Atlantic Charter and again in the Potsdam declaration. But this provision, far from arousing suspicion, should reassure us for it promises, in effect, that the Japanese themselves will decide their form of government without outside interference. And who can believe that the Japanese people would choose anything but their Emperor system?"

Then the foreign minister warned that there was "strong opposition among some of the Allies to Japan's imperial system. But," he said, "the Anglo-American leaders have managed to restrain it to the extent that Byrnes' reply evidences. If we should now demand revisions in it, it is most probable that we will fail. And if we persist in debating the point, it is quite likely that the harsher opinions among the Allies will then be given free reign and a demand to abolish the Imperial house will be the upshot. In such an event, we must be resigned to a complete break in negotiations."

Togo had scarcely stopped talking before War Minister Anami ripped into his carefully constructed presentation. As expected, the military attack was focused on Byrnes' words "subject to" (totally unacceptable; compromised the Emperor; reduced His Majesty to a lackey) and the referendum on Japan's form of government (this rejects our request for assuring continuation of the Emperor system). Though he was bitter in his rejection of these points, Anami's mild tone of voice and reasonable attitude made the content of his attack seem softer.

His points were echoed by two other cabinet members, Home Minister Abe and Justice Minister Matsuzaka: Since Japan's national polity had been handed down by the gods, it could not be put up for decision by the people. The Empire's fighting men cannot bear the humility of being forced to give up their weapons.

The discussion staggered up and down over these metaphysical and ego-shattering promontories with Togo rebutting the arguments and Yonai backing him up. About 4 P.M. Togo put in a call to Matsumoto at the Foreign Office. "The situation looks extremely bad," he reported. "It's a difficult problem. The atmosphere at the meeting is definitely against acceptance of the Allied note." Obviously it would be best to wind up the meeting without a formal vote—perhaps recess it and work for some change in the situation. Matsumoto urged Togo to come back to *Gaimusho* after the meeting so they could plan further moves. The foreign minister agreed and, in low spirits, returned to the conference.

About an hour later the premier, seeming to tune in on the debate for the first time, put down his cigar and said with great feeling "If disarmament is to be forced on Japan, there is no alternative to continuing the war! To be disarmed by the enemy would be unbearable for a Japanese soldier and under such circumstances the Allied reply is unacceptable."

Stunned by this, Togo realized in a flash that his position was untenable. To prevent bringing the matter to a vote now, when Suzuki could and might cast his weight against the Allied reply, Togo stalled for time. "As the *official* reply of the Allies has not yet arrived, we had better postpone our discussion until after it is received." All of those present knew the formal Allied reply would be coming in at any moment. Suzuki therefore acted upon the suggestion, recessing the meeting until the official note should have been received later that evening.

Beside himself with exasperation, Togo herded the premier into his office. Once behind closed doors, the foreign minister exploded. "What are you thinking of?" he asked the docile old salt. "I completely disagree with you. This is no time to bring up the question of disarmament. Incessant bandying of words over the ultimatum from the enemy is profitless. Unless we are prepared for a breakdown of negotiations, there is no alternative but to accept their reply as it stands. As the premier is well aware, the Emperor wants to end the war. It goes without saying that his opinion, as Commander-in-Chief, should prevail. But the question now at issue involves the very existence of the Imperial house. I warn you," and here Togo slowed his words, emphasizing each one, "if you and the cabinet insist on continuing the war I will be forced to report my opposing view directly to the Emperor!" White with rage, Togo stalked from the room.

Neither Togo nor Suzuki wanted this for it would automatically bring down the Suzuki government. To prevent such a collapse they would have to reconcile their views. The foreign minister, depressed and shaken in the face of this crisis, drove the few blocks to his office and called Matsumoto in. Recapitulating for the vice-minister, he said: "With this turn of events, resignation from my post as foreign minister might be the only course left open for me."

Completely taken off balance, Matsumoto pleaded, "It will be ruinous if you resign. Everything will be thrown into confusion. Please rest this evening. Let's start afresh tomorrow."

Then Matsumoto had an inspiration that would insure an overnight respite. "Although the formal reply has not arrived yet, it will probably come in some time this evening. Since it is disadvantageous to push it through under the present circumstances, let us put it out as if it arrived tomorrow morning and distribute it with that receipt date." Togo, half-listening, wanly nodded his agreement, then left for home.

The vice-minister grabbed the telephone and called the chief of *Gaimusho's* telegraph section, Akira Oe. Matsumoto carefully instructed him about handling the expected official message from the Allied powers via Sweden or Switzerland. "In any case," he cautioned, "stamp the receipt date as of tomorrow morning, *August 13*, and hold it until then." The vice-minister repeated his directions to be sure he was understood.

Meanwhile, Togo made a way-stop at the palace. Realizing he would bring the government crashing down if he went directly to Hirohito, Togo called on Kido. The privy seal recorded in his diary:

1830 hours. Togo called and said the prime minister had agreed with Hiranuma's opinion and Togo is worried about future prospects. I feel extremely anxious.

But Kido's thoughts were somewhat less constricted: "Togo called and surprised me by telling me that the prime minister too, apparently approved Hiranuma's opinion. Togo felt very uneasy about amicably concluding peace negotiations. If they broke down, I thought, Japan would have to face a situation far worse than that which could confront her if she had gone on fighting to the bitter end without interruption. I felt I had to do everything possible to make the government proceed toward the peace goal. I had Matsudaira [Kido's secretary] telephone the premier to ask for an interview. The prime minister (also) wanted to see me and promised to call later."

Reassuring the foreign minister, Kido told Togo that the Emperor had already made up his mind about the surrender, and the privy seal would talk to Suzuki and impress him with this fact and the need to wind up the matter accordingly. Togo, still depressed and skeptical, piled into the limousine and drove home to the heights of Azabu and his waiting, affectionate, nonpolitical terrier.

Soon after the cabinet meeting adjourned, Domei foreign editor Hasegawa once more was called upon to ride up Kasumigaseki hill. He was summoned by an irate minister of finance, Mr. Hirose. He asked Hasegawa to come and bring the English original of Byrnes' message and his translation. It was a command appearance.

The editor pedaled his battered bicycle up to his appointment and, like a Christian tossed to the lions, was shown in to see the fuming finance minister. Though Hasegawa tried to explain the meaning of the Allied note, the bureaucrat was in such a lather he heard practically nothing. "This is against the Japanese Constitution," he ranted. "Under these terms they can take over the Emperor. . . ."

Hasegawa, attempting to reason with him, said "But we have been defeated in this war, therefore we have to accept." This was simply a red flag, and the bull roared even louder. "It was," says Hasegawa ruefully, "typical of the mentality or psychology of our people. We couldn't see that we were actually defeated."

If one of the "insiders"—a cabinet minister—could not see this, how could one expect any greater insight on the part of the millions who read and believed only what they were fed? When Hasegawa left to cycle back to Domei headquarters the finance minister was still chewing up the walls, rejecting the insulting enemy terms.

At 6:40 P.M. on the twelfth the telegraph key at *Gaimusho's* cable section chattered with the long-awaited official Allied reply, forwarded via Sweden. According to instructions, section chief Oe put it aside and stamped it 7:10 A.M., August 13. Immediately afterward a wire from Japan's minister to Sweden Suemasa Okamoto came clicking in. Addressed to the foreign minister, the cable was referred to Matsumoto, who called for a copy and read it eagerly.

Okamoto reported "It appears as if the U.S. is having a very difficult time in harmonizing the opinions among various Allied Powers regarding the reply to Japan. The Soviet Union and China are opposed to the retention of the Emperor system. The London *Times,* too, published an editorial calling for the abolishment of the deified-Emperor system."

To Matsumoto the cable seemed heaven-sent. First of all, it fit exactly the observations and thinking of top *Gaimusho* officials. As the vice-minister saw it, "If we were to plan further negotiations, Truman would have to make clear his attitude concerning the Emperor system, which he had expressly left untouched. Then, since the guarantee of the Emperor system could not be positively promised under the present circumstances, the negotiations would probably be broken off completely."

The description from Japan's minister to Sweden, thought Matsumoto, did an excellent job of explaining the current atmosphere among the Allies and would impress the premier with the urgency of accepting the terms. The vice-minister hailed his limousine, rushed to the *kantei,* and scurried to Suzuki's office. He was on intimate speaking terms with the Admiral.

Now the vice-minister burst in on Suzuki. He explained that a cable had just come in and handed it to the premier, who scanned it. "Since the international situation is as Okamoto states," Matsumoto said formally, "please give full play to your great statesmanship at this time."

Suzuki looked at the diplomat with his blank, nonplused expression and shrugged his rounded shoulders. "I have the same idea," he muttered, handing back the cable, "but as the war minister and Mr. Hiranuma are making strong representations to the Emperor, it's a very hard problem."

Matsumoto left, filled with foreboding. He had known old Suzuki for years, and in the crisis-packed four months since April, when Suzuki had become premier, the diplomat had observed the old man's unpredictability. He often came out forcefully in favor of one policy and then went full speed, crablike, in a different direction. Sometimes he did nothing but "tread water."

The vice-minister had rushed to the premier's residence to stiffen old Suzuki's spine. Now, discouraged and limp, he returned to his make-shift office.

Whisking into Kido's room like a huge black-feathered bird settling for a landing, premier Suzuki arrived in his cutaway, trailing cigar smoke. In his open, blunt way, the old man told the privy seal about the day's consultations. Kido thought he seemed much annoyed at the arguments of the faction which had set itself up as guardians of the national structure.

Kido, the Emperor's eyes-and-ears, commented "I don't intend to belittle the argument of those who are anxious to guard the national polity so jealously. But on the basis of careful study, the foreign ministry assures us that there is nothing objectionable in the paragraphs in question. It would get us no place if we allowed our moves to be swayed by opinions of individuals. Therefore, I think we have no alternative but to trust the interpretation of responsible authorities, in other words, the foreign ministry. If the Potsdam declaration is rejected at this stage and if the war continues, Japan will have to sacrifice additional millions of innocents, due to bombings and starvation. Even if a serious disturbance occurs on the home front because of accepting the Potsdam terms, we shall have only to sacrifice our lives. Without wavering or hesitation, let us carry out the policy to accept the Potsdam declaration!"

Suzuki had sat transfixed throughout Kido's oration, drinking it all in. He was moved deeply. Perhaps Kido's call to a meaningful and noble sacrifice in behalf of the Emperor's desire for peace stirred the old warhorse. Perhaps the vision of preventing his countrymen from descending into the Stone Age finally got across. Whatever the specific, Kido reports, "I felt greatly reassured to hear the premier say emphatically in reply 'Let us do!' " The privy seal took this to mean endorsement and felt self-satisfaction as old Suzuki gathered himself together and ambled out to "do" or die.

Confidently, Kido telephoned Togo at his home. With a slight note of triumph, the privy seal reported that he had had "an unusually frank talk" with the premier and had been able "to refresh his determination." Suzuki now understood the situation and was willing to go ahead on the basis of the Allied reply. He was, said Kido, not the sort of man to oppose the Emperor's will. Nevertheless, both Togo and Kido went to bed that night with fingers crossed.

One important action planned by Kido and the Emperor was the rallying of the imperial family around Hirohito's decision. Thus a family council had been scheduled, and while the cabinet was whacking away at the Allied terms, the Emperor was talking to his close relatives. The princes of the blood had assembled in the chamber off the imperial library and Hirohito explained to them the object of his decision. He then asked them to unite solidly, as one, to assist him in this dark hour.

Kido, who heard about the meeting from its principal performer, understood that it was a huge success. The Emperor told him that there was an open discussion and the princes had pledged their support.

That same evening, when General Anami visited Prince Mikasa, his purpose was twofold: to learn from the Prince what had gone on at the family council and to implore him to ask the Emperor to change his mind. The war minister drove to Mikasa's palace with his secretary, Colonel Hayashi. He went in to see the Prince jauntily and full of confidence. He returned to the car chastened and quiet. On the trip back to his official residence, Anami confided to Hayashi. "Prince Mikasa severely scolded me, saying 'since the Manchurian Incident the army has not once acted in accordance with the Imperial wish. It is most improper that you should still want to continue the war when things have come to this stage.' " These words, says Hayashi, "struck the war minister very hard."

At both the war ministry and GHQ confusion was the order of the day. Top officers were in constant meetings. Most section chiefs were nowhere to be found. Underlings visited friends in other units and telephoned to their own sections occasionally to find out what, if anything, was wanted of them. Rumors swept the military establishment in waves. One that further inflamed the outraged army men had it that the "Badoglio" faction planned to kill the war minister. Twenty *kempeitai* were sent to guard Anami's official residence and fend off the assassins.

At the navy building the situation was slightly more orderly. By evening many navy officers knew that there was a plan afoot in the army for a *coup* of some sort. The information was hazy but navy brass understood that the plan called for "eliminating" members of the pro-surrender faction. "Large-scale use of force"—six battalions of the Imperial Guard Division—was planned, it was heard. Then word came that the plan had been shelved "since it was recognized that Byrnes' reply would naturally be rejected because of its extremely unfriendly tone."

August twelfth was a Sunday. Anami was a family man. Like any civil servant, he looked forward to his weekends with his wife and children. There had been precious little family time in recent weeks. Now determined to spend a few moments with them, the war minister directed his driver to take him to the family home in the Tokyo suburb of Mitaka.

No time this Sunday to take the boys to the beach or to the horse races. The races were another wartime casualty. They had long been shut down. Nor was there time this Sunday to pile the family in a car and go off on a carefree spin around the dusty outskirts of Tokyo, even if the roads had been drivable. There was not much time for any private activity. The family outings they had enjoyed in the past were another wartime casualty. There was a clear view of the top of Mount Fuji and a rosy sunset, however.

Anami had the children take their hot baths, then intended to have dinner with the family. But the word had been passed among his subordinates, friends, neighbors, and adherents that the war minister was at home this evening. Many of them took this literally to be an "at home," and called in groups.

It was like a New Year's reception all over again. Even Lieutenant Colonel Ida and Major Hatanaka struggled with the battered transportation system and made the twenty-mile trek out to Mitaka to verify that their adored leader was being guarded well and was safe. Anami welcomed them about 9 P.M. as he had the others, with easy conversation and some sake and cigarettes. It was late when the last visitor left the modest combination Western-Japanese stucco house and disappeared down the street in the maze of near-identical blocks with their near identical houses for the return trip to Tokyo.

The family man had missed dinner with his family. His two schoolgirl daughters were in their *futons,* fast asleep. His youngest son, still in junior high school, was also in bed when Anami finally made the rounds to see his offspring sleeping peacefully. Two were missing: the oldest boy, who was in the army serving as an air force technician. The second son had been a soldier in China and had been killed just four years ago August 14.

From his father, a pious Buddhist, Anami had learned to give little attention to food, so he did not feel he had missed a special dinner. Wartime rations made anything special impossible, anyhow. He had missed a quiet time with his loved ones, however. In the morning, in good spirits as usual, Anami took his modest breakfast and bade farewell to his family. Word had come that a Big Six meeting was to be held at the premier's residence at 8:45 A.M. that morning. But Anami had errands he wanted to take care of before that.

Bidding farewell to his wife, the General climbed into the staff car. Glancing back, he saw his wife's slight, stooped figure in the entryway. Her features bore the stamp of resignation typical of Japanese wives. He smiled and waved through the car window. Across her face there was not so much as a flicker of change. She raised her hand automatically as the auto disappeared from her life around a corner a block away.

Chapter 16

Carp on the Chopping Block

At his quarters on the imperial palace grounds on August 13 Marquis Koichi Kido, lord keeper of the privy seal, had an early caller. At 7:30 A.M. the war minister arrived at Kido's suite of offices in the imperial household building.

Kido's sparsely furnished office was as anonymous in character as any built in the 1920s in Liverpool, Schenectady, or Brussels. For this confrontation of two key antagonists in the ripening tragedy an appropriate setting would have been an inn or a teahouse, with spectacular view of a river or lake, a *koto* mournfully drifting ancient sagas through elegant sliding doors on which the famous Forty-seven Ronin sally forth to immortal vengeance. Kido's office, with its businesslike air, lacked the trappings of *Kabuki*-style high drama.

Yet the ingredients of drama were there. In the lull between moves in their conflict the warlord in his impeccable uniform faced the imperial factotum in his kimono. About Kido there was something of the terrier in appearance. He lacked the size and weight of a bulldog, but made up for it with calculation and speed.

Kido was recognized as a leader of the peace faction and had been called a "false counselor" to the Emperor. Until two days before, he had been guarded by fifteen policemen. But then, for his own safety, the privy seal decided to move into the imperial household ministry building, remaining within the confines of the palace walls.

Anami and Kido had known each other for years, since both had served the Emperor in the early thirties. Kido was chief secretary to the lord keeper of the privy seal at that time and served also as

234

counselor to the household ministry; Anami was an aide-de-camp to His Majesty and a colonel of infantry. In the imperial household "family" they met frequently during this period and often ate together "in the same dining room" (as Kido put it).

They respected one another as individuals and as adversaries. Neither knew it at the time, but this was to be their last meeting.

When Kido looked at Anami he saw the figurehead of the military masters of the country, the apex of opposition to the Emperor's declared will. For His Majesty had told the war minister and the other members of the Supreme Council for Direction of the War more than seven weeks ago to end the war. Three days before, on August 10, he had expressly told them he favored accepting the Potsdam declaration. Now here was Anami, the standard-bearer of the opposition, full of bounce and smiling brightly at him. Did the General have something fresh to propose?

Anami's face went long. He spoke gravely. Kido knew (because both Togo and Suzuki had told him) that Anami had led the attack on the Allied reply all day August 12. "Japan will be destroyed," the war minister boomed in a voice of doom, "if the Allies' demands are accepted." Nothing new there.

"We must by all means have the Emperor reconsider and conduct a final decisive battle in the homeland." Nothing new in that—just what the military had been advocating for months.

"What do you think? Pessimism in war never yields good results. If Japan makes one last effort, it will not be impossible to end the war more to our advantage." The war minister plugged his mouth with a cigarette as he awaited Kido's reply.

It was, thought Kido, a typical Anami statement—involuted and inexact, based on emotion and wish rather than reality and logic. Kido had no more faith in maxims than in amulets. Kido believed the evidence of his own eyes and the statistical reports he had received. He had little use for unsupported wishful thinking.

The privy seal respected Anami's strength of character and was past the stage of temporizing. He felt sure that if he spoke his mind Anami would not bring harm to him, regardless of how distasteful the message might be. In his recent talks with Anami he had been candid but discreet. Now, when he sensed that there was a real chance for peace, he did not intend to be coy.

"That will not do," Kido countered, his large eyes calmly surveying the war minister. "After reading the Foreign Office research reports on the note, I cannot see how this [Allied] reply is going to harm us. We can get as many different opinions as we want, but we cannot bother with so many conflicting, ill-informed views. Our only alternative is to abide by the opinions of the responsible authorities [meaning the Foreign Office experts]."

Shifting his ground, Kido adopted Anami's premises: "But suppose the Emperor did change his attitude and rescind Japan's peace proposal of the tenth. Suppose he issued a proclamation for a final decisive battle. Remember, Japan has already notified the Allies that we are willing to accept the Potsdam terms. If the Emperor should now turn his back on this official note, the Allies and the rest of the world then would regard him as a fool or a lunatic. It is unbearable to have His Majesty insulted that way. You may have your own ideas, but I have no alternative but to follow my own policy."

The war minister snorted smoke like a thwarted dragon. Suddenly his frown evaporated. His expression reversed. Anami laughed. "I understand your position quite well, Kido-san. I knew you would say something like that." He hesitated, then spoke solemnly. "But the atmosphere in the army is indeed tense."

Stubbing out his cigarette, he rose to his feet and was on his way all in one motion.

It had been a civilized meeting with no surprises. Each had confirmed the opposition of the other. Had that been Anami's purpose in calling on Kido? Or was it to alert the privy seal and the Court to his slippery position, struggling to restrain the army? Kido pictured Anami forcibly holding the lid on a furiously boiling cauldron. The key question was could he keep the lid on long enough?

In the premier's official residence on this hot August morning the office of the chief cabinet secretary, Hisatsune Sakomizu, was functioning full blast before 8 A.M. Sakomizu was in a tight spot.

From the start of the Suzuki administration the military had looked at the cabinet secretary with suspicion. In their view the premier, like the Emperor, had his false counselors—and chief among these was Sakomizu. It was significant, therefore, that Sakomizu's name shared billing with Kido on those posters that had erupted in train stations and on crowded corners in recent days. Kido, Sakomizu, and others of the peace faction should be killed on sight as traitors, spat the placards. Now the cabinet secretary was seated at his desk busily working on details of the approaching cabinet meeting. There had been rumors that the young officers were reaching the boiling point and that *coup d'état* attempts were imminent. Other rumors simply reported that assassination lists had been drawn up and described who had "made the team." The guard around Sakomizu had been increased and bookcases and filing cabinets had been moved to block entry to the offices of key officials whose lives might be in danger.

Into Sakomizu's office this morning stamped a lieutenant bearing an armload of papers. He stopped directly in front of the secretary and, when Sakomizu looked up, contemptuously spilled the papers onto the desk in a cascade that flooded it and pushed Sakomizu's other work to the floor.

The cabinet secretary sprang up, trying to ward off and catch the falling papers. By then the military man had emptied his hands. He looked at Sakomizu defiantly, did an about-face, and stalked out of the office without a word. Picking up the papers, the cabinet secretary noted that they all were top-secret, dealing with the need to fight the war to final "victory." Sakomizu got the message.

No sooner had that special delivery been put aside than the cabinet secretary found himself facing Lieutenant General Sanji Okido, commander of the dreaded *kempeitai*. This instrument of oppression had been developed to a degree that terrified all Japanese. General Tojo, as prime minister, had used it increasingly in the first three years of the war. But even in the early thirties the *kempei* had a well-deserved reputation for ruthlessness and brutality. Tens of thousands of Japanese and endless numbers of Chinese and Koreans had been arrested, confined, tortured, and held without recourse on suspicion of subversion, disloyal thoughts, anti-war utterances, and disrespect for the Throne. Four months before, less than two weeks after he became war minister, General Anami had authorized the *kempei* to round up 400 well-known Japanese for "end-the-war" sentiments. Among these were a high-ranking judge and the former ambassador to England, Shigeru Yoshida. This had sent a shiver of fear through all peace advocates. Sakomizu had reason to believe that his own name was on the *kempei's* list, for future action. So, looking up now into the face of the *kempei* chief, the cabinet secretary could not avoid an inward shudder. But it was prime minister Suzuki Okido wanted, not Sakomizu. The cabinet secretary wondered, with mounting concern, why the *kempei* chief wanted the old man. He told Okido that Suzuki had not yet arrived, but that he believed the premier would be going directly into a meeting of the Big Six when he did come. The meeting was scheduled for eight forty-five.

The General was insistent. He demanded to see Suzuki as soon as possible. But as time drew near for the meeting of the SCDW and the premier had not arrived, Okido impatiently called Sakomizu aside.

"If Japan surrenders," the head gendarme rasped, "the army will rise. This is certain. Has the PM confidence that he can suppress the revolt?" This was a curious question, which seemed more threat than query. After all, Okido was head of the police agency of the army, the very organization charged with maintaining order in the military.

"The *kempei* is receiving reports almost hourly from regiments all over the country. They all point to an insurrection." Okido glowered at Sakomizu, and it was obvious that he was indicting the premier and the peace faction for this military unrest. "We cannot take the responsibility for what happens," he snapped. "The *kempeitai* urges that the war be continued. Tens of millions of lives may be sacrificed, but we must not surrender!"

Sakomizu promised to relay this news and advice to the premier, and the General marched pompously to the door. There he stopped, turned around, and fixed the cabinet secretary with a glare full of significance—a look that said "I know where you stand, you know where the troops and I stand. Be sure that the premier understands this thoroughly also." Then he was gone, leaving behind a faint air of brimstone.

Sakomizu's morning experiences were an ominous prelude to what promised to be a climactic day. A showdown was inevitable on this August 13. The unofficial Allied reply that had tied the cabinet in a knot all day the twelfth would have to be answered one way or another now that the official note had been received.

The question of the hour this morning of the thirteenth was whether the prime minister had stopped revolving and, if so, at what point. Would he now reverse himself again and come out for acceptance of Allied terms at the SCDW and cabinet meetings that day? If he did not, the peace advocates would be up against a roadblock that would prevent surrender.

At eight forty-five the six members of Japan's Supreme Council for Direction of the War filed into the small top-security conference room in the bomb shelter beneath the premier's official residence.

As they sat down around the green-felt-covered table, War Minister Anami with General Umezu, the army chief of staff, and Admiral Soemu Toyoda, navy chief of staff, were ranged against Foreign Minister Togo and Admiral Mitsumasa Yonai, the navy minister. Suzuki, the hoary premier, enigmatically sipped his green tea and seemed to watch the proceedings without seeing.

The meeting had scarcely opened when the two chiefs of staff were summoned to an immediate audience with the Emperor. Toyoda and Umezu left at once and faced the Emperor at nine o'clock. Hirohito was accompanied, as usual in such audiences, by his military aide-de-camp. Wearing his uniform of Grand Marshal of the Army, the Emperor stood and spoke in measured cadence.

"A peace proposal is now being discussed with the Allied nations. What is your plan as to the air operations we will conduct while the negotiation is in progress?" Looking through his thick, black-rimmed glasses at Umezu and Toyoda, the Emperor-god examined the two trigger men before him. Each was in command of hundreds of thousands of Japanese troops and either could issue battle orders that would disrupt or destroy the negotiations. He was asking them now about Japan's remaining striking force in order to get a commitment that would serve as a safety catch to prevent those triggers from being pulled. In his customary oblique fashion, Hirohito was trying to indicate his interest in the safety of the negotiations and in their success.

Speaking for the navy chief of staff as well, General Umezu replied. "We shall refrain from making aggressive attacks. Only when we are attacked and when there is need for defensive measures, we shall return fire."

The Emperor studied the General and his colleague. Umezu's answer, if both army and navy stuck to it, would suffice. Hirohito nodded and the audience was ended. The two military leaders bowed their way out and sped back to the SCDW meeting.

Meanwhile, Sakomizu had been active. The cabinet secretary had carefully kept track of enemy newspaper and radio reactions. From these he knew that Allied patience was running out. On August 12, American broadcasts stated that Japan had not responded to the Allied note sent the day before. Japan's peaceful intentions were therefore doubtful. By the morning of August 13 the American broadcasts were even more contentious, accusing Japan of deliberately delaying. They threatened a rain of atomic bombs on Japan's cities unless she surrendered promptly.

These views were the consequence of no word, official or unofficial, having been sent by Japan to the outside world to indicate that the new Allied terms were even being discussed. Sakomizu, alarmed, decided that it was important to spike the suspicions of the Allies and indicate Japan's sincerity. He could not send any official notice, of course—that would have to have government sanction and go through the Foreign Office. But he could send unofficial word via short-wave radio through Domei. Earlier that morning Sakomizu had asked Domei to send a news story on its overseas transmission.

Afterward, the San Francisco station repeated the report in English. Domei had said (at Sakomizu's instruction) that the Japanese cabinet had decided on peace and was now discussing procedure. This, reported Domei, was the only matter yet outstanding. Obviously the cabinet secretary had stretched the truth considerably.

The Japanese army and navy, monitoring major radio stations of the U.S. and other nations, had immediately pounced on this statement. A phone call to Domei quickly pinpointed the source of the information and angered some of the activists enough to make them call on the cabinet secretary to intimidate him. Several army officers broke into Sakomizu's office. One ranted "On what authority did you give such a broadcast?" "You are a traitor!" another screamed. Sakomizu tried to calm them, but after much cursing and threatening they rushed noisily out as quickly as they had come.

The SCDW meeting resumed. The discussion was like some ritualistic dance by a small group of sophisticated birds. One pounced on a phase of the question, waltzed it in one direction, only to have it seized by another who trotted it diagonally toward another star. Then a third introduced another theme and contrapuntally backed through the preceding variations in a fugue of pros and cons, and the movement stopped only when a recess was called. It was hypnotic; it was maddening; it was like a debate among semanticists; it was without climax or end; it was thoroughly Japanese. While aboveground their world was in ashes and their countrymen were reduced to garbage-sifters and ragpickers, they continued this ritual dance in their isolated, insulated cubicle.

The war minister and the chiefs of staff wanted the Allies to state that the Emperor would not be ordered about by the Supreme Commander, that the Emperor system would not be a matter for the plebiscite, that there would be no occupation of the main islands and that the Japanese armed forces would be allowed to disarm themselves voluntarily.

Togo and Yonai believed that to demand any one of these, much less all of them, would result in collapse of negotiations and continuation of all-out Allied warfare on Japan. Togo agreed to query the Allies about the disarmament and occupation questions, but refused flatly to make these part of Japan's conditions for accepting Allied terms.

The debate flickered back and forth over the statement that the Emperor would be "subject to" the occupation commander and over the provision that Japan's government would be decided by "the free will of the people."

War Minister Anami, jaw set, slapped the felt tabletop ponderously and said flatly that occupation of the homeland and disarmament, except by Japan herself, were out of the question.

Yonai had been sitting mute, chin in hand, following the proceedings glumly. Now he spoke at last, tersely as always. "These are problems which have already been settled by the Imperial Decision [August 10]. Therefore anyone who revives these arguments is a rebel against His Majesty." There was a gasp, then silence. Anami fumed and Toyoda shook his head vigorously.

But Umezu imperturbably dodged the implication of Yonai's bluntness. "We are not arguing against the spirit of the Imperial decision. It is only natural that we should demand changes of wording so Japanese may clearly understand the terms. We have to avoid one-sided interpretations."

This colloquy seemed to stir the old premier and he peered through a cloud of cigar smoke to ask testily "Do the military leaders intend to upset our efforts to end the war by deliberately grumbling about Byrnes' reply? Isn't it all right if we interpret it as we see fit?"

Togo took a deep breath of the stale, humid air. At last the old man had come down off the fence. Although this was not an unequivocal statement of support for accepting the Allied terms, it would do. So now the balance seemed restored—three to three.

The debate continued. Anami led the opposition. Umezu followed his lead, but concentrated on the technical difficulties of disarming and occupation. He considered these extremely delicate, if not insurmountable. Toyoda proved unswerving and, though he had no fleet, his forensic powers were undiminished. It was unthinkable, he almost chortled, that the Allies would continue to fight rather than bargain just because Japan wanted to clarify terms. After all, Japan had signified that she wanted to end the hostilities.

Toyoda later described his thinking: "When a customer buys a potted plant from a nurseryman at a fair, once the nurseryman decides his customer is willing to buy, he does not give up easily. If the customer complains about this and that, he does not cut short his sales talk. He may pretend to be uncompromising but at the bottom of his heart he usually remains patient and waits until he succeeds in selling the plant. If he is not willing to reduce the price first asked for, he will probably wait until the customer gives in and agrees to meet the price. If he is willing to reduce the price, he will probably compromise a little before long."

Some might have questioned how potted plants related to warfare and who was the buyer and who the seller in the surrender negotiations, but not Toyoda.

The fugue of frustration continued until almost 2 P.M., when the premier, out of patience and cigars, called a halt. The SCDW was hopelessly split. Suzuki announced a cabinet meeting for three o'clock and adjourned the session.

As Togo was collecting his papers, Anami moved briskly around the table to Suzuki. The war minister stood before him, practically nose to nose. He referred Suzuki back to the Imperial Conference of August 10: "The Imperial Decision should not have been asked for before we had reached agreement. That mistake must not be repeated!"

Anami's purpose was clear: He was underlining the army's anger at changing the ground rules in this way. He was warning Suzuki not to attempt this again. It was a heavy-handed threat.

Togo picked up the gauntlet and spoke stiffly. "The high command is trying to upset the negotiations. We have to let the Allies know our intentions quickly. Therefore we must decide the matter promptly." Togo was defying Anami and the military. He was saying that if they blocked agreement the prime minister and the peace faction would not hesitate to call on the Emperor again for a "decision."

So saying, Togo gathered up his papers and brief case and hurried from the room. He drove through waves of summer heat to the palace and reported to the Emperor the official text of the Allied reply. He also enumerated the difficulties Suzuki was having with the military. Hirohito approved Togo's stand, told him to buck up the premier, and again urged the foreign minister to do his best to settle the matter.

At army GHQ the young officers were goading one another to reject any truce or surrender. Reports of frenzied groups of military men scheming ways of hoisting the bloody shirt filtered through to the Foreign Office and prime minister's staff. According to the information reaching Togo and Sakomizu, literally scores of officers in the middle ranks were planning to:

· Call upon the Emperor to issue a proclamation of full, all-out war at all costs.
· Have the war minister order the whole army to fight to the last man.
· Announce a state of martial law throughout the nation, with the war minister also taking over the home ministry (with its control of every domestic policeman in the nation).
· Cooperate with the "war party" in the navy to defy any end-the-war orders.
· Suppress the peace faction ruthlessly.

One report said the army hotheads were going to use hand grenades instead of machine guns to keep order and planned to destroy the peace faction if the masses became agitated. Another account said the officers were feverishly trying to enlist support for their schemes. And, though they struck some responsive chords among navy counterparts, Yonai's tight grip on that service and the strong discipline maintained there prevented joint ventures from blossoming.

Toyoda, Anami, and Umezu were all under intense pressure from their jingoistic junior officers. So bold were these fanatics that they even tried to block Foreign Office radio contact with Switzerland and Sweden, the nations through which Japan was conducting the formal surrender negotiations.

While the foreign minister was at the palace, the war minister was besieged with callers. Anami was very approachable. Now, at this moment of deep unrest, his office was the chief dispensary of encouragement, sympathy, and determination. Dozens of young officers called on the war minister. They simply jumped the military chain of command, ignored their section chiefs and department heads, and went directly to the minister to register their feelings and secure his promise that there would be no surrender.

Had Anami not been robust he would have been worn down completely by the daily deluge of callers and their diverse demands. One of his significant meetings that afternoon was with the army chief of staff, General Umezu, and the commanding officer of the Eastern District Army, General Shizuichi Tanaka. Tanaka was responsible for all of Tokyo and central Honshu.

A hard-bitten disciplinarian, Tanaka's career included years as a professional iron fist. He had been in charge of suppression as head of the *kempeitai* and later as military chief in the occupied Philippines until malaria sent him back to Japan and his present post. Now he reported to Umezu and Anami that there was growing confusion in the army and among the people. Always one for the simple, drastic solution of problems, Tanaka urged that now was the time for martial law. Furthermore, the pacifists were stirring up trouble and should be rounded up immediately. Anami and Umezu assured Tanaka that they would keep his recommendations in mind, but that was the extent of their action for the moment.

The ferment in the army and navy had not gone unnoticed by the Court. But though he was titular commander-in-chief, the Emperor could not issue a simple command to his armed forces to stop their agitation. Orders were issued by his qualified, loyal representatives, the army and navy chiefs of staff, in his name. So one of the circuitous methods Hirohito used to cope with this condition was to send for all the imperial princes, the privy council, fleet admirals, field marshals, and others of influence. To these he told his determination to end the war and his reasons for accepting the Potsdam declaration. This action helped kill attempts to claim that the Emperor's true wishes were being circumvented by "treacherous advisers."

Hirohito also sent his brothers to trouble spots. Prince Mikasa, an officer on the army active duty list, was dispatched to GHQ. Among others, he spoke to Takeshita's superior officer, the chief of the Military Affairs Section. Mikasa's tirade was clearly audible in the next office. "The attitude of the young men in the army is wrong," Mikasa charged. "Anami's attitude is also mistaken."

Takeshita recognized that the Prince (therefore the imperial family and the Emperor) was reproaching the army for disobeying His Majesty's expressed wish that the war be ended by accepting the Potsdam terms. Then Takeshita heard the section chief reply "It is because they are thinking only about the national polity."

That this was also a concern of the Emperor and had been basic in his decision to end the war was conveniently overlooked by the army men. They thought theirs was the only true vision of their country. The Emperor's sight, they believed, was distorted by those "clouds around the Throne"—the members of the peace faction.

At 3 P.M., in the full heat of the sultry August day, Premier Suzuki convened his cabinet and Sakomizu read the official reply from the Allies. The old admiral asked his cabinet ministers for their views. Ten of them agreed that the terms should be accepted immediately; three opposed Byrnes' note. The ritual dance had begun once again, but with more birds.

Shortly after the session started the war minister slipped out, went to Sakomizu's office, and asked him to call the chief of the Military Affairs Bureau, the policy-making nerve center of the army. When Lieutenant General Yoshizumi answered, Sakomizu turned the receiver over to Anami. The war minister's next words stunned the cabinet secretary.

Anami jauntily told Yoshizumi "The cabinet meeting is now taking a favorable turn. One minister after another is coming to understand your opinion, so I want you to do absolutely nothing until I return. The chief cabinet secretary is right here. If necessary, ask him about the conference."

Sakomizu had been in the meeting and knew that the situation was directly contrary to Anami's description. Far from moving toward the military's position, the cabinet was ranged against it three or four to one and no shifting of ground was evident. What could Anami be thinking of? Sakomizu stared at the war minister in astonishment, about to protest. But Anami froze him with an intense frown and a deliberate nod.

However, Yoshizumi accepted Anami's statement and Sakomizu was not called to speak. The situation in the army must be incredibly tense, thought the cabinet secretary, to require the war minister to telephone his closest, most trusted subordinates with a false story such as this. Anami was simply dampening the fuse, at best.

The war minister returned to the cabinet meeting and so, a bit later, did Sakomizu. Togo noticed that the war minister seemed to have less zest for controversy than he had in the morning. True, the heat was upsetting, but they were all suffering from that. Anami seemed pensive and Togo thought he fell into reverie from time to time. There was no lessening of opposition to the enemy's terms, however. Both the home and justice ministers staunchly rejected the Byrnes note.

Togo did not know it at the time, but Anami had shortly before received additional discouraging advice. On August 10 he had secretly sent for Yosuke Matsuoka, Japan's prewar foreign minister who had so ably assisted the military in bringing about the Axis alliance and in alienating the democracies. Anami asked him if there was any possible diplomatic way out of Japan's dilemma. Matsuoka, mortally ill, was living south of Tokyo. He came to the capital, spent two days seeing friends to familiarize himself with current conditions, then reported to the war minister: There were no diplomatic measures nor miracles that could save Japan now.

Suddenly Sakomizu was called out of the cabinet room. He found in the hall a reporter from the *Asahi* newspaper whom he knew well. The chief secretary had found it useful to build up his own sources of information by subsidizing and entertaining reporters so that they would feed him tips on important matters, particularly about the military. Now the reporter handed Sakomizu a piece of paper. "Do you know about this?"

The cabinet secretary scanned it. It was an imperial General Headquarters communiqué carrying a release time of 4 P.M., August 13, and read:

The Imperial Army and Navy having hereby received the gracious Imperial Command to protect the national polity and to defend the Imperial Land, the entire armed forces will single-heartedly commence a general offensive against the Allied enemy forces.

A general offensive! The starch went out of the cabinet secretary.

"This announcement has been readied for publication at *Asahi* and is scheduled to be broadcast on radio stations at 4 P.M.," the reporter went on. Sakomizu looked at his watch. It was then three forty-five. If this was true, the negotiations were over, the war would be renewed with an intensity and bitterness that would make *Gyokusai* inevitable, because the Allies would never believe any future peace move by Japan.

Sakomizu leaped for the meeting room and moved to Anami's side. He put the paper before the war minister and whispered in his ear. "What about this?"

Anami's eyes widened as he read it. He wheeled in his chair and looked Sakomizu full in the face. "I have heard nothing about this," he said. "Announcements from Imperial GHQ are not under the jurisdiction of the war ministry, but of the army general staff. Contact General Umezu immediately!"

The cabinet secretary seized the paper and carried it around the table to the director of the Cabinet Planning Board, Lieutenant General Ikeda. Ikeda had heard nothing about it either, but like Sakomizu was galvanized by its threat. Both of them rushed from the room. While the debate droned on, the central action of the war at that moment focused on a telephone. Ikeda hastily called General Umezu to find out about the command.

Umezu was astonished. He had never heard of such a command and knew nothing about the communiqué. He ordered Ikeda to take steps to kill it and said he would do likewise. So began a frantic race to call the newspapers, radio stations, and Domei. The calls took agonizing minutes, but the phony order to attack was finally spiked just seconds before its four-o'clock release time.

Sakomizu later discovered that this harrowing announcement had originated in the press section of Imperial GHQ and had been okayed by the vice-minister of war and vice-chief of staff. They did not think it necessary to clear it with their superior officers, Anami or Umezu, nor did they hesitate to construct such a monstrous falsehood—even incorporating in it the Emperor's endorsement—and broadcast it to the nation and the world. It was a desperate act of now-desperate men. It illustrated the deterioration of discipline in the army. It also indicated that ending the war was going to be a feverish race. Who could predict what the hotheads would dare next? And who could be sure that their next bombshell would be defused in time?

All afternoon the war ministry and Foreign Office had been shuttling messengers to Anami and Togo with ammunition for their opposing stands. Monitored radio broadcasts of news, comments, and editorial opinion from world capitals were grist for the mills and were fed to the opposing sides as fast as translations could be made.

Anami passed around copies of a *New York Times* editorial of August 11 as an example of "the intolerably malicious and sacrilegious attitude of the U.S." The editorial said that the Emperor should be retained because a "discredited god" would be more desirable than a "martyred god" from the American standpoint.

Togo turned the war minister's point to his advantage. This attitude, he said, favored Japan because it showed that the Allies would not tamper with the Emperor system.

The editorial in the New York *Herald Tribune* of the same date was another matter. It said categorically that the Supreme Commander of the Allied Powers would "rule" Japan. Anami and his adherents triumphantly pointed to this as positive proof that Byrnes' phrase "subject to" meant the Emperor would be a lackey.

Togo contested Anami, the *Herald Tribune,* and the interpretation of the phrase. After two solid days of grinding away at this semantic gem it still remained a very rough stumblingblock.

While the cabinet was mired in its ritual of wrangling, Colonel Makoto Tsukamoto, a square-headed, raw-boned army officer, arrived at the squat stone building known and feared by every Japanese—the headquarters of the *kempeitai* in Tokyo.

Tsukamoto was about to make his first report on his new assignment, as ordered. He had been transferred from Japan's army in Formosa to serve as a senior member of the Eastern District *kempei* in central Honshu. Eager, garrulous, and hail-fellow, Tsukamoto was perfect for the stool pigeon job.

August 12 was his first day on duty and he had spent it gumshoeing about Imperial GHQ looking up people he knew, such as Lieutenant Colonel Masataka Ida of the Army Affairs Section of the Military Affairs Bureau. Young Ida had been stationed on Formosa also, but had been ordered to Tokyo several months ago.

On this afternoon of the thirteenth, Tsukamoto was reporting straight to the top, to Lieutenant General Sanji Okido, commander of the entire *kempei*.

"On the morning of the twelfth," the informer began with relish, "Lieutenant Colonel Ida said to me 'Now the conflict between the army and navy has been abolished. The navy has split into two factions and the Naval General Staff has moved to Ichigayadai [where the army GHQ was located]. We are developing a plan to overthrow the Suzuki cabinet and form a radical government headed by General Anami. Moreover, because of this, plans are being readied to declare martial law."

Warming to his subject, Tsukamoto continued enthusiastically. "The feeling predominates [among young officers] that 'the Suzuki cabinet is a Badoglio-like cabinet, secretly conspiring with the U.S. and Great Britain, and its ringleader is chief cabinet secretary Sakomizu. The Emperor is being deceived by the cabinet's treachery. This cabinet must be dissolved and our national polity upheld.' I was told this by staff officer Ida." Tsukamoto paused momentarily for some sign of the approval he was sure the information and his diligence deserved. The grizzled *kempei* chief toyed with a naked short sword on his desk and his eyes drilled through Tsukamoto. But he said nothing.

The Colonel cleared his throat and plowed ahead: "Furthermore, Ida said 'The national polity must be maintained by advising the Emperor. General Anami is doing his best on this. . . . But there is danger that when worse comes to worst, the Emperor will be made a

Badoglio unless he is given protection. . . . However, Lieutenant General Mori, commander of the Imperial Guards Division, is a problem, for he tends to do just as the Emperor bids.'

"At this point," said the *kempei* agent modestly, "I made a bid to preserve my self-respect by saying 'The army must always act in unison and if the Emperor expresses his will, the army must abide by it.'

"Ida ignored this and continued. 'Although the minister of war feels the same way we do, chief of staff Umezu is cautious and, therefore, we cannot settle the matter.' "

"I asked him 'How do you know the intentions of the minister of war?' Ida replied 'Lieutenant Colonel Takeshita is in constant contact with him.' "

General Okido brought his fist down on his desk. "The minister of war has no idea of executing an all-out army *coup d'état!*" he thundered.

The informer's report confirmed all the wild rumors Okido had heard, and he barked "Now just what is everyone thinking, after the situation has come to this? The minister of war and I have considered the matter from many angles. But we [Japan] are like the carp on the chopping block. Now is not the time to start kicking and struggling!"

(This was a far cry from Okido's own belligerent threat to Sakomizu just seven hours before. Then he favored sacrificing "tens of millions of lives" rather than surrender. Just where would he stand in another seven hours?)

It was now nearly 7 P.M. in Tokyo's dusty, bedraggled streets, and the ninety-degree heat had faded slightly. The muffled *tunk, tunk* of temple bells could be heard from many directions. In the cabinet room, the heat was still on and the cabinet debate sputtered soggily.

Suzuki finally decided that this meeting had accomplished as much as it could—which was to say almost nothing. The premier wearily polled his cabinet informally, and found that Togo, Yonai, and eight others favored acceptance of the Allies' terms. Anami and the home and justice ministers wanted further negotiations; the munitions minister couldn't make up his mind, and one other minister gave his proxy to Suzuki. It was a hung jury, and as in jury trials unanimity, not a majority, was required for a decision. But unlike a trial, this case could not be dismissed. Thus another day had been lost in this futile exercise. A precious day.

Drooping and discouraged, the aged premier faced his hopelessly split cabinet. He put down his cigar and addressed his official family frankly (one of the few times he had done so on this subject):

"I admit that when I first read the Allied reply I did not see how it could be accepted. I was resolved to fight to the last, scorching the earth behind our heroic defenders."

However, he had reread the note again and again. So doing, he had at last decided that the Allies had no sinister purpose in mind. His Majesty's heart cried out for one thing only—the end of the war and restoration of peace. As premier, said the old Admiral, his desire and duty were to follow the imperial will. Therefore he would report on the cabinet meeting and again ask His Majesty to give his gracious decision. With that Suzuki adjourned the meeting.

He had, in effect, put the military on notice that if a *coup* was to be attempted it must be before the Emperor handed down his decision in another Imperial Conference such as the one on August 10. The bitter-enders must therefore strike quickly. Or they had to prevent or delay convening of such a conference. They could block it by withholding permission of either the army or navy chief of staff, for it could be convened only by written petition of the prime minister and both chiefs of staff. Of course, the Emperor could call an Imperial Conference on his own initiative, but that was rare and unlikely.

After the cabinet meeting, General Anami went around to the premier's office. The war minister found Suzuki had a visitor, a navy doctor named Kobayashi. Impelled to try and delay or prevent the Imperial Conference, Anami asked: "Mr. Prime Minister, would you please wait another two days before calling an Imperial Conference?"

Suzuki rejected the war minister's request. "Now is the time, Anami; we must not miss this opportunity. I am sorry."

Anami had made the effort and realized that further discussion was useless. He bowed and left silently.

Dr. Kobayashi was puzzled. "Why not wait for a while? Would it matter so much?"

The old Admiral heaved a sigh and replied "Any delay would be dangerous. If we miss this chance for ending the war, the Russians may come not only into Korea, Manchuria, and Sakhalin Island, but into Hokkaido [the northernmost home island of Japan]. This would be a fatal blow to the very foundation of our country. No, we must settle this business while the negotiations are confined to one primary party, the United States."

"But Mr. Prime Minister, General Anami may kill himself," Kobayashi observed.

"Yes," said Suzuki, thoughtfully, pausing at the door. "That is possible. I am sorry." He nodded to the doctor and left the room.

As the war minister went from the cabinet meeting to calm his nerves with his daily *kyujutsu* (Japanese archery) exercise in the garden of his official residence, Togo drove through the rubble of Tokyo to a dinner party to inaugurate the new official residence of the foreign minister, replacing the one destroyed in a fire raid. He expected a relaxing occasion, though it had its duty aspects. Still, it was a respite from the eighteen-hour days he had been putting in trying to outmaneuver or convert the militarists. Rigid and stand-offish though he was, Togo was looking forward to unbending a bit with friendly companions for a change.

The foreign minister had been at the party only a short while when he was called to the telephone. Umezu and Toyoda wanted to see him immediately. Togo was reluctant to leave a party that had been planned weeks before. He did not relish traveling across the city to argue still more with the general and the admiral. He was doubtful that there was anything to discuss that had not already been exhausted in the talkathons of the past week. The chiefs of staff were insistent. Hesitant to spurn any opportunity, no matter how slight, that might wind up the debate, and determined to avoid giving the military any grounds whatsoever to complain that he had been uncooperative, Togo agreed at last to see them at the premier's residence at nine o'clock. At that very moment Anami was receiving the delegation of conspirators, as noted earlier.

Sakomizu had been asked by the chiefs of staff to make the arrangements for their meeting with Togo. He anticipated an icy confrontation. So, to soften the atmosphere, he furnished tea and a bottle of whisky that had been carefully cached away for an important occasion such as this. But the cabinet secretary's hospitality was spurned by the chiefs of staff, who pointedly refused to touch the rare delicacy.

Umezu and Toyoda apparently wanted Togo to change his mind about widened negotiations with the enemy. Two hours were spent in a closet review of the situation with no visible results. The only accomplishments were psychological: the subordinates of both Umezu and Toyoda at army and navy headquarters, respectively, were aware of this conference. They believed that progress was being made in forging conditions that would save the military from humiliation and the nation from disgrace.

It was nearly eleven o'clock when Togo, Umezu, and Toyoda prepared to leave. Just then Vice-Admiral Onishi burst into the room. He seized Toyoda's arm and wailed that he had just come from Prince Takamatsu, the Emperor's younger brother, whom he had tried to persuade to influence the Emperor and Admiral Yonai in favor of a decisive battle in the homeland. Far from enlisting Takamatsu, he found himself on the receiving end of a severe tongue-lashing: On the contrary, the Prince had crackled, you are the ones who should reconsider, not Yonai. You bring no workable plan to save the situation; you are incapable of winning the decisive battle, and because of its record of not measuring up to its promises, the navy has lost the confidence of the Emperor.

Onishi, the developer and high priest of the *kamikaze* corps, was in tears.

The suicide specialist then pleaded with the two chiefs of staff. Whether the American reply was acceptable or not was beside the point, Onishi cried. The fundamental issue was that the armed services had lost the confidence of the Emperor, their Commander-in-Chief. Therefore, he entreated, "we must submit to the Emperor a plan to gain victory and ask his reconsideration. If we are resolute and are prepared to sacrifice twenty million Japanese lives in a *kamikaze* effort, victory shall be ours!"

General Umezu and Admiral Toyoda observed Onishi as though he were some extraordinary specimen they were seeing for the first time. Their silence was eloquent response. Onishi turned to Togo. "What is the foreign minister's opinion?" he demanded.

Togo said quietly "If only we had any real hope of victory, no one would for a moment think of accepting the Potsdam declaration; but winning one battle will not win the war for us."

With that the foreign minister left, amid heat lightning and sputtering showers. He stopped at the nearby foreign ministry office to go over the telegrams from overseas posts and transcripts of broadcasts from foreign countries. Japan's peril was growing, the messages indicated. Her thin stock of international tolerance was being dissipated rapidly by the continuing delay.

Driving home, just as elsewhere in the Tokyo night Anami was arriving at his midnight rendezvous with the conspirators, Togo pondered. "Even if we offered the sacrifice of twenty million Japanese lives, they would but fall easy prey to machines and gunfire. We could bear anything if it promised a return; but the arrows and bamboo spears of which the military men are prating promise none." He shook his head. The soldiers' ignorance of the nature of modern warfare was beyond his understanding.

Admiral Onishi's day was not quite ended, nor was Sakomizu's. The cabinet secretary was still in his office trying to devise a way out of the stalemate. He had attempted repeatedly to get permission of the chiefs of staff to call an Imperial Conference immediately. Umezu and Toyoda refused even to discuss it. The longer such a showdown could be delayed the better it suited them. Now Sakomizu sat reading the translations of foreign broadcasts that were increasingly vitriolic about Japan's stalling. He had just concluded that there was nothing to be done until morning when Onishi thrust himself in, sobbing.

To Sakomizu, an old friend, the navy vice-chief of staff lamented "We have been trying sincerely to win a victory. But now, at this final stage I see that earnestness was not enough. If we concentrate with our present determination, we are bound to think of a plan to turn the war in our favor." Taking the cabinet secretary's hands in his, Onishi wept. "Here, now," he cried, "can't we find some way to continue the war?"

But Sakomizu knew all too well that Japan could not afford an Onishi victory. Such slaughter would be more costly than defeat. Japan was indeed a carp on the chopping block.

As Onishi and Sakomizu talked, a tiny piece of paper scarcely larger than a man's hand was being loaded on an enemy bomber hundreds of miles away. Though neither man could know it, in the morning that paper would settle the question that gnawed at each of them.

Chapter 17

Panic in the Morning

At the war ministry the early sun on August 14 found certain members of the Military Affairs Bureau already at their offices. This was to be *the* day. The time for the takeover was scheduled—10 A.M. The agenda promised a busy day: at 7 A.M. the war minister and Colonel Arao were to see the chief of staff General Umezu, and enlist him in the effort.

The conspirators, in anticipation of Umezu's blessing, had put in calls to the commanders of the Imperial Guards Division, the Eastern District Army, and the *kempeitai,* requesting them to come to Anami's office shortly after seven o'clock. Thus, when the war minister returned with Umezu and the army high command in his pocket, he could order the Guards, the Eastern District Army, and the *kempei* to cooperate and the *coup* would tick over smoothly when ten o'clock struck.

Takeshita, Inaba, Hatanaka, Shiizaki, Ida, Arao were all on deck, preparing the orders that would have to be issued to consolidate the takeover, orders for the disposition of troops, and directives to round up the peace faction. The key order (ready to sign) was the one initiating a state of martial law. When Anami put his seal on that, the action could begin

While his junior officers were thus preparing things for his assumption of power, the key man in these grandiose plans was, as usual at this hour, standing in his garden in the prescribed stance, loosing shafts at the straw clout that served as his target. Signs of worry were absent from his brow. His eye was unclouded. He did, however, require fourteen shots to group five arrows to his satisfaction. From the serenity of the minutely pruned and lovingly tended garden, Anami hurried to his breakfast date with Marshal Hata, commanding officer of the Western District Army. The war minister had asked Hata to fly to Tokyo from his headquarters in Hiroshima to report on the atomic bomb's effects and to urge Hirohito to reject the Allied reply.

Hata told Anami that the bomb had not affected the roots of sweet-potato plants just an inch or so below the surface of the earth and that the blast had been reflected by white clothing. Thus, he stated, defenses were possible against the bomb. Delighted, Anami insisted that Hata tell this to the Emperor to encourage him to resist the surrender talk.

The war minister then hurried to his appointment with Colonel Arao at the war ministry building. Arriving at his office, Anami was instantly surrounded by his coterie of eager, energetic protégés. They were brimming over with confidence and could scarcely wait to touch off their scheme to save Japan from shame. Koko Arao reminded Anami that it was nearly seven and that they had a date with Umezu. The two officers left the war minister's office with every encouragement but out-and-out cheers ringing in their ears. At this moment Anami's prestige was at a pinnacle. He was omnipotent. If he had suggested painting the Diet building purple, the young tigers would have been out with buckets and brushes within minutes.

In a matter of moments Arao and Anami arrived at the chief of staff's office nearby. Umezu stood as they entered and motioned them to chairs as an aide brought in the indispensable green tea. The plan for clamping martial law on the capital, changing the government, and "neutralizing" the peace faction was presented by Colonel Arao as it had been set before Anami the night before. The meeting was short, the discussion brief. Umezu, the "man who would not cross a bridge unless he sounded every stone before each step," turned thumbs down.

That was what Anami told the conspirators when they flocked into his office upon his return. "The *coup*," said the war minister, "will have to be abandoned. The chief of staff disapproves." (The war minister later told his brother-in-law Takeshita that Umezu had gestured disapprovingly and said "employment of armed forces in the sanctuary of the Palace would be a sacrilege.") Meanwhile, Lieutenant General Tanaka, the ferocious commander of the Eastern District Army; Lieutenant General Mori, scholarly chief of the Guards Division; and Lieutenant General Okido, the brusque *kempeitai* head, were waiting in the anteroom in response to the summons from the war minister's office.

The conspirators then confessed to Anami that they had called these commanders in the war minister's name and scheduled a 9 A.M. senior staff meeting in anticipation of Umezu's consent to the coup. Instead of blasting them for their unauthorized actions, Anami, softhearted as usual, forgave them and called in the three officers. He admonished them to take thorough security precautions because the over-all situation would reach a critical stage that day or the next. This was the exact opposite of the order the plotters had expected Anami to give, but was consonant with the decision by Umezu.

There was one crucial chore yet to take care of. At 9 A.M. all war ministry senior section members assembled. The war minister then spoke to them briefly. "The army should act in unison," he warned, "because Japan is now facing the critical situation. Strengthen your unity. Beware of any undisciplined acts. Those who consider any arbitrary actions will have to carry them out over my dead body." For emphasis, Anami swatted his knee with a short swagger stick he was carrying. Thus ended his instructions to staff members and the hope of the plotters for an easy takeover by means of a martial-law edict.

But hope, like a live coal, burned on in the minds of the conspirators. Takeshita and Inaba compared notes with Hatanaka, Ida, Shiizaki, and others. The war ministry men railed at Colonels Hara and Hosoda—who served under Umezu, not Anami. Why had they not secured the chief of staff's cooperation? The colonels had intended to talk with Umezu that morning, but now, mysteriously, he was nowhere to be found. Rumor had it that Umezu was in audience with the Emperor.

Colonel Ida came up with the theory that the chief of staff had been subverted the night before by Suzuki, Togo, and Sakomizu, with whom (the army men believed) Umezu had conferred at the premier's residence. This supposition fed the strong misgivings the plotters now harbored about Umezu. They simply could not understand why the chief of staff had opposed the plans. Anami had not taken time to explain and by then Colonel Arao was busy elsewhere.

A short time later, Hosoda and Hara excitedly burst into Take-shita's office with word that they had finally managed to get to Umezu when he returned to his office. They had sounded him out and the chief of staff said he was not absolutely opposed to a *coup*. On the strength of this report, Takeshita hurriedly drew up "Employment of Troops Plan No. 2" and rushed off to find Anami to gain his approval. He knew that the war minister had gone to the premier's residence and, hailing a staff car, Takeshita took off after him. His luck was poor, however, for he arrived minutes after Anami had left for the palace with the other cabinet ministers.

Takeshita sped off in pursuit. He was determined not to lose the war minister now.

When the cabinet meeting had recessed on August 13, Admiral Baron Kantaro Suzuki, prime minister of Japan, wearily set ten o'clock the next morning as the time for resumption of debate. At that time, he hoped, they would resolve once and for all to accept the Allied terms, as the Emperor wished.

Before dawn on the fourteenth, seven B–29s loaded with 5 million small blue papers, 4" x 5", took off from Saipan. Their mission was to drop these leaflets on Tokyo, Osaka, Nagoya, Kobe and Kyoto. When these cities were in their bombsights, each plane toggled out the handbills that proved to be among the most explosive cargoes they had ever carried.

The leaflets were propaganda and they papered whole sections of these cities. Their message was direct:

To the Japanese People:
These American planes are not dropping bombs on you today. American planes are dropping these leaflets instead because the Japanese government has offered to surrender and every Japanese has a right to know the terms of the offer and the reply made to it by the U.S. Government on behalf of itself, the British, Chinese and Russian [governments]. Your government now has a chance to end the war immediately. You will see how the war can be ended by reading the two following official statements:
[Here the leaflets carried the August 8 message of the Japanese govern-

ment to the Allies and the text of Secretary Byrnes' note dated August 11.]

Bearing one of these messages, a chamberlain of the Imperial Household Agency scurried down the halls to the room of the lord keeper of the privy seal. Kido, in his pivotal role of coordinator and adviser, counselor and strategist, had gone to bed convinced that the fourteenth would end the suspense. He was sure that his pep talk had put prime minister Suzui back on the track. He was certain that Suzuki would do his best to push through acceptance of the Allied terms at the cabinet session on the fourteenth. If that didn't work, a full-scale meeting of the SCDW—with the secretaries and the Emperor—might. And even though the high command was increasingly opposed to another meeting of the full SCDW, as a last resort the Emperor could call a "command attendance" Imperial Conference even without the customary petition for a meeting from the premier and chiefs of staff.

From the standpoint of lining up support for the Emperor's decision, nearly everything was in order. The Emperor had now talked in person with the *jushin* and such venerable leaders as Count Makino, the former privy seal. He had brought the princes of the blood into his confidence in the imperial family conference and come out with unanimous if not enthusiastic endorsement. Opinion leaders and experts such as the former foreign minister, Shigemitsu, had been consulted and all had heard from His Majesty's lips his determination to end the war. He had scheduled an audience that morning with the top-ranking officers of the navy and army, Fleet Admiral Nagano and marshals Sugiyama and Hata.

The unknown quantities were the armed forces (but Yonai seemed to be in control of the navy situation) and the Japanese people. If the army and the people would just remain dormant or docile until the Allied terms were accepted and the Emperor announced it by radio, all might be safe. It was a big if, but with a little luck it might be managed.

Now, as Kido sleepily groped his way out of bed, the chamberlain thrust into the privy seal's hands evidence that their luck had run out. The propaganda leaflet blew the cobwebs out of Kido's brain. "One look," he says, "caused me to be stricken with consternation. In the past two or three days the military services had gradually stiffened their attitude. The SCDW meeting had been postponed because of this. Now, here, such leaflets were being distributed at this juncture! If they should fall into the hands of the troops and enrage them, a military *coup* would become inevitable and make extremely difficult the execution of the planned policy [the surrender]. It would bring about the worst possible situation for our country."

Kido rushed to the phone and called to arrange a special audience with the Emperor and the time was fixed for eight thirty. Practically frantic with a severe attack of jitters, the privy seal could see Japan being plunged into chaos if this information was allowed to catalyze the already yeasty situation. There was now no margin for Suzuki to convene another interminable session of the cabinet debating society. There was not time to hope that sweet reasonableness would bring the Big Six to a favorable decision on this in short order. Therefore, the government had to act *now*.

When he popped into the *Gobunko* and faced Hirohito, this is exactly what Kido told him. The only way out, advised the nervous privy seal, was to stick to the decision: Summon the Big Six plus the cabinet and tell them, as Hirohito had on August 10, that their Emperor wanted immediate cessation of hostilities. His Majesty, Kido reports, "grasped the situation fully and ordered me to make arrangements with the prime minister." The privy seal withdrew from the audience (it had lasted a total of five minutes) and was about to hurry back to his office to call Suzuki.

Here luck was with him. The old admiral had decided to start his day with a call at the palace. Coincidentally, he arrived as the privy seal came from his audience. In a small room of the imperial library, Kido sat down with Suzuki and asked him if a meeting of the SCDW had been set. "A harried expression flitted across his face," says Kido, and the old man wheezed "I'm having a hard time. The army wants me to wait until one o'clock while the navy asks me to postpone the meeting without setting a specific time."

Kido scanned the premier's weatherbeaten face, handed him the propaganda leaflet, and asked if he had seen it yet. Suzuki had not. The privy seal told him the frightening news that American planes were scattering these all over Japan and outlined his fears. "To tell the truth, I had an Imperial audience just now concerning this subject. I told His Majesty of the extreme urgency of the situation and advised him to summon the members of the SCDW and the cabinet in order to direct them to accept immediately the reply of the Allies and bring about peace. His Majesty agreed and instructed me to consult with the premier. If you have no objection, let us make arrangements toward that end."

Suzuki shrugged his bent shoulders and raised his bushy brows. "Though I am sorry to trouble the Emperor, the attitude of the army and navy in the past two or three days makes me feel there is no other course than to request the Emperor to take just such steps. I would like to be received in joint audience with the privy seal at once to report the circumstances and receive the Emperor's approval."

Kido quickly called a chamberlain to ask His Majesty to see them and at eight forty, for the first time in Japanese history, the privy seal and the premier had a joint audience. Suzuki reported to Hirohito the troubles he had experienced in the past four days and formally requested that he call an Imperial Conference. In view of the urgency, the Emperor ordered it for 10 A.M. It was to be the first such meeting since December 1, 1941, when war was approved. This short lead-time was unprecedented. However, since the cabinet members expected to reconvene at that time at the premier's residence, most of them would be available. It left only the military and navy members of the SCDW and Baron Hiranuma to alert. At nine thirty-five the audience ended and Kido and Suzuki trotted and shuffled respectively, to their next tasks. The premier drove directly back to his office building and hurried to his room, calling for Sakomizu.

Suzuki ordered the cabinet secretary to notify the cabinet members and the SCDW of an Imperial Conference at ten o'clock at the palace air-raid shelter. It was now nine forty-five, and most of the ministers were already on hand for the scheduled cabinet meeting. "At the conference," Suzuki said, addressing Sakomizu, "the Emperor will proclaim an imperial rescript. Is the draft ready?"

Sakomizu was taken completely off balance. Since the August 10 Imperial Conference he had been laboring over a draft of a rescript with Tajiri of the Greater East Asia Ministry and Kihara, an *Asahi* reporter and close friend. But it was in rough draft and there was not a chance to type it in fifteen minutes. Furthermore, a rescript could only be issued after it had been considered and approved by the full cabinet. Then it would be submitted to the Emperor for his approval and afterward signed by the cabinet ministers. Only then was it issued.

But an imperial rescript to be prepared for issuance in just fifteen minutes! Impossible! "There must be a mistake," the cabinet secretary stammered, turning pale. "We haven't finished the draft and no cabinet minister has even seen it yet. If you are correct, the consequences will be terrible. Practically no time is left, and suicide will be my only way out for my failure." Sakomizu was practically speechless. "Are you sure that the Emperor said he would issue a rescript this morning? Surely the prime minister must be misinformed. . . ."

This was not something that could be left to chance. Suzuki drove back to the palace, hurried to Kido, and at nine fifty verified that the rescript was to be issued later. The privy seal also recommended that Suzuki close off debate in the Imperial Conference in order to end it quickly. The old man nodded agreement and plodded back to his car and drove once again to his office building, where Sakomizu was feverishly working on the rescript.

Suzuki pulled his aide aside and grinned. "It is as you said. The Emperor expects the cabinet to draft the rescript, which will be issued later." Sakomizu laughed nervously, thinking of the big job still ahead and the significance of the paper that would end Imperial Japan.

Within minutes the official summons to an Imperial Conference arrived from the Court. It extinguished the buzz of conversation in the ministers' lounge and talk was reduced to whispers. "Be at *Fukiage goin* of the Imperial Palace at 10:30 A.M.," read the message. "Informal clothing is permissible."

Only Suzuki and Togo were in court dress. The rest of the ministers were wearing whatever seemed comfortable for the intense midsummer heat. Many were in open-necked shirts; some were even without jackets. A few were wearing the khaki "national uniform"—the all-purpose jacket. The ministers were mortified at showing themselves at Court in such casual clothes.

Sakomizu and his assistants moved among the men and reassured them that special permission had been granted for them to go "as is," since it was an emergency. But most felt keenly that it would be disrespectful to appear in the Emperor's presence in such informal clothing. So there was a comic interlude as ministers who had dressed for the midsummer heat furiously buttoned up open collars, changed suits or jackets with their secretaries or staff men, borrowed neckties and even trousers, and pinned the ceremonial badges on their khaki jackets. Anami and Yonai, in their military uniforms, were amused at the pandemonium.

As the ministers completed their preparations they climbed into their cars, gathered in the forecourt of the *kantei* and set off for the palace. The procession was as prominent and somber as a funeral cortege, moving down the near-deserted streets to the plaza in front of the palace, then through the gate to the Fukiage garden. Once again the leaders picked their way single file down the wet, mat-lined stairway and through those massive bank-vault doors to the conference room. Once again the hall was set with the golden screen back of the simple wooden chair and the small table with the brocade on it. But this time, for the larger group, two rows of tables at right angles to the Emperor's table had been set up, with chairs facing the center of the room. In addition to the fifteen cabinet ministers there were General Sumihisa Ikeda, the Planning Board chief; Baron Hiranuma, the privy council president; Metropolitan Police chief Machimura; Legislative Bureau director Murase; and Cabinet Secretary Sakomizu. In addition, the two chiefs of staff and the heads of the army and navy military affairs bureaus, General Yoshizumi and Admiral Hoshina, were on hand. They took their seats according to Court precedence and a brittle silence settled over the room.

It was a silence of hope and foreboding, of pent-up anxiety and attenuated torture. The anxiety was about the future; the torture was the life endured for the past fourteen years. Could there be any in that room who did not know, logically as well as instinctively, that this was the moment when the great division between Japan past and Japan future would be drawn? With their ingrained appreciation of poignancy, what member of the Yamato race could fail to have his life's quota of it in living through this moment?

The silence, like that before the clacking of the wooden blocks preceding a *Kabuki* performance, was fecund with expectation and the reining in of emotions. The men sat tense and at attention. They cursed the heat, damned the humidity, and endured the mosquitoes. But they could not control their own bodies—first one coughed, then another, then it was epidemic, and the attempts to stifle the coughs increased the tension.

Sakomizu, sandwiched between generals Yoshizumi and Ikeda, scanned the faces around him. Yonai had his usual wry grimace; behind his round glass windows, Togo was not at home. Machimura was sweating profusely. Abe looked more froglike than ever. Umezu sat frozen, like carved ivory dressed in khaki. Anami was breathing heavily. Toyoda seemed oblivious, staring into space.

Then, through the door on the left, the Emperor entered, followed by General Hasunuma. The twenty-four men in the room got to their feet and bowed low, eyes on the floor at their feet. Hirohito was wearing his army uniform, as he had on August 10. After he was seated the conferees resumed their seats.

Suzuki, his mouth an inverted crescent and his brows like divots of gray above his tiny eyes, stood and addressed the Throne. He diagrammed the lack of progress of the past four days, reported that the cabinet was still split on the question of accepting the Allied terms, though roughly 75 per cent favored acceptance. The Big Six also were split, he reported. Then the old man summarized the majority and minority positions. "Thus," he said, "because support was not unanimous, I wish to apologize sincerely for the serious crime of troubling Your Majesty with this matter. Now, will you please listen to those opposing the terms and then grant us your Imperial decision." With that he called upon army chief of staff Umezu.

The general, with his dour mask, began. "I apologize for the unfavorable turn of events which must be a disappointment to Your Majesty." Then he launched again the familiar military argument: "If Japan is to accept the terms of the Potsdam declaration at this time, the preservation of our national structure becomes a grave issue. Under existing conditions, the national polity would be destroyed. Therefore we would like to determine once more the real intentions of the United States. We have lost the war anyway, so if we can be sure of maintaining our national structure we are ready to resign ourselves. However, if our national polity cannot be preserved, we must be ready to sacrifice the entire nation in a final battle." Umezu sat down. His face during his entire speech had shown no more emotion than if he were asking for a second bowl of rice at dinner.

Suzuki now called upon Admiral Toyoda, who rose and echoed Umezu. He was less emphatic, but said that Japan could not bear to "swallow" the American reply as it stood. "There is no certain assurance that we can win victory by continuing the war, but in view of the fact that we have once resolved to fight a decisive battle on the homeland with the entire nation prepared for suicidal warfare, I cannot see why we cannot resolve to negotiate on such a matter as the national polity." Though his words were tough, Toyoda later wrote that they were "in no way to be construed to mean that he advocated continuing the war." (He had simply unleashed his *haragei* again.) He was certain that another request to the Allies would not disrupt negotiations, and even if it was ignored, he believed it had to be made "because if not, Japan's future position would be very unfavorable."

It was then Anami's turn; he played the same tune, but with much emotion, his chest heaving and his eyes welling with tears. "If it is impossible to question the Allies again about the safety of the Emperor system," the war minister concluded, "it would be better to fight on, for there are still chances to win. And if not to win, at least to end the war on better terms than these."

Anami sat down and the premier faced Hirohito. "There are no other views to present."

The Emperor had been sitting rigidly erect, gloved hands in his lap, as he observed the three military men. He followed their statements, fastening on each word, examining them for evidence of new reasons for delaying the end. But the arguments were stale and empty. Now the Emperor-god gripped the arms of his chair, rose, and spoke.

The sounds of heavy breathing came from his listeners as they gasped for air in the humid dungeon.

"I have listened carefully to the arguments opposing Japan's acceptance of the Allied reply as it stands. Now I shall express my opinion." For a moment, all breathing in the room seemed suspended.

"It was not lightly, but upon mature consideration of conditions at home and abroad and especially the course of the war that I commanded the Potsdam proclamation be accepted. My mind is unchanged. I believe it is impossible to continue the war any longer." Hirohito's metallic voice faltered momentarily and there was weeping among those who heard.

"I have carefully studied the Allied reply and concluded that it virtually acknowledges our position in the note sent several days ago. In short, I believe the reply is acceptable. Though it is understandable that some should distrust the Allied intentions, I do not believe the reply was written with malice."

It was, after all, coming down to a matter of trust, and the Emperor was willing to place his in the Allies if it meant peace *now*.

"To my mind, it shows the enemy's peaceful and friendly intentions. But unless the war is brought to an end this instant I fear that the national polity will be destroyed and the nation annihilated. If the people, the domain, and the Imperial family survive, however, we can yet hope to rebuild the nation in the future. Therefore, the faith and resolution of the whole nation are vitally important . . ." The words were choking him now. The tips of his white gloves wiped tears and and sweat from the Emperor's cheeks and glasses. His breath, too, was irregular; in the room some of his listeners were sobbing outright.

At the Imperial Conference on August 10 he had been vehement about the inadequate preparations of the military for the enemy onslaught. His fury at the thought of subjecting his people to attack by atomic bombs, hordes of ships, planes, and conventional bombs was unmitigated by the heroism implicit in meeting the overwhelming attack with superior spirit but inferior weapons and defenses. Now he submerged any bitterness that might remain. His voice was strained and his words were spoken in clusters. He halted now, searching for phrases. The gloved hands again touched the imperial cheeks. His audience was shaken. Some held handkerchiefs to their eyes, others mopped their brows. One or two sniffled. The weeping was contagious among them.

Hoarsely His Majesty continued. "I fully understand how ignominious it will be for the officers and men of the army and navy to be disarmed by the enemy and see their homeland occupied. It is painful for me to issue the order for this and to think of my loyal and trusted servants being accused as war criminals. However, in spite of these feelings, I cannot stand putting my people to further suffering.

"I appreciate the people's determination to sacrifice themselves for the nation and the sake of their Emperor. My heart grieves for those who died on the battlefields and their bereaved families. I am deeply concerned for those who lost their homes and livelihood during this long war. But continuing the war would bring death to tens, perhaps hundreds, of thousands of people. Our nation would be completely devastated and reduced to ashes. The reconstruction of a peaceful

Japan will be a difficult and lengthy task. However, I believe it will be accomplished through the strenuous efforts and cooperation of our people. I am ready to do whatever I can do."

Here again there was a pause, as Hirohito collected his thoughts and applied a check rein to his emotions.

"This decision is like the one forced upon my Grandsire, the Emperor Meiji, who had the fortitude to endure the humiliation of the Triple Intervention [when France, Germany and Russia forced Japan to return the Liaotung Peninsula to China after her victory in the Sino-Japanese war in 1894–1895]. As he endured the unendurable and suffered the insufferable, so shall I and so must you."

By now the leaders of the Japanese Empire were crying unabashedly. Two of them, Education Minister Ota and Welfare Minister Okada, had slid to the carpet, out of control. There, forearms on the floor, they wailed and hid their faces in their hands.

Hirohito continued. "I bid you join me, my ministers of state, and carry out my wishes faithfully. Accept the Allied reply forthwith. In order that the people may know of my decision, I request that you prepare at once an imperial rescript to this effect. When the previously uninformed citizens suddenly hear of this it may come as a great shock to them. If it is desirable, I am ready to speak to my people over the radio. I am also prepared to go anywhere to talk personally to the troops if requested."

The Emperor knew all too well how easily in the past his wishes had been attributed to his advisers; this time he was giving the military and the ultras no room for such tactics. He was saying, in effect: There will be no excuse for the troops misunderstanding my intentions since I am willing to speak to them myself. Into the minds of his listeners came the spectacle of the being who was worshiped on hands and knees going out to his people to beseech them to understand his will, to accept the defeat that had cost so dear.

The sobs of many of the conferees were convulsive as the Emperor went on. "Finally, I charge every one of you to exert himself to the full so that we may meet the trying days which are ahead." His Majesty's gloves, wet with tears, once again brushed his cheeks and glasses as he sat down. In the room the only sound to be heard was that of weeping.

This ordeal was over for Hirohito. That he was willing to sacrifice even himself was the core of his statement. All in that room had heard and read the radical statements from the enemy press and radio about trying the Emperor as a war criminal, or sending him as a prisoner to China, or de-deifying him if not dethroning him. In spite of the ambiguous Allied assurances and the *Gaimusho* interpretation of the terms, no one could be certain that the man-god commanding the surrender would live to survive it. He was, perhaps, the last Emperor of Japan. Hirohito had placed his head on the block.

As the leaders of the empire struggled to control themselves, Premier Suzuki got up hesitantly. Promising to submit a draft rescript to His Majesty as soon as possible, Suzuki again apologized profusely to the Emperor for troubling him for a decision. Moving to the place directly before the center table, the prime minister bowed low, and with his right hand described a broad arc from his heart. At this signal the Emperor rose from his chair and paused. His weeping counselors hauled themselves to their feet, helped their neighbors up, and bowed, Hirohito, having made the hardest decision and longest personal statement of his life, turned his back on the ministers and left the room followed by General Hasunuma, who was hastily stuffing a handkerchief back into his pocket.

General Anami, stumbling out of the conference room, spotted his secretary, Colonel Hayashi, waiting expectantly in the anteroom. The General motioned to Hayashi to follow and headed into the men's room, wiping his eyes as he went. Inside, he told the Colonel that the Emperor had commanded that the Allied reply be accepted. "Hayashi," he choked, "there is one last bit of advice I want to ask of you. The Imperial decision has been made, but according to intelligence there is a large American convoy outside of Tokyo Bay. What do you think of the idea of proposing peace after striking the convoy?"

Thunderstruck, Hayashi's congenital look of bewilderment went even more blank. Could the war minister be serious? After the Emperor himself had called for accepting the enemy's terms did Anami actually mean to flaunt that decision and destroy the negotiations by attacking the nearest enemy task force? Could the man be twitting his deadly serious secretary with a macabre joke? Hayashi responded as though Anami must mean what he said.

"Your idea is absolutely mistaken! In the first place, the Imperial decision has been given and in the second, even though there is a rumor of an American convoy south of Tokyo Bay, there has been no confirmed report from the air patrol units. Therefore it is a mistake to think of such a thing!"

"I still believe," Anami contended, "that we should deal one last decisive blow to the enemy before proposing peace."

The secretary suggested that the war minister discuss it with General Umezu before taking any drastic action, and he and Anami joined the band of cabinet ministers climbing dispiritedly out of the dank bunker into the brilliant summer daylight.

In his staff car in the parking lot, surrounded by the timeless serenity of Fukiage garden's giant pines and eternal stones, Lieutenant Colonel Takeshita sat smoking, impatient to change Japan's future. As executive officer of the war ministry *coup d'état* group, Takeshita knew what backing the *coup* had and how it was to operate. More than that, he was vital to its success because he was the link with the war minister, his brother-in-law, who was the kingpin in the plan.

Takeshita's special relationship gave him nearly free access to Anami, and in twenty years of friendship he had developed a close understanding of the General, whom he served as primary confidant. Vigorous, aggressive, and opinionated, the younger Takeshita functioned as a special kind of valve: He transmitted information upstream to Anami from his fellow junior officers and he fed downstream "informed estimates" of the war minister's thinking to these same young tigers. Thus he played a key role as information broker. But because of his own convictions, his drive and boundless ambition, he did more than that. Takeshita shaped the attitudes and views of both Anami and the junior officers by his actions and interpretations. He was the epitome of the second-echelon "influential person" who operates just outside the spotlight of responsibility.

Chain-smoking nervously as he waited for the conference to end, Takeshita reviewed the situation. The *coup* plans had ground to an abrupt halt when Anami and Colonel Arao returned from meeting Umezu with word that the chief of staff would not cooperate. The carefully timed meeting of Anami with the commanders of the

Guards, *kempeitai,* and Eastern District Army was wasted, as was Anami's address of instructions to war ministry section chiefs. The strike that should have occurred at 10 A.M. was scrapped.

But when two of Umezu's own staff later talked with their chief and found him "not absolutely opposed" to a *coup,* it meant that all plans could be activated again—but for a later jump-off time. Takeshita had followed the scheme of the earlier *coup* and changed the title and time. But basically it was identical: it called for the war minister to proclaim martial law and assume power. Then there would be a roundup of the peace faction and renewed commitment to all-out war. There would be no skin-saving, ignominious surrender. The national structure, the Emperor system, would be defended fanatically until the Japanese were obliterated or the enemy gave iron-clad guarantees that the system would be preserved.

The *coup* and its consequences promised not a long future, but a glorious one to all who had been taught that sacrificing one's life for the Emperor and joining the guardian spirits at Yasukuni Shrine near the imperial palace is the highest possible calling. Death was not to be feared, but to be embraced, if it could be a meaningful end. After all, the two and a half million souls deified at Yasukuni now protected the sacred nation and received the homage of all Nippon, including the imperial family. And each of those souls had once been a living being who had sacrificed his temporal life for the higher good of the nation. Those were souls of patriots just since 1869, when Emperor Meiji established Yasukuni as the national shrine. Even the name gave one something for which to sacrifice proudly: *Yasukuni*— "to bring about peace and tranquility in the country."

To Takeshita, grinding out a cigarette butt and lighting a fresh one, the *coup,* in addition to its simon-pure motivation, offered an unlikely-to-be-repeated opportunity to be next to the most powerful man in Japan—the new Shogun, Korechika Anami. For there could be no question about it, in the name of the Emperor the *coup* would displace the Emperor. The army knew by now that the Emperor was serious about surrender. But if he insisted on it even after the *coup* swept aside his "false advisers," Anami would be forced to overrule or ignore him. Thus the nation would step back into the pattern that had existed for centuries, when the Shogun ruled and the Emperor held court and performed religious duties in isolation.

Anami, Takeshita knew, was a man of action, not contemplation. He was neither administrator nor intellectual. His instincts were open and clear. He was proving a natural politician in his role as war minister, but this was because of his magnetism, not any comprehensive program or beliefs. The man's directness, his warmth and spontaneity were engaging and attracted even those who opposed him most. But he needed trusted advisers, lieutenants, dedicated helpers. And there, without question, Takeshita stood in the front rank.

Suddenly, blinking like moles, the cabinet ministers began to emerge from the bomb-shelter entrance. At first it appeared that their eyes were adjusting to the blinding sun of midday, but as the Colonel moved to the doorway to find Anami he quickly realized the men were crying. The war minister emerged like the rest, shaky and wiping his eyes. General Yoshizumi followed him. Takeshita saluted Anami and asked for an on-the-spot interview. The General waved him aside, saying that he had to go to the *kantei* immediately.

Not to be put off, Takeshita followed the war minister's car to the prime minister's office building.

In his staff car in the caravan from the Imperial Conference to the premier's, Anami and Yoshizumi rode glumly. The war minister's eyes were puffy and he glanced absently at the passing moat. "I leave the rest to you with confidence," he told Yoshizumi quietly. "I can't live in this world any longer."

Not surprised at Anami's words, Yoshizumi presented the only valid argument in such circumstances—the appeal to a greater duty. "The mission before us is much harder. It is possible that army and navy personnel may revolt, so much is expected of you to control the situation successfully." This really did not qualify, in Anami's eyes, as a greater call than responsibility for Japan's defeat.

"I have given my opinions to His Majesty according to my convictions, but things have come to this pass. I don't know what excuse to make to the Emperor, nor can I remain in this world any longer in the light of my responsibility for our defeat in this war."

"You must reconsider," Yoshizumi urged. "Your leadership is needed for the peaceful return of our millions of loyal troops. . . ." But the war minister was beyond such arguments.

At the *kantei* in the foyer, waiting reporters knew from one glance at the procession of weeping, shaken, and broken men what must have happened at the Imperial Conference. There was little conversation among the politicians.

Sakomizu drove up and hit the pavement running. On the way to his office he spotted Kihara, who had been working with him on the draft rescript. "Come," he beckoned. "We have a huge job to do in a hurry." Inside his office the cabinet secretary told the reporter that the Emperor's decision had all but settled things. Further, His Majesty had offered to broadcast to the troops, so a message would be needed as soon as Kihara could get it on paper. The reporter pitched in and began writing this announcement while Sakomizu went on to attend Suzuki and set up the cabinet meeting.

The cabinet ministers went in to a luncheon of black bread and whale meat. Most were too overwrought to eat, but old Suzuki managed to finish a comfortable portion of each.

Anami was not among the diners. He was in another room with his brother-in-law.

Takeshita poured out to Anami his news that Umezu was not opposed to the *coup*. He pleaded with the war minister to seize the moment, to take command and prevent the occupation and war-crimes trials that would destroy the national structure. Takeshita spread before the General a rejuvenated plan for him to lead the takeover of the government of Japan. Still reacting from the emotional impact of the Emperor's final command, Anami read the plan hastily, leaned back, and closed his eyes. After a moment of silence he spoke. "Nothing further can be done. A final decision has been reached by the Emperor and an Imperial rescript ending the war is about to be promulgated."

Tenacious to the last, Takeshita refused to be turned aside. He knew that the war minister could still halt the surrender machinery. Since the Emperor's words would have to be acted upon by the cabinet to make the decision legal, the Colonel urged Anami to block this. "I understand that navy Vice-minister Onishi summoned navy officers and told them that if the Imperial decision was made to end the war we must keep fighting even at the risk of being called traitors, for the sake of greater justice. I earnestly beg you to resign from the cabinet."

By this action the army would again have the upper hand, for it would write its own conditions for supplying a war minister to the new cabinet, and the new premier would have to accept them or resign. It meant, in effect, that the army would decide not only the policies of the succeeding government, but would withhold its nomination of a war minister until it approved of the premier selected. In other words, the army could hold out for appointment of one of its own as premier . . . and if the young tigers had their way, it would.

Anami nodded and called his secretary, Hayashi. "Get me an ink slab and paper. I intend to write my resignation. Check on the procedure." The Colonel was at the door when Anami halted him. "Never mind," he called, waving Hayashi out.

(The secretary, having experienced the war minister's changes of mind more than once, followed through anyway and sought information on the resignation process. He called the cabinet secretariat and spoke to the chief of the general affairs section. "To be frank with you, the war minister has expressed his desire to resign and I wish to know the procedure for turning in a resignation."

Sakomizu's assistant told Hayashi "You don't have to be in any hurry to do that. The Suzuki cabinet is expected to resign *en bloc* tomorrow.")

The war minister explained his action to his brother-in-law. "Even if I resign, at times such as this the Imperial rescript can probably be issued without me. But if I resign, I will lose my prized privilege of appearing before the Emperor."

To Takeshita, Anami looked pathetic and his words seemed to mean "I will not be able to see my good friend, the Emperor, any more if I resign." The young tiger, now convinced that the war minister would not lift his hand against the Emperor's decision, was overcome with despair. The final gambit had been refused. Takeshita left Anami and drove back to army headquarters at Ichigaya Heights, filled with foreboding. He had failed. So far as he was concerned, the chances for a *coup* and continued resistance were now over.

A short time later Anami drove back to his office in the war ministry building. For a man to whom death in the service of his Emperor-god is the highest calling, the conference had been the height of tragedy. It meant that he, Anami, had failed his fellow officers and particularly his devoted young tigers, for the Allied terms were accepted, not rejected. Now there would be no all-out battle in which to demonstrate the superiority of Yamato spirit over the enemy's material advantages in weapons. Anami had failed his Emperor in not throwing back the enemy or convincing His Majesty that he had a workable plan to do so. Anami had failed the army by losing the Emperor's confidence in the service. So ran his thoughts. And on that road there was but one destination.

The privy seal had been on edge from the time the Allied propaganda leaflet was put under his nose the morning of the fourteenth. As the Imperial Conference actually got under way, Kido could hardly contain himself. He had spoken with His Majesty for two minutes just before he went to the air-raid shelter for this historic event. Then Prince Mikasa called for him and Kido met the Prince in the "resting room for princes of the blood." Mikasa had been a stalwart in working for peace and in using his position as an army officer to influence the military.

At noon Kido had a summons from His Majesty; he raced to the *Gobunko* to hear what had happened at the conference. Still shaky from his experience, Hirohito was outwardly composed, but he could not contain his tears or control his voice. Kido, stricken with awe at the spectacle of his sovereign in a condition he had never witnessed before, lowered his eyes and his head as the Emperor recounted the high points of the meeting. The 124th Emperor of Japan told his chief counselor how he had followed Kido's advice and by so doing placed the lives of his subjects and the continuation of the Yamato race above his own life, his position, and the sanctity of the imperial house. From this point on, he said, the future is in the hands of the Allies.

Once out of the imperial presence, Kido the ever-efficient administrator took the reigns from Kido the dedicated retainer of the Emperor and began making necessary arrangements with all his considerable energy. With the grand chamberlain and the chief aide-de-camp he conferred about an imperial message to the troops, to quiet them and keep them in line. Then at 2 P.M. he had another audience with His Majesty. (The Emperor was calm now, his poise restored, and he was determined to see it through.) They conferred about procedures and schedule.

At two forty-nine, while Kido was leaving His Majesty and General Anami was arriving at the war ministry, Domei News Agency broadcast a special announcement on its overseas radio programs beamed to America. It was terse. There was a moment of silence, then the excited voice of the announcer broke into the regular program: "Flash! Flash! Tokyo, August 14—It is learned an Imperial message accepting the Potsdam proclamation is forthcoming soon." The announcement was followed by a brief silence. But those few words were enough to loosen all the bells in all the Allied nations.

Half an hour later Prince Mikasa called at Kido's room and brought him up to date on current conditions in the army.

Twenty minutes after that, when the Prince had left, Kido bustled along to the aide-de-camp again and learned that both the army and navy ministers had personally pledged that they would keep their troops under control.

Kido then sped to Ishiwata, the household minister, to confer about recording the Emperor's rescript.

Machimura, Tokyo's police chief, came to Kido's office and reported on peace and order in the city. Things were under control at the moment, but the conditions were dangerous, he said. Before dawn, more posters had been put up in central Tokyo on telegraph poles and in the subway and train stations. They branded as traitors the cabinet ministers favoring peace. Thus, observed Machimura, the rightists have begun to agitate. If they linked up with the military— serious trouble!

Next Prince Takamatsu arrived. He was fearful that fanatics in the navy might break loose at any time.

Following Takamatsu, Prince Konoye called on Kido. Konoye unpacked some of his standard worries about a "Communist uprising" by leftists in the army and the populace. Then the Prince asked his old friend if the palace was safe. He had heard, he explained, that the Imperial Guards Division was rebellious. Kido had heard no such rumors and pooh-poohed them: "True to its name, the Guards Division will never resort to any unlawful action."

In a few short hours the privy seal found out how wrong he was.

Chapter 18

Sunset for Samurai

At army GHQ, August 14 had begun with "an atmosphere of relative tranquility" according to Lieutenant General Torashiro Kawabe, its vice-chief of staff. But after the word of the Imperial Conference reached headquarters this quiet evaporated. "Tense emotion and excitement" prevailed. "I could sense this," Kawabe reports "by looking at the eyes and mouths of those passing me hurriedly in the corridors."

The war ministry and army GHQ were churning like a hive of wet hornets when, about 1 P.M., word raced through the building that General Anami had returned from the palace. The young tigers flocked to his office and crowded to greet him.

After a short wait, the General appeared. He was noticeably pale but seemed composed. Those closest to him observed that he was choked with emotion and was straining to control himself. Colonel Masataka Ida, Takeshita's subordinate, described the mood: "Anxious to know whether the news was good or bad, the officers, tense because the fate of their fatherland was now to be decided, held their breath to hear him speak, and their eyes suddenly glistened.

"Before long the minister said quietly and simply 'It was decided at the Imperial Conference this morning to terminate the war. I must apologize for not meeting your expectations.'

"All were dumfounded and their bodies seemed to stiffen. For a moment silence reigned, a stillness like that in mountain recesses. It was suddenly broken by a loud wail and [the officers] awoke to the fact that they were now faced with the stern realities of defeat. It was Hatanaka who first burst out crying.

276

"I could not help asking 'For what reasons did you change your resolve, Minister?'

"I shall never forget [his] expression at that time. After closing his eyes for a short time, trying to suppress his emotion, he replied resolutely: 'I could not resist the Emperor's own desires any longer. Especially when he asked me in tears to forbear the pain, however severe it might be, I could not but forget everything and accept it. Moreover, His Majesty said he was confident that the national polity would be guaranteed. Now, if you try to rise in revolt, kill Anami first!'

"By these words we were all made silent and quietly left the war minister's room."

After Anami broke the bitter news to his coterie of junior officers, the chief of the army Operations Department stuck his head into General Kawabe's office and suggested that something be done to make sure the top-ranking army leaders coordinated their actions. The purpose was to prevent some splinter movement, resistance, or *coup*. The army vice-chief of staff agreed readily, remembering that five of the army's top leaders were in conference at that very moment in Anami's office.

Kawabe buttonholed Vice-minister of War General Wakamatsu and that military bureaucrat concurred. Kawabe describes how the generals' agreement was secured:

Together we entered the war minister's reception room where the generals were gathered. Anami was not present, out on some official business. Speaking in a tone calculated to attract the attention of the four generals, I said, "I wish that you take advantage of this meeting to discuss matters concerning the immediate coordination of minds among you five top-ranking army leaders." Marshal Hata turned toward me and said "That is of the utmost importance." Wakamatsu and I sat down side by side on two empty chairs. For several seconds no one said anything, so I spoke again, saying "Under the present circumstances, I do not think that the situation calls for any discussion or consideration. I think the only thing for the entire army to do is obey loyally the Imperial decision."

General Umezu nodded assent; General Doihara, chief of Military Training, murmured "That's right"; Hata faced me and said clearly "I agree with you." Marshal Sugiyama, commander of the Western District Army, said nothing and showed no indication of his feelings, but I felt that he did not disagree. I said to Wakamatsu, "Let us record this unanimity of feeling in writing and have each general sign it."

Wakamatsu instantly agreed. He stood up, left the room and went to the ministerial office next door. Some time passed but he did not return, so I went over and looked into the office. I saw that Wakamatsu and Colonel Arao were trying to find the right phraseology for the statement, so I approached the desk where they were working and recommended that the statement read simply "The army will act in accord with the Imperial decision to the last."

Colonel Arao wrote those words, the date and names of each general on a single sheet of paper. Wakamatsu took it into the room and showed it to the generals. No one raised any objection. Each man placed his signature or affixed his seal on it. War minister Anami, who came in at just this point, also placed his signature on it without voicing any objections.

Umezu turned to Wakamatsu and me and said "Members of the air units are likely to cause trouble, so you had better show this to the commander of the army air force in particular. Wakamatsu immediately took the document to air force headquarters in the building next door and had the commander, General Kawabe [Torashiro's brother] affix his seal to it.

This step was taken to reaffirm the unwavering loyalty to the Imperial will under these extraordinary circumstances, not to mention the purpose of making it a self-disciplinary measure to prevent even the least confusion in the command psychology of the top leaders. It was a precautionary step designed to prevent even the slightest error in the course of action of the entire army.

But how effectively would these army leaders be able to control the troops under their command?

The young tigers clustered in groups and commiserated dolefully. There were schemes, theories, plans, fantasies, suggestions rational and irrational. The word was officially passed that the war minister would address all section heads at 3 P.M. in Conference Room I. Colonel Ida, for one, could not bear to hear Anami say those despicable words again. To him it seemed vastly more important to decide how the army would conduct itself in this situation. "There are more than a few people in history whose attitude was admired by posterity even though they were defeated in war," he considered. "And in this unprecedented national emergency we should take such measures as would make the end of the Japanese army a noble one."

This mature though painful view was admirable; how to implement it was the question. After concentrating on it in his office, Ida concluded that the troops should assume their responsibility for the defeat "by killing ourselves in apology to the Emperor and the Japanese state. If all the personnel on Ichigaya Heights [the GHQ and war ministry site] killed themselves by *harakiri* in turn, their sincerity would certainly move Heaven."

For Ida this was a moment of *satori,* of sudden and intense personal enlightenment in the Zen sense. "When I reached this conclusion," he reveals, "I felt relieved. My mind, which had been troubled since the ninth of August, suddenly cleared and I became conscious that I had awakened to the realization that death was glorious. As my last service, I decided to submit to the war minister this plan for the suicide of the entire officer corps."

Acting on this resolution, Colonel Ida left his office and moved about among his fellow officers, exchanging opinions and discussing the path to follow. The result was disillusioning. "To my regret," he discovered, "only 20 per cent of them agreed with me. Ten per cent advocated going underground to establish a long-range plan and the remaining 70 per cent were undecided. Some officers were apparently busy with routine work and this 'usual state of affairs,' even on the last day of the glorious Japanese Empire, made me feel hopeful and, on second thought, miserable." Ida went back to his room and stayed there "meditating, chatting, or discussing."

Meanwhile the plans for execution of the "Second Troop Employment Plan" were inflaming some of the young tigers. A new convert to the scheme was Colonel Sato, chief of the War Material Preparation Section, who two days before had tried to stop the *coup* plans in Anami's office. Now Sato was demanding immediate action. Hatanaka, Shiizaki, Hosoda, and Hara also were absorbed with the plot. Hatanaka was raring to go. He and his associates had approached members of the Guards Division two days before and were in contact with the commander of its 2d Regiment.

But the imperial decision and Anami's announcement had cooled the ardor of others among the conspirators. Takeshita and Arao withdrew. Inaba argued with Hatanaka and tried to discourage the plot. He was sure it would fail now that Anami had refused to go along with anti-peace moves. Inaba advised the plotters to act as the war minister directed. But Hatanaka was equally convinced that the men he had contacted would follow when the signal was given. He was also sure he could play on Takeshita's patriotism and self-interest to bring Anami into the *coup* at the propitious moment.

For Hatanaka there was no turning back. He had committed himself fully to the *coup* in his discussions with more than a dozen key officers. His *giri* to his name—his duty to admit no failure—drove him on like the fuel in a rocket, inextinguishable once ignited. In Japan, where shame is and always has been a cardinal force, Hatanaka could not simply drop the *coup*. He would never be able to look in the eye those who knew of his leadership in the plot. Better to perish!

Four and a half miles west of Ichigaya Heights the navy's scientific leaders had assembled at the Naval Technological Institute in the Meguro section of Tokyo. They were, at last, to hear the official report of Professor Asada about the explosion that had wiped out Hiroshima. His route from the devastated city to this presentation to navy brass had been indirect.

After traveling from Hiroshima to Osaka (roughly 215 miles) by night train on August 11, Asada reported to Naval Guard Headquarters. He told the officers the results of his observations and research in Hiroshima and the inescapable conclusion: The city had indeed been destroyed by an atomic bomb, just as the enemy declared. The navy men urged Asada to take his evidence to navy GHQ. He agreed.

Asada had returned to his laboratory at Osaka University and was putting things in order after his four-day absence when he received a visitor, Lieutenant Saito of Etajima Naval Academy. Saito was a former pupil and told his professor that he was on his way to Tokyo to report to navy GHQ for his commandant. Saito's commanding officer had studied the information about the Hiroshima blast and had come up with the deduction that the bomb used there was a mixture of magnesium and liquid oxygen. Therefore, he reckoned, there was, relatively speaking, nothing more to fear in it than in conventional bombs.

Asada was staggered. "If this report reached navy GHQ earlier than mine, they would believe the academy commandant. The report of a mere university professor would not have been believed by the navy." This, he resolved, must be prevented at all costs, for there had been rumors and reports of short-wave broadcasts from America that Tokyo would be atom-bombed on the seventeenth and Osaka on the twenty-first of August. And the American president had threatened to rain such bombs on Japan. Though Asada doubted that wholesale atomic bombing was possible, he believed the U.S. might have five or six of them. And if they were used on cities prepared only for conventional types of bombs, the devastation and slaughter would be impossible to calculate.

When the Professor's scientific devices had corroborated that the bomb was a nuclear device, he had used navy facilities to cable Tokyo this fact and urge circumspectly that the war be ended immediately. Now his former student was about to deliver a message that would encourage continued—and suicidal—resistance. Asada told Saito the results of his investigation and went over the evidence with him. He convinced the young officer of the truth of the atomic bomb and the urgency of presenting that truth to navy GHQ before some other theory was presented and adopted. For, once adopted, a theory, right or wrong, would have to be maintained by the self-protective military men.

Saito agreed to delay his trip, allowing Professor Asada to reach navy headquarters first so that he could present his report before Saito's liquid-oxygen theory hit navy brass.

Again traveling by night, Asada arrived in Tokyo the morning of August 14. Before an audience of admirals just after noon, the Professor described his investigation, cited the scientific evidence he had actually gathered with his navy team, and reported that it was without question an atomic bomb. There was, he told them, no means of coping with this weapon.

If he thought this news would panic the navy men into an immediate rush to sue for peace, Asada could not have been more mistaken. Faced with his data, "the conclusion of the naval authorities was indeed horrible," he says. "It was to isolate all Japanese physicists in the caves in Nagano Prefecture to have them produce atomic bombs. They planned to drop them on America. The navy had no intention of surrendering."

When the Suzuki cabinet finally assembled at 1 P.M. August 14 in the premier's office building, the first order of business was the formal decision to accept the Allied terms, as "counseled" by His Majesty. The legal papers were brought in by Sakomizu and signed by each of the fifteen ministers. Thus Japan formally accepted the Potsdam declaration.

At this point, when the decision was legally completed by the cabinet, Foreign Minister Togo telephoned his vice-minister, Matsumoto, and directed him to prepare a note of surrender to the Allies. Another memorandum, incorporating the points desired by the military, had been drawn up at Togo's instruction and this was circulated to the heads of the army and navy for their approval. It was then sent to the Allies. The key points were:

1. Since the occupation's purpose is to achieve the objectives of the Potsdam proclamation, the Japanese government desires that the Four Powers rely on Japan's good faith and facilitate execution by Japan of its obligations so as to prevent complications.
   a. That advance notice of entry of fleets or troops in Japan proper be made, so that reception arrangements can be made.
   b. That occupation points be limited to the minimum number and selected to leave cities unoccupied and occupation forces as small as possible at each point.
2. Disarming of 3,500,000 officers and men overseas. Suggest the best way be by command of His Majesty, the Emperor; the Japanese forces to disarm themselves and surrender arms of their own accord. It is hoped that the Hague Convention would be applied and "honor of the soldier" respected, allowing them, for instance, to wear swords.
3. Because some troops are in remote places, allow reasonable time before cessation of hostilities.
4. Either the Allies take steps or give Japan facilities for shipping food and medical supplies to distant Japanese forces, and to transport the wounded.

This remarkable message from vanquished to victor seemed perfectly logical to Japan's military. They seemed oblivious of the fact that Japan's stock of "good faith" had been systematically dissipated in the fourteen years beginning with the Manchurian Incident. What remained went up in smoke at Pearl Harbor. In this category Japan was bankrupt. But what the Japanese really meant in this note was that they were terrified that some flare-up beyond their control might occur as the disarmament and occupation began. Their unfortunate choice of words, however, failed to convey this.

To the Allies, the request for advance notice of fleet and troop entry to Japan smacked of a trap. Yet all responsible Japanese leaders were quite sincere in believing that police protection and adequate preparations would be mandatory to prevent mishaps when the occupation forces came ashore.

The suggestion that occupation points be minimized in number and garrisoned outside the cities with the smallest number of troops possible also suggested trickery to suspicious Allied leaders. Naturally the defeated nation would like to have the fewest possible foreign troops on her soil, and she would prefer to have them tucked inconspicuously out of the way in the rural areas. To have the occupation forces in the capital and major cities, controlling the air, land and sea traffic and communications would be against the wishes of any nation. Yet Togo and the military had valid reasons for wanting to minimize friction and avoid displays of armed Allied might that they feared could incite the populace.

Point 2, about the troops overseas disarming themselves, seemed ludicrous on the face of it. How could anyone seriously propose that the Allies stand by patiently while the unsupervised Japanese carefully, at their own pace (probably very slowly) stacked arms? Some might "forget" to turn over their weapons. Others might put them away for a rainy day. And, again, this "voluntary" disarming would feed the myth that in reality the Japanese army and navy had not fought the final battle for which they supposedly were prepared because the Emperor had directed them to halt, not because they were beaten.

Realist that he was, Togo knew that there was precious little chance of the Allies accepting this suggestion. He included it because the military demanded it and because he recognized the highly sensitive nature of this particular matter. In ancient Japan the samurai traditionally was recognized by his swords. The right to carry weapons was his alone and this placed him clearly and definitely in the social structure—at the top. The successors to the samurai, the army and navy, jealously maintained their right to wear weapons, especially the coveted swords. Tradition spoke through these strips of the finest consecrated steel encased in handsome wooden scabbards. The cult of the sword stretches back into the misty prehistory of Japan, when the Sun Goddess presented a sword to her grandson. One of the three sacred treasures of Nippon was and is this sword. Swords of iron were in use in the Japanese islands at least six centuries before Christ. Sword-making was always one of the noblest of trades and was indulged with religious fervor.

When putting the edge to the blade, the smith donned the kimono of a court noble, hung up the *shimenawa* (a plaited straw rope with pendants of straw and paper, traditionally placed above the doorway at New Year's), symbolic of purity and prayers to the gods, and shut himself off from the world for the delicate and secret task. It was a near-sacred rite. The swordsmith was required to be of highest character and absolutely dedicated to his craft. The sword was emblematic of purity and justice, and it was believed that if evil thoughts entered the head of the smith during the forging they would affect the blade and its owner. Such a sword would never be of good purpose.

In ancient times a samurai would swear by his weapon; so binding was this oath that it could be broken only by death. The sword was literally a sacred weapon, intended for conquering evil and meting out justice. On the two to three-and-a-half feet of superb steel in the long sword (*tachi* or *daito*) or short sword (*katana* or *shoto*) the finest craftsmanship and skill were lavished. For centuries Japanese blades were famed throughout the Orient. There developed, naturally, a fine appreciation of these works of art.

The Japanese army officer's dress uniform was incomplete without one of these choice weapons. Furthermore, for this *sine qua non* of the military man, the Japanese officer willingly might spend ten months' salary or more and if necessary mortgage his house and land, repaying the purchase price over many years. With these strong economic, historic, and emotional ties to his sword, the military man was, Togo and the cabinet ministers knew, not likely to turn over his sword without a struggle. After all, in their grandfathers' day it was the edict that samurai could no longer wear swords that touched off the Satsuma rebellion against Emperor Meiji. Give up his rifle, his pistol, his machine gun or mortar, yes. But a family heirloom? Not easily.

Consequently Togo included a specific request that the honor of the soldier be respected and the troops be allowed to retain their swords.

Togo's "hope" that Article 35 of the Hague Convention would be applied could only raise hackles among the Allies, for the flagrant and scornful refusal of Japanese commanders to abide by the Convention in the treatment of Allied war prisoners had been protested formally again and again without result.

On the face of it, Item 3 appeared an out-and-out attempt to allow the fighting to continue until the local Japanese commanders decided to call a halt. It had little possibility of acceptance, but in reality it was an admission that many Japanese garrisons were out of contact and, as had been the case with the military for a generation, almost beyond the control of the central authorities.

From the standpoint of Togo and the civilian cabinet ministers, it was obvious that it would take time to convince the troop commanders that the surrender was the genuine wish of the Emperor and the sincere command of the military authorities. It was planned that Hirohito's brothers would be dispatched to the remote areas to carry the imperial word that the surrender was legitimate. It was believed that this would be necessary because of the technical problems of radio communication and the necessity of vouchsafing the truth of the surrender with the highest available authority.

Military leaders calculated that it might take from two days to several weeks to bring the word to the troops, depending on how remote or fanatical they were. (Later events proved that their fears were well founded. In some outlying, bypassed garrisons, the surrender orders were contemptuously ignored as crude Allied tricks and the fighting continued for weeks.)

Togo's Item 4 was a straightforward request for humanitarian action to save the lives of Japanese troops. It also was a humiliating admission that Japan, once possessor of the world's third largest fleet, now was reduced to begging for shipping facilities to take care of emergency needs, to say nothing of normal requirements.

The army and navy leaders willingly approved Togo's draft memo. The realists among them feared that it had little chance of acceptance; the less pragmatic thought it covered some of the most urgent matters in a satisfactory way, though they would have enlarged its scope and increased the bill of particulars if Togo had allowed it.

The foreign minister must have known it was unlikely to be accepted favorably by the Allies. Perhaps he was simply going through the motions to satisfy the military. At any rate, he shot this arrow into the air the following morning and it fell to earth unheralded, unanswered, he knew not where. (The approved text was sent by Togo on the fifteenth. It was the last official note from Imperial Japan to the enemy. This note had a curious fate. Undoubtedly it was received by the Allies, but it apparently elicted no response. Perhaps it was considered gratuitous and too incredibly impertinent to answer. Perhaps it was simply lost in the shuffle. Its fate is unknown and no reply is on record.)

The cabinet ministers heard Information Bureau president Shimomura describe the plan to broadcast the Emperor's voice to the people, carrying the Imperial rescript directly to his subjects. These leaders of the government shivered at the thought of what the people might do if they learned of the surrender. They were unanimous in wanting the Emperor to broadcast, for it was crucial that the word get to the public throughout the Empire simultaneously and fast, and that the decree have clear and unmistakable imperial backing. The words of any human being other than the Emperor would be given no credence by a people who still believed their armed forces were winning. In fact, these misled people would consider such a message an affront to their intelligence and it would inspire immediate riots, probably a manhunt for the unlucky bearer of such information, and popular revulsion against the government and all its leaders. There would be *uchikowashi* (literally "smashing-up") throughout the land on a scale that would make the terrible food riots of the eighteenth and nineteenth centuries seem like fraternity initiation rites.

So the cabinet approved the scheme for the broadcast. Meanwhile, the imperial household ministry had been making preliminary arrangements for the Emperor to speak to his people via radio. About noon Chamberlain Kato of the imperial household telephoned the Information Bureau and asked Mr. Usaburo Kato, chief of the First Department of the Bureau, to come to the palace to discuss a broadcast by the Emperor to take place about 6 P.M.

Information Kato piled into a car and drove to the palace to discuss this unprecedented event with Household Kato. With only the barest skeleton of facts to go on, Information Kato jumped to the conclusion that the Emperor was going to announce his abdication, *à la* Edward VIII of England!

Back at the Information Bureau, Kato called NHK, the Japan Broadcasting Company, to bring them into the picture. NHK's president, chief engineer, and domestic bureau chief went to the Information Bureau and were told that an imperial rescript would be issued by His Majesty, that he would broadcast it, and that it was to be a recorded announcement. The recording staff should report to the imperial household by 3 P.M.

While the cabinet was approving the broadcast, at Radio Tokyo, the chunky black building on Hibiya street just a block from Hibiya Park and Domei headquarters in Hibiya Hall, preparations began. An engineer named Nagatomo was told to prepare for a remote recording session by 3 P.M. Although he didn't know where the recording was to be made or what was to be recorded, Nagatomo suspected that it was important and might even involve the Emperor. So he commandeered the best microphone in the station (Mazda Type A) and secured two sets of K type, No. 14 recording machines and supporting equipment, testing each component.

Nagatomo selected three associates for the recording team and reported for duty. His superior objected to such a large crew, but Nagatomo insisted he must have four to insure a good recording. If they should fail, he said, they would have to commit *harakiri*. This was a shrewd ploy to insure that he had enough helpers, and also to confirm his suspicion that the recording involved the Emperor. He won. The four engineers, under Mr. Takajiro Kondo, were picked up in household ministry cars, along with NHK president Ohashi and Bureau Chief Yabe. They had all been given special dispensation to wear ordinary clothes, so instead of formal attire they were clad in the national uniform—the khaki jacket with ceremonial badge.

At the palace, they went directly to the second floor of the huge household ministry building and were taken to the imperial audience room of the administration suite. The microphone was set up in the administration room and the recording machines in the audience room. One of the chamberlains asked if the Emperor could listen to the recording afterward and the broadcasters suddenly realized that they did not have a playback machine with them.

In a ministry car Nagatomo sped to the nearest place such a machine was available: the secret broadcasting room NHK maintained for emergency purposes in the basement of the Dai Ichi Insurance Company building, the starkly modern office building just across the moat. In this building General Shizuichi Tanaka, commander of the Eastern District Army, had his headquarters on the sixth floor. It was probably one of the safest spots in the entire city, and had been chosen by NHK for its emergency installation for that very reason.

As the NHK engineer headed for the basement of the Dai Ichi building, a rather willowy young officer wearing war ministry insignia strode resolutely into the monumental entrance. Directly to the elevators and up to the sixth floor offices of the *Tobugun* (Eastern District Army) commander he went. The effeminate face and quiet manner masked the obstinate will and fanatical drive of Major Kenji Hatanaka.

Aware that Takeshita, Inaba, and Arao had abandoned all plans for a *coup,* Hatanaka had seized the reins and was moving on his own to prevent the sacred land from falling to the infidels. He was determined to carry out the plot as planned. Or, failing that, to execute a *coup* as close to the original as possible. He had already secured pledges of cooperation from second- and third-echelon officers of the Imperial Guards Division. His friends were working on General Umezu and hoped to bring GHQ along. He would prevail on Ida and Takeshita to get the war minister and bring him into the action. But now Hatanaka was about to pull the *Tobogun* into the scheme. Because of its control of the entire Tokyo area, the Eastern District Army was vital to the plan.

In the orderly room outside the office of the commanding officer Hatanaka told the duty officer that he wished to talk to General Tanaka. The orderly looked at the slight figure in rumpled khakis and asked Hatanaka's business. The Major refused to divulge his purpose except to the General himself. There followed a verbal scuffle in which Hatanaka wouldn't describe his business and the orderly therefore wouldn't allow him to see Tanaka. The heat of the exchange finally pierced the walls and the General came to the door to investigate the commotion.

Tanaka's blazing eyes, long, pointed mustaches (left over from his Kaiser Wilhelm and Emperor Taisho days) and his constant attitude of exasperated outrage made him formidable under the best of circumstances. His voice was capable of only two modulations—quiet and gentle or FULL BLAST *and* ANGRY. Having been interrupted by the argument, Tanaka was a veritable reincarnation of a Japanese god of wrath and destruction as he appeared at the doorway. He cut loose with modulation number two, bellowing "What's going on here?"

Told that Major Hatanaka wanted to see him on unstated business, Tanaka placed his hands on his hips and roared "You fool! Why have you come here? I know what you are after . . . you don't even have to open your mouth . . . get out!"

Obviously Tanaka had been forewarned, and there was little Hatanaka could say. He turned pale, bowed rigidly, and left quietly. There would have to be another approach to the *Tobogun,* he thought. It was too important to cross off just because of this temporary setback. Hatanaka headed back for Ichigayadai past the blocks and blocks of fences and wires that separated street and sidewalk from bomb craters and gaping pits where once Japan's most modern office buildings had been. The next step in his scheme was to enlist the help of his fellow officers at the war ministry.

War Minister Anami left the cabinet session about three o'clock to return to the war ministry. When the General stepped out of the cabinet meetings, business was over, for literally nothing could be transacted without him. Thus there was a recess until he returned.

At three thirty Anami assembled all war ministry section chiefs and heads of offices, schools and facilities under ministry jurisdiction. "This decision was made by the Emperor," he told them, "and the entire army must act in complete accordance with it. The Emperor is especially worried about the military. He said he would, if necessary, send a special Imperial rescript to the army so that all of his loyal soldiers and subjects would understand. Just one way is left. The only path for the army is to follow the Emperor's wishes and carry out his will."

The General paused, seeming to reflect for a moment. "From now on Japan will suffer much agony. But even if it means sleeping in the fields and eating stones, I charge you to do your utmost to preserve the national polity."

General Yoshizumi followed, with a description of the Imperial

Conference and a recapitulation of the Emperor's line of thinking as he had expressed it in his decision. Then General Wakamatsu, responding on behalf of ministry personnel, pledged cooperation of all in carrying out the Emperor's decision.

Anami went to his office and instructed his secretary to bring him two pieces of white paper. Colonel Hayashi delivered them to the war minister, believing that at last Anami was going to resign. But no, Anami carefully put the papers aside, then called to Hayashi to follow. He hustled out to the limousine and back to the premier's residence to carry on with the cabinet meeting. Nothing more was said about the papers or about resigning.

As they waited in the improvised broadcasting studio in the Emperor's offices at the household ministry, the radio team, accustomed to split-second timing and a life in which each day is a series of deadlines, began to get edgy. They sat. They stood. They checked out the microphone, the turntables, the connections, the amplifiers. They smoked, sat, and stood some more. There was no word about recording, and no sign that it would be imminent.

There were good reasons why they could not be told when the recording would be made. One reason was that the cabinet did not receive the draft of the rescript from Sakomizu until 4 P.M. Another was controversy about what should and should not be in the rescript.

While the cabinet was beginning to go over the draft rescript in earnest, another meeting was just starting a few hundred yards away. Professor Asada was conferring with executives of the home ministry about the atomic bomb and means of coping with it. He learned that not only military minds were impenetrable. The conclusion reached by the civilian bureaucrats seemed utterly incomprehensible to him: "Japanese people should wear white clothes. White reflects radiation. A man clad in white will not sustain burns at a distance, but will be burned if his flesh is exposed. Since white material is unavailable, people are to be instructed to use bedsheets to make clothing. The war will continue."

Meanwhile, both General Umezu and General Anami acted to keep the army in line. If words could contain the young tigers, the two men would have had them on snaffle bits.

At army GHQ Umezu, as chief of staff, had assembled all the officers about 1:30 P.M. to explain the Emperor's decision at the Imperial Conference. "The army," he had said, "had no alternative but to obey faithfully and carry out the Imperial will."

By late afternoon a joint notice from Anami and Umezu, the two top army leaders, was radioed and dispatched to all army operations commanders under the Emperor's direct command. It read, in part:

1. Negotiations have taken place with the enemy on the basis of our conditions that the national polity be preserved and the Imperial domain maintained. The stipulations laid down by the enemy, however, rendered the realization of these conditions extremely difficult, and for that reason we vigorously and consistently maintained that these stipulations were absolutely unacceptable. Although we reported to the Throne to this effect on various occasions, His Imperial Majesty nevertheless has decided to accept the terms of the Potsdam declaration. . . .

2. The Imperial decision has been handed down. Therefore, in accordance with the Imperial will, it is imperative that all forces act to the end in such a way that no dishonor shall be brought to their glorious traditions and splendid record of meritorious service and that future generations of our race shall be deeply impressed. It is earnestly desired that every soldier, without exception, refrain absolutely from rash behavior and demonstrate at home and abroad the everlasting fame and glory of the Imperial Army.

(At 4:30 P.M. Navy Minister Yonai pulled in his principal staff members and told them to take all the precautions possible to make sure the Emperor's will in accepting the Potsdam terms was obeyed. Yonai also ordered the major naval commands within Japan to send their executive officers to navy GHQ at once for further instructions.)

Nevertheless, the buzzing of the drones at Ichigaya Heights reached fever pitch. Rumors were germinated, propagated, and devoured only to be spewed forth again magnified and embellished: An enemy task force was said to be standing by off Tokyo Bay with landing forces ready! The landing of U.S. troops was expected momentarily! Enemy paratroopers were on the way to take over key airports!

In the lower echelons particularly, soldiers left their posts to pack up their paltry personal belongings and get their families out of the invasion path. Others simply left and headed for the provinces. Even the *kempeitai* guards assigned to Anami slipped away, deserting yesterday's idol.

Those who stayed on duty began to pull out files and haul them into the yard in a monumental "evacuate and burn" operation. Some pulled out their sake bottles instead and anesthetized themselves. Others, like Ida, debated with themselves whether to choose self-immolation. Still others went off the deep end. One of these was Lieutenant Colonel Oyadomari, chief of the Military Information Bureau.

In G-2, the Intelligence Department of army GHQ, the crew assigned to translation of English-language newspapers and radio broadcasts was in an uproar, like all other units on Ichigaya Heights. The officers were in an intense bull session when the door flung open and Oyadomari lurched in, eyes blazing. Slung at his side was his dress sword, the two-handed *daito*. Around headquarters it was unusual to wear this except on dress occasions for it was clumsy and caught on door jambs and chairs.

Oyadomari pulled his sword and yelled at the translators. "You defeatist bastards!" All eyes focused on him, and all talking stopped.

Brandishing the long, curved blade, he waved it at the men in the room and howled "You're the reason we've lost! All along you've said we would lose. Now it's happened. Are you happy? Hunh? Are you pleased with yourselves? Hunh?"

One of the men, Lieutenant Sadao Otake, murmured to the man next to him "Don't make a move and don't say anything or he'll cut loose." The razor-sharp tip of the sword made the circuit of the room slowly, menacing each man, one after another. Oyadomari held the sword point a fraction of an inch from each officer's nose in turn as he went on with his tirade.

Tears were streaming down the Colonel's cheeks as he vented his misery on these immobilized targets. They were a suspicious lot, as viewed by the ultras. Many of the translators were Nisei (born outside Japan of Japanese parents) who had returned to Nippon for one reason or another and been assigned to the unit because of their language skills. They were not under any cloud until the war began to go against Japan. Then, as they sent in their translations of enemy victory claims and production reports, jingoists who had access to the information or the scuttlebutt based on it began to point the finger of doubt at the intelligence officers.

Oyadomari, who came from Okinawa, was one of the most ardent patriots and the loss of the war after the loss of his home island was too much for him. "You goddamned dogs!" he continued, moving toward the door. "You deserve to die for misleading us. . . ." He returned his sword to its scabbard as the translators remained frozen. "Go ahead, glory in our defeat, you traitors!" he shouted as he stumbled weeping from the room.

The Suzuki cabinet's major job that frantic afternoon of August 14 was to shape the message that would be handed down to future generations as the imperial rescript ending the Pacific War. It was no easy chore, as Sakomizu could testify, because it had to be couched in official Court language called *kanbun*. It served a purpose such as Latin does in the West—it was intended to inform contemporary Japanese and at the same time be a statement for the ages in a language that was not transient.

The chief cabinet secretary had been working on the rescript since the Emperor's decision August 10, as we know. With the help of Kihara of the Nippon *Times* and Takeda of the Greater East Asia Ministry, the edict was now in draft form. Sakomizu had studied *kanbun*, but because of the importance of this message, he purposely checked the draft with two noted scholars, professors Kawada and Yasuoka. These men suggested changes and added phrases and expressions.

Sakomizu passed around copies of the draft to the cabinet ministers and it was open season on the language, expressions, terminology, even the cadence of the message.

The first axe fell when War Minister Anami read the phrase "the war situation is getting worse day by day." This, he insisted, had to go. It was a slur on the fighting men of Japan and did not accurately reflect their strong resistance and offensive actions on the China fronts and in the islands. No, he would not stand for any such phrase as this.

Yonai spoke up, taking the opposite view. "We should never change this part. Absolutely not!"

The cabinet secretary offered a weak substitute, with the help of other ministers. The wording they devised (which rings absolutely false in the final rescript) was "the war situation has developed not necessarily to Japan's advantage." Anami endorsed this. Yonai objected violently. However, the prime minister, still afraid that Anami might hand in his resignation and bring the whole house of cards down, sided with the war minister and agreed that the ambiguous second phrase should be used.

As the discussion wore on, the agriculture minister, Ishigeru, singled out the expression *shinkio-ho-jite* for deletion. The meaning of the phrase is "the faithful," in the sense of followers or those loyal and faithful to the Emperor. Ishigeru pointed out that this phrase would provide ammunition to the conquerors, who might be seeking evidence that the Emperor and the religion were identical. They might, he feared, use it as proof that the Emperor was god. The phrase was cut.

Unfortunately, this deletion ruined the rhythm of the sentence. Since the meter is very important in *kanbun,* something had to be done. This crisis was overcome by the insertion of some strictly poetic expressions that were practically meaningless. They restored the classical rhythm pattern without affecting the content of the edict.

Three or four of the ministers fastened on the word *gimei* immediately preceding the statement "endure the unendurable." *Gimei* is an ancient, special word that means "it is the will of the god [in this case the Emperor] that such-and-such be done." But the word was so obscure that even some of these men did not recognize it. Others insisted on scratching it because it appeared also to deify the Emperor. It was changed to *jiun,* a word in contemporary usage, much more passive, meaning "it has already been decided and it is our destiny to do such-and-such." Since this was used before the phrase "we must endure the unendurable," it meant "under these circumstances we must. . . ."

One highly significant change was suggested by War Minister Anami. The general was openly skeptical about the Allied occupation. And, as he had demonstrated again and again, he distrusted the terms the Allies had set out in the Potsdam declaration and subsequent notes. Therefore he urged that the Emperor use the words "having been able to safeguard and maintain the structure of the

Imperial state. . . ." This, he believed, would tell the Japanese and the world that the Emperor had kept the national polity intact and anything that happened to it afterward would be the handiwork and the responsibility of the Allies.

At the household ministry, the fidgeting broadcasting team was offered supper by one of the chamberlains. They ate in two shifts, expecting to be called at any moment for the feature event. But no call came. No information or hint seeped through. The reason was that the cabinet did not finish its editing session until eight thirty. It was then that Sakomizu's revised, final copy was at last approved.

Now, with the fruit of his four months as prime minister clutched in his weathered hands, Baron Suzuki drove once more to the palace. Received at once by Hirohito in the imperial library, Suzuki placed in His Majesty's hands this truly awesome statement. It was nine hours since the Emperor had directed that this action be taken, and now he found many of his words in the rescript. He was pleased that it emphasized his interest in peace and avoided recrimination. Its basic feature was the wish to bring about peace for all ages to come, for Japan and the whole world.

There was no mention of revenge in the message. After the Sino-Japanese war in 1894–1895, the joint pressure of three nations forced Japan to return the Liaotung Peninsula to China. At the time, Hirohito's grandfather had issued an imperial message explaining his action and containing words that were easily interpreted as a call to avenge this embarrassment.

Sakomizu, no shrinking violet, later said of the rescript which he had labored to frame: "It was a very difficult task for me to prepare that rescript. When I read it again later on, I could not but wonder myself how I could compose such excellent sentences. It was so magnificently made that I was surprised at myself." In its avoidance of cant and the spirit of retaliation, it is a remarkable document.

Hirohito approved the rescript, signed it with his hand and his official seal was applied. He and Suzuki spoke briefly about the broadcasting arrangements and the Admiral, hopeful that his harbor was nearly in sight, brought the edict back to the cabinet meeting.

Shortly before 10 P.M. the sirens howled and the recess in strategic bombing of Japan was over. President Truman had grounded the

B–29s on August 10 when he saw the Domei dispatch about Japan's acceptance of the Potsdam terms. But Japan had dilly-dallied in answering Secretary Byrnes' note. The President had loosed the B–29s again to help the enemy decide. Now they were over Tokyo as the final decree was about to be approved and issued. Lights throughout the area had been turned off at the first sound of the sirens. Blackout conditions were in effect until the all-clear.

Only the signatures of the cabinet members were needed on the document to ratify it. The fifteen men affixed their seals. After the countersigning, Anami strongly advised that the Emperor's broadcast of the rescript be made the following day. To those who had locked horns with the military and knew so well their delaying tactics, this had sinister overtones. It was by now known to most of the leaders that conditions at Ichigayadai were confused, if not absolutely out of control. Was the war minister stalling for time to protect some threatening action?

Anami argued convincingly that a broadcast before daybreak might cause civilian riots or some unforeseen outbreak by the army. Shimomura suggested the following noon and the cabinet agreed.

But that was not all. When this technicality had been settled, the war minister threw up another roadblock. He demanded that the acceptance of the Allied terms be presented to the privy council before announcement. His basis was that the surrender was in the nature of a treaty between sovereign states.

The privy council had been created in the time of Emperor Meiji by an imperial ordinance that gave it six areas of jurisdiction, among which the fourth was international treaties and agreements. No laws could be enacted or rescripts issued without privy council approval, according to this ordinance. Suzuki's attempts to finesse the privy council by including its president Baron Hiranuma in the Imperial Conferences were now challenged by Anami.

Again the suspicion arose that the war minister was stepping on the brakes to give some irregular action time to ripen. A call was sent out for the expert on such matters, Murase. As director of the Bureau of Legislation, Murase gave his interpretation of the privy council powers and a compromise was agreed upon. The rescript would become effective with its publication the night of the fourteenth, but the privy council would review the entire matter the morning of the fifteenth, just for form's sake.

The text was then passed on to the Printing Bureau for publication. It was set and printed as an extra of the *Official Gazette* at 11 P.M. and this time (the twenty-third hour of the fourteenth day of the eighth month of the twentieth year of the reign of Showa) became the official termination point of the Pacific War for Japan.

This cleaned up the cabinet business, and as the ministers sat around the conference table talking of the momentous actions that day, General Anami, replete in his formal dress uniform complete with decorations, dress sword, white gloves, and hat under his arm, marched over to Togo and stood at attention before him. In the most formal manner, the war minister addressed his persistent, now-victorious adversary: "I have seen the foreign ministry's draft of the note to the Allied Powers about the occupation and disarmament and I am grateful beyond expression. If I had known the matter would be handled so satisfactorily I would not have had to argue so strongly at the Imperial Conference."

Togo, unbending and wooden to the last, answered as if responding to a legal summary. "While I resisted proposing those points as conditions for accepting the Allied terms, I had no objections to presenting them as the *desires* of the Japanese government."

Anami, still on his formal best behavior, said "I am much indebted to you for all that you have done."

"I felt that he was overly polite," Togo noted. "But at any rate we all parted with smiles, saying to each other that it was good that it was over."

For Anami there was still one more stop to make at the *kantei*. It was by then after 11 P.M., and the official notice had been published. Sakomizu and Suzuki were seated alone in the prime minister's room. They were teary and tired, glad that the worst was over, yet deeply pained that the arduous, murderous war had inflicted such cost on Japan. There was a knock at the door and Anami entered, with sword and hat under his arm. He stopped in front of Suzuki, stood stiffly at attention and said "Since the question of ending the war first came up I have presented many arguments opposing it. I am afraid I have troubled you very much. I apologize now from the very bottom of my heart. My true intention was always to maintain the national structure, that is all. I had no other purpose. Please understand this point."

Anami's eyes were overflowing. Suzuki arose and came over to the general. Awkwardly, he put his hand on Anami's shoulder, saying "I understand it very well. But Anami, I am sure that the imperial house will be protected because the present Emperor earnestly performs the sacred rites and observances for the imperial ancestors in both spring and autumn [in other words, because the Emperor is so devout]."

"I believe so too," choked Anami, tears coursing down his cheeks. He bowed low, then turned and left the prime minister's room quietly. Sakomizu walked silently with him to the front door. With a perfunctory good night, Anami climbed into his staff car and drove off to his office at the war ministry. Sakomizu returned to Suzuki, who was at the window. The premier turned to the cabinet secretary and said softly, "Anami came to say goodbye."

The odyssey of Professor Asada and his precious burden of scientific data about the Hiroshima bombing was not yet ended. It had been arranged that he report his findings to the navy high command. The conference was held in the navy ministry air-raid shelter. The section chiefs and department heads of the navy were assembled to hear Asada.

The Professor glanced up at the ceiling and noticed water dripping from it in several places. He looked at his audience of top navy brass and observed that they were drooping, silent, and some were sobbing. It was then that he learned Japan had surrendered.

Navy officials advised Asada to stop at Ookayama Naval Base outside of Tokyo overnight. They insisted that he leave the city as soon as possible, because there would be a very important announcement on August fifteenth and it was likely that there would be riots in Tokyo. They might strike the government offices and army and navy buildings and it was best to get out of town.

Asada went to Tokyo station. Its brick shell was still standing, but its roof and insides had burned and it was patched back together with corrugated steel and make-do furnishings. Only one train was running and it was scheduled to leave at ten thirty. The Professor observed:

The train was more than overcrowded. People were even lying on the luggage racks, arms stretched out against the ceiling to keep themselves from falling out. The sailor who escorted me to the station looked for space in each of the coaches and finally found a place in the last one. I learned that it was to be used exclusively by the navy, so I got aboard. At Ofuna [eleven miles from Yokohama] a large group of navy officers came on board my coach. They were heading for Korea. Finding me there, they demanded that I get off. However, one of the officers who had been aboard from the start, directed his flashlight at his shoulder straps. The officers who had come aboard at Ofuna were all lieutenants; he was a lieutenant commander, so they saluted him and stopped reprimanding me. Thus I was able to stay on.

When the train approached Odawara [fifty miles southwest of Tokyo], I saw the town was being air-raided and flames were bursting out at many places. It was the night of August 14.

Back in Tokyo there were flames also, but not from air raids. These were fires set by the Japanese themselves, and they flared in the dark landscape almost everywhere there were government offices. These were the flames consuming the history and future of Imperial Japan.

Flickering firelight played across the war minister's face as he stepped out of his car at the war ministry building in Ichigaya Heights. The scene was straight out of the sulfurous park near Beppu on the Inland Sea. Or it might have been part of Dante's hell. On every side sparks and fire leaped upward in the sultry air from piles of books, documents, files, and papers—the archives of the ministry and IGHQ going up in smoke. As Anami walked into the building there was an unreal quality to the whole scene. Men he recognized were rushing here and there, some with bundles, others with stacks of papers, some empty-handed, running back to gather more papers to fuel the flames. There was an air-raid alert on, but nobody seemed to notice.

Feeling the futility and fatigue of it all, Anami plodded to his office, nodding at those who spoke and saluted. In an unfocused way, the war minister moved about his quarters, rummaged through his desk drawers, called in Colonel Arao, and asked where General Yoshizumi was.

Arao explained that Yoshizumi had gone to his family in Chiba City for the night, that the general had not slept for the past five days. Anami gave Arao a cigar. Then a score of the young tigers crowded into the minister's reception room. They were not the same. The spirit had changed. Already there was a quality of bewilderment, of "How could it turn out this way?" in their attitudes.

Instead of unanimous outrage, indignation, and vows to reject peace, there were conflicting views. Some of the men spoke to Anami of suicide; others maintained that they should head for the hills and scorch the earth. A few spoke with the old fire, talking of rounding up the traitorous peace faction. But none who looked out on the fires of Ichigaya Hill that night could see hope in them. They were the flames not of energy but of despair and guilt.

Anami was too choked with his feelings to say much. But he managed to tell them "This war has been given up. Leave the rest to me." His brooding and his words chastened them, and they drifted out of the office. The war minister bundled up his belongings, carefully including the short ceremonial sword in its polished cherrywood scabbard, and left the building. The mad scramble from files to fires to files was still on as he put the bundle in his staff car and drove back to his official residence in Miyakezaka.

The Emperor was anxious to record the imperial rescript so that it could be checked over by the radio specialists and prepared for broadcast the following noon. But when he was about to leave his quarters in the *Gobunko* for the imperial administration room in the household ministry building the air-raid sirens wailed their despairing warning that *Teki-san* (Mr. Enemy) was coming over again. There was an inviolable rule that the Emperor was not to venture outdoors while an air-raid alert was on.

Hirohito waited patiently for an hour, but finally turned to Chamberlain Irie and insisted on driving to the household ministry. He believed that the sooner the recording was made the sooner the suffering of his people would end.

So Irie called the car and he and the Emperor drove slowly, in total darkness, across the palace grounds to the hulking household ministry building. It was 11:25 P.M. Hirohito was wearing his army uniform. He climbed to the second-floor administration room and was impatient to get on with the job.

The standing microphone was placed in front of two embroidered lion screens. By the window stood Information Minister Shimomura, Household Minister Ishiwata, and five chamberlains in a row. In the next room the recording gear was set up and in addition to the eight men from NHK there were three from the Information Bureau.

Hirohito asked whether it was necessary to test. There was a hasty conference between one of the chamberlains and an engineer. It was decided that Chamberlain Toda had a voice similar to the Emperor's. Toda was asked to read a few lines from the newspaper for a test.

Then, with everything in order, Shimomura bowed to the Emperor and Hirohito, holding a copy of the rescript, read his unprecedented message to his subjects. His voice was high and strained and tremulous. Then there was a definite change, and the tone became softer and more relaxed. It was all over in about five minutes.

"Was it all right?" asked the Emperor. The engineers were consulted and Nagatomo judged that technically the recording was good but there were some places where the words were unclear. The Emperor's voice trembled somewhat, but it would have been imprudent to say so to a god. Hirohito spoke to Shimomura: "My voice was a little low for this one, so let's take another." He was quite concerned about the intonation.

The second recording went smoothly. But when it was over the Emperor noticed that he had skipped a conjunction and he requested a retake. This third time everything seemed to go well. Nagatomo verified that the take was satisfactory. (As the recording session ended, B–29s were dropping their fire bombs on Takasaki, a city sixty-three miles northwest of Tokyo.)

With the two recording machines, an original and a spare record were made of each of the takes. After the third time through the rescript, the Emperor went back to his car before the A disc of the last take could be replayed. Nagatomo judged the quality of the record to be very bad, and ruled that the B disc would be used for playback purposes and the original A take would be used for broadcast.

It was 12:05 A.M. of August 15 when the Emperor drove back in his blacked-out limousine through the palace grounds.

The recordings were carefully put in motion-picture cans and these in turn placed in cotton bags. Then followed a discussion between the chamberlains and the broadcast staff about storing the records until broadcast time. The chamberlains suggested that the NHK men take the records back to the radio station with them.

The radio men, with more wisdom than they realized, refused on the ground that it was dangerous at the station. Their obstinacy probably changed the course of history, very likely saving tens of thousands of lives. Finally the chamberlains agreed to take custody of the discs, and they were turned over to Mr. Takei. The radio men arranged to come and pick them up at 11 A.M. Takei gave the recordings to Chamberlain Tokugawa for safekeeping, and that meticulous aristocrat took them to the room of the Empress' ladies-in-waiting and put them in a safe in the bookshelves, covering the safe with books afterward.

Tokugawa then went to the aide-de-camp's room, where soldiers were on duty at all times. He had heard the air-raid siren again and asked the noncommissioned officer on duty what the situation was. The targets, he learned, were beyond Tokyo. The soldier also reported that the Emperor had retired at 12:50 A.M. Tokugawa left chamberlains Toda and Mitsui and went to bed. He dropped off to sleep about one thirty. His sleep was brief; his nightmare began when he awoke.

Chapter 19

Tigers Strike

The distance between traitor and patriot is often impossible to measure. Yesterday's traitor frequently becomes today's patriot. In America, as an instance, those the Tories saw as the traitors of 1776 were the patriots of 1781 and vice versa, by the painful, bloody, and shattering process of revolution. The winners' patriotism and courage have been judged ever since by reason of their success. Had they missed their mark, no matter how narrow their failure, history would have condemned them to a minor place in the record of Britain's colonial empire and branded them the traitors they surely were from the British viewpoint.

The distance between Washington's emergence as a hero instead of a traitor was one not of miles and time and blood, battles with Congress, the enemy, and the elements. That distance could be calculated only with the painstaking entry of infinite details that were factors, ranging from George III, his Parliament and armed forces to the personality quirks of his generals, as well as the more easily assessable statistics and records of such fundamentals as matériel, money, and manpower on both sides.

Even so, the result would be inadequate. It could scarcely pinpoint the moment the metamorphosis took place as exactly as the cold, harsh, black–white judgment of the turning point of the American Revolution—the point at which the Colonials began winning and the British forces began losing. Washington the hero was a product of victory.

Our purpose here is not to equate Japanese such as Anami and

Hatanaka with Washington and Hamilton any more than America 1781 with Japan 1945. It is difficult enough to grapple with a value system and mores so alien both to the Westerner and even to the Japanese of a generation later as were those prevailing in Imperial Japan at its end. It is asking too much to compare across cultures and time the men involved. But we may note with empathy that the men we view as the defeated and as the obstinate stumblingblocks to Allied victory were patriots. Their patriotism took expression in ways characteristic of Japanese throughout the ages, but ways better suited for feudal times in Nippon alone than in the twentieth century on a world stage.

After his stinging rebuff by General Tanaka, the commandant of the Eastern District Army, Major Hatanaka scurried back to the war ministry building the afternoon of August 14. He went over his plot with three other young tigers: his co-worker Lieutenant Colonel Jiro Shiizaki and two staff officers of the Imperial Guards Division, Major Sadakichi Ishihara and Major Hidemasa Koga (son-in-law of General Tojo, the former premier). They agreed that there was still a chance of jolting the army to final unified battle against the enemy if the Emperor's broadcast could be forestalled.

To accomplish this they would cut off the Emperor from the outside world and halt the broadcast. This was all-important, for if the radio carried His Majesty's words, tantamount to imperial command, it would be impossible to rouse the army against his will. Therefore, Hatanaka and his comrades planned to deploy the Imperial Guards Division during the night, seize the imperial palace itself and its precious inhabitant, and take over domestic broadcasting by occupying the headquarters of the Japan Broadcasting Company at Radio Tokyo.

They all realized that the odds against them were high, but the stakes were astronomical. If they succeeded, the Japan they knew would continue until it won or went under in the final struggle against the enemy. If they failed, their lives would constitute a small sacrifice and the nation would recognize their heroism and honor them. What greater opportunity could any patriot ask?

Around 4 P.M. on the fourteenth Hatanaka sought out Lieutenant Colonel Ida, who had been in his room since his realization of the profound glory suicide promised. Now Hatanaka suggested that they go up on the roof of the ministry building for some fresh air and a talk. Once up on the deck, looking out over the ruins of the capital, across to Yasukuni Shrine, to Akasaka palace grounds, and the gray-black granite walls of the imperial palace itself, Hatanaka asked Ida his plans. Like a new convert to religion, the baby-faced Colonel fervidly told Hatanaka his idea for wholesale suicide of war ministry and GHQ staff officers in atonement for the defeat.

Wide-eyed with surprise, the Major replied thoughtfully *"Harakiri* of all officers would be the 'most beautiful end of the Imperial army,' as you say. Perhaps it would be the best way. But I think it is easier said than done. I wonder whether all the officers will have enough determination to execute such a plan at the last moment."

"It will be enough," Ida replied, "if ten or twenty volunteers, if not all the staff officers, die in a group." Hatanaka nodded in pensive silence. Then, acting as though he had suddenly resolved on his own course, the Major confided "I cannot agree with you because your suggestion is impracticable. But we should not sit back and do nothing. Should we accept the Imperial surrender rescript for the sake of safeguarding the national polity? Or should we reject this way of ending the war and fight to the finish? Which is better? Only results will show, and it is beyond men to predict results. Therefore we should leave everything to fate. I would rather take the best way left for a Japanese to take, even at risk of incurring the stigma of traitor, than safeguard the national polity with 'outside help.' "

Warming to his subject, Hatanaka's eyes shone and in his passion he was eloquently persuasive. "We don't know what course fate will favor, but Heaven's judgment will depend on what we do. And since our action, whatever it is, will stem from unalloyed loyalty, we need not be ashamed.

"Ida-san, I believe we should camp in the imperial palace, cut off all communication with the outside, and help His Majesty in the final effort to solve the situation. This, I believe, is more proper than the mass suicide of all officers.

"Contact with the Imperial Guards Division has already been established. All necessary preparations have been completed. The successful action of a minority is bound to trigger the uprising of the whole army. I am sure success will be ours if the whole army rises and acts. I wish you, Ida-san, to join in our plan."

But Ida was not so easily swayed. "I fear that we would have no power to move the army, now that the war minister has decided against a *coup*. Before, I thought that a takeover would be possible only if the war minister resolved to carry it out, but any attempt now would be futile."

Hatanaka had an answer. "After all, the minister is a human being. He is not absolutely impossible to convince. Tonight is the only chance left and it would be neglect of duty on our part to waste in idleness the remaining hours that Heaven has given us. After all, this is not an ordinary affair, but the most crucial question our country has ever faced. Each and every one of us should sacrifice himself and give the best that is in him at such a momentous time. If we do not, what will posterity say about it? Indeed, we must give our all and leave the rest to Providence!"

Ida was drawn by Hatanaka's persuasiveness and hamstrung between logic and emotion: "Of course, human powers are limited. The present situation is in itself a problem beyond human judgment. He is right who advocates peace and so is he who favors resistance. I really do not know what is the best way for Japan. Therefore I would not try to stop you from carrying out your plan. Only the gods know whether it will meet with success or failure. If you wish to do it, by all means go ahead. As for me, I am quite conscious of the way I should go. However, depending on the circumstances, I may, perhaps, respond to your friendship as a comrade of ten years' standing." In other words, the Colonel didn't say yes, he didn't say no.

"I understand your point of view, but as for me, I'll do my best and leave the rest to Providence." With that, Hatanaka hurried away.

Ida went off to dinner, a bath, and early bed. He was awakened at 10 P.M. by Hatanaka and Lieutenant Colonel Shiizaki. The two men excitedly outlined their plan. "We have roughly completed our preparations but we need one thing: your support to help persuade General Mori, commander of the Imperial Guards Division. You must come with us and induce him to join us."

With this, says Ida, "I became so inspired by them that I made up my mind to abandon my cherished [suicide] plan." Before taking such a serious step, Ida told his friends "Well, I'll go with you. But in this critical time we must judge quickly and accurately whether our attempt will succeed, because it is not our true intention to cause public disorder by going to extremes. Therefore, if we feel we have failed, we should resign ourselves and [commit *harakiri*]." All agreed that this was reasonable.

Like the Three Musketeers facing insuperable odds, the trio went to the Guards Division headquarters. There they met majors Koga and Ishihara, who had already prepared a divisional order that required only the signature of the unit commander, General Mori. Once issued, it would put the *coup* in motion.

But they knew that Mori's cooperation was not likely to be automatic. He might in fact be quite difficult. Hatanaka had known Mori from his days at the Academy, where Mori had served as instructor. The General's whole career reflected his solid character. He had a reputation for being strong-willed, calm, and incorruptible. At the Academy Mori had been called *Osho-san,* a term that means, roughly, "father superior" or head monk. He was monkish in his devotion to duty and in helping the young men who seemed to him serious and worthy of help. He was part of the army elite without being in any of the contending army cliques. Only men of top leadership potential were chosen for the staff of the Academy. This was true to an even greater degree of the Army Staff College faculty, of which Mori was a member at a later time. Then his selection as commandant of the Imperial Guards was a signal honor. All the officers and men of the unit were hand-picked, superior types. After all, their duty was to protect the Emperor-god and the imperial family.

The conspirators realized as they arrived at Mori's orderly room that they might have a formidable task ahead of them. The air-raid sirens began to bellow and whoop. The B–29s were coming again to burn off more of Japan—perhaps to strike the area around the palace. Just a few hundred yards away the broadcasting team was making final adjustments on the recording equipment as the Emperor prepared to drive from his quarters in the library to the household ministry building. And a scant half-mile farther away, Sakomizu was giving the approved, final version of the imperial rescript to the printers for publication as an official document of the nation.

With Koga and Ishihara, Hatanaka, Shiizaki, and Ida sat and talked outside Mori's office. The General was with his brother-in-law, Lieutenant Colonel Shiraishi, who had flown in that morning with

Marshal Hata from Hiroshima. As the time dragged on, the plotters became increasingly nervous about the *coup* and the delay in seeing Mori. Finally, visualizing the opportunity slipping through their fingers, Hatanaka, Shiizaki, and Ida took the initiative and barged into the General's room.

From behind his desk Mori rose and snapped "What are you doing here at this time? The threesome lost their tongues for the moment, but Hatanaka found his voice and said "General, we have come to ask you to lead the Guards Division against the surrender. If the Guards rise, we are sure the whole army will follow suit."

"You are asking me to use my men in an unauthorized scheme?" Mori asked evenly. "How can I do such a thing without an order from the Eastern District Army?"

Hatanaka looked at his watch. It was after midnight now. He pulled Ida aside. "I must go out briefly, as I have something absolutely necessary to do. Please look after things while I am away." He left Ida and Shiizaki to continue the discussion.

Patiently the two conspirators reasoned with Mori. "At first," says Ida, "he was strongly opposed to us, but eventually he said that though he understood us, he would have to go and worship at the Meiji shrine to help him make up his mind." It took Mori nearly an hour to come to this point. To the plotters it seemed an eternity.

Meanwhile, Takeshita was at home in bed, repeating the pattern of previous nights: rolling and tossing, thinking and cursing fate. But not sleeping. Shortly after midnight, Hatanaka arrived, directly from General Mori's office.

Reluctantly pulling himself out of bed, Takeshita went with Hatanaka to the veranda, where there was now a lovely view of the bright, almost-full moon. This was the time for that most delectable activity, moon-watching. In fact, August was known as the month of *tsukimizuki,* moon-viewing. The fifteenth of August was traditionally the occasion for gathering with friends, sitting quietly with tea or sake, watching the full moon soar into the heavens. Observing the silhouettes first, then the countryside transformed by the mellow orb, was a favorite midsummer pastime in calmer times. But moon-watching was not the immediate purpose of Takeshita's caller.

"The war minister has given his speech and says that the war is over," mourned Hatanaka. "Everything is over. But do you think it really is?" Takeshita answered that he believed it was, indeed, over.

Hatanaka was unwilling to leave the discussion on this note. He argued and pleaded with Takeshita to consider the consequences for the nation, to think of honor, humiliation, the future of Japan. He told the Colonel that they had determined to go ahead with a *coup* regardless, and urged him to join them. But the former firebrand said he saw no hope for it. To succeed, a *coup* would have to have the whole army, not just parts of it. And obviously, Takeshita said, the army is not going to join in. "You cannot possibly succeed," he went on, "therefore give up the idea . . . there is nothing to be done now; it is too late."

"All right," said Hatanaka. "I understand. But we are going ahead anyway. Already the officers and men of the Second Imperial Guards Regiment are ready to participate in the uprising along the lines we had discussed previously. From this point on we will carry forward by ourselves."

One thing they needed desperately from Takeshita, however; it was his influence with his brother-in-law. "Please use your persuasion to win over the war minister so that he will take control of the situation after the *coup*," Hatanaka entreated. Takeshita finally promised to "exhort" the war minister to do so if the *Tobugun*, the Eastern District Army, also rose simultaneously. Hatanaka said the strike was timed for 2 A.M., and he stepped from the house into the moonlight and, amid the sudden wailing of the air-raid sirens, climbed into the staff car and sped off.

"After he left," says Takeshita, "the thought in the back of my mind that General Anami might commit suicide became very strong and I felt that I had to go and see him."

By the time Hatanaka reappeared in General Mori's room, accompanied by Major Koga, it was 1:30 A.M. The distant crackle and thunder of the air raid could be heard, and within the palace walls the recording had been finished and the Emperor had retired for the night. Precious time had trickled away. Hatanaka felt extreme pressure to act and act quickly before all was lost.

"Your Excellency," he said to General Mori, very formally, "have you reconciled yourself to the humiliation of surrender, which Japan now faces? The Emperor, who is all-wise, would surely continue the war if it was not for the advice of a few treacherous counselors around him. The orders you will issue to the division will save our country. They have already been drafted by Major Koga. . . ."

Mori called in Colonel Mizutani, his chief of staff, and told him that he planned to visit the Meiji shrine to help him decide on the right course of action. Mori asked the Colonel what he thought of the *coup* plan. Mizutani replied that he didn't know enough about the scheme. The General pointed at Ida and ordered him to go with Mizutani and tell him the details of the plot.

They left Mori's office, went to Mizutani's room, and Ida unfolded the plan to him as instructed. Meanwhile, Hatanaka was rapidly narrowing the General's room for maneuvering.

"The Emperor thought out and made a decision to save the Yamato race and our country," Mori intoned. "I am the commander of his personal bodyguards, the Imperial Guards Division, and I can only respect and follow his will. Though you men are in a hurry, I cannot decide such an important question on such short notice. I will have to meditate at the Meiji shrine and consult the commander of the Eastern District Army.

"We have already seen the *Tobugun* commander," Hatanaka cut in. "He doesn't seem to understand our intentions."

"If that is so, all the more reason why I cannot consent."

"We are asking you for your own decision, sir. If you issue the orders we are certain the *Tobugun* commander will sanction them!"

This was too much. Mori's patience was by now exhausted. "No!" he roared "Since the Imperial decision has already been given, I will not act against His Majesty's will!"

"You mean in any case?" Hatanaka queried.

"No, never!"

At this point, according to Ida, an officer wearing air force insignia burst into Mori's room, calling "Is the matter all settled, Major Hatanaka?"

"No, not yet," was the reply.

"Day will break if you delay any more." He turned to the General. "Why are you hesitating?"

"Who is this brash upstart?" thundered Mori.

"I am Captain Shigetaro Uehara of the Air Force Academy. I came here because I heard that the Imperial Guards had risen."

"What are you talking about! That is not His Majesty's wish!"

Without taking his eyes off the General, Uehara spoke deliberately to Hatanaka. "Major, we must take final measures."

"Your Excellency," said Hatanaka, "I beg you to reconsider."

The General shouted "No matter how many times you may ask me, I will not change my mind!"

"I cannot avoid this action," cried Uehara, sweeping his sword from its sheath. "It is for the good of the country."

The Captain rushed at Mori and Colonel Shiraishi leaped in front of the General, pulling his sword and shouting "You mean to kill him!" Uehara's thrust drove his sword point into Shiraishi's chest and the Colonel's left arm dropped uselessly as, off balance, he lashed out wildly at Uehara with his long sword.

At the same instant Mori sprang to his feet, stumbling against his chair. "You fool! What are you doing?" he cried.

Uehara's sword flashed again and hacked through the right side of Shiraishi's throat and breast. There was a crimson eruption, up, forward and outward as knots of blood flew from the gaping wound. The man's body doubled up and hit the floor at Mori's feet.

Simultaneously, the sharp blast of Hatanaka's pistol reverberated in the room. General Mori clawed at his chest and pitched forward over Shiraishi's body.

(This was an end almost foreseen by Mori when he had been appointed commandant of the Guards Division in March 1945. His statement to his stepbrother, Lieutenant General Yamaoka, at that time was prophetic: "If peaceful surrender . . . actually comes, belligerent groups are not likely to remain quiet. Even if headquarters orders them to surrender peacefully, they will be sure to entreat the Emperor to continue the war. I am quite aware that the function of the commander of the Imperial Guards is very important. It goes without saying that my chief function will be to protect the Emperor, even with my life. I know the responsibilities of a subject to a sovereign and am prepared for the worst even if it means my death.")

Uehara and Hatanaka saluted the dead officers and left the room. Ida and Colonel Mizutani rushed out of the latter's office; they saw Hatanaka, pale, buttoning his holster as he emerged. "I have just disposed of him," Hatanaka admitted, "for fear that we might waste more precious time here." Uehara followed, matter-of-factly replacing his hastily wiped sword in its sheath.

Mizutani and Ida went to the door and looked into the abbatoir.

The desk, floor, and walls were splattered and blotched with blood. The bodies were crumpled in a heap where they had fallen.

Mizutani said, tentatively, "This should be reported to *Tobugun* Headquarters." Hatanaka readily agreed and urged that Ida go with Mizutani to "report." Ida knew that the Major's purpose in sending him was to secure the cooperation of the *Tobugun* in the *coup*. It was now just 2 A.M. The air-raid all clear had not yet sounded. Koga and Ishihara, who produced copies of a document headed "Division Order 584," huddled with Hatanaka. The order read:

August 15, _____ [there was a blank, for the time to be inserted], Imperial Guards Division Order.

   1. The Division will smash the strategy of the enemy and uphold the Emperor to safeguard our country.
   2. The commander of Infantry I will occupy the Palace and safeguard same. A company of soldiers will occupy the Tokyo Broadcasting station and block its broadcasting.
   3. The commander of Infantry II will occupy the outer area of the Palace and block outside intrusion.
   4. The commander of Infantry VI will remain at present duty.
   5. The commander of Infantry VII will occupy the Nijubashi [double bridge] Gate and block any entrance into the Palace.
   6. The commanders of GK and TK will move forward to Daikan Street and remain there.
   7. The commander of Artillery I will remain at the present post.
   8. The commander of Engineering I will remain at the present post.
   9. The commander of Signal Unit will cut off all communication to the Palace except the line to the Palace from the Division.
   10. The commander of the Mechanized Battalion will guard the Palace with its full strength.
   11. The Division Commander will be at the Division Headquarters.

[signed] *Mori*
Division Commander

While Hatanaka, Shiizaki, and Uehara hurried to the palace grounds, majors Koga and Ishihara filled in the time—0200 hours—took Mori's chop (signature seal), and put his official signature on the false orders, thereby authenticating them. Then they rushed the orders to the various commanders by messengers.

At the palace grounds, Hatanaka and his companions arrived at the command post at the Nijubashi gate. Two battalions of the 2d

Infantry Regiment of the Guards were assigned there. Hatanaka told the commander, Colonel Haga, that he and Shiizaki had been attached by army GHQ to the Guards Division and that a divisional order was being issued even now, directing that the palace be isolated and secured. Minutes later an adjutant from division headquarters arrived and handed the false order to Haga.

The Colonel instantly did as directed and issued the necessary commands to his troops. The massive palace gates thudded shut and all traffic immediately stopped. Troops at the gates were reinforced and others were deployed about the palace grounds. The palace was cut off. The *coup* was under way, at last.

Chapter 20

The Mourning-Keeper

There are ancient Chinese reports on the customs of the primitive tribes of Japan in the third century A.D. Because a significant portion of the land apparently was ruled by a woman at the time, the Chinese called it the "Queen Country." Chinese observers told of a striking custom of that land, having to do with a "mourning-keeper," and described his function:

They appoint a man whom they style the "mourning-keeper." He is not allowed to comb his hair, to wash, to eat meat, or to approach women. When they are fortunate, they make him valuable presents; but if they fall ill, or meet with disaster, they set it down to the mourning-keeper's failure to observe his vows, and together they put him to death.

In the 1,600 years following this report Japanese life and customs had become exquisitely refined. From eating with their hands from crude wooden trays the people had progressed to the delicate ritual of the tea ceremony. And from destroying 1,000 of the retainers of a dead ruler in ceremonial self-immolation, they had advanced to ceremonies that called for symbolic grief rather than actual self-destruction. From the raw scapegoat treatment of the third century had evolved an intricate and subtle guilt-expunging system in the twentieth.

Near Kyoto, the ageless, longtime capital of Japan, there is a Zen Buddhist temple resting on a forested hillside. In it one steps into a world of silence, serenity, eternity. Within its rectangular court, separated from the temporal world outside by a roofed plaster wall, there is a celebrated garden. It is no ordinary garden, for this is Ryoanji, where the entire yard is covered by sand surrounding five islands of moss and stones.

From these simple, pedestrian ingredients, the master designers of 1499, the date of the temple's construction, conceived a work of art that strikes the consciousness as surely and forcefully as switching on the lights in a dark room.

It is a masterpiece of calculation, of juxtaposition and control of elements. For here every tiny grain of stone is regimented into serried rows, carefully raked and maintained by the monks. Like a miniature field of plowed sand, the rows run parallel to the veranda of the temple and undulate rhythmically and monotonously until they intersect the concentric curves of the furrows of sand that surround the five islands like suddenly dehydrated waves. And then the straight rows resume their unhurried, immemorial march to the far edge of the garden.

But it is the rocks themselves and their interrelationships that give this daring arrangement of materials the tension, the impact, the sublime qualities that make the sight of Ryoanji ineradicable. Given the theme of the Buddha and his two consorts, the inspired artists who created the garden placed their carefully selected rocks so that they can be seen as apexes of interlocking triangles, to symbolize this triumvirate.

Choosing with unswerving attention to total effect, the designers found stones contrasting in texture, outline, and mass. A low, heavy pyramid of rock in the right foreground takes the eye into the composition, carries it to an island of two smaller stones in the right middle distance, then to a closer central group of three. The eye moves then to the left rear to a long, narrow cluster of gray rock and then comes to rest in the left middle distance on a heavily crenellated fist of stone, taller than all the rest.

As to the composition, the inquiring mind is challenged. The dull mind is terrified. Both see the garden and ask the same question: Why? But to one the composition is rich with infinite meanings and interpretations. To the other the garden is a nightmare enigma of brain-wracking obscurity, so utterly obvious that any effort to see more is incomprehensible.

If the interested but uninitiated may find easy landmarks in the garden, the most likely one is the central group of stones. Here the Westerner may see a figure, of monumental proportions, head bowed, cloak clutched about him, Atlaslike in the infinite load he bears. Though the sculpture is nature's, the treatment is familiar: we see it in Goya's cape-wrapped men; in the sculptures of Giovanni Pisano, the Balzac of Rodin. At the base of the large figure are two compact stones as attentive as two smitten retainers.

This one rock, this pillar, this anchor, is pivotal. About it swirl and eddy the frozen waves, the conjecture, the inspiration and the watch-like movement of the design. Without that stone, that balance-wheel, the composition flies apart by centrifugal force, like a pinwheel.

In the final days of the Japanese Empire in 1945, many believe War Minister Korechika Anami played such a role.

Shortly before midnight, as Major Hatanaka was rendezvousing with his compatriots at Guards headquarters, the war minister drove the four blocks from the premier's office building to his official residence in Miyakezaka for the last time. He was satisfied that he had fulfilled his duty in speaking to Togo and Suzuki. The slate was now clear with them. He was glad that the distasteful business of preparing the formal papers—the rescript, the orders to the troops—had been completed. But to think about the Emperor broadcasting that message to the nation and the world tomorrow at noon—that was too much.

Anami marched into his quarters in his usual no-nonsense way, took his short sword into his room, and went directly to his habitual hot bath. Afterward, the medical corpsman who attended him asked if Anami wanted his "fatigue-relieving" vitamin shot as usual. He did, and received it. Whether it was the shots, Zen, the archery or some simple inner security, Anami during these trying days was relaxed and appeared rested and completely healthy, unlike his brother-in-law Takeshita, who was twenty years younger.

The Colonel had been worrying himself to a frazzle. He couldn't sleep, had lost weight, was nervous and irritable. Takeshita was a familiar sight around Anami's menage. When he hopped out of a staff car at the front entrance to the war minister's official residence about 1 A.M. the *kempei* guards saluted and the maid welcomed him tensely. They were glad he had come because it seemed to them His Excellency was preparing to commit suicide.

("Ever since he became war minister," Takeshita reports, "I was aware of his having secretly determined to commit suicide at the last stage of his duty. Anami seems to have known that there was no hope of winning the war, and that it could not be ended without extraordinary measures. After August 9 the time had suddenly become ripe for his suicide. From about the tenth on, his intentions had been so clearly evident that I had called the matter to the attention of Colonel Hayashi, his secretary.")

Takeshita knew his way around the house. He kicked off his shoes and went straight into the interior. He found Anami in the rear, in his bedroom. It was a traditional Japanese room, with *tatami* floor of straw mats, a *tokonoma* niche with scroll painting, vase, and flower, a wooden chest, sword rack, and a kimono stand. The bed was made up—the *futons* were on the floor. Anami was seated outside the huge mosquito net, which was suspended from the ceiling.

Brush in hand, the war minister looked up belligerently and called out accusingly "Why did you come here?" As his brother-in-law approached, Anami rolled up the paper he had been writing and put it on a shelf. He stared at Takeshita and quietly said "I am thinking of commiting *seppuku* tonight, according to my predetermined plan."

"It may be all right for you to commit suicide, but it doesn't have to be tonight, does it?" asked the Colonel.

Apparently relieved by Takeshita's approving attitude, the war minister went on. "To tell the truth, at first I thought you were going to give me trouble by trying to stop me or interrupt. I'm glad you approve. And I'm glad you are here—you can assist me."

Anami had beside him a small wooden tray with a bottle of sake and some cheese on a plate. He called the maid and ordered two glasses. She looked at the sake bottle and at Anami—"Sake cups?" she asked.

"No," Anami laughed, "beer glasses, not sake cups." She soon returned with the glasses.

Pouring them two-thirds full of sake, Anami offered one to his brother-in-law. "I decided on tonight," he explained matter-of-factly, "because the fourteenth is the anniversary of my father's death. The twentieth is just as good a day because it is the anniversary of my second son's death. But I can't bear to listen to the Emperor's broadcast tomorrow, so I'd better do it tonight." The two men began drinking in earnest.

In the household ministry building 50 yards inside the palace gate, the Emperor's recordings had been safely tucked away. The chamberlains, the chief aide-de-camp, and the lord keeper of the privy seal had gone to bed. The NHK and Information Bureau personnel were packing their recording gear in their autos. A quarter-mile away in his living quarters in the imperial library building the Emperor had retired more than an hour ago and was, presumably, fast asleep.

At 2 A.M. the president of the Information Bureau, Shimomura, and the president of the Broadcasting Company, Ohashi, decided that they were no longer needed and went to their car. The air raid now seemed to be many miles west of Tokyo, but the all-clear had not yet sounded. The two men climbed into their car and slowly drove, without lights, through the soft summer blackness. When they arrived at the Sakashita gate, it was shut tight. As they waited for it to open, soldiers with fixed bayonets jumped from the darkness onto the running boards and ordered the driver to proceed to the guardroom at the Nijubashi gate. There, to their astonishment, Shimomura and Ohashi were ordered out of the car and marched to the guard post at bayonet-point. Their fears grew as they were commanded to be silent. The two men were searched and their car was examined minutely. It was then that they realized the hunt was on for the Emperor's message. They were shut into a room of the guard house and sentries were posted at the door.

Minutes later they were joined in confinement by the NHK engineers and the Information Bureau specialists who had followed in other automobiles. All told, there were eighteen men herded into detention. Their captors ordered them not to talk to one another. Guards with bayonets at the ready made sure that the command was obeyed. In Shimomura's mind one question loomed over all others: What will happen now to the Emperor's broadcast? Will it be put on the air as scheduled or destroyed by these rebels?

Outside, in the palace grounds, platoons had been deployed to cover the key points—bridges, gates, road intersections, building entrances—surrounding the huge household ministry building, the library, garage, and other structures, and the grounds themselves.

In the blacked-out palace nerve center, the household ministry building, Hatanaka, Shiizaki, and Uehara were leading squads of Colonel Haga's troops in a search for the Emperor's recording. They cut the telephone lines, knocking out communication with the outside world. And they rounded up top members of the palace staff, including the chamberlains and General Hasunuma, and grilled them about the location of the Emperor's recording.

An orderly came to the Nijubashi gate and broke the silence forced on the imprisoned civilians. "Which of you is in charge of the broadcast-recording project?" he snapped.

Mr. Yabe, the chief of domestic broadcasting, spoke up. The orderly told him to follow, and, escorted by armed guards, took him to the regimental headquarters. There, a major was dispatching several officers on specific tasks. Finished, he turned to Yabe.

"I understand you made a recording of the Emperor's statement. Did the recordings come out all right?"

"Yes, everything came out fine."

"What did you do with the records?"

"I asked the imperial household ministry to keep them."

The Major turned to two officers and commanded them to find the records, using Yabe as a guide. He warned them to take good care of the discs.

One of the officers, a battalion commander, mustered four officers and forty soldiers and they escorted Yabe to the household ministry building. The detachment was halted on the wide, sloping approach to the building and the commander ordered his troops to load their rifles. Yabe had been impressed with the size of his escort; he now was doubly impressed by their "determination." They took him inside, and he could see soldiers with flashlights coming and going up the staircases, to and fro in the corridors and lobbies. He could hear the sound of furniture smashing and glass breaking close by as well as in distant rooms.

Questioned about the recording session, Yabe described the process. When it came to the key question, "Where are the records now?," Yabe said, truthfully, "I do not know, I turned them over to one of the chamberlains."

This was like telling an alcoholic that the key to the wine cellar had been given to one of the monks in a monastery. There seemed to be chamberlains by the dozen. *Which* chamberlain? Yabe said he didn't know the name (and all chamberlains looked alike, didn't they?). The soldiers began to be ugly about the matter, and since Yabe didn't recognize the names, they brought the chamberlains before him, one by one. And one by one the broadcaster insisted that they hadn't shown him the right one. Exasperated, the officers sent Yabe back to the guardhouse to rejoin the other detainees.

Meanwhile the search went on. The troops ransacked the rooms of Chief Chamberlain Fujita, went through his desk, and forced open his safe. Like locusts they went through the kitchen and the pantry, the furniture repair and the storage rooms, the offices and bedrooms, parlors and closets, ripping and tearing and destroying all before them.

Meanwhile, at the war minister's residence, in the isolation of General Anami's room the sake-drinking was interrupted shortly after 2 A.M. by the crackle of gunfire from the direction of the palace. Takeshita, remembering Hatanaka and the revolt, then told the war minister of the *coup* effort by the Major and Shiizaki. He mentioned that the 2d Guards Regiment was part of the uprising and that the plan was to bring out the whole division. Anami was singularly unmoved. He did not leap to the telephone to order the plot crushed. He remained seated on the *tatami* and continued drinking. "Even though the Guards Division rises, Tanaka's Twelfth Area Army probably will not join it. If it doesn't, there is nothing to worry about. The attempt will collapse." He was completely calm and showed no hint of emotion. "Anyway, my suicide will atone for that also."

Anami continued to down rice wine by the glassful, one after another. Takeshita cautioned him. "If you drink too much, you may fail in your attempt."

Anami shook his head. "If you drink a lot of sake, the circulation of the blood is speeded and increases bleeding. This makes death more certain. Besides, no man who has reached the fifth rank in *kendo* needs to worry!" he laughed.

"You were writing something?"

"Yes, my will." Anami took from the chest a scroll of paper which he handed to his companion. It was addressed to the Emperor and was in the form of a *waka,* a thirty-one-syllable poem:

> Having basked in the limitless benevolence
> Of the Emperor,
> I cannot find words to express my gratitude
> In my final hour.

[s] *Korechika*

Takeshita recognized this as the same *waka* Anami had written when he was sent to the China front, years before.

The General picked up his brush and wrote on another paper:

> Confident of the imperishability of our
> God-protected land . . .

The telephone interrupted and Takeshita took the call: "General Mori, the Guards Division commander, has been killed by rebels." Takeshita passed this word along to his brother-in-law. But even this news did not move Anami to action. "My suicide," he commented, "is to expiate for his assassination as well."

At the Emperor's quarters in the *Gobunko* the staff and the retainers were wide awake. About 3 A.M. an army officer had appeared at the library door and demanded of the chief of guards that his five men surrender their weapons. The guard chief, disturbed, told Chamberlain Irie of this request. Irie, Mrs. Hoshina (the Empress' chief lady-in-waiting), and the other attendants, electrified by this threatening request, conferred about a reply.

They decided to tell the officer that the palace guards wore their weapons—sabers—on authority of the director of the Palace Guard Bureau and any order to disarm would have to come from him. The guard chief passed this word along and the staff held their breath while the army officer mulled it over. He accepted the explanation and moved off. There was a rustling in the darkness beyond him that indicated he was not alone.

Now thoroughly apprehensive, the staff quietly closed all the steel shutters on the windows and doors, to block any possible forced entry. There followed a frenzied, inconclusive discussion about where to hide the Emperor if rebels came for him. They decided not to awaken His Majesty—yet.

On this night of August 14, from the Eastern District Army command post on the sixth floor of the Dai Ichi building none of the rebel action was visible. The first indication that something was up came when one of General Tanaka's senior staff officers telephoned the Guards Division headquarters on a minor question shortly after 2 A.M. Division staff officer Koga answered. The caller was startled to hear Major Koga weeping. Then the Major begged his caller to have the *Tobugun* rise in protest against the surrender.

Only minutes later, Colonel Mizutani and Lieutenant Colonel Ida arrived from Guards headquarters. Mizutani, pale and gasping, went directly to the chief of staff and with him awoke General Tanaka.

At the same time, Ida went with two of the *Tobugun* staff officers, Colonel Fuwa and Lieutenant Colonel Itagaki, to the now-vacant office of the chief of staff. There Ida passionately pleaded the case for an uprising to reject the surrender. He went through the many arguments in its favor, from sacred honor to protecting the national structure. But when he had finished, his ardor and his eloquence had fallen short. The *Tobugun* officers not only said no, they said absolutely not. Recognizing a dead horse when he saw one, Ida decided to beat it no more. Instead, he hustled back to the palace, to tell Hatanaka of this failure.

Meanwhile Mizutani, having recounted the events of the last two hours to his commanding general, fainted.

About this time Hatanaka's cohorts struck simultaneously in three places outside of Tokyo to prevent the Emperor's broadcast. A small group of soldiers took over the NHK broadcasting stations at Hatogaya, Koshigaya, and Niigo. They occupied the stations, preventing transmission at two of them. At the third, staff members told the troops that broadcasting was impossible anyway because there was no electric current. They purposely neglected to mention that the station had its own generators. (At any rate, the rebel soldiers believed the statement and waited around harmlessly for nearly twelve hours.)

Lieutenant Colonel Ida, having failed completely in his mission to rally the *Tobugun* to the uprising, arrived at the palace to tell Hatanaka to abandon ship. He found Hatanaka in front of Colonel Haga's 2d Guards Regiment command post. Ida confessed his failure, told the Major that there was absolutely no hope for the *coup* now that the Eastern District Army would not join in. "Resign yourself to fate," Ida advised, "and take steps to withdraw the troops before something serious happens. I will go and see the war minister and tell him the whole situation."

Hatanaka, too deeply mired to extricate himself, watched silently as Ida hurried toward Anami's place in Miyakezaka.

Anami and Takeshita at this time were proceeding with their sake-drinking. The war minister asked his brother-in-law to deliver final messages and do some last errands. He had words to convey to family, relatives, friends, and army colleagues. Takeshita made notes about them and afterward faithfully delivered the messages and executed Anami's requests. All but one. That one was deliberately unheeded by Takeshita. It was Anami's stern admonition to Takeshita to "kill Yonai!"

The war minister began his suicide preparations. He talked as he put on a new shirt of pure white. It had been a gift from the Emperor when Anami was an Imperial aide-de-camp, he explained. He took up his sword. "In case I should fail in the attempt, would you please finish the matter? But I know I will not fail. I have two short swords for *harakiri*. Since I am an army man, the correct way technically would be for me to commit *seppuku* with a military sword. But I am not a coward, even though I am going to use the short sword instead." (The official military sword in use at this time was the long, curved sword, too clumsy to use for ceremonial *harakiri*. Therefore, Anami planned to use the short sword, about fifteen inches long,) "The other one I will give to you as a last memento."

It was nearly 3 A.M. and the sirens were sounding the all-clear when the vice-minister of the imperial household awakened two of the chamberlains and told them the building was surrounded by troops. The three went downstairs to the staff room maintained by the military and naval aides-de-camp and reported to Vice-Admiral

Nakamura, one of the aides, that the ministry had been occupied. The room of Chamberlain Tokugawa, who had squirreled away the precious recordings, was nearby, so they awakened him and warned him of the dangerous situation.

Tokugawa went into the corridor with his flashlight and was standing there when Household Minister Ishiwata came bustling up with his secretary and a group of ministry personnel. Realizing that Ishiwata (as one of those "close to the Throne") would be a prime target of the rebels, Tokugawa ran to the chamberlains' office and directed the man on duty to open the air-raid shelter, called the Safe Room, in the basement. Then he quickly led Ishiwata down there. The route took them through so many rooms that only an experienced guide could possibly find it. Between them they decided that five raps on the door would be the "safe" signal, and Ishiwata was to open only if he heard this sign.

In another part of the vast building, the lord keeper of the privy seal, Kido, was dozing lightly. Just above the threshold of consciousness he realized that the radio had stopped. It was really a speaker, piped from a central source, tuned to the Japan Broadcasting Company's Tokyo station day and night. But it had stopped sometime after midnight. Something in his brain told him that this was unusual, but he was too tired to fight off sleep and investigate.

At 3:20 A.M., when Chamberlain Toda padded into Kido's room and whispered that part of the Imperial Guards Division had started a rebellion, Kido awakened instantly. The hair on the back of his neck went stiff. The life expectancy of privy seals was not great. They had been magnets for assassins in recent years. Kido lost no time in dressing. Toda, meanwhile, told him that the building was cut off from the outside world—no telephone, no wires, no wireless, no way through the cordon of troops. Furthermore, the imperial library was surrounded also and it was therefore impossible to reach its precious occupant, the Emperor.

As the most obvious rabbit in what he expected to be a deadly earnest "hare and hounds" hunt, Kido knew he had to hide somewhere, and quickly. Toda had a brilliant idea: how about the court physician's room, posing as the night doctor? Kido hurried along to the infirmary. But he had no more than arrived than he began to have misgivings. He felt uncomfortable in the masquerade and decided it was too vulnerable. Furthermore, he remembered papers that must not fall into the hands of rebels.

Toda meanwhile had rejoined Tokugawa and told him about the clever ruse. Tokugawa strongly suggested—strongly enough to send Toda running—that Kido be directed to the Safe Room also. As it happened, Tokugawa met Kido on the stairs as the privy seal returned to his room to dispose of the valuable documents. Kido scooped up the papers, rushed to the *benjo,* tore them to bits and flushed them. Then he followed Tokugawa through the maze of rooms to the Safe Room. As he joined the household minister there, Kido, with an eye to the future, told Ishiwata: "We don't know when we may be discovered and killed together, but history has already changed its course. Even if we are killed now, it won't matter, for the war is being brought to an end." Tokugawa swung the door shut, and the two fugitives prayed that there were no bloodhounds among their pursuers.

It was now three forty and Lieutenant Colonel Ida had arrived at the war minister's residence. He was shown in, at Anami's request. Ida found the General wrapping his abdomen with the traditional length of white cloth, preparing for his *harakiri.* Anami looked up at Ida and said "I have made up my mind to commit suicide now. What do you think about it?"

Ida replied enthusiastically "I think it will be a good thing. I will join you in death!" The war minister, suddenly stern, admonished Ida harshly: "Survive me and serve your country!" The two of them then wept in each other's arms. (Takeshita states that Hatanaka and Ida were special favorites of the war minister and that Anami's command sprang from his affection for Ida.)

"The minister smiled," reports Ida, "and offered me a drink. While drinking several cups of sake, we three talked, sometimes tearfully, sometimes lamentably, about the course the army had followed in the past.

"Then I considered it worthless to report the circumstances of the *coup* to the war minister because I understood his mental state . . . his determination to kill himself. The minister cautioned that however painful the situation might be, we should not die uselessly so that we might survive to devote ourselves to national rehabilitation. I bade him farewell and walked out toward the front door. But, as I found no car there, I waited helplessly, imagining the suicide of war minister Anami."

Inside the palace grounds, when Chamberlain Tokugawa arrived back at his room in the household ministry building Toda met him and breathlessly recounted how he had tried to reach the *Gobunko* to alert the Emperor's retainers to the dangerous situation. Toda had come within sight of the library, but was stopped by troops who prevented him from reaching it and sent him back. It was now about 3:50 A.M. Tokugawa suggested that they try again, via the short cut using the new road by the Dokan moat. At the Kaintei gate there were the usual sentries plus army officers new on the scene. The chamberlains were challenged. Halted and examined closely, Tokugawa insisted that they had business with the imperial residence staff at the library. His firm tone and patrician manner turned the trick, and they were passed.

Now Tokugawa and Toda reached the door to the *Gobunko* and, recognized, were quickly pulled inside. They reported to Irie and Mrs. Hoshina the rebel takeover of the ministry building, their isolation and the room-by-room search that was under way for the recording and Kido and Ishiwata. Also, they mentioned that Chamberlain Mitsui had been beaten by the soldiers. This sent a shiver of fear through them.

Returning from the Emperor's quarters to the ministry building at four ten, Tokugawa and Toda walked via the path along Momijiyama —Maple Hill—and the moat. They came to a point where they could see the ministry building and noticed machine-gun positions set up outside the entrance to the building and glimpsed officers and soldiers there. When they arrived at the building they were challenged by officers, but after a few words were allowed to enter.

They went directly to the duty room of the aides-de-camp and reported that they had contacted the *Gobunko*. But when Toda asked about the situation in the ministry building the aides requested that he and Tokugawa leave the room. The military aides were afraid that their conversation would be overheard by the rebels. A soldier with rifle and bayonet was patrolling the corridor and room entrance, but he did not challenge the chamberlains.

Minutes later Tokugawa was in the corridor looking into the aides' room. A rebel officer with a squad of men challenged him excitedly. Tokugawa told him that the actions of the rebels were deplorable, and the officer whipped out his sword and brandished it under Tokugawa's nose as he ordered his men to hold the chamberlain. Tokugawa was then grilled by a second lieutenant, next a captain, and then other officers.

In the midst of this a wild-eyed officer rushed up shouting "Slash him. Cut him down!" Tokugawa calmly replied "What's the use of cutting me down?" Since no good answer could be thought of, the knifework—and Tokugawa—were spared. The chamberlain practically shouted his replies so that the interrogation would be heard by the aides-de-camp on duty in their room just behind him. He believed both his voice and that of the nervous officer with the unsheathed sword were heard, but there was no help from the aides.

While he was being questioned and badgered about the location of the privy seal and the recordings, there was constant traffic through the corridor by rebel officers and men. At one point a palace guard passed. Tokugawa called to him and ordered him to report his predicament. The rebels held the guard, but the chamberlain insisted that the guard had his duties to perform and should be allowed to go his way. For his remarks, Tokugawa was slapped by a rebel non-com, but the guard was released. And so, after they had quizzed Tokugawa fruitlessly for half an hour, the officer ordered him released as well.

The chamberlain immediately went inside the aides' room and asked one of them what measures were being taken against the uprising. The aides did not know. They were cut off from the outside world also. But one aide, Nakamura, called Tokugawa aside and spoke to him in secrecy. Nakamura had discovered that the rebels had overlooked an important link. They had cut all lines but one. It was the direct telephone wire with the navy ministry. With the greatest care and stealth Nakamura had successfully reported the situation to the navy without drawing the attention of the rebels. There was, after all, a glimmer of hope.

As the Emperor's hand-picked bodyguard regiments ransacked his imperial household ministry building and consolidated their grip on Broadcasting House, other rebels struck in two widely separated parts of Tokyo. The rebel targets were Prime Minister Suzuki, Privy Seal Kido, and Privy Council President Hiranuma.

Two trucks and a car pulled up at No. 1, Nagata-cho, the premier's official residence, about 4:30 A.M. Out jumped a band of more than forty soldiers and students, armed with machine guns, rifles, and swords. Swarming through the gate, they opened fire with the machine guns, spraying the front of the building.

In his upstairs front room, Cabinet Secretary Sakomizu was sound asleep. The rattle of gunfire penetrated his consciousness and he began to boil with rage even before he opened his eyes. "What stubborn people—we have already surrendered and still they strafe us!" he steamed.

At that moment his brother's fear-laden voice cut through the haze and brought him fully awake. "Brother! They have come! They have come!" Sakomizu's younger brother had spent the night in the next room.

"What is it? What came?" Sakomizu asked, struggling to put on his trousers. His brother reported that the street at the gatehouse was crawling with armed men, some of them in army uniforms. Sakomizu stuck his head out the window, saw three machine guns positioned at the front gate. Significantly, they were pointing *at* the *kantei,* not away from it. A burst of fire from one of the weapons chiseled chips of masonry from the building façade. One of the bullets struck next to Sakomizu's window just after he had ducked inside.

His thoughts flew back to the 2–26 Incident, that February day in 1936. He had been there as private secretary to his father-in-law, Admiral Okada, prime minister at the time. Troops had surrounded the building then and come in after the premier, leaving only after they had riddled Okada's brother-in-law in the mistaken belief that they were killing the prime minister.

Sakomizu thanked the gods that Baron Suzuki had decided to spend the night at his home in Koishikawa. At least he was safe for the moment. The cabinet secretary wriggled into his shirt, grabbed his jacket, and telephoned the Suzuki residence to warn of possible attack. He then summoned his aide, the chief of the General Affairs Section, told him the situation and that he was going to attempt to escape from the building. The aide cautioned him, fearing he might be caught.

"If I stay, I will surely be caught, and if I am caught I will surely be killed. That would be a dog's death—a meaningless end." Sakomizu instructed his colleague to do whatever the attackers said, to offer no resistance. There would be no need to resist.

With his brother and a policeman Sakomizu went to the underground office level of the building and headed down the corridor of the buried passageway that exited on the street behind the residence. Remembering that in 1936 the troops had surrounded the residence and posted guards at each door, Sakomizu asked his brother and the policeman to investigate before they set foot outside. All clear, they signaled.

They tried the gate, to make their getaway from the grounds. It unlatched but would not budge. Peering over, they found that burned and rusted iron, salvaged from the fire raids, had been piled up all along the wall and against the gate, holding it shut. They heaved against the door and moved the pile of metal enough for a person to squeeze through the opening. The policeman led the way. There was a huge, metallic crunch as he leaped out onto the iron. No time to stop. Sakomizu and his brother squeezed through and bounded from the metal accordion to the street. Following his brother, Sakomizu and the policeman ran full speed down the avenue toward the Patent Bureau building. The street was deserted. They gained the corner, raced down the next block without interference, and soon were safe in the metropolitan police offices, talking with the Police Commissioner.

By now the attackers had overwhelmed the guards at the premier's office building and had learned that Suzuki was not there. Enraged, they poured gasoline over the porch and entryway and set it afire. Then they climbed back in their vehicles and sped off. As they disappeared from view, the building staff set to work dousing the flames and in short order had put them out. The damage was slight.

Three miles away, on the other side of the imperial palace, beyond the military headquarters on Ichigaya Heights, is the ward of Koishikawa. There, at prime minister Suzuki's home a panic-stricken comedy of errors was being played.

Sakomizu's telephone call had routed the household members from their beds. As Captain Takeo Sasaki of the 3d Army Division Headquarters in Yokohama led his contingent of assassins across the winding streets and potholed roads from the premier's official residence to the premier's private home, all was confusion at that destination. In the house were the Admiral, his wife and brother, Mr. Sato (of Suzuki's cabinet family) and his wife, plus two clerks, a maid, a chauffeur, and a policeman.

Suddenly the building seemed to become the setting of an impromptu vaudeville skit as kimono-clad bodies darted hither and yon, in and out of doors and hallways, windmilling their arms as they narrowly kept their balance, and squealing and grunting as they pushed past one another. Suzuki, in the midst of the turmoil, held up his hands to halt the traffic. "Please calm down, everybody," he pleaded. "I was safe during the Japan-China war, the Russo-Japanese war, and the 2–26 Incident. Since you are with me, please relax, calm down." This brought the pell-mell action to a halt and everyone quickly dressed and rushed out to the car.

As they were cramming into *Kakoka* #1, the official limousine, Mrs. Suzuki realized that the Admiral's frock coat had not been packed. It was necessary for cabinet meetings and Court. The maid was sent back for that. Mr. Sato then recalled a bag of important documents and ran back for them. At last they were all jammed into the car. Then came the problem of starting it.

Usually the chauffeur turned the car around each night before killing the motor, so he could start out rapidly in the morning by coasting down hill. But not last night. Now, loaded with six people, the car was headed uphill. But it was too spavined and winded to make the grade. So fifteen men of the police detachment guarding Suzuki set their shoulders to it and pushed the car up to the crest of the hill. The old limousine gathered speed on the downhill run and chugged off under its own steam.

By the time the guards returned to the Suzuki house from the hilltop, the assassins had roared up in front. With machine guns and rifles at the ready they hopped out of the trucks and the car and surrounded the guards. Some, brandishing swords, entered the house looking for the premier. They searched the place from top to bottom, intimidating the staff members.

While the rebels took over his house, Baron Suzuki drove to his sister's house about a mile and a half away in the Hongo section of Tokyo. As they unloaded the car, one of the clerks telephoned the premier's house to tell the staff that they had arrived safely. When the phone was answered the clerk blurted "Here we are at Hongo." The voice on the other end asked "Are you Kantaro Suzuki?" Stricken with fear that he had given the game away, the clerk ran to Suzuki to tell him that the murderers now knew he was here.

So the car was packed once again and they all jammed into it and set off for Suzuki's brother Takao's place in Shibashi district. They resolved not to telephone anyone when they arrived.

The rebels, finding no premier and determined to vent their spleen, ejected the staff from Suzuki's house, doused it with gasoline, and lighted it. It went up like tinder.

Back in their trucks once again, they set off for another destination—and another target. This time they were after the scalp of the president of the privy council, Baron Hiranuma, farther north in Yodobashi Ward.

The right-wing, ultranationalist leader had finally emerged from the family bomb shelter at 3 A.M., when the all clear sounded, and had gone to bed. At 5:30 A.M. when another air-raid alarm roared, the old man's grandniece Setsuko—with whose family Hiranuma lived—squinted at the sky and decided not to go to the shelter. Suddenly there was a clatter and the sound of motors and voices nearby and when Setsuko peeked out the window she was horror-stricken. At the gate of the compound a gang of soldiers and armed men was jumping out of trucks. Some were coming into the yard while others had the police guards at gunpoint.

The police, hands above their heads, were being harangued by an army captain in uniform, the same Captain Sasaki who had just come from Suzaki's house. "Don't you know what a *blank* Hiranuma is? You don't? I'll tell you! He is a traitor—a notorious leader of the pro-Anglo–American group, working to destroy our sacred land. Guarding an arch-traitor! What kind of thing is that! You should be ashamed!"

Setsuko remembered that one of the guards had said several days before that some incident was likely. And just yesterday Japanese army planes had circled low and threateningly over the place. A guard had thought they were going to be bombed, but nothing happened. Now some of the rebels, carrying gasoline cans, hurried up to the house. The woman pulled her children with her, awoke the nurse, and told her to get out with the youngsters, then she tore to Hiranuma's room. He was not there.

Flames and smoke seemed to explode in the house and a voice shouted "We can't find him." Setsuko ran outside as another rebel answered "It doesn't matter, in a minute he'll be burned to death anyway." She hoped and believed that the old man must have escaped somehow. The police guards were still immobilized with their hands in the air and Setsuko scurried to the garden of the building next door. The children were there and a policeman guarding this Immortality Society headquarters whispered to her that Hiranuma, its president, was hiding inside. He had fled through the one exit the rebels overlooked—the gate between the two gardens.

The house burned to ashes, and the gang, satisfied that this time they had been successful, piled back into their vehicles and drove off again.

While Kido was locked in the Safe Room at the household ministry building at dawn, a fanatical band of civilians in league with Hatanaka descended on the privy seal's home in Akasaka ward. They surrounded the house and, armed with swords, grenades, and revolvers, attacked the place hoping to get a shot at Kido. Police guards stationed there put up a fight and in the battle drove off the attackers. In the melee one of the guards was nicked by a sword.

(The following morning the same superpatriots tried to get Kido again. This time they called at the home of his brother, suspecting the privy seal might be staying there. His niece answered the door and a ceremonial tray with a small swordlike object was given to her for her uncle. It was meant to "invite" Kido to commit *harakiri*—or the gang would finish him off. The assassins left quietly when told that Kido was not staying there.)

Dawn's light began to change the war minister's residence from black to gray. General Anami had just put on his full-dress military jacket complete with decorations when another thought came to him. He unbuttoned the jacket and took it off. Then he carefully folded it, crossing the sleeves in the back. He placed it tenderly in the *tokonoma* alcove and between the sleeves and the jacket itself placed the photograph of his dead son. "After the *seppuku*," Anami called to Takeshita, "please put the jacket on my body."

His brother-in-law nodded, then noticed how Anami had placed the photograph of his dead son. He recalled, as he observed this, that General Nogi, that national hero of the Russo-Japanese war, had committed *harakiri* in the manner of ancient royal retainers when Emperor Meiji was buried. And Nogi, who had sent his sons into battle and sacrificed them both, was found with the photos of the two dead boys in his hand. Tears sprang to Takeshita's eyes and he was choked with sympathy.

The maid reported that General Okido, the chief of the *kempeitai*, was in the reception room. "You see him," Anami directed Takeshita. It would hardly do for a man who had ceremonially prepared himself for suicide to receive all callers and he did not intend to change clothes or leave the room at this stage.

Takeshita went to the reception room, where only two nights before he, Arao, Inaba, Hatanaka, Shiizaki, and Ida with such high hopes had unfurled their plan before Anami. Okido was there, full of information about the *coup*, the slaughter of Mori and Shiraishi, and the attempt to halt the Emperor's broadcast. The *coup* was now being crushed, he said, by General Tanaka and the *Tobugun*. Distracted and filled with mixed emotions at this news, Takeshita hurried the *kempei* chief out.

While Takeshita was listening to General Okido, Colonel Hayashi ran in from his quarters next door. Excitedly Hayashi rushed through the house to the war minister's room, carrying news about the revolt of the Imperial Guards Division. Arriving at the entrance to Anami's room, Hayashi stopped short. The war minister was beyond taking a hand in suppressing the revolt. The Colonel withdrew, and as he came to the reception room, told Takeshita that Anami was committing *harakiri*.

The practice of *harakiri* had flowered during Japan's medieval period. It was the accepted way of the aristocrat to elude capture or humiliation at the hands of an enemy. And it was a privilege of the upper classes. The form was well established by the fifteenth century. Every year for centuries afterward some 1,500 Japanese are reported to have committed *seppuku*.

There were two types—voluntary and obligatory. Voluntary *harakiri* is more recent and has been the exit for men who had private debts to settle, who were protesting the actions of officials or the government, or who were expressing loyalty to a dead superior.

Obligatory *harakiri* was abolished in 1868, but was for centuries the acceptable way to dispatch an official or noble who was guilty of breaking the law. The offender received an exquisitely phrased letter from the ruler hinting that his death would be welcome. To make sure he got the import of the note, a jeweled dagger accompanied the message.

Carrying out this "command," the condemned man would have built a dais about four inches high and this would be placed in a temple or his castle grounds and covered with a red rug. With his second, or assistant, the guilty one would seat himself, clad in his ceremonial court clothing, on this rug. His friends and officials would form a semicircle seated about him and the dagger would be presented to him with deferential bows. The condemned man would confess his guilt publicly, take up the weapon, and make the cut across the belly from left to right, then up.

It was the responsibility of his second to make certain that the suicide neither survived nor lingered. His actions varied, depending on the individual and situation. Often he would wait until the belly cut had been completed, then, using the two-handed great sword, decapitate the suicide with one swift stroke. The ruler received the bloody dagger as proof that the offender was no more.

In some cases, by prearrangement a tray with a fan would be extended to the suicide, and as he bowed and reached for the fan his second would bring down the *tachi,* lopping off his head. This streamlined method had numerous advantages (not the least of which was speed), including certainty and painlessness.

When Hayashi and Takeshita went into the war minister's room they found Anami sitting cross-legged, in the prescribed position. But he was not in the room on the tatami mats. He was on the wooden veranda that bordered the room, beyond its sliding doors. By the etiquette of *seppuku,* this was very significant. Usually *harakiri* was committed in the house. However, a sinner would normally commit *harakiri* on the ground. If the sinner had pure motives or the authorities sympathized with his case, he might be allowed to separate himself from the earth, sitting on a straw mat, or low dais.

The veranda of a traditional Japanese house is, in effect, a wooden porch extending outward from the *tatami* rooms a few feet into the garden on each side. Wooden shutters closed off Anami's veranda from the garden for privacy and protection. These shutters were used only at night and were thrown open during the daylight hours. At this moment of the night-morning the shutters still were closed.

The garden was patrolled constantly by sentries guarding the war minister. So Anami rejected going into the garden itself. Seeking to classify himself as a sinner, but one whose motives were pure, he had placed himself on the veranda. It is technically a part of the garden and served the General as an approximation of the sinner's position out of the house but separated from the ground.

Anami was caught in a complex web. He was atoning for sins of omission as well as commission. He was assuming guilt for failure of the army to win the war, for inability to execute His Majesty's wishes and for opposing his desires, for the army's headstrong disobedience ever since the Manchurian Incident in 1931. He also shouldered culpability for the attempted *coup,* though he was not to know for certain whether it would succeed or not. To his officers and men he was apologizing for failing to realize the impossible achievements they expected of him, ranging from winning the war to taking over as Shogun.

To the young tigers particularly, his suicide was an evasion of the role of Saigo they had determined for him. And yet Anami's ceremonial suicide was his way of trying to bear the burden of responsibility for their irresponsibility.

At the moment of decision, the war minister simply could not bring himself to lead a *coup.* He realized, perhaps more clearly than the conspirators could appreciate, that to participate in it would brand him a traitor. Furthermore, the mark would apply as well to his family, his sons and daughters and their offspring. The very name *Anami* would be anathema. For a man who had served his Emperor with love and devotion in the highest posts possible for a military man this was simply too much.

The man's words, his *haragei,* came back to haunt him and add to the weight he felt. He had, after all, managed to revive the belief of the people in the army to a considerable extent in the face of stiff criticism about failure to pour everything into the defense of Okinawa.

The war minister was facing the palace, short sword gripped firmly in his powerful right hand. He was just completing the excruciating belly cut, *kappuku,* when his brother-in-law returned. The technique calls for thrusting the sword through the abdominal wall just below the lowest left rib, drawing the blade through the stomach from left to right, then jerking it upward abruptly in a right-angle turn.

As Takeshita hurried to his elbow the war minister was searching the right side of his neck with the fingers of his left hand, trying to locate the carotid artery. Still the soldier, Takeshita summarized General Okido's report on the palace uprising, then asked "Shall I serve as your second?"

"No," panted Anami. He thrust the dagger into the right side of his throat without help. Then he collapsed, falling forward toward the palace. There was a sudden flood of blood, spreading crimson and viscous on the polished wood of the veranda floor.

While Tokugawa and other chamberlains were undergoing their private ordeals and the ministry building was under siege, the rebels were active in another part of the capital. At Radio Tokyo, the headquarters of NHK, the Japan Broadcasting Co., there had been tremendous excitement on the fourteenth. The grapevine had it that the Emperor was planning to broadcast either the fourteenth or fifteenth! All those who caught wind of this and could be spared at home hung around Japan's radio city all day and into the evening. Some gave up and went home, but many stayed on, convinced that His Majesty would come even during the night if the occasion was so important. They wanted to witness the historic event. So the swanky lounges, couches, upholstered chairs, even offices and desks were covered with sleeping Japanese when the first rebel soldiers pushed in.

The NHK building had been completed in 1939. It was a showplace of modernity. Its studios and furnishings, its stages, equipment, arrangement of facilities, and its traffic in the arts and information services marked it as a major exhibit of modern Japan. By 1945,

NHK's transformation was symbolic, perhaps, that the geisha had turned into a drab by now. The station carried propaganda and exhortation, distorted news, and little entertainment other than propaganda plays. The main entertainment consisted of music programs. Everything else was gray; even the exterior of the building was a flat charcoal gray. The electric shortage curtailed radio listening, especially during the day. But with the uncertain publication and distribution of the four-page newspapers, NHK's broadcasts were increasingly the topical cement that bound the nation together.

Having surrounded the building, the rebels moved inside and rounded up all staff members, on or off duty, domestic and international, and locked them in Studio 1, the huge room reserved for symphony and theatrical broadcasts. It was 4 A.M. when they took over, but it was not until five o'clock that the operation moved ahead.

At the Nijubashi guardroom, a rebel officer came in, singled out the chief engineer of NHK among the prisoners. He ordered him to keep his mouth shut and climb into the waiting auto. They drove slowly through the gate and the palace plaza, to Hibiya-dori avenue, and along it past the park to the NHK building.

Once inside, the rebels asked for the office of the chief of broadcasts. It was upstairs, and the engineer was taken there and locked in with others who already were confined.

At this moment a young NHK employee managed to sneak out of a side entrance to the building and run to the Dai Ichi hotel two blocks away. There the department heads of NHK were staying. The news of the takeover of the station set off a debate among them as to what action to take. They decided the most important thing was to contact NHK's president, who presumably had decided to remain at the palace overnight after the recording session. They had absolutely no hint that the palace was occupied also. So they sent a messenger to the palace with word for the NHK executive. But the messenger was caught at the palace gate and his note never reached the radio people who were still sweating it out in the guardhouse.

At 5 A.M. Major Hatanaka and two soldiers entered Radio Tokyo's second-floor Studio 12. The Major was carrying a paper on which was a "manifesto" and he ordered the engineer on duty to prepare for broadcasting. While they were talking, an army announcement was being broadcast. The engineer told Hatanaka that no broadcasts could be made while army announcements were going out. The Major was incensed and stormed out of the studio. The engineer, fearing what might come next, fled.

Hatanaka went to the news room and insisted that he be put on the air. He was refused by the assistant news chief, backed up by others who were with him. Hatanaka returned to Studio 12 and found there an announcer named Tateno. The Major drew his pistol, brandished it at Tateno, and demanded that the poor man let him broadcast. Nimbly, Tateno said "We must consult army headquarters while an army announcement is on the air, and if your broadcast is to be on a nationwide hookup we must make technical contact with all the local stations." Tateno simply was stalling for time. Hatanaka argued with him violently, demanding that the microphone be opened so he could read his manifesto.

Meanwhile, the engineer in the main control room received word to cut off the line between the studio and the transmitter. Thus even if Hatanaka and his colleagues took over the studio, from then on the line would be dead. However, Hatanaka and the other rebels had no clue that the line was cut. They wasted precious time calling Eastern District Army headquarters several times for permission to broadcast, but though they talked to a higher echelon each time, the response was *no*. Hatanaka was left fruitlessly waving his script, which began "Our army, safeguarding the Palace. . . ." Outside, the air-raid sirens howled. *Teki-san* was coming visiting again with his cargoes of death.

In the war minister's room Colonel Hayashi was with Takeshita, watching General Anami's white shirt soak up blood like a blotter, observing the man's final agonies while the U.S. Navy deck planes roared over the capital.

As he promised, Takeshita went to the *tokonoma*, took up the general's jacket and draped it about Anami's shoulders. On the *tatami* near the man he placed a scroll given to Anami by Prince Kan-in when he was army chief of staff, and beside this scroll Takeshita carefully put the two wills Anami had left. The second read:

Confident of the imperishability of our god-protected land, with my death I respectfully apologize to the Emperor for the great crime.

[s] *War Minister Korechika Anami*

In his death throes, General Anami writhed and threshed about, splattering his blood and staining the two wills.

Suddenly the telephone bell sliced through the morbid fascination of Anami's aides. It broke the hypnotic tension and Takeshita snapped to as Hayashi answered the phone. Moving to Anami's body, he put his ear close to the General's mouth. He could hear hoarse, labored breathing, but was certain Anami could never survive. However, the minister apparently had missed the carotid artery. Takeshita picked up Anami's limp hand which still held the knife. He closed his hand over Anami's, then plunged the blade into his brother-in-law's neck, severing—so he thought—the artery.

On the telephone was the vice-minister of war, Wakamatsu, calling Takeshita. The Colonel went to the phone. He told Wakamatsu that Anami had just committed *seppuku* and that it was all over with the minister. Wakamatsu insisted that Takeshita report immediately to the war ministry.

At Wakamatsu's insistence, Takeshita left the war minister to be cared for by his adjutant, Lieutenant Colonel Kobayashi, and drove off to the ministry.

Kobayashi called the ministry's chief of medicine, who came with a team of three medical orderlies. Anami was still breathing when they arrrived. It was 8 A.M. when his breath and his life officially stopped. An autopsy revealed that he died from loss of blood, primarily from the cervical vein, not the carotid artery, which was intact. The warrior's body was cleansed and purified and placed in the war ministry building with a small altar beside it.

Takeshita reported at once to Lieutenant General Wakamatsu when he arrived at the ministry building. Lieutenant General Yoshizumi was there, talking with Wakamatsu about Anami's end and his motivation in committing suicide. The Imperial Guards uprising was still uppermost in their thinking, and they conjectured that this had caused Anami to end his life in guilt and shame. Takeshita felt resentment rise within him.

"What do you think Anami meant," asked Wakamatsu, "in his will where he says 'I give my life to atone for the great crime'?"

"I don't believe there is any connection between the Palace Incident and Anami's suicide at all," protested Takeshita. "Since the Manchurian Incident, the China Incident, and finally the Greater East Asian War, Anami—as leader of the army—wanted to atone for the past and present of the army. So, representing the whole army, he apologized to the Emperor. He had decided on suicide without any knowledge of the incident and even after he learned of it he was confident that it would be suppressed before it became serious. Suicide was in his mind from the time he assumed office as war minister. Moreover, the fact that he was careful not to mention himself in his address yesterday afternoon (using the pronoun *you* instead of *we*): 'You officers, even though you may have to sleep on grass and eat stones. . . .' should have shown that he was bent on self-destruction."

The two older men seemed unconvinced by Takeshita's argument. General Wakamatsu had insisted that the Colonel report to him immediately as a precaution against Takeshita rushing off to some rash act. He might even, Wakamatsu reasoned, rejoin the conspirators in their audacious attempt. Better to keep an eye on this man, especially now that his brother-in-law was not around to control him.

Without the balance-wheel, there was no knowing what would happen to the military machine. Perhaps, like that garden at Ryoanji, it might fly apart by centrifugal force, now that the unifying figure was no more.

Chapter 21

Tanaka

From the Dai Ichi Insurance Company building one can look out across Hibiya-dori, the broad avenue with streetcar lines that separates the palace plaza from Tokyo's workaday world of business and banking. Beyond Hibiya-dori is the mossy moat, then the imperial plaza with its trees, park, and parade ground, the low black-stone walls marking out the inner moat, and across its green waters the soaring parapets of the palace walls enclosing the huge palace grounds.

From the plaza there are two major gates, each massive—at least fifteen feet tall and more than twenty feet wide. Each is covered by a tiled roof in the ancient style. Each gate is approached by a bridge across the inner moat. Once drawbridges, these are now permanent and built to handle automobile traffic. The first of these is the Seimon gate, nearest to Nijubashi the double bridge. The next is the Sakashita gate (nearest to the imperial household ministry). Most of the palace traffic flows through the Sakashita and Seimon gates.

By 2:30 A.M. on the fifteenth the commander of the 7th Regiment of the Imperial Guards arrived at *Tobugun* headquarters. In his hand he had a report and "Division Order 584." He had deployed his troops as ordered, but he had decided that he ought to verify this order. The order itself was attached to his written report.

Immediately the *Tobugun* chief of staff, General Takashima, tried to telephone each of the Guards regiments. However, he was unable to raise an answer except at the 2d Regiment. There he managed to get across part of his message to a staff officer, telling the man that Order 584 was spurious and should be disregarded.

Tobugun officers Colonel Fuwa and Lieutenant Colonel Itagaki took off immediately for the Guards Division headquarters to investigate the report of General Mori's murder. Pulling up beside the building, they found it pitch-dark. As they were about to enter General Mori's office, which they knew well from previous visits, an armed guard materialized from the darkness and challenged them. He refused their identification and rejected every reason they offered for entering. They asked him to call his commanding officer and suddenly Major Ishihara appeared out of the shadows. He had been assigned to the Guards Division only a few days before and was very unsettled.

Major Ishihara allowed Fuwa and Itagaki to enter the room and see the bodies of Colonel Shiraishi and General Mori. He then escorted them to another office. There the Major was so fidgety and excitable that Fuwa thought for certain the man was going to pull his sword and cut them up if there was even the slightest provocation. Ishihara said he was going to remove the bodies and dispose of them properly, then go to the palace.

The telephone rang. Colonel Fuwa was ordered to return to *Tobugun* headquarters at once. Back at the Dai Ichi building, Fuwa reported to General Tanaka. He confirmed that Mori was dead and that the *coup* had moved to the second stage—the execution of the plan. General Tanaka vowed "I will go to the Palace . . ." but his chief of staff stopped him. "Day will break soon; please wait a few minutes, Your Excellency. It is very difficult to control men in the dark."

"Oh, I see," Tanaka agreed and sat down. He pondered his next move. As commander of the Eastern District Army Tanaka had plenty of troops at his disposal to overwhelm the Guards Division in a fire fight, if necessary. But the General rejected the use of sheer power at this time. The palace was too sensitive a mechanism and the Emperor too valuable to endanger with a pitched battle. Furthermore, in Japan's current critical situation the last thing any sane man could want would be a confrontation in which armed Japanese troops faced one another and fought it out.

No, he would have to overcome the uprising by other means. Luckily, he knew some of the Guards officers. A number of them had served under him at one time or another. He would try to reach them and reason with them rather than use military muscle.

General Shizuichi Tanaka was an anachronism. He was straight out of the Japanese age of chivalry, when real men were samurai and the samurai were the lords of creation. But he had an overlay of Edwardian paternalism that complicated his character.

In his youth Tanaka had earned his degree at Oxford. It was he who headed the Japanese troops in London's World War I victory parade, astride a chestnut mare. Carrying the flag proudly, Tanaka's Hindenburg mustache was as much an object of interest as the Rising Sun banner. He had later served as military attaché in Washington. This background of service in the two democracies was a double kiss of death in an army striving to imitate the fascists and Nazis and using its political power to push the nation into alliances with the ascending stars of the dictator states. Like almost all Japanese officers with American or British experience in the thirties, Tanaka found himself swept into a corner while key posts went to men with German or Russian service.

Pro-American, Tanaka was decidedly unhappy with the army's involvement in politics and opposed its action in pushing through the Axis treaty. He was home in bed on December 8, 1941, when his young son rushed in with the news of the war. Tanaka's head was under the *futon* as his son gushed "Father, Japan has gained a great victory by attacking Pearl Harbor." The General rolled over, still hidden under the quilt.

"Declaration of war!" the son went on. "Have you heard the news extra? About the great victory at Pearl Harbor?" Turtlelike, Tanaka stuck his head out of the *futons* and spat "I know that Japan acted foolishly. Do you expect Japan to win over America? I'm afraid not! What will become of Japan?" Then up over the face came the covers again.

Tanaka had a reputation as a tough soldier, and had served in responsible posts that required his particular brand of toughness. He had been head of the *kempeitai* on two different occasions. Thus he was accustomed to using the iron fist. This background earned him assignment to head the Japanese forces in the Philippines in 1944, when that subjugated nation showed signs of restiveness under the "benevolent" East Asia Co-Prosperity policy. Malaria sent Tanaka back to Japan for recuperation and later to his present assignment, where his roar and his mustache were equally famous.

Now, in the little time left before dawn, General Tanaka tried again to reach Colonel Watanabe, commander of the 1st Imperial Guards Regiment, but the telephone was dead. Tanaka stood and called to his adjutant, Colonel Tsukamoto, "I am going to the Palace; prepare the car and give me my pistol. I fear that something serious might happen to the Emperor."

"It is still dark, General," Tsukamoto demurred, "and the rebel soldiers might not see the commander's flags on the car." Tanaka, impatient, paced around the room. Soon, though it was no lighter, Tanaka again called to Tsukamoto and requested his pistol. The adjutant declined again to get it, saying it was his duty to guard Tanaka and therefore the General would not need the weapon. The General insisted and Tsukamoto hesitated. Finally, firmly, Tanaka demanded his sidearm and commanded "Now let's go, Tsukamoto!" It was just after 4 A.M.

Tanaka, Tsukamoto, and Fuwa climbed into one staff car and four MPs followed in another. The General directed the driver to avoid Sakashita gate and make for the 1st Regiment Headquarters. Its commander, Watanabe, had served under Tanaka before and therefore it was a logical point to start, even if the regiment was involved in the uprising.

As they drove up to the gate, the early light was just cracking the solid blackness of night. In the heavy grayness they could see troops in full battle gear beginning to march out of the gate.

Directing the car to the regimental headquarters, Tanaka spotted Colonel Watanabe, the commanding officer, armed and just fastening the chin strap of his steel helmet as he came out of the building. The General called to him. "Watanabe! I'm lucky to be in time. That order you received was false. Call back your troops and let's go to your headquarters."

Watanabe did as ordered, and his single command removed 1,000 troops from the *coup* at a stroke. When the Colonel came into his orderly room he was accompanied by Major Ishihara, the jumpy staff officer from Imperial Guards headquarters, one of Hatanaka's conspirators. This was pointed out to General Tanaka, who blasted Ishihara: "This is one of the men who has done it! Arrest him." He ordered the *kempeitai* to be called to take Ishihara and went on lambasting the Major for his part in the incident. Fuwa sat beside Ishihara, half expecting the man to lash out violently in some way, and fully ready to subdue him. But the Major sat quietly, if sullenly, until a *kempeitai* warrant officer arrived. Fuwa went with them to MP headquarters.

With the 1st Regiment stabilized, Tanaka again telephoned Colonel Haga, commander of the 2d. This time he succeeded in reaching the Colonel, told him of the false order, and commanded Haga to meet him at Inui gate. Tanaka and his adjutant jumped in the staff car and sped to Inuimon. The huge doors with their iron bosses, studs, and hinges were shut fast. Though quiet, the situation looked dangerous. When the car pulled to a stop in front of the gate two guards challenged. The driver told them it was the *Tobugun* commander and they presented arms. Colonel Tsukamoto, Tanaka's aide, suspected treachery. The whole atmosphere, he thought, seemed too quiet. Perhaps they were waiting for the General to enter on foot, only to mow him down. Tsukamoto ordered the gates flung open.

As the mammoth doors of Inuimon creaked and slowly lumbered open, Tanaka and Tsukamoto could just make out at the guardhouse the figures of Colonel Haga and others. The General jumped out of the car and strode through the gate, his mustaches jouncing. The 2d Regiment, he knew, was short of officers and many of its companies were led by young captains and lieutenants, men who conceivably might be easy marks for the rebels to enlist. Calling to Haga, Tanaka discovered that the officer had already informed Major Hatanaka that the 2d Regiment would not follow rebel orders another moment.

Now Tanaka demanded that Haga return his troops to their normal guard duties, and the Colonel promptly sent runners to his units with orders to withdraw from the palace grounds and pull back to routine duty stations.

Tanaka then took one of Haga's battalion commanders as an escort and rushed to the palace guard command post near the Nijubashi bridges. Here the General came face to face with the rebel leaders—Hatanaka, Shiizaki, Koga, and Uehara. Tanaka transfixed them with a roar as he ordered them to assemble the troops inside the gate in the half-light. Then he launched a harangue that ranged from god to mother to country and particularly stressed the Emperor and the pain it had given His Majesty to decide to end the war. He described explicitly how the plot had failed completely and called on the rebels to realize their error and give up willingly.

Demanding that they expunge the stain they had made on the honor of the army by disobeying the Emperor's will, the General reduced to tears these men who only minutes before had been willing to suppress the peace faction and drive Japan to self-annihilation. Tanaka left little doubt that the only acceptable way to pay for their transgressions was with their own lives, in the "true *bushido* spirit" (*bushido* was the supposed code of honor of the samurai, which included loyalty, truth, sincerity, and readiness to die for honor). And, since the four rebels nodded their agreement and indicated that they would do the honorable thing, Tanaka did not arrest them but let them go so that they could commit *harakiri*.

By now Tanaka was sure that the situation at the gates was under control. At this point an army staff car arrived and was halted by the sentries. Colonel Tsukamoto challeged it, and three war ministry officers stepped out—Colonel Arao and lieutenant colonels Shimanuki and Ida. General Tanaka stalked over to them and examined the trio through narrowed eyes.

Colonel Ida recalled later that Tanaka told them "though the situation within the Palace has already become so calm and quiet that one could feel at ease, no one but those of the Imperial Guards Division will be permitted to enter there."

Colonel Tsukamoto's description is more colorful: "Out of the car came three officers of the Military Affairs Bureau, one of them covered with blood, showing that he had been present at the killing of Mori. 'General,' they said, 'we have come to lead the Guards Division!'

"The Hindenburg mustache of the General seemed to move a bit, then he roared 'No! Not a single man except those assigned to the Imperial Guards may pass here. Return at once!' They went back quietly, but it was indeed a hairbreadth event. If they had entered the gate before the General arrived, the situation would have been most unfortunate."

"Close the gates and don't let anyone in," ordered Tanaka. Then, at last, freedom came for the eighteen prisoners in the Nijubashi guardhouse. Some time after the palace grounds had become thoroughly light in the morning sun they had heard the commotion outside the guardhouse that signaled a change of some kind. Groggy from lack of sleep, they were released at about 7 A.M.

Meanwhile, Tanaka had hopped into his staff car and was off for the Emperor's quarters to check on his safety and report on conditions.

Inside the besieged household ministry building word had come through aide Nakamura's secret telephone line that some time after 4 A.M. General Tanaka had left to put down the rebellion. Chamberlain Tokugawa, who visited Nakamura about five fifteen, felt relieved and returned to his room about five-thirty. He noticed, as he left the aide's room, that there was no longer a sentry in the hallway. That was a change for the better, at least.

About 6 A.M. Tokugawa discovered that there was another telephone to the outside in the aides' room in the bomb shelter under the *Gobunko*. Chamberlain Mitsui headed for the library and when he reached it found the grand chamberlain and the lord steward to Her Majesty had arrived there from their sleeping quarters. They used the phone to call out and learned that Tanaka was already at the palace grounds quelling the uprising.

The retainers decided that now the Emperor should be awakened. It was six-forty—twenty minutes before his usual awakening time. (He had adopted a policy of never emerging before 7 A.M. out of consideration for his Court family and retainers. Otherwise they would have had to be on duty all night in case he might appear.)

There is no report on the Emperor's reactions, his appearance, change of expression (if any), or words in response to the information that "his" imperial bodyguards had risen in revolt and occupied the palace grounds, had ransacked the ministry building, and were hotly pursuing his privy seal, his household minister, and the recording of his rescript in deadly earnest. A *coup* or an army maneuver—these were possibilities he and Kido had discussed. They were calculated risks. It was the dawn of a new day all right, but the kind of day Hirohito had feared. The fear was not for himself; he was beyond that. It was now for the survival of his subjects. His thoughts could not have avoided fleeting recall of the nearly succesful rebellion of February 26, 1936. Would the ship of state right itself this time?

More important still—would the whole peace negotiations be wrecked?

Hirohito commanded that General Hasunuma come to him immediately. Chamberlain Mitsui rushed off to fetch the aide.

As General Tanaka drove through the palace grounds to check on Hirohito's welfare and pay his respects to his sovereign, his staff car practically flattened a chamberlain rushing down the road from the *Gobunko*. It was Mitsui hurrying to find General Hasunuma.

In a vignette reminiscent of Stanley meeting Livingstone in mid-Africa, Tanaka sprang from his staff car, bowed low to the chamberlain, who returned the greeting somewhat apprehensively. The General then produced from an inner pocket an oversized name card and with a flourish presented it to the surprised chamberlain. In quick succession Tanaka then inquired about His Majesty's health, stated the uprising had been crushed, and asked where he could find chief aide-de-camp Hasunuma.

Since Mitsui also was on his way to the aide, Tanaka invited him into the staff car and they drove directly to the entrance to the ministry building. There, clusters of troops were packing up machine guns and ammunition boxes and carrying gear away from the emplacements so hastily established only a few hours before.

The chamberlain led Tanaka to the rooms where Hasunuma had been held incommunicado by the insurgents. With the aide, Tanaka hastened to the imperial library to report to the Emperor. However, the chamberlain stationed at the door to the *Gobunko* looked out into the morning mist and, seeing two soldiers marching resolutely to the Emperor's quarters, slammed and bolted the door. Even when he peered out at Hasunuma, whose face should have been familiar, and Tanaka, whose mustache was celebrated, the near-sighted retainer seemed to see only two more rebel soldiers. At length the two loyal generals were identified and received by His Majesty. Tanaka told him the events of the night and the measures taken and was thanked by his sovereign.

At 7:47 A.M., leaving the Emperor, Tanaka assembled the chamberlains, stewards, and retainers in the chamberlains' room of the library and addressed them with his version of an inspiring "virtue will triumph" pep talk.

While General Tanaka was on his way to assure Hirohito that the revolt was over, at Radio Tokyo, rebel troops guarding the broadcasting plant inside and out had suddenly downed their arms, put away their bayonets, and taken off for their regiment. As they moved out, a small contingent of MPs moved in to guard the station.

The most important matter there was repair of the cut line. This was restored with a temporary splice and NHK went back on the air at 7:21 A.M. Announcer Tateno's voice went out over the nation: "We now have a special announcement. The Emperor will graciously promulgate a rescript. [Pause] The Emperor at noon today will graciously broadcast, in person. This is a most gracious act. All the people are requested to listen respectfully to the Emperor. [Pause] Electricity will be supplied to all districts that do not normally have the supply during the daytime. We especially request government offices, business offices, factories, railroad stations, post offices to make use of all available receivers so that all citizens can listen to the Emperor's broadcast. The most gracious broadcast will be at noon. Moreover, in some parts the newspapers will be delivered after 1 P.M."

Now the attention of the nation was focusing on the unprecedented, mysterious event.

Meanwhile, General Tanaka, accompanied by General Hasunuma, proceeded to make a top-to-bottom inspection of the huge household ministry building. He made sure that the recordings were safe, ordered the telephone lines restored, saw to it that all those detained by the rebels were released, and that the soldiers cleaned up and cleared out.

By 8 A.M. Chamberlain Mitsui was reassured that peace and order had indeed been restored. He went to the Safe Room door and knocked slowly and distinctly five times, the agreed-upon all-clear signal. Nevertheless, Kido and Ishiwata were understandably anxious when they came to the door and finally unlocked it. Mitsui gave them a hasty résumé of the night's harrowing history. Kido learned from one of his staff that the rebels had searched the privy seal's office six separate times looking for him, and that they had used every kind of threat on his aides to reveal Kido's hiding place.

As the privy seal was leaving his dungeon, General Tanaka was driving through the palace plaza, across Hibiya-dori to his office in the Dai Ichi building. It was eight o'clock when the General walked into his inner office, returned his pistol to Tsukamoto, shed his cap and jacket, and faced the day's routine.

Meanwhile, Kido and Ishiwata hurried to the library to pay respects to the Emperor and learn what had to be done now. Hirohito seemed composed and he was as determined as before to go through with the day's scheduled events—the privy council meeting and broadcast of the rescript. The privy seal was relieved. He knew his god. Nevertheless, it was reassuring to find him unshakable, even in the aftermath of the night's events.

Chapter 22

Sacred Crane

As the danger of an army takeover dwindled, the Emperor-god's retainers faced some problems in arranging for his broadcast. They still had to move the recordings from the household ministry building to the broadcasting studios. It seemed eminently possible that some of the dissidents might be lying in wait, ready to pounce on the records and destroy them. As the night's events had demonstrated, the discs were worth many times their weight in blood to desperate men.

Three household ministry officials met at 8:30 A.M. to consult on the matter. Mr. Takei and chamberlains Mitsui and Okabe decided that stratagem was necessary to foil any attempt to intercept delivery of the recordings. So it was that the records were removed from the hidden safe in the Empress' office room and the two film cans placed in their containers for delivery.

An imperial household ministry limousine pulled up at the door of the building and Mr. Takei, proudly bearing a formal tray with the Emperor's crest, emerged. In the tray was a fine silk brocade covering the film can with the recording inside. With just the right touch of ostentation, Takei entered the limousine and drove at a leisurely pace through the Sakashita gate, across the imperial plaza to Hibiya-dori avenue, and over to the Dai Ichi Building, where he stepped out of the highly conspicuous palace limousine. Again the flourishes and pompous touches, the "highly important-mission" manner. Takei advanced up the short flights of steps, between the square, forty-foot granite columns, into the modern interior. As if the tray and the limousine were not sufficient, he identified himself and asked to be taken to the basement. He arrived there without incident and delivered the precious can of records to an NHK staff member assigned to the secret standby studio. Relieved, Takei retraced his steps, popped back into the limousine, and sped back to the palace.

Meanwhile a car from the Metropolitan Police office had been sent to the ministry. It pulled up at the entrance to the building, and a man in a humble worker's uniform shambled out and got in. He carried his lunch bag with him. He was driven to NHK headquarters directly, and then two policemen accompanied the worker to the executive floor. There the lunch bag was turned over to NHK President Ohashi by the "worker," Chamberlain Okabe. The bag contained a movie-film can in which was the good recording of the rescript plus the less desirable first takes. Takei's record was the standby, inferior one.

The household ministry had delivered the goods to the broadcasters. It was now up to the broadcasters to deliver them to the people.

There was one formality to complete on this day—the meeting of the privy council to secure its technically necessary approval of the peace move. The meeting had been set for 10 A.M. in the palace. But the rebel uprising had caused so much damage that the cleanup had not been completed by that time.

Finally, at eleven o'clock the thirteen privy councilors and their president, Baron Hiranuma, picked their way down the damp stairs to the bomb shelter under Fukiage Garden. To the historic room where the Emperor had stated his decision on two occasions they went and sat at the same two rows of tables as had the Imperial Conference participants just twenty-four hours before. Outsiders (other than privy councilors) included in this conference were Premier Suzuki, Foreign Minister Togo, and the director of the Bureau of Legislation.

Once again the Emperor entered with the chief aide-de-camp; he took his place at his table before the golden screen, and the meeting officially began. Baron Hiranuma read the Emperor's message to the council.

I have ordered the government to inform the Allied forces of our acceptance of the Potsdam Declaration. . . . Although such a decision should be made with the advice of the privy councilors, I asked the advice of only the president of the Privy Council because of the urgent need. I hope you will approve this action.

By the time the meeting was fairly under way and Baron Hiranuma had called on Togo to recapitulate the sorry chain of events that had led to this moment, the time for the Emperor's broadcast was nigh. Hirohito rose and left the room as the councilors bowed. The meeting was recessed so that all could listen to the broadcast of the Emperor's words.

Across the nation, loyal subjects were drawing to their radios like iron filings to magnets. The special ration of electricity was scheduled to make the widest reception possible. Trains were halting in the nearest stations so passengers could hear the words of the voice never before broadcast. The Japanese have a legend that the Sacred Crane is heard, though invisible above the clouds. The crane, symbolic of the Emperor, would now be heard in a way never dreamed. But what was his message to be? Rumor and conjecture were rampant.

In Tokyo, not far from Ichigaya Heights, Father Joseph Roggendorf, of Catholic Sophia University, asked his students and friends what they had expected the Emperor would say in his broadcast. Most thought His Majesty would announce that Japan had dropped an atomic bomb on Washington in retaliation. Mentioned next most often was a new, even more stringent mobilization of the entire nation against the Russians. Some spoke of a warning from the Emperor that the enemy had landed, at last, on sacred Japanese soil. None, he found—not one—expected the sovereign to declare the war ended.

Across the land, many thought his address was to be a declaration of war against Russia. No, others insisted, it would be an exhortation to fight to the last man. Could it be that Hirohito would abdicate? Or was the merger of army and navy (so long talked of but never achieved) to be announced?

At government offices, all employees assembled in auditoriums or clustered about radio sets in groups. In village market places farmers and townspeople had been gathering for hours, walking miles to hear the historic words and the Voice of the Sacred Crane.

Meanwhile, at Radio Tokyo, a call came in from the Information Bureau recommending that the broadcast be aired from the secret studio in the second basement of the Dai Ichi Insurance Company Building. But NHK's chief engineer Arakawa decided against this, since they were protected in depth: the NHK building and studios were now under guard; there were spare records in the Dai Ichi studio if needed; and conditions were now calm and safe.

It was decided that the big event would take place in Studio 8, since so many people wished to be present for the occasion. VIPs from the Information Bureau, from the household ministry, from NHK—and every Radio Tokyo staff member with enough pull to get in—had flocked to the studio. The doors to the studio were guarded closely by military police who doublechecked those who entered. And the control room too was jammed with NHK staff members wishing to share this historic moment.

At eleven forty-five the studio alert went on, and Mr. Ohashi, NHK's president, brought from the safe a beautiful simple wooden box inside which was an elaborate embroidered silk wrapped about the film can containing the records. Ohashi presented it, with a low bow of respect, to the head of the news department, who responded in kind. He turned it over to one of the newsmen (specially selected for the honor) with an exchange of bows. The records were carried ceremoniously to the control room, and as the newsman handed them to the engineer, again with low bows, there was a sudden commotion in the studio.

An army lieutenant was on his feet, shouting. ". . . if this broadcast is the end of the war . . . then I will slash everybody here with my sword!" He lunged toward the control room, drawing his army sword, but just as he headed for the studio door staff officer Suzuki grabbed him, pinning his arms. The army man was disarmed and turned over to the MPs.

The engineers opened the package, removed the discs and tested the all-important third take. It was judged to be satisfactory; the stand-by sign went on in the studio while all over the nation work came to a standstill. As noon came, Announcer Wada introduced the national anthem, the *"Kimigayo."* As the mournful strains of the anthem died out the announcer, in a formal introduction, told the nation that the Emperor would now speak.

The sounds that followed—historic, epochal, unprecedented—were a surprise to all, a shock to most, and almost unfathomable to many. The Emperor's slightly metallic voice was high and its cadence unfamiliar. This was particularly so since the message had been written not for immediate understanding of the masses, but for the ages. Thus the obscure expressions puzzled scores of thousands who listened with unswerving attention to the Sacred Crane as had Moses to the Sermon on the Mount.

"To our good and loyal subjects," the Emperor began. "After pondering deeply the general trends of the world and the actual conditions obtaining in Our empire today, we have decided to effect a settlement of the present situation by resorting to an extraordinary measure. We have ordered Our Government to communicate with the Governments of the United States, Great Britain, China, and the Soviet Union that Our Empire accepts the provisions of their Joint Declaration."

Throughout the land, those who connected this statement with the Potsdam terms began to weep. But most of their countrymen did not yet realize what His Majesty was telling them. Hirohito went on, and the key phrases told the story:

"The war has lasted for nearly four years. Despite the best that has been done by everyone . . . the war situation has developed not necessarily to Japan's advantage, while the general trends of the world have all turned against her interest. Moreover, the enemy has begun to employ a new and most cruel bomb, the power of which to do damage is indeed incalculable, taking the toll of many innocent lives. Should we continue to fight, it would not only result in an ultimate collapse and obliteration of the Japanese nation, but also it would lead to the total extinction of human civilization. Such being the case, how are we to save the millions of Our subjects; or to atone Ourselves before the hallowed spirits of Our Imperial Ancestors?

". . . The thought of those . . . who have fallen in the fields of battle, those who died at their posts . . . or . . . met . . . untimely death and all their bereaved families, pains Our heart night and day. . . . The wounded and the war-sufferers . . . are the objects of Our profound solicitude. The hardships and sufferings to which Our nation is to be subjected hereafter will certainly be great. . . . However it is according to the dictate of time and fate that We have resolved to pave the way for a grand peace for all the generations to come by enduring the unendurable and suffering what is insufferable."

Hirohito now reassured his people and raised a hand in warning: "Having been able to safeguard and maintain the structure of the Imperial State, We are always with ye, Our good and loyal subjects, relying upon your sincerity and integrity. Beware most strictly of any outbursts of emotion which may engender needless complications, or any fraternal contention and strife which may create confusion, lead ye astray and cause ye to lose the confidence of the world. . . . Cultivate the ways of rectitude; foster nobility of spirit; and work with resolution so ye may enhance the innate glory of the Imperial state and keep pace with the progress of the world."

Kazuo Kawai, then editor of Nippon *Times,* describes the reaction to the broadcast:

The response of the listeners was practically uniform throughout the whole nation. In virtually every group, someone—generally a woman—broke out in a gasping sob. Then the men, who with contorted features had been trying to stay their tears, also quickly broke down. Within a few minutes almost everyone was weeping unabashedly as a wave of emotion engulfed the populace. It was a sudden mass hysteria on a national scale, but a hysteria held to a strangely subdued, muted, minor key. Never had so many Japanese undergone such a simultaneous emotional experience; never had the nation been spiritually so united as in this response to the Emperor's voice.

At the home ministry, as at other major government organizations, employees were assembled in the auditorium listening attentively to the Emperor's words. As the broadcast began, most of them thought he was encouraging the nation to prepare to fight "the decisive battle in the homeland." Until he had spoken for a minute or two there was dead silence. Then, as they realized that the subject was surrender, listeners began to sob and crying spread throughout the audience.

On his train from Tokyo, Professor Asada focused his attention on the broadcast with all his might, as did his fellow passengers. However, there was a great deal of static throughout. Many who listened cried *"Banzai!,"* thinking the message was a declaration of war against Russia. As the train pulled into Nagoya shortly after the broadcast ended, the passengers were shocked to hear children shouting from the platform "Japan was beaten, Japan was beaten!" It was then that the travelers knew for certain the real meaning of the Emperor's broadcast. The hurrahs turned to tears.

In war plants, where work had stopped so that all might hear the Emperor's words, there were the same mixed interpretations and reactions. Nowhere did His Majesty use the word *surrender*. However, as the rescript neared its final sentences, sobs and tears sprang irrepressibly from listeners. They were tears as much of relief as of grief. It was the end of fourteen years of war. Whatever was to come could scarcely be harsher. As soon as the broadcast ended, factories all over the nation shut down. At that moment none knew if it would be permanent or not. The patriotic posters on the fences and walls exhorted PRODUCE PLANES!, but there was no need now. Millions of steadily employed, conscientious workers were without jobs in an instant. There were no *Banzais* in the factories.

At Imperial General Headquarters of the Japanese army, the leaders had decided that the humiliation of surrender would be faced as a group. The orders had been distributed on the fourteenth. All officers were to report in "A-type" formal, dress uniform, complete with decorations, white gloves, and the ceremonial sword of the samurai.

At noon, the rows of officers in the drab auditorium stood facing the platform from which a loudspeaker showered the voice of their Emperor on them. On the dais were the top echelon of the army, including the chief of staff, General Umezu, and the field marshals, highest generals, and commanders. The Emperor's words took some time to sink in, but when they did, the white gloves soon became damp with tears. And when His Majesty spoke the words "We have resolved to pave the way for a grand peace for all the generations to come by enduring the unendurable and suffering what is insufferable," nearly every officer, including the steely leaders on the platform, was sobbing.

The dream of conquest was shattered. The prospect of survival was tenuous. These men knew well the aftermath of defeat and occupation from their experience as the conquerors and occupiers of the

Philippines, Dutch East India, Malaya, Burma, Indo-China, Manchuria, Korea, and Chinese provinces and cities. To many, the thought of occupation by the Allies equated directly with Japanese occupation of conquered territories. To those who thought of Nanking at this moment, the immediate future was a prospect truly as horrifying as any possible human experience.

In that Chinese city during the first two months after its capture, the victorious Japanese troops indulged in an unrestricted orgy of drunkenness, looting, murder, and rapine. Literally tens of thousands of women were raped and an estimated 200,000 helpless civilians— men, women, and children—were slaughtered simply because they tried to stop the looting, or stood in the way on the sidewalk, or in some manner were unfortunate enough to upset the Japanese conquerors. The victors so eagerly and enthusiastically wielded bayonet and bullet that the streets of the city were filled for weeks with human carcasses, the stench of death, and the reek of rotting human flesh.

To Second Lieutenant Sadao Otake, an American Nisei trapped in Japan when the war broke out and drafted into the army as a translator in the sixth section of G-2, army intelligence, the occasion of Hirohito's broadcast was the fulfillment of his predictions. As he stood in the ranks of the choking, crying leaders of the Imperial Japanese Army, listening to the Emperor's pronouncement of failure on his loyal troops, he found himself incensed at these once-powerful men, crying *now*. "What the hell have they been doing for the past ten years?" he said to himself.

The specters of Bataan and Khota Baru, of Mukden, Nanking, Shanghai, Teintsin, Balikpapan, Hong Kong—the sites of Japanese wholesale atrocities against unarmed civilians and helpless prisoners of war peopled the minds of some of the officers. The list of places that had felt the unrestricted wrath of Japan's soldiers of occupation was almost a catalog of the places conquered. No wonder there was fanaticism in the army's determination to fight to the end. None of the military men wanted Japan to suffer the treatment they had meted out to conquered peoples.

After the final words of the Emperor echoed through the auditorium, the officers were dismissed. Some returned to their offices to work on the huge task of informing the overseas troops and planning for the surrender. Many took off.

Lieutenant Otake, after checking in at his desk in the research and analysis branch, left Ichigaya early and headed for home, across the city. He waited and waited for the tram. There were few except at commuting times, when they jammed the tracks. Now, in early afternoon, they were scarce. Finally his streetcar came and he jumped aboard. It was almost deserted, and he felt uncomfortably conspicuous in his best uniform with white gloves and that long, curved sword. A middle-aged woman on the car looked at him, clattered over on her clogs. Her *mompei* (baggy quilted trousers) marked her as a worker. She tugged at his sleeve. "Why did we lose the war? Why did we lose? I gave my son in the war. Why can't we fight on? What's the matter with you people?" Otake could only tell her that it was the Emperor's decision, because the odds were so hopeless.

At home in the outskirts of Tokyo, the young Lieutenant found his father. The older man, like thousands of others, now had two families: in Tokyo, his daughter at the university and Otake at GHQ; in the country, his wife and daughter-in-law, living with his brother. He was forced to spend his time commuting between the two, bringing food to the city folk and family possessions for bartering to the country. He had just returned from the country, on the single inbound train of the day. For six months he had been commuting so, under increasingly difficult conditions: it required a ticket, purchased beforehand, and the ticket could be bought only with permission of the military authorities. Those who had relatives in the officer corps had a clear advantage.

Tired from his enervating trip, the older man looked up from the chair where he had dropped after unloading his pack of sweet potatoes. "I can't believe it. We can't have lost the war."

Sadao stood before him in his ceremonial uniform and tried to make his father understand. "It's true, Dad. Didn't you hear the Emperor's address on the radio today?"

"No, I just came from the country on the train."

"Well, it was broadcast at noon. It's true!"

"Ahhh, you're lying! You've always said we were going to lose the war. You shouldn't say those things."

"But Dad, we *did* lose the war."

The father quickly began to sob. He was motionless, and the tears ran down his cheeks unchecked. Though the sight of hundreds of his fellow officers crying had not affected him this way, seeing his father in tears triggered an inescapable feeling of loss in Otake. The young Lieutenant found that he, too, was crying.

Father Flaujac, director of the Catholic Bethanie Institution for tubercular patients, made sure that the loudspeakers were in order before the Emperor's broadcast. They were the same speakers that four years before had announced "the great victory of Pearl Harbor." Now they played the somber imperial message to a beaten, demoralized audience. "After His Majesty's broadcast," noted Father Flaujac, "there was a burst of sobs from the whole audience, women and men . . . yes, it was finished in humiliation, that was the first feeling . . . it was finished . . . the war. The burden so heavy to carry had been unloaded. . . . Damocles' sword which hung every day over our heads had been taken down, the atom bomb vanished. Finished! The people breathed with a sigh of relief and were not in the mood to commit a mass *harakiri*."

Within minutes after Hirohito's broadcast the plaza in front of the palace was crowded with hundreds of citizens. Kneeling, they faced in the direction of the unseen Sacred Crane somewhere inside those eternal walls. Young and old, men and women, civilians and uniformed men, they wept. Some cried uncontrollably, foreheads to the paving stones; others, almost hypnotized, focused on an infinity beyond Nijubashi bridge, tears coursing down their cheeks. There were the fanatics, for whom sharp steel gave the only release. Some performed their *harakiri* on the plaza, surrounded by throngs of weeping, stricken subjects. More took to the woods surrounding the plaza and in this comparative privacy satisfied their feelings of *giri* to themselves with a blade or pistol. Among these were Major Hatanaka and Lieutenant Colonel Shiizaki. Major Koga returned to General Mori's office for his admission of guilt and failure, and there ended his life with a bullet. Two days later Captain Uehara killed himself at the Air Academy.

If there ever was a "lame duck" session of any deliberative body, it was the reconvening, after the Emperor's announcement of Japan's defeat, of the privy council. Technically, it was up to this body "of personages who have rendered significant service to the State" to give the Emperor their "valuable advice."

Though not typical of the appointees, one of the councilors was the seventy-year-old General Baron Shigeru Honjo, who as commander of the Kwantung army in 1931 brought off the Manchurian Incident. He successfully established Manchukuo, Japan's puppet state. General Honjo became a privy councilor when he retired from the army in 1936. It was a fitting reward for his honorable service, as things went in those days.

With a president, vice-president, and up to twenty-five councilors appointed by the Emperor for life, the privy council had been moribund for months. But at this critical time, cool heads thought it wise to do as General Anami had demanded and follow all the prescribed steps in legalizing the surrender. To do so would forestall later claims of fraud or deceit.

So Baron Hiranuma called the councilors to order and Premier Suzuki deferred to Foreign Minister Togo to brief the fourteen men. Togo picked up the traces and patiently steered through the history of Japan's Soviet maneuver, the Potsdam declaration rejection, the two atomic bombs, and Russia's attack. He told them of the Emperor's August 10 Imperial Conference and the one the morning of August 14.

Then (as though they could do anything about it at that stage) General Honjo and his fellow councilors began to pick and chew the provisions of the Potsdam declaration and the Allied note. They denounced the occupation, the idea of voting on the national form of government, the horror of giving the Communists a legal foothold. They were incensed about the subordination of the Emperor to the Supreme Commander of the Allied Powers and practically shrieked that Japan's economy would be wrecked by having to pay war reparations.

Suzuki, Hiranuma, and Togo had been through this to the point where it was stifling to wallow in it this last futile time. But Togo bore the brunt and evenly, unemotionally responded to each question, no matter how impractical the query. At least one of the councilors, Mr. Fukai, had a grip on the realities of the situation. In contrast to the resentment and grumbling of his fellows, Fukai said "In order to make a decision we should compare continuing the war to . . . accepting the Potsdam declaration right now. I am very pleased with the Emperor's decision and the great leadership of the prime minister and foreign minister and others who approved this decision." This reasonable remark became the sense of the meeting.

The privy council adopted the Emperor's decision and president Hiranuma closed the session at 1:30 P.M.

At two o'clock the final meeting of the Suzuki cabinet was called to order by the old sailor. Looking haggard and worn, wearing the morning coat retrieved at such peril earlier that day, Kantaro Suzuki called on Togo—who appeared almost fragile now, a shell of his former self. Still stony in demeanor and as imperturbable as during the most hectic days of negotiation, Togo reported. "Our desires were transmitted to the U.S. early this morning but we have not received any reply as yet. This morning, however, we received the American proposal on how to go about ending hostilities through the Japanese embassy in Switzerland."

Navy Minister Yonai was next. All navy posts, he reported, had been notified through an imperial order and navy orders, setting the cease fire for about ten thirty. Yonai was worried about the time orders would take to reach all echelons. "The Allied Powers have stated in their communiqués regarding the termination of hostilities that we must cease fire within twenty-four hours. We must, however, consider the lower echelons and the time relationships." It would, he judged, take two days for all units in Japan to be notified; six for those in Manchuria, China, and southern seas; and it would take twelve days for the word to reach the cut-off, beleaguered troops in New Guinea and the Philippines. These facts, it was decided, should be given the Allies to prevent some serious misunderstanding or incident.

Suzuki then took over. Lifting his prominent eyebrows to their full height, he told the cabinet about Anami's last call the preceding evening. "War Minister Anami faithfully complied with the cabinet policies. The cabinet would have collapsed immediately had the war minister submitted his resignation. Because Anami did not resign, the Suzuki cabinet was able to attain its major goal, namely termination of the war. For this I shall be ever grateful to the war minister. General Anami was indeed a loyal and industrious person, a rare soldier. He was an admirable minister and I grieve for his death very deeply."

Suzuki's eulogy put the ministers in a somber mood, but there was work to be done.

Perhaps one of the most popular actions of Suzuki's government was its last one. The cabinet decided that goods stockpiled for the military should now, immediately, be distributed to needy civilians, since the invasion threat was no more.

So food, clothing, blankets, and other urgently needed goods were ordered given out to the people. This, Suzuki judged later, definitely helped to quiet unrest and was a real "hit."

The premier turned to the final item of consequence on his agenda: resignation. The old man believed it necessary to draw a distinct line between the war period and the peace with a change of government. His work was done. Now it was possible to do what would have been an act of criminal irresponsibility as recently as twenty-four hours before. The cabinet could resign now—in fact *should*—said Suzuki. He was guilty as premier and the ministers as his cabinet were guilty of troubling the imperial consciousness with the necessity to do what the cabinet should have done—choose peace.

"It has been decided to cease fighting. I am ashamed to think that I troubled His Majesty twice for his august decision. Therefore I will tender my resignation. Now that the war has ended, the cabinet should be changed, but I am uncertain as to when this should be done. There does not seem to be a better time than now. In this regard it is indeed sorrowful that the war minister is not with us today."

To the Japanese people, accustomed to the fall of a government when a wrong policy or a split in the government made it impossible to carry on, there might have been doubts because of this resignation. The doubts might have attached to the decision to end the war. However, foreseeing such an event, newspaper editors carefully explained to their readers that "the resignation implies no political criticism on the policy or methods of the Suzuki cabinet. It implies no lack of respect or confidence on the part of the people. It implies no opposition from any quarter to the ending of the war. . . . The resignation is solely a moral matter." And the moral question was

Suzuki's action in drawing the Emperor into the machinery of government, an unforgivable act!

So Suzuki brought his unsought high calling to a creditable close. He was received in audience by His Majesty and there tendered his resignation formally. The Emperor, whose prestige and power had been brought to a modern pinnacle by the Admiral's actions, thanked him: "You did very well, Suzuki." He thoughtfully repeated it, in case the premier's ear had not caught it. To the plain, unvarnished old man it was like a benediction. Suzuki was asked to stay on until a successor could be chosen. And that choice was Kido's province.

In choosing the new prime minister, Marquis Kido asked His Majesty's permission to consult only the president of the privy council rather than go through the process of polling the entire group of senior statesmen. Hirohito approved, in the interests of speed.

At four-thirty the old warhorse Hiranuma met with Kido, and they talked at length. Finally they decided to recommend Prince Higashi-kuni (Hirohito's uncle-in-law) with Prince Konoye as his adviser. This princely cabinet would presumably have strengths unlike any previous government.

First of all, the royal family would be in charge of the government —through Higashikuni—for the first time. The new premier would be almost above reproach, and certainly above danger. Suzuki and other commoners were exposed to the possibility of gunfire, knives, and bombs as potent if extreme ways of indicating disagreement. But use force on a member of the royal family? Hardly. Blue blood was as impervious a shield as one was likely to find.

Second, the experience and still considerable prestige of Prince Konoye would be invaluable to the new government.

Kido visited the Emperor at six-thirty, told him the conclusion Hiranuma and he had reached, and formally recommended the two princes to lead the incoming government. His Majesty approved and Kido hopped to make the necessary arrangements.

By now literally scores of thousands (some estimated hundreds of thousands) had made their way to the imperial plaza outside the Nijubashi bridge to the palace. With low bows and tears and *harakiri* they apologized to the Emperor for their failure, for their inadequacy, for the inexcusable indignity of Japan's defeat. The crowds were orderly and subdued, the people almost as if in trances; so quiet, yet so driven. Tears and blood flowed throughout the evening and into the night.

The impact of the Emperor's rescript on his loyal armed forces was, in many cases, traumatic. Lieutenant Colonel Masataka Ida was not alone in being thrown completely adrift. His actions following the imperial broadcast were no more extreme than those of hundreds of his fellows. At 2 P.M. he began working on his will, convinced now that his first idea—mass suicide of all officers—was best. At 5 P.M. he went home for a last dinner with his wife. There he changed into a new uniform, told his always-obedient spouse that on the morrow she should call at police headquarters and claim his corpse. He was resolved, absolutely resolved, to offer the Emperor his apologies and follow Hatanaka and Anami in death.

Ida arrived at the ministry of war building at 8:30 P.M. and entered the room where the bodies of his former associates were lying in state for the wake. Ida went through the ritual, clapping hands to summon the spirits and meditating before each coffin.

Though he sincerely wished to hold a wake at the remains of his friends, Ida's primary purpose was, as he had told his wife, suicide. For hours he stuck around the ministry building in the vicinity of the three dead officers. He was waiting until everyone was asleep so that he could slip into the war minister's deserted room and kill himself. But every time he thought there was an opportunity it was spiked by the arrival of a Major Sakai. Sakai seemed to be hovering about him. Ida, fed up, finally asked why the Major was shadowing him. Sakai told him he had been ordered to keep Ida under surveillance. "If you want to commit suicide, you will have to kill me first."

Suicide was one thing; murder was another. Ida found Sakai tenacious and determined. He simply would not leave the would-be suicide alone. Finally Ida gave up the idea and settled down to talk the night out with Sakai.

The following morning, Ida's wife and father called at military police headquarters for his remains, as instructed. They were not in the morgue, and the MPs could find no information about anyone fitting Ida's description. It was not until later in the day that Ida rather shamefacedly showed up at home, having concluded that, as Anami said, there *is* life out of death—in his case, Ida's life out of the deaths of his friends.

The words that put a period to that climactic day were those of the tired helmsman who had steered Japan to this destination. Admiral Baron Kantaro Suzuki, the prime minister, spoke to the nation that same evening at seven-forty. Sakomizu and his collaborators had prepared a talk on the Emperor's decree.

"From the moment we stop grieving," Suzuki told his countrymen, "we must brace ourselves anew and forget the events of the past; we must eliminate selfish ideas and maintain and develop the eternal life of the people in our nation. For this purpose we must start to build a new Japan by fostering a new spirit, through self-government, creative power, and labor. The people must especially endeavor to advance scientific technique, the lack of which was our greatest shortcoming in the recent war."

It was a typical Suzuki statement, full of generalities, and exhortation. Only the final sentence rang a practical note in a welter of amorphous homilies. The old man's *haragei* was not in use. He meant what he was saying, but who could believe him—or anyone? Only hours before Suzuki had spoken confidently about defeating the enemy. Now here he was, leader of the defeated, talking about "the eternal life of the people." What did he mean?

Actually, Suzuki was trying in his usual ambiguous way to reassure his fellow countrymen, to quiet them and call upon them to accept the inevitability of defeat stoically but peacefully. As usual, the response to his words was mixed. Not a few, in spite of the admonition of the Sacred Crane, reacted violently. Some, contrary to all expectations, even went so far as to threaten the new premier, Prince Higashikuni. Though warfare was ending, peace within Japan itself had not yet been won.

Chapter 23

Hitobashira

In August 1945 the U.S. Office of Strategic Services rushed out a secret "research and analysis" memo on Japanese reactions to the surrender. The OSS document said:

It has often been observed that, in an unexpected or new situation, many Japanese exhibit uncertainty to a degree abnormal for most Occidentals. Under these conditions their behavior may be characterized by anything from extreme emotional apathy and physical immobility to uncontrolled violence directed against their persons or almost any object in their environment. The fact of surrender presents such a new situation, and one which for years the Japanese have been taught to avoid beyond all others.

This perception proved to be astonishingly accurate, as events in Japan were proving, even as the memo was being written and distributed to American government leaders.

General of the Army Douglas MacArthur, the Supreme Commander for the Allied Powers, proudly boasted just two months after Hirohito's historic broadcast that the occupation of Japan had been accomplished without a shot fired or a drop of Allied blood shed. It was true, and it was a spectacular feat. MacArthur had reason to gloat, for he had ventured one of the most breathtaking gambles in all history: with a token force he had landed at Atsugi airfield, next to Tokyo, in the midst of a nation that still had nearly four million men carrying weapons in the homeland alone, not to mention overseas forces.

MacArthur had read the cards correctly, and he won his gamble brilliantly. There were no incidents, no attempts on the conqueror or his troops. But that there were none was due mainly to the vigorous leadership of the Emperor and the efforts of the top government and military leaders to control the people of Japan. It was far from easy. The nation was seething beneath the surface, though it might have appeared placid to casual observation. All that would be required to make it boil over, it seemed, was a touch of heat—just a small amount in the critical places.

With the enormous responsibility of surrendering this nation of eighty million souls peacefully, the Emperor was filled with anxiety that peace and order might break down and that some military incident might kick off new hostilities.

The first order of business was the armed forces. It was absolutely necessary that they put down their weapons and obey orders. Therefore Hirohito dispatched, on August 16, three of the imperial princes to carry the word to troops overseas.

Radio and written messages would not suffice. It was too easy for the diehards to discount them as the work of "traitors around the Throne." Only the direct word vouchsafed by the Emperor's close relatives would convince the skeptics that Hirohito himself, of his own free will, had made the fateful decision. So Prince Takeda was flown to the headquarters of the Kwantung and Korean armies; Prince Kan-in went to the Southern Army and 10th Area Fleet headquarters. Prince Asaka was sent to the China Expeditionary Army and the China Area Fleet. Their missions were successful with only minor exceptions.

To clinch this and to demonstrate his concern for his loyal soldiers and sailors, the Emperor issued a special imperial rescript—a cease-fire order—to the armed forces the following day. It was full of admiration for the loyalty and bravery of the imperial forces and, significantly, did not mention the atomic bombs but did specify the Soviet attack as a reason for ending the war:

. . . The Soviet Union has now entered the war and in view of the state of affairs both here and abroad, we feel that the prolongation of the struggle will merely serve to further the evil and may eventually result in the loss of the very foundation on which our Empire exists. Therefore, in spite of the fact that the fighting spirit of the Imperial army and navy are still high, we hereupon intend to negotiate a peace . . . for the sake of maintaining our glorious national polity. . . .

Both the army and navy sent out instructions to their officers and men to supplement this special message. The chief of the Naval General Command tried to answer the doubts of his men:

. . . I wish to make it clear that I am absolutely convinced of the fact that the recent Imperial decision was made solely of His Majesty's own free will. Therefore, if you harbor a suspicion of the circumstances which led up to the proclamation . . . and give rein to your personal views or some biased opinions or are misled by rumor, act rashly or blindly, you will only bring about unnecessary trouble. Or if, for instance, you were to agitate the popular sentiment by indulging in irresponsible assumptions, it would not only make it difficult to cope with the situation but serve merely to benefit the enemy, and will on no account meet His Majesty's wish. Again I demand that all officers and men under the Naval General Command renew their conviction that they are loyal fighting men of His Majesty in the grave crisis we face today. I ask that all the commanding officers under my command understand my intent and exhort their subordinates of every rank to fulfill it, so that no one will commit any indiscreet act.

Both army and navy headquarters were apprehensive about how the troops would take the surrender. The army on the eighteenth and the navy the following day sent out orders intended to soften the blow. They instructed, in part:

Military personnel and civilians attached to the armed forces, who come under the control of enemy troops following the promulgation of the Imperial rescript, will not be regarded as prisoners of war. Nor will the surrender of weapons or any other act performed in accordance with enemy directives handed down by Japanese superiors be considered surrender.

Since the term *surrender* did not exist in the military lexicon, the brasshats hereby drew up their own definition. It was one that made surrender palatable by refusing to recognize it as surrender!

Though Suzuki addressed the nation calling for calm and cooperation, and after him the home minister, the president of the Information Bureau and the head of the Great Japan Political Society, and other prominent persons did likewise, violent incidents continued to erupt. These protests ranged from stoning Sakomizu's family in their country refuge immediately after the Emperor's broadcast to large-scale actions involving hundreds of men.

In one of the random outbursts, a noncommissioned officer demanded that his commanding officer swear to battle the American troops when they came ashore, regardless of the Emperor's words. When his commander refused, the noncom drew his sword and killed him on the spot.

There were isolated instances of attacks by Japanese aircraft on Allied positions or ships, particularly in the islands. Many of the *kamikaze* pilots felt that they could not survive with the burden of shame they bore. They had an obligation to the spirits of their comrades who had died on suicide missions.

On the seventeenth, Privy Seal Kido had an emergency call from the Court, asking him to come to his office at once. There he learned that a contingent of more than 200 (one report said 400) soldiers from the Army Air Signal Training Division stationed in the nearby town of Mito was advancing on Tokyo by train. The troops debarked and went to Ueno park in the heart of the city, where they took over and camped in the Imperial Museum of Art.

At this news Kido conferred with the home minister and others, and the army moved to suppress the rebels. Troops from the Imperial Guards Division and the 12th Area Army were sent to deal with the recalcitrants. It took two days of alternate threats, cajolery, and actual armed assaults to dislodge them (during which Major Ishihara, one of Hatanaka's co-conspirators, commanded a loyal unit of troops and was killed by rebel fire). Finally they agreed to return to Mito and went back by train on the nineteenth. Their commanding officers, of course, committed *harakiri* to atone for the disorder.

The incidents were by no means limited to troops in uniform. The assassins who tried to finish off Kido on the mornings of the fifteenth and sixteenth finally took over the summit of Atago Hill, about a half-mile from the imperial palace. From this point Tokyo Bay and Mount Fuji can be seen, and it was here that a shrine was established in 1603 to protect Edo Castle (now the imperial palace). All of these facts were important to the murky philosophy of the thugs who holed up here. They turned out to be members of a fanatical society, the "Revere the Emperor—Expel the Barbarians Society," *Son-Jo* for short.

Armed with grenades, pistols, and swords, they held off the police from the eighteenth to the twenty-second, maintaining that the peace order was really a conspiracy by politicians. Police and friends pleaded with them for days to give up and disperse, but, after carefully writing out individual poems and wills, the twelve simultaneously pulled the pins on grenades, joined hands and blew themselves up in what was intended to be a heart-rending protest against the surrender.

There were outbursts in the provinces also. In Matsue, a city in Shimane Prefecture in the far west of Honshu, civilians launched a multipronged attack on local institutions. Led by young men in their late teens and early twenties, some forty extremists attacked the post office, prefectural government building, power station, newspaper office, and broadcasting station. They tried to set fire to the government offices and succeeded in cutting the radio station off the air for more than three hours. This band included ten women; they carried rifles and explosives, proving that the army (the only source of such weapons) had assisted and given tacit approval of the action.

Perhaps one of the gravest disturbances took place almost as soon as the new prime minister was installed. Prince Naruhiko Higashikuni became Suzuki's successor and concurrently war minister at 11:45 A.M. on August 17. Prince Konoye was made his deputy and was thought to be the real power in the new cabinet. After all, he had been prime minister twice before, even though his record was one of weak accommodation of the extremists in and out of the military.

Higashikuni, bearing the rank of general in the army, had the confidence of the military; as an imperial prince and uncle of the Empress he had the confidence of the Court and the public. He was a figurehead in the true sense, behind which, Kido's theory held, all factions would rally.

Nine years before, at the time of the celebrated 2–26 revolt, it was reported that Higashikuni was in his palace, drunk. To one who called on him at that critical time he said "The junior officers who joined the insurgents are paying much respect to Prince Higashikuni. They may call on the Prince in order to win him over. In such a case you must receive them with utmost hospitality."

This opportunistic attitude won him the instant dispatch of a protective-preventive guard of loyal troops. Thirty soldiers and two tanks were sent to Higashikuni's palace to discourage the "paying of respects." No one called.

Evidently Hirohito had not heard of this particular incident when, two days later, on February 28, 1936, he spoke of recent actions by princes of the blood: "Takamatsu is best in behavior, Chichibu is better than at the time of the May 15 [1931] Incident. . . . Higashikuni has good sense."

Higashikuni's selection as premier in 1945 shows the foresight of Kido and the mechanics of the process of finding a new premier. It also throws considerable light on the situation at this vital moment.

An Imperial messenger was sent to me on the thirteenth of August 1945, [Higashikuni tells us] to advise me to succeed premier Suzuki who was retiring shortly. I declined the request. I knew I was not fit for such a job as premier. And again the Emperor sent me a messenger on the following day, urging me to assume the post. Again I declined. I said "I object to being appointed to the premiership." I said this because my father had a bitter experience before. . . .

Then, on the fifteenth, I was asked by the Emperor to come to his Palace. I went there. . . . The Emperor strongly advised me to assume the post of premier. He said: "There is nobody who would agree to take this job; even if there was, one could not locate him. American troops will enter Japan soon . . . I have been advised that in case Japan does not respond . . . it would be considered by the Allies as a delaying tactic to put off ending the war; in that case, American troops will make an offensive, instead of a peaceful entry into Japan." The Emperor was very worried about it. He strongly requested that I, as prime minister, would smoothly negotiate with Gen. MacArthur. Hereupon I decided to accept the request, saying that in this case I must.

The Emperor looked very exhausted due to the agonies of the war. He had become so thin and worn out that it pained me even to look at him.

Hirohito charged the new premier to "respect the Constitution fully and strive hard to cope with the situation by enforcing discipline in the army and maintaining law and order throughout the country."

The Prince's experience within forty-eight hours of taking office was hair-raising not only to him but also to those who had thought his rank would quiet the opposition to surrender. Installed in the premier's official residence, he had callers.

"After I organized my cabinet a group of army officers came to me, carrying pistols and swords, and said they opposed ending the war. (The Prince was concurrently serving as war minister.) They asked me to withdraw the decision to surrender. I said that I could not. One . . . said that all the military men (I do not know whether he meant it), especially the young officers, were against ending the war. . . . They were planning to call all the forces in and around Tokyo to gather in the palace plaza in front of the Nijubashi bridge that night and asked me to be present there. . . . If I did not agree with them, they would kill me. They said that they were going to enter the palace to recommend [rejecting the surrender] to the Emperor and in case he did not agree, they would back [*sic*] him up, and would start the war again."

The center of the ferment was, as so often before, the army, whose junior officers still were unconvinced that the national structure would survive surrender and occupation. They had set midnight August 20 as the jump-time for this *coup*. And they had dispatched army trucks and vehicles to the countryside to recruit and gather up rebel forces and bring them back to Tokyo. They were to assemble at the imperial palace and strike at midnight. It was this grand design that the delegation of officers described to Higashikuni at their meeting.

The Prince, however, rejected their scheme "with thundering words," as he put it. He "reprimanded them with a harsh voice, warning them that they must not say such things." Apparently his technique plus his status did the trick. "They said that they understood the situation and asked me to broadcast the reasons for the end of the war every half-hour until midnight. So I hurriedly wrote a draft of my talk and did so."

Higashikuni's speech was aired from six o'clock on, every hour. It contained this significant bit of wishful thinking: "So far as the preservation of our national structure is concerned, I have a positive and definite plan, so you must all behave with the utmost calm, maintaining a dispassionate attitude." Since there was no explanation of the whys and wherefores of the Prince's broadcast, thousands who heard his words were completely puzzled by them. (All during this period the censors made sure that no word of the incidents and unrest appeared in the newspapers or was uttered on the radio.)

The malcontents to whom the announcement was directed took heed. Instead of a huge rally of disgruntled and dangerous army men in the plaza at midnight, only scattered groups of diehards with no coordination and little cohesion showed up. The expected *coup* collapsed then and there, without any violent action.

The following day Higashikuni's military callers again paid their respects. "Those officers came to me again to say that all the troops that gathered in the plaza had dispersed and asked me to feel at ease since all of their plans, such as occupation of the palace, had been abandoned."

Though this particular *Putsch* fizzled, there were sporadic outbreaks in many parts of the nation. The situation was tense, to say the least. The people of Japan were near panic. Rumors swept across Tokyo like waves. One had it that the Chinese were landing troops in Osaka. Another reported that more than 50,000 American soldiers had come ashore at Yokohama and were swarming across the land like locusts, looting, raping, and robbing without stint. Another rumor, that the Americans were in Sagami Bay (just outside Tokyo Bay), was more accurate. But the fleet was assembling for the surrender ceremonies, not for landing operations.

Those who could were leaving the cities in droves. And in the country there was consternation. The radio and newspapers attempted to quiet fears, but some of the attempts were ludicrous in hindsight. (An article in one newspaper advised women "When in danger of being raped, show the most dignified attitude. Don't yield. Cry for help." Needless to say, all females between puberty and senility who could, headed for the hills.)

In some prefectures the people lost their heads. Kanagawa, the province next to Tokyo, borders both Sagami Bay and Tokyo Bay. It includes Yokohama and many suburban towns whose workers commute daily to the capital. In this prefecture the officials recommended that women and children be sent to the provinces from the main cities and towns, such as Yokohama and Kamakura. This advice was seized upon by local neighborhood associations as though it were an official directive. They circularized their areas so thoroughly and effectively that citizens, thinking it was a compulsory evacuation, clogged the streets and roads. This spectacle shook the authorities out of their lethargy and they notified the local mayors to quiet the terror-stricken people and induce them to return to their homes.

It was difficult to bring the people to their senses when they were easy prey for wild rumors and were assailed by supposedly authoritative messages, such as the leaflets circulated by diehard groups.

From airfields dotted about the nation bitter-enders dropped handbills urging opposition to the surrender. Some even talked about a "government of resistance." The army and navy men, as members of centralized national organizations, clung to the structure they knew and dreaded the "nothingness" that was about to descend on them.

Prompt action by the army quickly grounded most of its planes. On the fourteenth General Yoshizumi had ordered all military aircraft disarmed and their fuel tanks removed. In general the order was effective.

Not so in the navy. The 302d Air Group at Atsugi airfield, the secret port built for the defense of Tokyo and the training of navy *kamikaze* pilots, refused to acknowledge defeat. The commandant, Captain Yasuna Kozono, led a group of diehards in flying over Atsugi and Tokyo, buzzing the nearby towns menacingly, and scattering leaflets. The handbills called the surrender decision false and used the old buncombe that it wasn't really the Emperor but the "traitors around the Throne" who wanted to give up.

The final batch of 2,000 men had all but completed *kamikaze* training at Atsugi when the war's end came. But so hopped-up and determined to smash the enemy were they that, led by Kozono, they boasted they would torpedo the Allied fleet in Tokyo Bay and that they would blow its flagship, the battleship *Missouri,* out of the water.

Kozono was one of the ablest navy aviators and had maintained the high quality of planes and personnel at Atsugi in the face of general deterioration of both throughout the country. It was but one of the strange interludes in this uncertain time that Captain Kozono absolutely rejected defeat. He refused orders to ground his pilots. He ignored the command of the navy minister. He would not talk on the telephone to his superior officers.

Now Atsugi was vital. It was the military airfield closest to the capital. MacArthur had directed that it was to be made ready for his arrival and it was his personal choice as the landing point for the vanguard of the occupation forces.

But Kozono was immovable. Even the threat of force from the

marines at nearby Yokosuka Naval Station did not stir him. It was at this point that navy GHQ arranged for Prince Takamatsu, a good friend of Kozono, to talk with him by phone. The problem was to get the Captain to speak with the Prince, and so Captain Oi, Kozono's roommate at the Naval Academy, was sent to reason with him.

Told by the Atsugi watch officer that the Captain had gone mad, Oi was suspicious and asked the executive officer to see the commandant. Taken to Kozono's bedroom, Oi entered and found him stretched out with two medical officers flanking him. Kozono, under sedation, was babbling incoherently about Amaterasu, the Sun Goddess.

Oi prevailed on the executive officer to go to the telephone and talk with Prince Takamatsu, who confirmed the Emperor's decision to surrender. Outside the headquarters, near a pond, the young officers of Atsugi were at the moment staging a mass meeting in the early twilight. They insisted that the war continue. The executive officer addressed them and told them that they must give in because the war was going to end by direct order of the Emperor himself. Oi returned to the navy ministry believing that Atsugi was now secure and that the matter was settled.

The next day he found out that his mission had failed. The young officers flew their planes to Yokosuka and other military airfields. Kozono was sent to a hospital (later he was tried by a court-martial and sentenced to long-term confinement).

Another of the navy holdouts was Captain Minoru Genda. It was he who had planned and actually signaled the flyoff of "Genda's circus," the bombers and fighters of the special squadron that struck Pearl Harbor. Famous in Japan for the stunning success of this attack, Genda at war's end had one of the few remaining units of fighter planes. Stationed on Kyushu, Genda's men were assigned to knock down American planes streaming across that island. It was an impossible task. They were outnumbered nearly a hundred to one, they had limited gasoline and trained pilots, and their planes were unable to reach the high-flying enemy bombers.

About August twelfth Genda had received word that acceptance of the Potsdam terms was near. He absolutely could not believe it. He flew to Kyushu headquarters and found out it was true. He tried to interest some of the officers there in continuing the fight nevertheless, but was rebuffed. He flew back to his base at Omura.

On the seventeenth Genda ordered his men to accept no orders but his, then flew to navy air headquarters at Yokosuka. He wanted to determine whether the surrender decision was the Emperor's or his advisers'.

When he landed at Yokosuka he found turmoil. There was a split between the *kamikaze* fliers and their superior officers. The Atsugi extremists had flown to the naval station to whip up support for their resistance. Several hundred members of the navy Special Attack Corps were there, being trained to pilot midget suicide submarines loaded with bombs to be used against the expected invasion fleet. Some of these *kamikazes* were swayed.

Meanwhile, Genda took his question to Tokyo, to Admiral Tomioka, chief of naval operations, who confirmed that it was the Emperor's will to end the war. Genda flew back to Yokosuka and told the young insurgents that the decision was truly the Emperor's wish, then flew on to navy airfields on Shikoku and Kyushu, relaying the message, giving it the impact of his own considerable prestige. He assembled his own squadron and told them the bitter truth. Thus his men accepted the end quietly, and when the hotheads from Atsugi later flew in to enlist them in continued war on the enemy Genda's discipline held firm.

The incidents at Atsugi had a decidedly unsettling effect on government leaders and the Emperor. It had been thought that the navy was firmly disciplined and that Yonai controlled the allegiance of commanding officers up and down the line. Both he and Anami had given Hirohito their word that they would take care to see that their troops accepted the surrender. Anami, of course, was gone, but the army was doing reasonably well to curb its ultras, considering the quantity of them and their positions of power within that service, where they had for years been the major force. In the navy Yonai was still the minister (Higashikuni kept Yonai on in his cabinet), and though it was known that there were diehards of the Onishi–*kamikaze* stripe, it had been thought that the commanding officers were seasoned men of moderate views, loyal to Yonai and the Emperor.

Events at Atsugi did not negate this reasoning, but did show the potential for havoc of even one holdout if he was obsessed and had a dedicated and highly mobile following.

To counter the infection being spread by the Atsugi flyers in their recruiting calls at airfields throughout the country, the Emperor sent his brother, naval captain Prince Takamatsu and Vice-Admiral Prince Kuni to navy commands in the homeland. Their purpose was simple—to reiterate forcefully to commanders and troops the absolute necessity of obeying the Emperor's surrender decision.

A second move by Hirohito was a further acknowledgment of the deterioration of discipline and the foresight of Anami, Umezu, Toyoda, and Togo in sending the note to the Allies about the delicate situation in Japan, a note that seemed such an insulting impertinence to Allied readers. The Emperor issued still another special message to the armed forces. It went out on August 25 and was unmistakably explicit:

To our trusted soldiers and sailors on the occasion of the demobilization of the Imperial army and navy:

Upon due consideration of the situation, we have decided to lay down our arms and abolish military preparations. We are overcome with emotion when we think of the precept of our Imperial Grandsire and the loyalty so long given by our valiant servicemen. Especially, our grief is unbounded for the many who have fallen in battle or died of sickness.

On the occasion of demobilization, it is our fervent wish that the program be carried out rapidly and systematically under orderly supervision so as to give a crowning example of the perfection of the Imperial army and navy.

We charge you, members of the Armed Forces, to comply with our wishes. Turn to civilian occupations as good and loyal subjects, and by enduring hardships and overcoming difficulties, exert your full energies in the task of postwar reconstructions.

Fortunately, by the time this message was issued conditions had improved tremendously. In fact, the situation was so much better that princes Takamatsu and Kuni were called back and their missions canceled.

There were still isolated pockets of resistance, however. The fanatical Atsugi *kamikaze* pilots continued their revolt almost to the moment of MacArthur's scheduled arrival (originally set for August

26). In fact, on the night of August 23 the Atsugi officers got together for a farewell banquet. The party was in one of the barracks. But, as Kato reports in *The Lost War,* at the height of the festivities a band of corps members, cadets, and enlisted men crashed the party to protest the demobilization order, scheduled to take effect the next day. They insisted on continued resistance to prevent the occupation. Attempts to restore order brought on a riot in which the furniture and windows were smashed, shots rang out, swords flashed, several men were killed, and many were hurt. The fighting spread. Other barracks were damaged and so were installations at the field. At one point the battle was so serious that the army MPs were called in, but the struggle cooled off and participants fled before the gendarmes arrived.

The next day, all of the navy *kamikazes* were moved out and the cleanup of blood and debris was rushed through in order to be ready for MacArthur's arrival just two days later. The field was then put under guard of the Boys' Corps, youths of fifteen to eighteen, and there were no more incidents at Atsugi.

One rough indication of the slackening of discipline is the record of court-martial cases at this time. Yonai announced officially that navy courts examined 2540 men for misconduct from mid-August to mid-October. They had, he charged, "taken advantage of the confusion following the termination of the war."

At the height of the Atsugi uprising Japan was ordered to send a team of representatives to Manila to receive the Allies' preliminary instructions for the actual surrender. Two planeloads flew on a secret course in specially marked aircraft. When only one returned on schedule, there was real fear that the other had been downed by army or navy air force rebels who had gotten wind of the mission. However, it turned out that the ship had been forced down by engine trouble and all aboard were safe. It limped in a day late.

The diehards were a genuine, frightening problem, nevertheless. Sakomizu tells of leaving the premier's official residence for the last time on August 17, after the new cabinet took over. He went out and walked about the rubble of the Marunouchi district, where the showcase buildings of Japan had once stood, and the Ginza, the burned-out shopping district. He was shocked to see on a telephone pole one of the posters reading *Kill Japanese Badoglios—Suzuki, Kido, Togo, and Sakomizu.*

The former cabinet secretary was staying with his father-in-law, Admiral Okada. But the local police station objected. "They said guarding Okada was already too much for them and they couldn't be responsible for another person who was on the blacklist. They asked me to go to another place," Sakomizu reports. "The Metropolitan Police requested Suzuki and me not to go out and not to stay at the same place more than three nights running."

Suzuki meanwhile received letters and telephone calls from people who demanded that he commit *harakiri* for his guilt in the defeat of the nation. He took these with equanimity. But the attacks made him conscious of his vulnerability, and he moved seven times to keep out of range of assassins.

All of this was a prelude to the landing of the Allied occupation forces. On General MacArthur's triumph in bringing ashore the conquering troops without firing a shot or losing a drop of Allied blood there was a high price. It was a price paid by the defeated and it was in lives. More than a thousand Japanese army officers (plus hundreds of civilians and navy men), from the war minister down to company grade, dispatched their spirits to the Yasukuni Shrine by taking their own lives.

There was nothing in the postsurrender world that promised to have substance. There was no thing or plan or banner to which one could rally, save the Emperor. Thus many preferred resistance or death under the Emperor and with a way of life they knew to living on with the Emperor and a radically changed existence they would find excruciating. What could be more excruciating than to be condemned to live in a society in which "equality" is the guiding principle instead of "proper station"? Hierarchy was the bedrock of Japanese society.

In few places in the world were relationships between family, neighbors, employers, clerks, workers, military, and each and every category of individual existence so elaborately identified and respected. "Righteousness in Japan," wrote Ruth Benedict in her classic *The Chrysanthemum and the Sword,* "depends upon recognition of one's place in the great network of mutual indebtedness that embraces both one's forebears and one's contemporaries." But in the U.S.A., hierarchy, "place," and "proper station" were (as all Japanese knew with attitudes bordering on contempt) practically nonexistent. To enforce "equality" in Japan would destroy the glue that held the society together. What would be left? Chaos. And no right-minded Japanese could willingly tolerate that.

There is almost nothing so abhorrent and impossible to endure for a Japanese as an unstructured situation. From birth to spirit world, each Japanese knows exactly what his position is in the family, the community, the nation. Now, with surrender and occupation all were to be cut adrift. Only the pole star, the Emperor, would remain. Everything else would be abolished, transformed, or at the mercy of the conquerors.

Of course the future of the armed forces was in doubt. Industry was to be shut down. The government was to be changed—the familiar institutions would be rooted out or drastically modified. And what about customs and social practices, religion? Would the conquerors impose their own value system on Japan? Would they eradicate state Shinto as the enemy leaders had often advocated?

With the victor's grip on the machinery of government, the courts, the law-enforcement procedures, would they not junk the traditional, the god-given ways of Japan and substitute their own? It could mean the end of the Japanese family—they might even emancipate women! They might take over the education system and convert young Japanese into parent-despising, English-speaking democrats instead of monarchists. And there was another great enigma, much to be feared: What role would the Soviets play in all this? Obviously the Reds would encourage a strong, disruptive Communist movement in Japan at the very least, and more likely they might try to take over the government by machination and intrigue.

In this welter of confusion many saw suicide as the only rational escape. Most of them took this action, the most extreme resort open to a human being, as an expression of guilt and protest, not as an aggressive striking out at society as in the West. It was not a ritual act demanded of them by the Emperor, the government, or the military system. Unlike the classic Western case where the condemned military officer is left alone with a bottle of brandy and a revolver, no overt pressure was put on Japan's officers.

Yet many responded to the defeat as others had to the 1932 London naval treaty that stirred such violent reactions in Japan. Then, as in 1945, many took their lives in the ultimate act of protest against a decision they could not change, a change they could not live

with. Now, at the war's end, others, in the spirit of earlier days, took
on their shoulders the responsibility for failure of their subordinates
(as did Anami) and ultimately themselves in their duty to the
Emperor. And, of course, there were some who so detested the
thought of standing in the prisoner's dock as accused war criminals
that they chose death before dishonor. (Prince Fumimaro Konoye,
the prewar prime minister, Kido's close friend, was one of these.
Notified by the occupation authorities in December 1945 that he was
to be arraigned as a war criminal, Konoye chose suicide rather than
trial.)

Early in this century a Japanese who borrowed pledged his *giri* to
his name to repay the loan. If he failed to pay up on New Year's day,
the traditional day for clearing debts, *harakiri* was often the socially
acceptable escape route for the debtor. Even today New Year's eve in
Japan does not pass without some suicides of this type. In 1945 the
officers, who had pledged to bring the Emperor victory in war,
"cleared their names" in the traditional samurai gesture.

Some made theatrical productions of their self-destruction. Vice-
Admiral Onishi, the navy vice chief of staff and "father" of the
kamikazes, ended his life the morning of August 16. The event was
carefully planned, and he had the foresight to call friends who were
articulate and influential before he pulled the trigger in his navy
ministry office. Onishi also made sure that his will was available for
publication.

In an emotional message to the memory of the special attack units
Onishi expressed his "heartfelt gratitude for having fought so well."
He apologized with his suicide to the spirits of his subordinates and
to their bereaved families. And to the youth of the nation he said
"Since our rashness in dying only aided the enemy, I will be happy if
you will learn from this lesson to obey His Majesty, to exercise
caution, and to endure hardships. Even under humiliation, do not
abandon the pride of being a Japanese. You are the flower of our
nation. Even in peace you must maintain the spirit of the special
attack unit and do your best for the welfare of the Japanese people
and for the peace of mankind."

The churning events of that time made it unlikely that Onishi would
get his much-desired hero's burial. Even he must have had little hope
that the navy would drop everything and render him homage. But he

was not only given short shrift, he was given a short shroud. His adoring followers were incensed that the glamor boy of the navy was placed in a coffin so small (they said) that his feet stuck out! Insult was added to this injury when Onishi's one-way trip was made unceremoniously by truck rather than hearse and cortege.

In contrast to Onishi's exit was that of one of his subordinates who decided on a matter-of-fact way out. Although navy GHQ had ordered on the fourteenth that all *kamikaze* operations should be suspended, the commanding officer of the 5th Air Fleet, based on Kyushu, listened to the Emperor's broadcast and decided to defy both navy and god. Vice-Admiral Matome Ugaki chose one final suicide attack on the enemy as his act of defiance. With ten other *kamikazes* following, he took off from Oita Prefecture airfield within hours of the Emperor's rescript. The eleven *tokko* planes headed for Okinawa, presumably to attack enemy ships. None of them returned. It had been Ugaki's duty to send *kamikaze* pilots against the foe and he thought it appropriate to perish as had his men.

Another type of finale was that of Marshal Sugiyama, who had held the topmost posts in the army and had been war minister prior to Anami. Sugiyama's quietus was carefully arranged for maximum symbolic effect. On the day his troops were demobilized the marshal killed himself with a bullet. His wife, by prearrangement, joined him in death, using the traditional ritual dagger in front of the Buddhist altar in their home. Thus the classic joint suicide of General Nogi, the Russo-Japanese war hero, and his wife after the funeral of Emperor Meiji was once again brought to mind.

General Tanaka, the hero of the August 15 incident, took a different route. He was ever prone to self-criticism, and was punctilious about guilt for things beyond his control. In this also, he was a throwback to a previous era. He had, for example, sent in his resignation when he was stricken with malaria in the Philippines. He was put on sick leave and his resignation was rejected.

Tanaka had been assigned on March 19, 1945, to command troops in the Tokyo area. Less than a month later the Meiji shrine burned in a fire-bomb raid and Tanaka, shouldering responsibility for this desecration, promptly turned in his resignation to the war minister. Anami declined to accept it.

By May 25, the west, middle, and northern parts of Tokyo had been turned to ashes by enemy bombers. On this date a fire raid whipped by a whistling windstorm made Tokyo a blast furnace. Although the palace grounds purposely had been spared throughout the war by Allied bombers, on this date wind-driven sparks and flames set fire to trees and buildings in the palace precincts. Ever intrepid, Tanaka rushed to the scene, took command of the fire fighting. It was a hopeless task to try to save the tinder-dry wood-paper-and-glass pavilions in a firestorm. The following day Tanaka sent in his resignation again. It was turned down by the war minister.

After the August 15 incident, the General apologized for his guilt once more with his resignation. This time the Emperor refused it.

Tanaka was mulling over dates for his own suicide and had narrowed the choice to four. He told one of his subordinates not to commit suicide and to dispose of unit colors. The banners, Tanaka told him, were a constant source of trouble. If the regimental colors had to be burned, the regimental commander and standard bearer should commit *harakiri* at a ceremony when the flags went up in flames. If burned at the divisional level, that commander must take responsibility for it. It would be best, he concluded, to supervise this at Eastern District Army headquarters.

"Anyway," he stated, "I will do my best to dispose of them by the time American forces have landed. If the war ministry supervised destroying them in one large bundle somewhere, my men would not worry about them. I have only to die, taking responsibility for this, as commander of the *Tobugun*. My men need not commit *harakiri*. I am going to write it in my will: 'I am committing suicide on behalf of my officers and men.' "

On August 24, Tanaka the fire chief rushed to put out another brushfire. Military cadets, led by a captain, occupied a broadcasting station in the town of Kawaguchi in nearby Saitama Prefecture. Tanaka plunged into the dissidents alone. His handlebar mustaches were flying and he fully expected to be shot. He harangued them, as he had the Imperial Guards, until they saw the error of their ways and gave up.

That night in his room in the Dai Ichi building, Tanaka retired at ten o'clock. His aide, Colonel Tsukamoto, in the next room, heard the General putting things in order, then the General's voice: "Thank you for your past kindnesses, Tsukamoto!"

The Colonel rushed to the door and heard a shot as he opened it. Tanaka was seated in a chair behind his desk, on which he had carefully placed a statue of Meiji, his wills, addressed to his officers and his family, a scroll bearing the Emperor's words to him on August 15, one *sutra*, cigarettes given him by the Emperor, his sword, cap, gloves . . . and false teeth.

Interestingly enough, *Asahi* reported General Tanaka's death the following month as follows in its news columns: Tanaka "committed suicide by shooting himself in the heart, taking the whole responsibility for the destruction by fire of a section of the Imperial Palace, having been unable to safeguard it from the bombings of the U.S."

Tanaka's own words to his regimental commanders were "I am very grateful to all of your regiments for keeping in strict order after the Imperial command to surrender. Now I have fulfilled my duty as Commanding Officer of the District Army. I am determined to lay down my life to beg His Majesty's awful pardon in place of you and all of your officers and men. I heartily hope that you and all your officers and men will strictly watch yourselves and guard against rashness and be devoted to the peaceful revival of our fatherland."

Tanaka, Onishi, Anami, Sugiyama were among the men at the top who ended their lives with the end of Imperial Japan. They were but a handful of those who chose death. The soil of the imperial plaza in front of the palace was drenched with the blood of suicides for days after the Emperor's broadcast.

They were *hitobashiras* all. In olden times, before the construction of a major building a human sacrifice was buried alive at the site. The sacrifice was made to appease the spirit of the place and to help the building endure, for it would rest on the shoulders of the *hitobashira*.

The suicides of the final moment of the Pacific War, the terrible toll of the long, bitter struggle, these could be counted *hitobashiras* —sanguine sacrifices to the new structure that was to rise. Whatever came after, it would be built on their shoulders.

Chapter 24

Survivors

What was the fate of the men who decided to "endure the unendurable" and rang down the curtain on Imperial Japan?

When Admiral Baron Kantaro Suzuki, the dedicated advocate of nongovernment, resigned as premier, he believed he had fulfilled the Emperor's wishes. For himself he wanted nothing more than peace and quiet. This was impossible. His past dogged him. Persistently for months and occasionally until his death he was assailed by curses and demands from extremists that he commit suicide for his "great crime."

The old man returned to the small town in which he had been born—Sekiyado, in Chiba Prefecture, north of Tokyo. There was no convenient way to get there, and he thought this would insure privacy. He was wrong. The place was full of relatives of his family, of childhood friends and their descendants. And he soon found that his home became a pilgrimage point for friends and acquaintances from Tokyo, for newsmen seeking a "how it really was" article, and for American officers who wanted to meet him.

Until his move to the provinces he had been guarded at his various homes (he moved frequently to prevent assassination, as we have seen) and in transit. At Sekiyado, at least, Suzuki felt secure. Uncomplaining and cheerful, he played cards, walked a great deal, and did brush calligraphy on small bits of paper which he gave to callers.

Suzuki's father had died of cancer of the stomach and the old sailor was convinced it would be some such affliction that would end his days also. On April 16, 1949, when he was in his eighty-first year, Suzuki passed away murmuring "Eternal peace, eternal peace." Cause of death: Cancer of the liver. For his tombstone he chose the posthumous Buddhist name "Humility." Suzuki sleeps in Jisoji temple in his home town.

Foreign Minister Shigenori Togo, that wooden-faced, driven man, was asked by Prince Higashikuni to continue as foreign-affairs chief in his cabinet. Togo declined—respectfully, of course. His reasons were valid and unsentimental: Premier Suzuki's resignation applied equally to Togo. Furthermore, though his conscience was clear about his part in the tragic events of late 1941, he foresaw that he might be charged as a war criminal, and this would inevitably embarrass the new government. So Togo turned back to his predecessor, Mamoru Shigemitsu, the foreign ministry reins. Togo addressed his colleagues of *Gaimusho* and the Greater East Asia Ministry briefly and said farewell forever to public life.

As he anticipated, Togo went on trial for his life before the International Military Tribunal for the Far East, better known as the Japanese or Tokyo war-crimes trial. The court was in session for two and a half years—from May 3, 1946, through November 12, 1948. Togo was charged with conspiracy to wage aggressive war and responsibility for atrocities. He was acquitted of any guilt on the atrocities charge and convicted of "crimes against peace" for his period as foreign minister from October 1941 to September 1942. He was, said the court, in a position in those months to play a leading role in Japan's design to wage aggressive war. Yet, when it came to sentencing, Togo alone of those so convicted received less than a life sentence. He was condemned to twenty years from the date of arraignment.

The term did not matter. His health was shattered. From the time he was arrested until his death he spent half his prison life in hospitals.

One has only to look at the pictures of Togo in his book *The Cause of Japan* to see how the man's life force literally drained from him in those frenzied months of 1945. From the cocksure, natty diplomat in his resplendent *Gaimusho* office in 1942 to the spent form soaking up sunshine by a window in September 1945 is a distance most mature men travel over a period of thirty years or more, the distance from vigorous masculinity to recumbent senility.

In a September 1945 photograph we see Togo (or is it a woman?) seated in a chair, his hair apparently white and thin; he is wearing those full-circle glasses (now with narrow rims). His cheeks are puffy; so are his eyes and lips. His chest is sunken and his neck is long with his head thrust forward seeking the sun. His hands are clasped. He is resting. Waiting. The spark is extinguished. The end is a foregone conclusion.

In Sugamo prison Togo diligently set down, without benefit of reference material, his record of the times and events in which he had played a part. His wife and daughter were allowed to visit him in hospital twice a month for a half-hour at a stretch. It was at their mid-July visit in 1950 that he gave them a package of notebooks filled with his writing and asked for their comments. It was his last meeting with them. He died on July 23, 1950, at sixty-seven.

The words that end his book are a fitting epitaph: "Vividly before my eyes is the scene of the Imperial Conference at which the Emperor decided for surrender, and my feeling of then returns to me: That while the future of Japan is eternal, it is a blessing beyond estimation that this most dreadful of wars has been brought to a close, ending our country's agony and saving millions of lives; with that my life's work has been done, it does not matter what befalls me."

General Yoshijiro Umezu, dour gray archetype of the bureaucratic military man, became overnight the most widely recognized, if not the most famous, Japanese soldier in the world. Although his name was unknown to or forgotten by those who saw the pictures of the surrender ceremonies on the deck of the USS *Missouri* September 2, 1945, his appearance was indelible. He stood wearing a rumpled jacket, boots and cavalry breeches, chest bedecked with braid and ribbons, on his head a campaign cap.

When the moment came, Umezu stepped forward and signed his name on the surrender document, representing Imperial General Headquarters. He used a borrowed pen for that ignominious task— on the way to the "Mighty *Mo*" he had discovered that his pen didn't work. It was Umezu's picture, at that nadir of his career, that was flashed around the earth as evidence that the fanatical Japanese military had at last admitted defeat.

Few could have resented the dirty job more than Umezu. To certify that the army would actually accept defeat it had to be an army man who endorsed the document—not, as Umezu had suggested, the senior armed forces representative available: Navy Minister Yonai.

When Umezu first heard that he had been designated to sign for the armed forces he rebelled and said if so ordered he would commit *harakiri* on the spot. But, like so many of his statements, this one was for public consumption and was overriden by the Emperor's direct "request" that he take this onerous assignment. It was more than disagreeable; it was a dangerous task as well. He and the other surrender delegates drove secretly—and fast, to avoid assassination—to the Yokohama-pier rendezvous for their trip to the dotted line.

Later Umezu presided at the ceremonies ending the Imperial Japanese army and was one of the "big fish" netted in the war crimes trial. He had been one of his country's most distinguished officers and had held most of the army's top posts: chief of staff, commander of the Kwantung army, vice-minister of war, head of the General Affairs Bureau of GHQ, chief of the Army Affairs Section of the war ministry.

The war-crimes court found Umezu guilty of conspiracy to wage aggressive war because he had been in a position (to cite only three examples) to plan and approve the operations against China in 1937, to produce the army's national policy plans of 1936 and the industrial mobilization plan of 1937 which, said the court, were prime causes of the Pacific War. Umezu received a sentence of life imprisonment. On January 8, 1949, at the age of sixty-seven, he died in Sugamo prison of cancer. He is survived by a daughter and a son.

Unlike Togo, the "white elephant," Admiral Mitsumasa Yonai, stayed on in Higashikuni's cabinet as navy minister, the only holdover from the Suzuki government. This was highly significant. It indicated official approval both of Yonai's policies and his firm hand on the tiller. He had proved steadfast in the darkest period; he was equally dependable in the emergent Japan.

Yonai presided over the liquidation of the imperial navy—a distasteful task for any career sailor. His words to his fellow navy men were candid, as usual, on that chill occasion in late 1945: "From the opening of the war the navy, especially the navy, made a great effort to be loyal and fought well. But finally we could not respond to His Majesty's wishes. . . . Not only do I feel responsible for this failure to the Emperor but to all of the nation. . . ."

It was notable that Yonai did not feel moved to commit *harakiri* for the navy's part in the defeat. And it was also notable that he was not accused of being a war criminal by the Allies. His record was clean. As he put it, "I think to this day that the basic war plan, as expressed by the scope of the initial advances, was not a proper plan in view of the situation, and our national war strength. I think it should not have been undertaken at all, and I firmly believe that, had I been premier at the time, we probably would not have had this war."

In spite of Anami's "deathbed" charge to his brother-in-law Colonel Takeshita to kill Yonai, the Admiral survived. He was not attacked, either by disgruntled navy diehards of the Onishi stripe or by army hotheads such as Takeshita and his friends. There is something formidable about a man who towers over his fellows physically, morally, and consistently, as did Yonai. And the very directness and vigor of the man, whether standing against the tide of jingoism or sweeping away the wineglasses at a state dinner and placing a quart of whisky on the table in front of him (and consuming the entire contents before the end of the meal) was enough to make would-be assassins think twice.

Yonai, after his public service ended with the phaseout of the Japanese navy, concentrated his attention on Hokkaido, the underdeveloped northernmost Japanese home island. With others he put effort into schemes to build up this "new" land. But, on April 20, 1948, in his sixty-eighth year, he died of pneumonia. He was survived by his wife, three daughters, two sons, and many grandchildren.

Admiral Soemu Toyoda, the navy chief of staff in Suzuki's cabinet, had been hand-picked by Yonai to help him bring the war to an end. Often, particularly at the meetings of the Big Six and the two Imperial Conferences, Toyoda acted as though he had been brought in not to end but to extend the war. Yet Yonai apparently tolerated Toyoda's direct opposition to his wishes. Why?

It is difficult, at best, to determine how much of a statement or action by a Japanese is *haragei* and how much is to be taken at face value. Toyoda was misread in both categories by his associates: "Some people may criticize me as having been a coward and irresolute," the Admiral commented. "As a matter of fact, the navy minister seemed displeased with my unexpected actions. But it does not matter to me what criticism may be flung upon me. I thought at the time that there was no other course for me to pursue."

He gives us an unusually candid behind-the-curtain view of his *haragei* in operation:

I felt that if a conflict developed between army and navy, the war would not be ended successfully. I thought that in order to prevent the army from revolting it was imperative for the navy to show a sympathetic attitude toward the army, and to persuade the army by saying that since the navy was making a great concession in agreeing to the peace, the army should also join in the move.

Since, seemingly, I took a stand in opposition to the navy minister it may appear that I broke the promise I had made to him when I became chief of staff, but I do not believe that I did. I was in complete agreement with the navy minister's opinion regarding the end of the war at that time and under those conditions. However, since Yonai made his stand exceedingly clear, I felt that if I were to follow his footsteps, the army would be left standing alone and it was unpredictable what attitude the army would then assume.

On the other hand, even if I showed sympathy toward the army, there was no fear that the peace faction would be overruled by the war hawks. Since the Emperor himself had made clear his desire for peace, my display of [a contrary] attitude would in no way jeopardize peace. Thus convinced, I acted somewhat in cooperation with Anami and Umezu, although it may be thought that I took too much of a roundabout way.

Toyoda, the plodding admiral without a fleet, turned out to have a keen and complex mind, as Yonai and the rest of the Big Six discovered. He, too, wrote a book after the war, to give his picture of the proceedings from the navy standpoint and to vindicate his actions. Typical of his approach is his stance on the question about guilt for starting the war:

I feel now and felt at the time that the country could have avoided the war if it had tried hard enough. . . . Our country needed at the time to avoid war; [we needed] the presence of a strong and wise statesman who could have led. . . .

There is a great doubt in my mind as to whether the government that was in power at the beginning of the war should alone be held responsible for the way that the war was started. I wonder whether we should not go back farther, even to the Manchurian Incident . . . [it] has always been my conviction that nothing can come from the combination of political and military power in one and the same hands. The army did participate in politics and that is not a recent phenomenon. It goes back as far as the Meiji era.

Because he was commander-in-chief of the combined fleet from early 1944 until he became chief of staff in 1945, Toyoda was tried in the Tokyo war-crimes trials for atrocities committed by Japanese navy personnel. He was the only Japanese leader acquitted of all charges.

At the time of the surrender he presented his samurai sword to U.S. Fleet Admiral Nimitz. After the peace treaty with Japan was signed in 1952 Nimitz returned the sword to Toyoda as a gesture of goodwill.

Toyoda outlived all other members of the Big Six. He finally succumbed to a heart attack in 1957 at the age of seventy-two.

Of the men who planned the *coup d'état* and expected War Minister Anami to become the new Shogun of Japan, four are very much alive and active at this writing.

Lieutenant Colonel Masataka Ida, the vacillating warrior who pingponged about Tokyo the night of August 14–15, 1945, leaped with ease from determination to commit suicide, to *coup,* to stop the *coup,* to suicide, and then to live after all. He was court-martialed for his part in the *coup.* Ida convinced the court that he had sincerely attempted to undo his error by trying to persuade Hatanaka to give up when he found that General Tanaka's Eastern District Army was not going to enter the plot.

Today, his name changed to Iwata, the former firebrand is a model of decorum and conformity. On a typical day you may find him in his gray-striped worsted suit, wearing a striped tie, at his office in Japan's largest advertising agency, where he is chief of the general affairs department. He looks and is well-to-do and middle-aged. His hair is rapidly giving up its foothold on his round head. His calculating eyes are ever mobile; his chin is slowly subsiding in a complacent curve that extends from lip to throat. A quiet-spoken man, he smokes cigarettes nervously and is the epitome of Japan's second-echelon businessmen, right down to the company button in the lapel of his suit jacket.

(It will be recalled that former *kempeitai* colonel Makoto Tsukamoto reported Ida's *coup* plans in detail to the *kempeitai* commander before the historic Imperial Conference. Tsukamoto is today one of Ida-Iwata's fellow workers at the Tokyo advertising agency.)

Colonel Okikatsu Arao, who, as a senior officer of the original *coup* group, had been its nominal leader, has also adjusted to the "horrors" of a drastically changed Japan. Like Ida-Iwata, he has buried the past. The very picture of the prosperous businessman, he dresses conservatively but well. He is director of a large auto agency in a major district of Tokyo. Business is thriving and so is he.

He is a diffident man on the subject of Japan at the end of World War II. Though he remembers well many of the events of that hectic final period, his memory is selective. He recalls nothing of the evening of August 13, 1945, when he called on War Minister Anami with the blueprint for the *coup;* nor today does he remember anything about his midnight meeting with Anami at the war ministry that same night. Yet he recalls vividly being called by Prince Mikasa the preceding night and his part in the preparation of the agreement signed by the top military leaders the afternoon of the fourteenth.

Arao's face is a mask—a broad, flat, oval-shaped expressionless visor covered with large-pored, waxy skin. The black hair is coarse and thin and streaked with gray. Only the eyes are ever alive—watching, watching. He may have perfected this opacity in the army, but it has been well applied to the automobile business, to his evident benefit.

The former colonel still maintains great respect for War Minister Anami. "It was Anami's greatness," he states categorically, "to bring the Japanese army to the war's end without incident." The irony imbedded in this testimonial either escapes Arao or is intended to influence the visitor to believe that this man could have played no role that would have been at cross-purposes to Anami's achievement.

Lieutenant Colonel Masao Inaba was, with Takeshita, one of the original planners of the *coup*. He abandoned the plot the morning of August 14 when he learned that General Umezu had turned thumbs down.

Lively and vigorous, Inaba should have found it easy to convert from his wartime job to peace. He had the skill to manage the war ministry's budget section and to prepare speeches for the war minister. One would expect to find him in a modern corporation where such ability is needed. Yet today he is still immersed in World War II.

It is not a flight from reality, however, but a professional interest. He is a civilian on the staff of the Land Self-defense Forces War History Section and has been working on the definitive Japanese history of World War II. He is to be found on the second floor of one of the drafty frame buildings in the old Imperial GHQ complex at Ichigaya Heights. There, in sweater and suit jacket, he eagerly reviews the events of twenty years ago as if they were yesterday's happenings.

Voluble, excitable still, Inaba's eyes dance as he discusses the clash of personalities and policies in the grand finale to the Pacific War. And he is not above sowing a few seeds of doubt about his contemporaries: He points out that there is still one survivor of the group involved in General Mori's murder. And he challenges the version of Mori's death according to which this survivor was out of the room at the time of the shot. The implication is that the survivor was one of the assassins and later hung the guilt on a dead companion.

Affable and interested, Inaba shuttles back and forth from the dusty reception room to the seedy halls in which stacks of documents and printed matter are kept. Anami remains one of his heroes. Inaba doubts the theory that the war minister committed *harikiri* in order to vanish immediately after countersigning the imperial rescript because he feared the young tigers would rise, forcing him to be their leader if he lived on. No, says Inaba, "Anami could trust his men to follow his orders absolutely. If he did have such a worry all he had to do was to express it clearly, which he would not have hesitated to do." A visitor is tempted to ask if Inaba means that they would have obeyed his orders as did Anami's dedicated disciples Hatanaka and Ida.

Lieutenant Colonel Masahiko Takeshita, whose words wounded his brother-in-law, War Minister Anami, and whose hand inflicted the final cut when he served as second during the war minister's *harakiri,* has remained an army man. Today, heavier, with rounder face, he seems temperate and is a jovial, extroverted host, even when the subject of the inquiry is Anami and the end of the war.

It is a period that is an open book, so far as he is concerned, and he is interested in it professionally and personally because of his nearness to the central mechanisms of that time. He has written about Anami and has addressed graduating classes of officer candidates in the Land Self-defense Forces about the late war minister.

Takeshita, the son of an army general as well as brother-in-law of the war minister, is today a general himself, in the Land Self-defense Forces. He is head of the Command and General Staff College, situated on the historic site of Imperial GHQ at Ichigaya Heights. And he still lives next door to his sister, Anami's widow, in the suburban Tokyo area of Mitaka.

Recently former Lieutenant Colonel Ida-Iwata told reporters that in looking back, he is more than ever convinced that but for the atom bombing of Hiroshima and Nagasaki and the Soviet attack, the military would have been successful in squelching the surrender rescript and continuing the war. He is equally convinced, he said, that the action he took was not wrong.

It is baffling to the Western observer to find these men who disobeyed their Emperor, their war minister, chief of staff, and their superior officers in planning or participating in a *coup* are still alive and at liberty. Not only are they alive; they are flourishing in positions of trust and importance.

The answer to this seemingly incomprehensible laxness on the part of responsible authorities is relatively uncomplicated. To the Japanese, the question of motivation still takes precedence over the mere technicality of legal guilt for a challenge to authority, no matter how dangerous and costly. "It was just a case of high-spirited youth," says one Japanese. "After all, their intentions were for the good of the country," states another. "Since they failed and there was relatively little damage done, why bother with them? Times have changed," advises a third. These views are typical.

Japan has moved on. The onetime conspirators have moved with the times. In the frantically industrious everyday life of Asia's most prosperous, advanced nation, they have sunk inconspicuously into the background.

Of those who contended for power in those climactic final days of empire, most have joined their ancestors. Two who still live are the former chief cabinet secretary and last lord keeper of the privy seal.

Hisatsune Sakomizu, the right-hand man to Premier Suzuki, weathered his wartime experiences well. A man with his intelligence, experience, drive, and political know-how was destined for a bright future. And his excellent connections, through his father-in-law Admiral Okada, were no handicap.

In his final cabinet meeting, Premier Suzuki followed the usual procedure and nominated for the House of Peers men who, the premier judged, had given outstanding service to the nation. There were five; Shigemitsu was one, Sakomizu another. The cabinet members approved unanimously. But such a cynosure without power was not for the kinetic young bureaucrat. He resigned from the Peers, ran for a seat in the Diet, and was elected. In 1967 he still held that office and his thick shock of unruly hair and bristling, arched eyebrows were familiar sights to visitors to the Diet.

Sakomizu played an important part in the history of Japan and managed to insure that he received his due by writing of his role. He was perhaps the first to bring out a report on the "secret history" of the end of the war. It ran in serialized form in a periodical shortly after the war's end and was later published in book form. He followed this with numerous articles on various aspects of the subject, which is perennially absorbing to Japanese. His latest work is *The Prime Ministry Under Attack,* a book published in 1965, covering the old ground from yet another angle. Throughout the years Sakomizu has spoken so often to so many groups on the way the war was brought to an end (never neglecting his own role) that his talks have a one-note quality. In fact, some of his countrymen comment caustically that Sakomizu is "still ending the war, *his* way." He appears to be in the prime of life, enjoying good health and still contributing his formidable energy and talent to Japan's peaceful progress.

What about Kido? Perhaps one of the most controversial and complex of Japanese, Marquis Koichi Kido, bearer of an honored name, closest confidant of the Emperor, completed more than five years as lord keeper of the privy seal. (In one of the early acts of the occupation, the Allies abolished the post of privy seal. In another, the Court titles and peerage were thrown out. So not only was Kido out of a job, he became a commoner overnight.) The divergence of opinion on his performance of duties as privy seal is enormous.

Hirohito, for instance, showed his gratitude and esteem on August 27, 1945. Kido received a call from Minister of the Imperial Household Ishiwata, his "cellmate" during the *coup* attempt two weeks earlier. This was an official call. Ishiwata was to notify him of the Emperor's decision to confer rewards on Kido for his services. The windfall: 20,000 yen, a box of canned food, and a barrel of refined sake. Though his diary is silent on his reaction, we can picture the privy seal at this revelation "filled with awe and trepidation," his almost invariable response to imperial initiative.

Kido's response to the war-crimes charges leveled at him by the conquerors was quite different. The indictment charged him with using his influence to advance the efforts of the military faction that was bent on war. There are many accusations in the indictment, —fifty-four in fact—four more than in the indictment against Tojo. However, the paramount fact is that the privy seal was acquitted of all responsibility for war crimes but convicted on other counts and sentenced to life imprisonment.

Harsh judgment of a vanquished foe? Consider:

Konoye and Kido . . . did not flatter the military but joined hands with it. The military used them as stool pigeons to lure the people. . . . Kido's weak points were these: He did not gather wise men together for discussion; he was not a type deliberate in council and prompt in action; he meddled too much with the government, compared with other privy seals before him, especially about personnel administration; he virtually isolated the Emperor from the people; he could not hold firm confidence, allowing the formation of the Tojo cabinet. . . . Kido became the single adviser of the Emperor. He should have opened the route for outstanding statesmen to approach the Emperor without difficulty. (Even the Emperor's brothers seldom had opportunities for heart-to-heart talks with him) . . . Kido shut up the Emperor too closely. He gathered too much power to himself. . . . He should have checked the birth of the Tojo cabinet (instead, he backed Tojo and recommended the Emperor appoint him prime minister because "Tojo can control the military").

Source? Kido's contemporary, the distinguished former editor of the *Asahi* newspapers, Information Minister Kainan Shimomura, in his book *A Secret History of the War's End*.

Kido wound up his voluminous presentation before the war-crimes trial with this statement:

It was my inward satisfaction that I was instrumental in saving another 20,000,000 of my innocent compatriots from war's ravages and also in sparing the Americans tens of millions of casualties . . . had Japan gone on fighting to the bitter end. . . . It is my sole consolation, that at the close of the war I was able to give full play to my bold activities under the august virtues of the Emperor [and] succeeded in preventing the Japanese mainland from becoming a battleground and saving lives of hundreds of millions of people.

That the determined little terrier played a key role cannot be denied. That the war ended only because of him is another matter. At any rate, he stayed out of circulation, locked in Sugamo prison, serving his life sentence until Japan shook off the occupation and became free and independent again. In 1956 Kido walked out of Sugamo free.

Since then he has lived quietly, out of the limelight. He sees his old friends frequently, seems active and healthy though frail, and at this writing is understood to be in good health for a man in his late seventies. His volumes and volumes of diary (literally more than 5900 entries and thousands of pages) covering the period from 1931 through 1945 have recently been published in Japan and are stirring up still more controversy about his role.

Once the Allied forces landed in Japan the anxiety among leading Japanese over the fate of the Emperor became intense. It was clear that the victors were going to arrest prominent Japanese and try them for war crimes. Would the Emperor be so ignominiously treated?

It was no secret that the Russians, Australians, and Chinese clamored for this. And in the United States, advocates of a "tough" peace called for Hirohito's trial or exile to China. General MacArthur recalled in his *Reminiscences* that "realizing the tragic consequences that would follow . . . I had advised that I would need at least one million reinforcements should such action be taken. I believed that if the Emperor were indicted, and perhaps hanged, as a war criminal, military government would have to be instituted throughout all Japan, and guerilla warfare would probably break out."

So when, after some weeks, the Emperor sent word that he wished to call on the Supreme Commander for the Allied Powers, MacArthur suspected it might be to "plead his own cause against indictment as a war criminal." He could not have been wider of the mark.

Everything about Hirohito's visit to MacArthur was unprecedented. *He* left the palace. *He* drove to meet MacArthur in the American Embassy. Dressed in top hat, striped trousers, wing collar, and cutaway (in civilian clothes for the first time in public in years), he presented himself to the victor. He had with him his grand chamberlain, his interpreter, and his doctor. Weeks of insomnia, added to the Emperor's chronic stage-fright at public occasions, caused him to tremble visibly. If MacArthur thought the Emperor-god was quivering with fear as the General lighted a cigarette for him, he found out almost instantly that he was one hundred eighty degrees off course.

Hirohito's words were not suggested by Kido or Togo this time. They were, according to MacArthur, "I come to you, General MacArthur, to offer myself to the judgment of the powers you represent as the one to bear sole responsibility for every political and military decision made and action taken by my people in the conduct of the war." This bowled the Allied commander over.

Here was the Emperor-god shouldering all blame for the entire war. As so many of his loyal subjects had given their lives for failing him, he was offering his life for his surviving subjects and for the memory of those who had sacrificed for him. He had said at the Imperial Conferences that he could not bear to think of those who had served him so loyally being taken by the victors and prosecuted as war criminals. He could not prevent the Allies from exercising this power, but he could offer himself in lieu of them, and he did. It was an action worthy of a god.

"This courageous assumption of a responsibility implicit with death," wrote MacArthur, "a responsibility clearly belied by facts of which I was fully aware, moved me to the very marrow of my bones."

The Emperor was not indicted as a war criminal.

On New Year's Day 1946, Hirohito, in accordance with tradition, released his annual poem in the nationwide poetry contest. It did not please SCAP (Supreme Commander for the Allied Powers—literally MacArthur, but used to refer to occupation headquarters in general). The Emperor wrote:

> Though bent with snow
> The pine tree remains green.
> People too, should
> Like the pine tree be.

Was this some thinly veiled call to resist the occupation? Not at all. Hirohito was realistic and farsighted enough to see that the impact of the occupation, even if a model of benevolence, was going to be profound on his country. He was urging that the Japanese character not be abandoned or warped by this new overlay of foreign influence.

Yet, inescapably, he too was influenced. Once again, as in the post-World War I period, the winds of *dem-mok-ra-sie* stirred the land (as Togo's studies had predicted). He, as the pace-setter, led his people in accepting it. He went about, visiting coal mines and factories, schools and hospitals and projects. He met the press and the people and, although it may have been excruciating to him at first, he soon became accustomed to it.

That same New Year's Day he followed the wishes of the occupation forces and issued an imperial rescript that shook the immemorial foundations of Japan and destroyed one of the prime elements in the structure of Imperial Japan. The statement said:

We stand by the people and we wish always to share with them in their moments of joy and sorrow. The ties between us and our people have always stood upon mutual trust and affection. They do not depend upon mere legends and myths. They are not predicated on the false conception that the Emperor is divine and that the Japanese people are superior to other races, and fated to rule the world. (The Japanese language version of the statement carried the words "the Tenno is not a living god.")

Thus he renounced his divinity—and the fundamentals underlaying *Hakko Ichiu*. He had turned his back on godship with misgivings. He had rejected manifest destiny and racial superiority without a qualm.

His doubts about publicly stating that he was not a god centered not about any belief that he was one, but about the confusion and reaction that might result from such action. Anyone with his credentials in biology must have abandoned conceptions of godhood at an early age.

The Emperor watched with extreme interest the press reports and monitored reactions that followed this announcement. He was apprehensive that there might be strong negative reactions. Response abroad was almost universally favorable, stating that this removed several of the bases of distrust of Japan and if followed logically inside the nation would wipe out some of the virulent beliefs that underlay Japan's expansionist adventures in the past. The Emperor was pleased with these reports and reassured about his act. So was SCAP.

Hirohito did not become a more active ruler as a result of his imperial "decisions" in 1945. His nature was against it, the Meiji Constitution was against it, his counselors opposed it, and the occupation made it impossible. It was in November 1946 that a new Japanese Constitution was promulgated. It superseded the Meiji document and put a fence around the Emperor, limiting his powers. The key paragraph, the sentence that revolutionized his relationship to his people is:

Chapter I. The Emperor. Article I. The Emperor shall be the symbol of the State and of the unity of the people, deriving his position from the will of the people with whom resides sovereign power.

This was a far piece from the Meiji Constitution, which had said "The Emperor is sacred and inviolable." But it fit the realities of twentieth-century life much better. Hirohito issued an imperial rescript making the new Constitution official. He said "I rejoice that the foundation for the construction of a new Japan has been laid according to the will of the Japanese people, and hereby sanction and promulgate the amendments of the Imperial Japanese Constitution. . . ." With this step Japan shucked off many vitally important feudal elements that had been institutionalized in the old Constitution. In a very real sense the new document was symbolic of the metamorphosis from that feudal era.

In recent years, with the romantic courtship and marriage of Crown Prince Akihito to a commoner, the center of public interest has shifted away from the Emperor to his athletic, handsome son, to the Prince's family and travels. But the Emperor is still head of the Japanese family. On ceremonial occasions, such as the opening of the Diet and the observances at the Yasukuni Shrine, he appears and goes through his paces. He continues his interest in marine biology and in 1965 published another book, this one about Pacific Ocean shellfish.

What his view is of contemporary Japan—prosperous, emancipated, with well-fed, healthy, busy citizens—the Emperor has not stated. Certainly he can have few regrets that he put his foot down on those two fateful days in August 1945.

For a fleeting moment in history, conditions made Hirohito the all-powerful Emperor-god, and for that moment he acted decisively as an Emperor-god should but seldom does. Because for that instant he was truly both Emperor and god, Japan exists today.

Bibliography

I. Records and Documents

CINCPAC (U.S. Navy Commander-in-chief, Pacific). *Report of Surrender and Occupation of Japan,* A16-3/FF12, February 11, 1946.

International Military Tribunal for the Far East. *Analyses of Documentary Evidence.*

———. *Exhibits.*

———. *Judgment.*

———. *Miscellaneous documents,* prosecution and defense.

———. *Transcript of Proceedings.*

Japan, Land Self-defense Forces Historical Division, Tokyo. *Publications, Records and Documents relating to events of August, 1945.*

United States Army, office of the Chief of Military History. *Interrogations of Japanese Officials on World War II,* 2 vols.

———. Japanese Monograph No. 119: *Outline of Operations Prior to Termination of War and Activities Connected with Cessation of Hostnities.*

———. Miscellaneous Documents.

———. *Statements of Japanese Officials on World War II,* 4 vols.

United States Army, General Headquarters, Supreme Commander for the Allied Powers, Counterintelligence Section. *The Brocade Banner: The Story of Japanese Nationalism.*

United States Strategic Bombing Survey (Pacific). *Interrogations of Japanese Officials,* 2 vols. Washington, D.C., U.S. Government Printing Office, 1946.

———. *The Effects of Strategic Bombing on Japanese Morale.* 1947.

———. *Japan's Struggle to End the War.* 1946.

———. *Effects of Air Attack on Japan's Urban Economy.* 1946.

———. *Effects of Bombing on Health and Medical Services in Japan.* 1946.

———. *Effects of Strategic Bombing on Japanese Morale.* 1946.

———. *Japan's War Economy.* 1946.

———. *Japanese Wartime Standard of Living.* 1946.

———. *Summary Report.* 1946.

———. *Effects of Strategic Bombing on Japan's War Economy.* 1946.

———. *The Campaigns of the Pacific War.* 1946.

United States Office of Strategic Services, Research & Analysis Branch.

———. *Japan: Winter 1944–1945.*

———. *Japanese Analyses of Defeat.*

———. *Japan, Conflicting Political Views.*

———. *Japan's Secret Weapon.*

————. *Japanese Reactions to Surrender.*

————. *Food Situation.*

————. *Wartime Distribution of Food.*

————. *The Japanese Emperor and the War.*

————. *Crisis in Japan.*

————. *Rival Cliques in the Japanese Army.*

Reports of Gen. MacArthur, vol. I and vol. I Supplement. Superintendent of Documents, Washington, D.C., Government Printing Office, 1966.

Supreme Commander for the Allied Powers, Report of Government Section. *Political Reorientation of Japan, Sept. 1945 to Sept. 1948,* vols. I & II. Washington, D.C., Superintendent of Documents, Government Printing Office, 194(?).

II. *Books, Articles, Documentaries*

Beasley, Wm. G. *The Modern History of Japan.* New York, Praeger, 1963.

Benedict, Ruth. *The Chrysanthemum and the Sword.* Boston, Houghton Mifflin Co., 1946.

Borton, Hugh. *Japan's Modern Century.* New York, Ronald, 1955.

Butow, Robert J.C. *Japan's Decision to Surrender.* Stanford, Cal., Stanford University Press, 1954.

————. *Tojo and the Coming of War.* Princeton, N.J., Princeton University Press, 1961.

Byas, Hugh. *Government by Assassination.* New York, Alfred A. Knopf, Inc., 1942.

Byrnes, James F. *Speaking Frankly.* New York, Harper & Brothers, 1947.

Cohen, Jerome B. *Japan's Economy in War and Reconstruction.* Minneapolis, University of Minnesota Press, 1949.

Colegrove, Kenneth W. *Militarism in Japan.* Boston, World Peace Foundation, 1936.

Churchill, Winston S. *The Second World War,* 6 vols. Boston, Houghton Mifflin Co., 1948–1953.

Craigie, Sir Robert. *Behind the Japanese Mask.* London, Hutchinson & Co., Ltd., 1945.

Craven, W.F. and J.L. Cate (eds.). *The Army Air Forces in World War II,* vol. 5. Chicago, The University of Chicago Press, 1953.

Feis, Herbert. *The Road to Pearl Harbor.* Princeton, Princeton University Press, 1950.

————. *Japan Subdued: The Atomic Bomb and the End of the War in the Pacific.* Princeton, Princeton University Press, 1961.

Fleisher, Wilfrid. *Our Enemy Japan.* Washington, The Infantry Journal, 1942.

————. *Volcanic Isle.* Garden City, N.Y. Doubleday, Doran, 1941.

Foreign Affairs Association of Japan. *Japan Yearbook* for the war years, Tokyo.

Fortune, editors of. *Japan and the Japanese.* Washington, The Infantry Journal, 1944.

Gaimusho. *Shusen Shiroku* [*The Historical Record of the Termination of the War*]. Tokyo, Shinbun Gekkansha, 1952.

Gayn, Mark. *Japan Diary.* New York, William Sloane Associates, 1948.

Gen. *Douglas MacArthur's Historical Report on Allied Operations in the Southwest Pacific Area, 8 Dec. 1941–2 Sept. 1945,* vol. II. General Headquarters, Supreme Commander for the Allied Powers. (MSS. in Office of War History, Department of the Army, Washington, D.C.)

Gibney, Frank. *Five Gentlemen of Japan.* New York, Farrar, Straus & Young, Inc., 1953.

Giovannitti, Len and Fred Freed. *The Decision to Drop the Bomb.* New York, Coward-McCann, Inc., 1965.

Grew, Joseph C. *Ten Years in Japan.* New York, Simon and Schuster, Inc., 1944.

Hattori, Takushiro. *A Complete History of the Greater East Asian War.* Tokyo, Masu Shobo, 1953.

Hayashi, Saburo. *Kogun: The Japanese Army in the Pacific War.* Quantico, Va., Marine Corps Association, 1959.

————. "General Anami at the End of the War." *Sekai* Magazine, Tokyo, Aug. 1951.

Hayashi, Shigeru (ed.). *Nihon Shusen Shi.* Tokyo, Yomiuri Shimbun, 1962.

Japan Broadcasting Co. (eds.). *History of Broadcasting in Japan,* vol. I. Tokyo, 1965.

Kase, Toshikazu. *Journey to the Missouri.* New Haven, Yale University Press, 1950.

————. *The Moment of Destiny in Japan's Diplomacy.* Tokyo, Japan Economic Newspaper Co., 1965.

Kato, Masuo. *The Lost War.* New York, Alfred A. Knopf, Inc., 1946.

Kawai, Kazuo. *Japan's American Interlude.* Chicago, University of Chicago Press, 1960.

————. "Militarist Activity between Japan's Two Surrender Decisions." *Pacific Historical Review,* vol. XXII, No. 4, Nov. 1953.

————. "Mokusatsu: Japan's Response to the Potsdam Declaration." *Pacific Historical Review,* vol. XIX, No. 4, Nov. 1950.

Kido, Koichi. *Extracts from the Diary of Marquis Kido, Feb. 3, 1931–Aug. 9, 1945.* University of California Photographic Service, 1948.

————, deposition of. International Military Tribunal for the Far East, Doc. 0002.

Kihensan Iinkai. *Biography of Kantaro Suzuki.* Tokyo, Totsuban Co., 1959.

Kodama, Yoshio. *I Was Defeated.* n.p. (Japan), Booth & Fukuda, 1951.

Konoye, Prince Fumimaro. *Lost Politics.* Tokyo, Asahi Shimbun, 1946.

————. *Memoirs, with Appended Papers.* Tokyo, 5250th Technical Intelligence Co., S.C.A.P., 1946.

————. *The Memoirs of Prince Fumimaro Konoye.* Asahi Shimbun, Dec. 20–30, 1945, as translated by Okuyama Service, 195(?).

Kurzman, Dan. *Kishi and Japan.* New York, I. Obolensky, 1960.

Lory, Hillis, *Japan's Military Masters.* Washington, The Infantry Journal, 1943.

MacArthur, Douglas. *Reminiscences.* New York, McGraw-Hill Book Co., 1964.

Maraini, Fosco. *Meeting with Japan.* New York, The Viking Press, Inc., 1960.

Matsuoka, Yoko. *Daughter of the Pacific.* New York, Harper & Brothers, 1952.

Millis, Walter. *The Forrestal Diaries.* New York, The Viking Press, Inc., 1951.

Mori, Motojiro. "Togo, Shigenori: A Tragic Character." *Kaizo* Magazine, Tokyo, Feb. 1951.

Morison, Samuel E. *History of United States Naval Operations in World War II.* Boston, Little, Brown and Company, 1948.

———. "Why Japan Surrendered." *The Atlantic Monthly,* October, 1960.

Morris, Ivan I. *The World of the Shining Prince.* New York, Alfred A. Knopf, Inc., 1964.

National Broadcasting Co., New York. NBC White Paper. *The Surrender of Japan.* Broadcast on TV Sept. 19, 1965.

Nishida, Kazuo. *Storied Cities of Japan.* Tokyo, John Weatherhill, 1963.

Nitobe, Inazo. *Bushido: The Soul of Japan.* New York, G.P. Putnam's Sons, 1905.

Niwa, Fumio. "Japan is Defeated." *Salon,* Aug., Sept., Oct. 1949.

Ohya, Soichi (compiler). *The Longest Day in Japan.* Tokyo, Bungei Shunju, 1965.

Okada, Keisuke. *Kaiko-roku* (Memoirs). Tokyo, Mainichi Shimbun-sha, 1950.

Price, Willard. *Key to Japan.* New York, The John Day Company, Inc., 1946.

———. *Japan and the Son of Heaven.* New York, Duell, Sloan & Pearce, 1945.

Reischauer, Edwin O. *Japan, Past and Present.* New York, Alfred A. Knopf, Inc., 1964.

———. *The United States and Japan.* Cambridge, Harvard University Press, 1957.

Roth, Andrew. *Dilemma in Japan.* Boston, Little, Brown & Company, 1945.

Russell (Lord Russell of Liverpool). *The Knights of Bushido.* London, Cassell & Co., Ltd., 1958.

Sakomizu, Hisatsune. *Secret History of the End of the War.* Tokyo, Jikyoku Geppo, 1946.

———. *The Prime Ministry Under Attack.* Tokyo, Kobun-Sha, 1965.

Sakonji, Masazo. "Mitsumasa Yonai and Korechika Anami." *Maru* Magazine, Tokyo, Sept. 1949.

Sansom, Sir George. *Japan: A Short Cultural History.* New York, Appleton-Century-Crofts, Inc., 1962.

———. *The Western World and Japan.* New York, Alfred A. Knopf, Inc., 1950.

Sherwood, Robert E. *Roosevelt and Hopkins.* New York, Harper & Brothers, 1948.

Shiba, Kimpei. *I Cover Japan.* Tokyo, Tokyo News Service, 1954.

Shigemitsu, Mamoru. *Japan and Her Destiny.* New York, E. P. Dutton & Co., Inc., 1958.

Shimomura, Hiroshi (Kainan). *A Secret History of the War's End.* Tokyo, Kodan-Sha Ltd., 1950.

————. *The August 15th Incident*. Tokyo.

Station JOTX-TV, Channel 12, Tokyo. Series: History of Showa; *The Emperor's Recording*. 1965.

Stimson, Henry L. and McGeorge Bundy. *On Active Service*. New York, Harper & Brothers, 1948.

Storry, Richard. *The Double Patriots*. Boston, Houghton Mifflin Company, 1957.

Suzuki, Bunshiro. *Miscellanies, Still and Active*. Tokyo, 1947.

Takagi, Yasaka. *Toward International Understanding*. Tokyo, Kenkyusha, 1954.

Terasaki, Gwen. *Bridge to the Sun*. Chapel Hill, University of North Carolina Press, 1957.

Togo, Shigenori. *The Cause of Japan*. New York, Simon and Schuster, Inc., 1956.

Tolischus, Otto D. *Through Japanese Eyes*. Cornwall, N.Y., Reynal & Hitchcock, Inc., 1945.

Tomomatsu, Entai. "Japanese Fatalism and Self-immolation." *Contemporary Affairs*, Tokyo, Dec. 1940.

————. *Tokyo Record*. New York, Reynal & Hitchcock, Inc., 1943.

Truman, Harry S. *Decision: The Conflicts of Harry S Truman*, television series: "Dialogue With the Future, Part II," Aug. 20, 1965.

Tsukamoto, Kiyoshi. *A Kogun Saigo No Hi*. Tokyo, Koyo-Sha, 1953.

United States Army Air Force. *Mission Accomplished: Interrogations of Japanese Industrial, Military and Civil Leaders of World War II*. Washington, D.C., U.S. Government Printing Office, 1946.

Whitney, Courtney. *MacArthur: His Rendezvous with History*. New York, Alfred A. Knopf, Inc., 1956.

Yoshida, Shigeru. *Kaiso Juen*. Tokyo, Shinako-Sha, 1957.

Young, A. Morgan. *Imperial Japan, 1926–1938*. London, George Allen & Unwin, Ltd., 1938.

Zacharias, Capt. Ellis M. *Secret Missions*. New York, G.P. Putnam's Sons, 1946.

Newspapers and magazines for the war years:

Asahi Shimbun, *Present-Day Nippon*.

Asahi Shimbun.

Bungei Shunju.

Chuo Koron.

Mainichi Shimbun, Tokyo.

Osaka Mainichi, *Nippon Today and Tomorrow;* 1939–1941.

Osaka Mainichi; issues for 1945.

Nippon Times, Tokyo.

New York *Herald Tribune*, New York and Paris editions.

The New York Times.

The *Times*, London, England.

Stars & Stripes, Armed Forces Far East.

III. *Interviews.* The following personal interviews were conducted by the author in Tokyo in 1965:

Ida/Iwata, Masataka	Niino, Hiroshi	Arisue, Seizo
Tokugawa, Yoshihiro	Ishii, Ken	Hayashi, Saburo
Takagi, Sokichi	Tsukamoto, Makoto	Hata, Ikuhiko
Takagi, Yasaka	Roggendorf, Fr. Joseph	Matsutani, Makoto
Suzuki, Hajime	Oi, Atsushi	Hasegawa, Saiji
Nakajima, Leslie	Anami, Mrs. Korechika	Abe, Genki
Umezu, Yoshikazu	Takeshita, Masahiko	Genda, Minoru
Otake, Sadao	Arao, Okikatsu	Ikeda, Sumihisa
Sugita, Ichiji	Inaba, Masao	Nishiura, Susumu
Ogawa, Masaru	Danno, Nobuo	Higashiuchi, Yosh

Transcripts of the following 1965 interviews were kindly made available by the National Broadcasting Company:

Arisue, Seizo	Sakomizu, Hisatsune	Higashikuni, Naruhiko
Abe, Genki	Hayashi, Saburo	Wachi, Tsunezo
Dooman, Eugene	McCloy, John J.	Asada, Tsunesaburo
Kido, Koichi	Matsumoto, Shunichi	Sato, Naotake

Interviews, interrogations and statements gathered by three major agencies provided a lode of material unmatched in any previous war in history. The statements and interviews were collected by General MacArthur's Military History Section in two volumes of unpublished "Interrogations of Japanese Officials on World War II" and four volumes of unpublished "Statements of Japanese Officials on World War II."

The second major source is the group of "Interrogations of Japanese Officials" by the United States Strategic Bombing Survey immediately after Japan's surrender. These are available in two volumes as cited above, and in additional, unpublished form.

The third extraordinary source is the massive literature of the Tokyo Trials— the International Military Tribunal for the Far East. This marathon legal event continued for more than two years and included testimony from nearly every significant figure in Japanese political and military life.

From these invaluable sources have come the actual words of the men who led Imperial Japan in its final days.

References

Chapter I

The descriptions and quotations come primarily from statements, interrogations and interviews with Okikatsu Arao, Saburo Hayashi, Masataka Ida, Iwata, Masao Inaba and Masahiko Takeshita. Major written sources include the books by *Gaimusho*, Kido, Sakomizu, Shimomura, and Togo listed in the bibliography.

Chapter II

Major sources for the action reported and statements quoted are the testimony, interrogations and interviews with Zenshiro Hoshina, Torashiro Kawabe, Ida, Sumihisa Ikeda, and Inaba. Primary written sources were the books by *Gaimusho*, Kase, and Morison.

Chapter III

The action and quotations are, in the main, from Koichi Kido, Matsudaira, Keisuke Okada, Naotake Sato, Kantaro Suzuki and Kenzo Tange. Written sources were Kido, Okada, the Sato-Togo diplomatic exchange, and the official Suzuki biography.

Chapter IV

Among those whose statements, testimony, and interviews provided the basic structure for the chapter were Eugene Dooman, Arao, Kawabe, Kido, Hoshina, Matsudaira, Shunichi Matsumoto, Mamoru Shigemitsu, Ikeda, Ichiji Sugita, Soemu Toyoda, Yoshikazu Umezu, Takeshita, Togo, Mr. and Mrs. Fumihiko Togo, Mitsumasa Yonai, Masao Yoshizumi. Written works, in addition to those cited above, included books by Hayashi and Grew, for the indispensable portions.

Chapter V

The main interviews, interrogations, statements and testimony used came from Togo, Toyoda, and Sakomizu. In this chapter the Sakomizu and Shimomura books were invaluable.

Chapter VI

The statements of Kido, Kiichiro Hiranuma, Ikeda, Sakomizu, Sakonji, Shimomura, Toyoda and Masao Yoshizumi were vitally important. Written material relied on heavily included the items cited earlier plus Kido's diary, books by Sakomizu, Shimomura, and Niwa's "Japan is Defeated" in *Salon*.

Chapter VII
Here again the interviews with and the testimony of Ikeda, Hiranuma, Sakomizu, and Toyoda were basic.

Chapter VIII
Here the books most used were by Byas, Beasley, Fleisher, editors of *Fortune*, Lory, Morris, and Sansom.

Chapter IX
The words of Kido, Kiyoshi Hasegawa, Ikeda, Matsudaira, Sakomizu, Sakonji, Kase, and Togo were most important here. Written material included Kido's diary and deposition, books by Kase, Sakomizu, Shimomura, and Togo.

Chapter X
The main sources were the interviews with or statements of Dooman, Kase, Matsudaira, Shigemitsu, Makoto Matsutani, Togo, Toyoda, and Yonai. Also important were books by Butow, Kase, Morison, and articles from Nippon *Times* and *Asahi Shimbun*.

Chapter XI
Again, primary material was derived from Seiji Hasegawa, Hiranuma, Kido, Sakomizu, Shigemitsu, Shimomura, Togo, Toyoda, and Yoshizumi. The written sources included the Sato-Togo exchange of messages and books by Butow, Byrnes, Churchill, Sakomizu, Shimomura, and Togo.

Chapter XII
Statements and interrogations of Seizo Arisue, Tsunesaburo Asada, Genki Abe, Kawabe, Kido, Dooman, Nishina, Sakomizu, Shimomura, and Togo, were fundamental to this chapter. Also important were books by Hayashi, Sakomizu, Shimomura, and Togo, Kido's diary, and articles from Nippon *Times* and *Asahi Shimbun*.

Chapter XIII
In this, major sources were statements of Arao, Asada, Kido, Ida, Inaba, Matsumoto, Seiji Hasegawa, Sakomizu, Shimomura, Togo, and Yoshizumi. Essential written sources were Kido's diary and works by Sakomizu, Shimomura, and Togo and articles in Nippon *Times*.

Chapter XIV
The basic material came from statements by Seiji Hasegawa, Hayashi, Ida, Inaba, Kawabe, and Takeshita. Also from books by Hayashi, Lory, Nitobe, Byas, Sansom, and Reischauer.

Chapter XV
Quotations from Seiji Hasegawa, Hiranuma, Hoshina, Kase, Ida, Hasunuma,

Hayashi, Kido, Ikeda, Matsutani, Togo, and Toyoda were indispensable in this chapter. Books used include those by Hayashi, Kase, Sakomizu, and Togo.

Chapter XVI

Main sources were statements by Hayashi, Kido, Ikeda, Matsumoto, Sakomizu, Togo, and Toyoda, and Makoto Tsukamoto. Written materials used included Kido's diary and books by Sakomizu and Togo.

Chapter XVII

The testimony of the following was paramount: Arao, Asada, Hayashi, Kido, Ida, Inaba, Sakomizu, Shimomura, Takeshita, Toyoda and Yoshizumi. Books consulted included those by Hayashi, Sakomizu, Shimomura, and the Suzuki biography.

Chapter XVIII

The spoken sources of primary importance were Arao, Asada, Ida, Inaba, Irie, Hoshina, Kawabe, Atsushi Oi, Sadao Otake, Togo, Yoshihiro Tokugawa, and Susumu Nishiura. Books that proved essential were those by NHK, Shimomura, and the Suzuki biography.

Chapter XIX

In this the statements of Ida, Inaba, Takeshita and Yamaoka were fundamental, as were the books by Sakomizu and Shimomura.

Chapter XX

Main spoken sources were Hasunuma, Ida, Sukemasa Irie, Sotaro Ishiwata, Tokugawa and Tsukamoto. Written sources included the books by NHK, Sakomizu, Shimomura, and Tsukamoto.

Chapter XXI

Testimony and statements used in this chapter came primarily from Asada, Fr. Flaujac, Ida, Kido, Otake, Togo, and Tsukamoto. Also used were books by Kase, Kawai, NHK, Sakomizu, and Shimomura.

Chapter XXII

Fundamental material came from statements of Hayashi, Higashikuni, Kido, Matsudaira, Otake, Sakomizu, and Yoshizumi. Books important to the presentation included those by Benedict, Hayashi, Kato and Kodama.

Chapter XXIII

In this, statements by Dooman, Arao, Inaba, Kido, Togo, Toyoda, Tsukamoto, Umezu, Yonai, and Yoshizumi, Sakomizu, and Shimomura were of prime importance. Written material used included books by Hayashi, MacArthur, Sakomizu, and Shimomura.

Chapter XXIV

Basic to this chapter were interviews with and quotations from Hayashi, Ida, Irie, Kido, Shimomura, Sakomizu, Takeshita, and Tokugawa. The books of importance were those by NHK, Sakomizu, Shimomura, and Tsukamoto's biography of Tanaka as well as the Suzuki biography.

Index

Behind Japan's Surrender: The Secret Struggle That Ended an Empire

by Lester Brooks
Foreword by Fumihiko Togo

In Japan, during the excruciating days between the first A-bomb, August 6, 1945, and the surrender, a wild drama of huge and tragic import was played out. This drama is the subject of this remarkable book.

Japan's emperor was Hirohito, descendant of the Sun Goddess, a quiet man of extravagant modesty and humility who seemed the last man on earth to lead a mighty empire into either conquest or disaster. Yet, by 1942 Japan's conquests bróught her an empire that ruled over one-sixth of the world.

Japan's prime minister during the crucial days before surrender was Admiral Baron Kantaro Suzuki, born in the last year of Japan's feudal era, 1867, hero of the wars of 1894 (against China) and 1904 (against Russia).

Around these two figures -- screening them from the world and also from Japan's 80,000,000 tattered, war-weary, half-starving people -- was the military elite, the powerful, dedicated group of officers who were sworn to conquest and self-hypnotized into a belief that Japan must be defended to the utter end, even if it meant the sacrifice of every soldier, every man, woman and child, every inch of their once-powerful land.

These men met in secret and schemed, plotted and debated while their countrymen suffered unprecedented bombings and devastation. They were neither blind nor fools. Rather they were men whom neither history nor experience could teach --

and it is their fantastic, desperate, last-ditch stand -- which one could too easily dismiss simply as fanaticism -- which Mr. Brooks describes in this book.

Besides being a breathtaking and fascinating account, *Behind Japan's Surrender* is also a magnificent piece of research. The author has used captured documents, Allied interrogations, the Tokyo Trials records and searching in-person interviews with surviving leaders. From these sources he has drawn their actual words. He has gone back into Japanese history to explore the drives, the ways of thought, the inner rhythm of the culture that led Japan into World War II and finally to its ignominious, abject and absolute defeat. He tells this story with rare wisdom and compassion, to make it a work unique in its genre.

Lester Brooks served in the Philippines and Japan in the U.S. Army during World War II. Stationed at MacArthur's SCAP GHQ across the street from the Imperial Palace in Tokyo, he traveled the length and breadth of defeated Nippon observing the wreckage of the once mighty nation. His subsequent years with the U.S. Foreign Service in the Orient and his extensive travels in Asia (including visits and research in Japan) provided him with rare background for this book. He lives in New Canaan, Connecticut and is the author or co-author of 14 other books.

(From the original edition's book jacket.)

Reviewing The Books

Japanese Surrender Story A Real Thriller

BEHIND JAPAN'S SUR- RENDER. By Lester Brooks. McGraw-Hill.

The chaos in Japan's government in the final days of World War II is depicted in great detail here. Although Brooks' research forms a solid factual basis for the account, the events themselves read like a fictional thriller.

He concentrates on the days just before and just after the official surrender of Aug. 14, 1945. Those who remember Hiroshima, Russia's declaration of war and the second atomic bomb at Nagasaki have heard only part of the story.

There was a struggle at the top which the author records almost hour by hour, centered around a handful of self-hypnotized military leaders who refused to face inevitable defeat.

The cabinet, led by an aging non-entity, was split into factions; so were the "Big Six" war leaders who actually ran the country; though a figurehead, Emperor Hirohito insisted on surrender. Almost until the final moment there was a chance that the war minister would accede to the demands of a group of rabid officers that he take power in a suicidal move.

The plan fizzled, but another handful of minor officers refused to give up. Their small revolt very nearly succeeded in preventing a broadcast in which Hirohito told the nation the war had ended. As a macabre counterpoint, the author describes the futile efforts of a physics professor, traipsing around amid the chaos, to make someone understand the meaning of the atomic bomb.

The author's main point is that it was Russia's entry into the Pacific War that swung the balance for surrender — that there had not been time enough for the significance of the atomic bomb to sink in.

Brooks presents, in prodigious detail, a bit of history that reads like wild drama, giving a graphic reality to the forces and personalities operating behind the scenes in the critical hours of Japan's surrender.

Miles A. Smith

—Associated Press